Contents

Credits

The author and publisher would like to thank the following individuals and organisations for permission to reproduce photographs:

Unit 1: p.1 Dean Mitchell. Shutterstock; p.3 Pearson Education Ltd. Jules Selmes; p.7 vario images GmbH & Co.KG/ Alamy; p.15 Sergey Lavrentev. Shutterstock; p.18 Monkey Business Images. Shutterstock; p.23 Janine Wiedel Photolibrary/Alamy

Unit 2: p.25 John Birdsall/John Birdsall/Press Association Images; p.27 Pearson Education Ltd. Rob Judges; p.29 John Birdsall/John Birdsall/Press Association Images; p.35 Pearson Education Ltd. Lord & Leverett; p.43 Lisa F. Young. Shutterstock; p.44 Pearson Education Ltd. Jules Selmes; p.47 Rex Features/Alix/Phanie

Unit 3: p.49 Stockbyte; p.51 Pearson Education Ltd. Studio 8 Clark Wiseman; p.55 PCN Photography/Alamy; p.57 Stockbyte; p.71 Jens Böttner/dpa/Corbis

Unit 4: p.73 MBI/Alamy; p.75 Pearson Education Ltd. Gareth Boden; p.81 Image Source; p.81 MBI/Alamy; p.81 Alex Segre/Alamy; p.83 Pearson Education Ltd. David Sanderson; p.95 Paul Glendell/Alamy

Unit 5: p.97 Yuri Arcurs. Shutterstock; p.99 Pearson Education Ltd. Studio 8 Clark Wiseman; p.101; Pearson Education Ltd. Jules Selmes; p.113 Pearson Education Ltd. Jules Selmes; p.113 Kurhan. Shutterstock; p.113 Pearson Education Ltd. Jules Selmes; p.113 jaymast. Shutterstock; p.120 Bananastock. Imagestate; p.122 Yuri Arcurs. Shutterstock; p.124 Pearson Education Ltd. Jules Selmes; p.128 Petro Feketa. Shutterstock; p.137 Pearson Education Ltd. Jules Selmes

Unit 6: p.139 Ryan McVay. Getty Images; p.141 Pearson Education Ltd. Studio 8 Clark Wiseman; p.151 Photodisc. Glen Allison; p.155 Heinrich Sanden/dpa/Corbis; p.156 ayazad.Shutterstock; p.183 Pearson Education Ltd. Lord & Leverett

Unit 7: p.185 IAN HOOTON/SCIENCE PHOTO LIBRARY; p.187 Suzanne Tucker. Shutterstock; p.212 IAN HOOTON/ SCIENCE PHOTO LIBRARY; p.213 IAN HOOTON/SCIENCE PHOTO LIBRARY; p.213 IAN HOOTON/SCIENCE PHOTO LIBRARY; p.214 AJ PHOTO/SCIENCE PHOTO LIBRARY; p.229 ERproductions Ltd/Blend Images/Corbis

Unit 8: p.231 Imagesource; p.233 Yuri Arcurs. Shutterstock; p.235 Monkey Business Images. Shutterstock; p.239 Pearson Education Ltd. Jules Selmes; p.240 Imagesource; p.240 Brian Goodman Shutterstock; p.240 Pearson Education Ltd. Jules Selmes; p.242 Mitchell Kanashkevich. Getty; p.250 Shutterstock; p.252 Pearson Education Ltd. Lord & Leverett; p.253 UpperCut Images/Alamy; p.259 PhotoAlto/Alamy; p.259 Ianni Dimitrov/Alamy; p.274 Pearson Education Ltd. Jules Selmes

Unit 9: p.277 Pearson Education Ltd. Lord & Leverett; p.279 Elena Elisseeva; p.289 Getty Images; p.292 moodboard/ Alamy; p.295 Richard Smith; p.299 Doug Steley A/Alamy; p.302 Paula Solloway/Alamy; p.307 Pearson Education Ltd. Gareth Boden; p.312 keith morris /Alamy; p.321 EugeneF. Shutterstock

Unit 10: p.323 Elena Elisseeva.Shutterstock; p.325 Pearson Education Ltd. Jules Selmes; p.329 Pearson Education Ltd. Richard Smith; p.332 By Ian Miles-Flashpoint Pictures/Alamy; p.336 Chris Howes/Wild Places Photography/ Alamy; p.350 Pearson Education Ltd. Mind Studio; p.355 Tim Pannell/Corbis; p.357 Photodisc. Keith Brofsky; p.358 Brooke Fasani/Corbis; p.363 Monkey Business Images. Shutterstock

Unit 11: p.365 and p.396 Regien Paassen. Shutterstock; p.367 konstantynov. Shutterstock; p.389 Corbis/ Reuters; p.389 MAURO FERMARIELLO/SCIENCE PHOTO LIBRARY; p.389 CNRI/SCIENCE PHOTO LIBRARY; p.390 BIOPHOTO ASSOCIATES/SCIENCE PHOTO LIBRARY; p.391 BIOPHOTO ASSOCIATES/SCIENCE PHOTO LIBRARY; p.401 EYE OF SCIENCE/SCIENCE PHOTO LIBRARY; p.401 JUERGEN BERGER/SCIENCE PHOTO LIBRARY; p.401 SCIMAT/SCIENCE PHOTO LIBRARY; p.401 DAVID SCHARF/SCIENCE PHOTO LIBRARY; p.405 Custom Medical Stock Photo/Alamy

BTEC
Level 2

edexcel
advancing learning, changing lives

HEALTH & SOCIAL CARE LEVEL 2

BTEC First

Elizabeth Haworth | Heather Higgins | Helen Hoyle
Siân Lavers | Carol Lewis

A PEARSON COMPANY

Published by Pearson Education Limited, a company incorporated in England and Wales, having its registered office at Edinburgh Gate, Harlow, Essex, CM20 2JE. Registered company number: 872828

www.pearsonschoolsandfecolleges.co.uk

Edexcel is a registered trademark of Edexcel Limited

Text © Elizabeth Haworth, Heather Higgins, Helen Hoyle, Siân Lavers and Carol Lewis 2010

First published 2010

13 12 11
10 9 8 7 6 5 4

British Library Cataloguing in Publication Data
A catalogue record for this book is available from the British Library.

ISBN 978 1 846 90681 7

Typeset by Phoenix Photosetting
Original illustrations © Pearson Education Limited 2010
Illustrated by KJA-artists.com
Cover design by Visual Philosophy, created by eMC design
Cover photo © Stuart Redler. Getty Images
Back cover photos © Pearson Education Ltd. Lord & Leverett / Pearson Education Ltd. Jules Selmes
Printed in Spain by Grafos, S.A.

Acknowledgements
We are grateful to the following for permission to reproduce copyright material:

The World Health Organization for details about the organization in Unit 3, http://www.who.int/about/history/en/index.html, accessed December 2009, copyright © World Health Organization; Dr. Marcus Smith for an extract in Unit 9 from "The energy cost of rock drumming: a case study" by Marcus Smith, Steve Draper and Chris Potter, European College of Sport Science (ECSS) 13th Annual Congress, July 2008, Estoril, Portugal copyright © Clem Burke Drumming Project, reproduced with permission; Table: 11.1 'Daily energy needs of babies and children' from Manual of Nutrition, 10th Edition, DEFRA, HMSO 1995; and Table 11.2 'Dietary Reference Values for vitamin C (mg per day)' adapted from Dietary Reference Values – A guide HMSO 1991; HMSO, Crown Copyright material is reproduced with permission under the terms of the Click-Use License; Little, Brown Book Group for Figure 11.3 'Food Combining for Vegetarian Protein' from The Optimum Nutrition Bible by Patrick Holford, Piatkus, a division of Little, Brown Book Group, 1997, reproduced with permission; and Food Standards Agency for a table in Unit 11 from The Balance of Good Health, Information for educators and communicators, 2001, http://www.food.gov.uk/multimedia/pdfs/bghbooklet.pdf, copyright © Crown copyright 2001.

Every effort has been made to contact copyright holders of material reproduced in this book. Any omissions will be rectified in subsequent printings if notice is given to the publishers.

Websites and Hotlinks
There are links to relevant websites in this book. In order to ensure that the links are up to date, that the links work, and that the sites are not inadvertently linked to sites that could be considered offensive, we have made the links available on the Pearson website at www.pearsonschoolsandfecolleges.co.uk/hotlinks. When you access the site, search for either the express code 6817V, title BTEC Level 2 First Health and Social Care Student Book or ISBN 9781846906817.
The websites used in the legislation grid (page 407 to 409) were correct and up to date at the time of publication. It is essential for tutors to preview each website before using it in class so as to ensure that the URL is still accurate, relevant and appropriate. We suggest that tutors bookmark useful websites and consider enabling students to access them through the school/college intranet.

Disclaimer
This material has been published on behalf of Edexcel and offers high-quality support for the delivery of Edexcel qualifications.

This does not mean that the material is essential to achieve any Edexcel qualification, nor does it mean that it is the only suitable material available to support any Edexcel qualification. Edexcel material will not be used verbatim in setting any Edexcel examination or assessment. Any resource lists produced by Edexcel shall include this and other appropriate resources.

Copies of official specifications for all Edexcel qualifications may be found on the Edexcel website: www.edexcel.com

About your BTEC Level 2 First Health and Social Care

Choosing to study for a BTEC Level 2 First Health and Social Care qualification is a great decision to make for lots of reasons. It is an area to work in which gives many varied opportunities for you to make a difference to people's lives in a positive way. At the same time you are gaining skills that you can transfer to other professions later. Working in the health and social care professions can also take you to different parts of the country and overseas. The opportunities are endless.

Your BTEC Level 2 First in Health and Social Care is a vocational or work-related qualification. This doesn't mean that it will give you all the skills you need to do a job, but it does mean that you'll have the opportunity to gain specific knowledge, understanding and skills that are relevant to your chosen subject or area of work.

What will you be doing?

The qualification is structured into **mandatory units** (ones you must do) and **optional units** (your school or college usually chooses the ones to be included in the programme). This book contains all 11 units, so you can be sure that you are covered whichever qualification you are working towards.

- BTEC Level 2 First **Certificate** in Health and Social Care: 1 mandatory unit and optional units that provide a combined total of 15 credits

- BTEC Level 2 First **Extended Certificate** in Health and Social Care: 2 mandatory units and optional units that provide a combined total of 30 credits

- BTEC Level 2 First **Diploma** in Health and Social Care: 4 mandatory units and 4 optional units that provide a combined total of 60 credits

Unit number	Credit value	Unit name	Cert	Ex. Cert	Diploma
1	5	Communication in health and social care	M	M	M
2	5	Individual rights in health and social care	M	M	M
3	5	Individual needs in health and social care	M	M	M
4	5	Ensuring safe environments in health and social care	M	M	M
5	10	Vocational experience in a health and social care setting*	O	O	O
6	10	Cultural diversity in health and social care	O	O	O
7	10	Anatomy and physiology for health and social care	O	O	O
8	10	Human lifespan development	O	O	O
9	10	Creative and therapeutic activities in health and social care	O	O	O
10	10	Health and social care services	O	O	O
11	10	The impact of diet on health	O	O	O

*To successfully complete this unit learners must complete 60 hours of work experience

How to use this book

This book is designed to help you through your BTEC Level 2 First Health and Social Care course. It is divided into 11 units to reflect the units in the specification. To make your learning easier we have divided each unit into a series of topics each related to the learning outcomes and content of the qualification.

Your teacher or tutor may have a copy of the mapping grid showing how the topics relate to the learning outcomes. You can also download this for free at www.pearsonfe.co.uk/btechsc.

This book contains many features that will help you use your skills and knowledge in work-related situations and assist you in getting the most from your course.

Introduction

These introductions give you a snapshot of what to expect from each unit – and what you should be aiming for by the time you finish it!

Assessment and grading criteria

This table explains what you must do in order to achieve each of the assessment criteria for each unit. For each assessment criterion, shown by the grade button **P1**, there is an assessment activity.

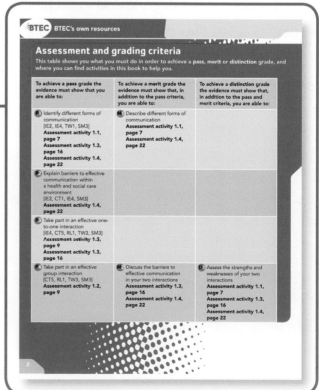

Assessment

Your tutor will set **assignments** throughout your course for you to complete. These may take the form of projects where you research, presentations, written work or research assignments. The important thing is that you evidence your skills and knowledge to date.

Stuck for ideas? Daunted by your first assignment? These students have all been through it before…

Unit 1 Communication in health and social care

How you will be assessed

The unit will be assessed by a series of internally assessed tasks. You will be expected to show an understanding of communication skills in the context of health and social care sectors. The tasks will be based on a scenario where you work in a local health or social care organisation. For example, your manager is concerned that learners on work experience placements from local schools and colleges do not have sufficient experience in using effective communication skills within a care environment. She asks you to produce training materials that can be used during the work experience induction session.

Your assessment could be in the form of:
- a written observation log based in health or social care settings
- training materials, such as leaflets and PowerPoint® presentations
- a training DVD demonstrating good practice in one-to-one and group interaction.

Laura, 16-year-old would-be nursery nurse

I really enjoyed this unit because it taught me some very useful facts about communication. When I went on placement to a nursery I knew to crouch down at the level of the children so I could look directly at them and not tower over them and frighten them. I also spoke quietly but clearly, so they could understand me and not feel intimidated. This meant they quickly accepted me. I also learnt to speak to physically disabled people directly, instead of to the person pushing their wheelchair. Lots of people do this and it makes the person feel unvalued and as though they are thought of as stupid when all that is different about them is that part of their body doesn't work very well.

I also enjoyed making observations of people communicating. It was actually really easy to see whether someone was doing it effectively or not. The use of body language was also very interesting and I have learned how to present myself more positively, which will be useful in everything I do, including job interviews in the future.

Over to you!
- What do you think you will need to do to get the most out of working in a group to carry out the required interactions for assessment?
- How can you make sure you communicate with others of all ages and abilities effectively?

Activities

There are different types of activities for you to do: Some are activities to deepen your knowledge of the subject and some are **assessment activities**. These are suggestions for tasks that you might do as part of your assignment and will help you develop your knowledge, skills and understanding, Each of these has **grading tips** that clearly explain what you need to do in order to achieve a pass, merit or distinction grade.

BTEC Assessment activity 1.3 (P1) (P3) (M2) (D1)

Do some research on a British Sign Language (BSL) website, and try to contact a local BSL association, to help you to produce a leaflet to teach basic sign language to a work experience student going to work in a nursery with a child using BSL. In the leaflet explain why it is important to learn the basics even if the student cannot learn any more than that in the time available. Learn some BSL yourself and use it in a role play to show the rest of your tutor group the basics such as hello and goodbye.

Grading tips

This assessment activity will help you gain (P1) and (P3) by showing that you can identify a different form of communication to overcome barriers to communication. In the role play you will be able to show basic sign language skills. To achieve (M2) you will have worked more independently and be able to explain why it is important to make the effort to learn the basics in this situation. In order to achieve (D1) standard you will have used a range of primary and secondary sources of information to complete the task and will have been able to give an accurate evaluation of your basic sign language skills.

There are also case studies that will give you an additional insight into the challenges you may face, and how to solve them, working in Health and Social Care.

Case study: Malik

Malik has not been in the UK long. He gets a job as a porter in a hospital but because his English is not very good he does not always understand what the other staff or patients have asked him to do. This has caused one or two arguments and he has come close to being sacked.

1. Suggest what Malik's employer can do to resolve this so that Malik can remain a porter.
2. What can Malik do to help himself?
3. How do you think (i) the patients (ii) staff (iii) Malik feels when communication fails like this?

Personal, learning and thinking skills

Throughout your BTEC Level 2 First Health and Social Care course, there are lots of opportunities to develop your personal, learning and thinking skills. Look out for these as you progress.

PLTS

This involves researching facts and generating ideas, so helping you to be an **independent enquirer** and a **creative thinker**.

Functional skills

It's important that you have good English, maths and ICT skills – you never know when you'll need them, and employers will be looking for evidence that you've got these skills too.

Functional skills

ICT functional skills will be developed by using ICT systems to research and produce evidence for your assessment activity.

Key terms

Technical words and phrases are easy to spot, and definitions are included. The terms and definitions are also in the glossary at the back of the book.

Key terms

Communication – the exchange of information between people

Context – the circumstances in which an event occurs; a setting

Just checking

These quick activities and questions are there at the end of each topic to check your knowledge. You can use them to see how much you have learnt as you work through each topic in a unit.

Just checking

1. List three different ways of adapting the environment to help overcome barriers to communication.
2. Why is timing important when giving someone information?
3. Describe how an electronic device such as a mobile phone can help overcome barriers to communication.

WorkSpace

Case studies provide snapshots of real workplace issues, and show how the skills and knowledge you develop during your course can help you in your career.

Extension activity

Extension activities at the end of each unit are designed to help you explore the content covered in more detail. They will also help you test your understanding of the unit.

Extension activity: Catching a bus

Sophie is 35 years old. She has been in a psychiatric hospital, after a complete mental breakdown, for fifteen years and is now preparing to live in the community. She has to learn how to catch a bus on her own again. Imagine she is coming to live in the area near your school and has to travel to a local town. You are her new care worker and are going to teach her how to cope with life outside the hospital. Remember that she will not know much about money and has only been on a bus a couple of times in the last two years, always accompanied by a care worker.

1. Sophie is not used to speaking to strangers. Write down what you would say to her.
2. Test out what you have written on another member of your group. Ask them to tell you honestly whether it would make sense if they were not used to catching buses.
3. Imagine how Sophie will be feeling about the experience of learning to travel to a nearby town by bus on her own. What are the barriers to communication for Sophie with (i) you (ii) the bus driver?
4. How can you help Sophie overcome each of these barriers?
5. Produce a reminder card for Sophie to have in her handbag, to refer to if she forgets what you have said to her.
6. How can you prepare her to cope when someone she has not met before sits on the seat next to her and tries to chat to her? To work out how you could do this think about a time when this has happened to you. Talk it over with a partner and role play the situation. Then write a list of practice opening lines to conversations that a stranger might use, such as, 'It's lovely weather, isn't it?' and then suggest what Sophie should say in response.

Edexcel's assignment tips

At the end of each chapter, you'll find hints and tips to help you get the best mark you can, such as the best websites to go to, checklists to help you remember processes and really useful facts and figures.

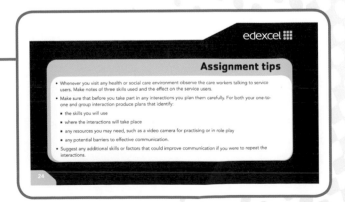

Additional documentation to help with unit work

At the end of the book you will find some documents, including a care plan and forms for taking measurements, which you can use to help you practice for your assessments. You will also find a very useful summary of all the important legislation that you will need to learn about as you work through the course.

Don't miss out on these resources to help you!

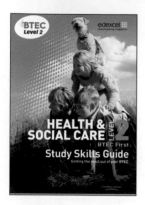

Have you read your BTEC Level 2 First Study Skills Guide? It's full of advice on study skills, putting your assignments together and making the most of being a BTEC Health and Social Care learner.

Hotlinks

There are links to relevant websites in this book. In order to ensure that the links are up to date, that the links work, and that the sites are not inadvertently linked to sites that could be considered offensive, we have made the links available on the Pearson website at www.pearsonschoolsandfecolleges.co.uk/hotlinks. When you access the site, search for either the express code 6817V, title BTEC Level 2 First Health and Social Care Student Book or ISBN 9781846906817.

Your book is just part of the exciting resources from Edexcel to help you succeed in your BTEC course. Visit www.edexcel.com/BTEC or www.pearsonfe.co.uk/BTEC 2010 for more details.

1 Communication in health and social care

Health and social care professionals need good communication skills to develop positive relationships and share information with people using services. They also need to be able to communicate well with people's families and/or carers and their own colleagues and other professionals. It is important therefore, if you are considering a career in health and social care, to gain the knowledge, understanding and practical skills needed to develop effective interpersonal skills.

There are several different forms of communication used in a health and social care environment. This unit looks at verbal and non-verbal communication methods. You will gain an understanding of the communication cycle, looking at how to make sure that communication is effective and messages understood at each stage. You will also learn to recognise a range of factors which may create barriers to communication. You will then consider ways in which these barriers may be overcome, including the use of alternative forms of communication.

You will be given the opportunity to observe and discuss communication methods used by professionals – skills which you will practise and refine. You will then demonstrate your communication skills in both one-to-one and group situations.

This unit has links with Unit 2 (Individual needs in health and social care), Unit 5 (Vocational experience) and Unit 6 (Cultural diversity) as it will develop your understanding of ways to adapt your communication to meet the individual needs of people using health or care services. These include cultural differences.

Learning outcomes

After completing this unit you should:

1. know different forms of communication
2. understand barriers to effective communication
3. be able to communicate effectively.

Assessment and grading criteria

This table shows you what you must do in order to achieve a **pass**, **merit** or **distinction** grade, and where you can find activities in this book to help you.

To achieve a **pass** grade the evidence must show that you are able to:	To achieve a **merit** grade the evidence must show that, in addition to the pass criteria, you are able to:	To achieve a **distinction** grade the evidence must show that, in addition to the pass and merit criteria, you are able to:
P1 Identify different forms of communication [IE2, IE4, TW1, SM3] **Assessment activity 1.1, page 7** **Assessment activity 1.3, page 16** **Assessment activity 1.4, page 22**	**M1** Describe different forms of communication **Assessment activity 1.1, page 7** **Assessment activity 1.4, page 22**	
P2 Explain barriers to effective communication within a health and social care environment [IE2, CT1, IE4, SM3] **Assessment activity 1.3, page 16** **Assessment activity 1.4, page 22**		
P3 Take part in an effective one-to-one interaction [IE4, CT5, RL1, TW3, SM3] **Assessment activity 1.2, page 9**		
P4 Take part in an effective group interaction [CT5, RL1, TW3, SM3] **Assessment activity 1.4, page 22**	**M2** Discuss the barriers to effective communication in your two interactions **Assessment activity 1.2, page 9** **Assessment activity 1.3, page 16** **Assessment activity 1.4, page 22**	**D1** Assess the strengths and weaknesses of your two interactions **Assessment activity 1.3, page 16** **Assessment activity 1.4, page 22**

How you will be assessed

The unit will be assessed by a series of internally assessed tasks. You will be expected to show an understanding of communication skills in the context of health and social care sectors. The tasks will be based on a scenario where you work in a local health or social care organisation. For example, your manager is concerned that learners on work experience placements from local schools and colleges do not have sufficient experience in using effective communication skills within a care environment. She asks you to produce training materials that can be used during the work experience induction session.

Your assessment could be in the form of:

- a written observation log based in health or social care settings

- training materials, such as leaflets and PowerPoint® presentations

- a training DVD demonstrating good practice in one-to-one and group interaction.

Laura, 16-year-old would-be nursery nurse

I really enjoyed this unit because it taught me some very useful facts about communication. When I went on placement to a nursery I knew to crouch down at the level of the children so I could look directly at them and not tower over them and frighten them. I also spoke quietly but clearly, so they could understand me and not feel intimidated. This meant they quickly accepted me. I also learnt to speak to physically disabled people directly, instead of to the person pushing their wheelchair. Lots of people do this and it makes the person feel unvalued and as though they are thought of as stupid when all that is different about them is that part of their body doesn't work very well.

I also enjoyed making observations of people communicating. It was actually really easy to see whether someone was doing it effectively or not. The use of body language was also very interesting and I have learned how to present myself more positively, which will be useful in everything I do, including job interviews in the future.

Over to you!

- What do you think you will need to do to get the most out of working in a group to carry out the required interactions for assessment?

- How can you make sure you communicate with others of all ages and abilities effectively?

3

1. Know different forms of communication

Key terms

Communication – the exchange of information between people

Context – the circumstances in which an event occurs; a setting

In this topic you will learn about why we communicate, why good **communication** skills are so important within a health and social care environment and the different **contexts** for communication. We communicate with others all the time, wherever we may be, often without even realising it and sometimes without intending to. This topic and the following topic will help you explore different forms of communication.

Interpersonal skills are those skills that enable us to interact with another person, allowing us to communicate successfully with them. Good communication skills are vital for those working in health and social care as they help them to:

- develop positive relationships with people using services and their families and friends, so they can understand and meet their needs
- develop positive relationships with work colleagues and other professionals
- share information with people using the services, by providing and receiving information
- report on the work they do with people.

Contexts

One–to–one communication

One-to-one means one person communicating with another person with no other people joining in. If you walk into a one-to-one job interview, the interviewer may say something like, 'Good morning, my name is … Please take a seat. Did you find us all right?' This is to make you feel relaxed and less nervous so you feel more confident and do your best. If you walked in and they immediately said, 'Sit down. Tell me why you want this job', you would be sitting down and starting to answer questions instantly so would be very on edge. It is the same in any conversation; it is important to create the right feeling by being

Activity: Group discussion

Sit in a circle in a group. Discuss the statement 'TV programmes such as *Casualty* or *Holby City* create the wrong impression of working life in a large hospital.' One person starts the discussion holding a ball or bean bag. When they have made their point they throw the ball to someone else in the group and that person responds to what they have said. The ball has to go to each person in the group before anyone who has already spoken

can speak again. When the discussion has finished discuss the following points in your group:

1. Did everyone join in properly? If not, why not?
2. Did sitting in a circle help? How?
3. How could you tell that someone was about to finish talking?
4. Did you find the ball made the task easier or harder? Why?

Figure 1.1: The communication skills needed by people working in health and social care environments

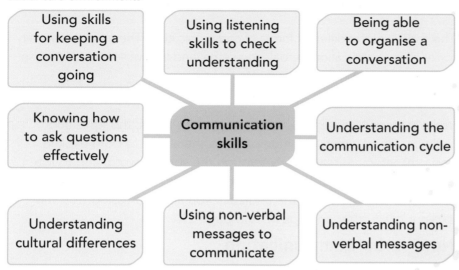

friendly and showing interest in and respect for the other person. The conversation needs a start, e.g. 'Hi', a middle, when you both discuss what you need to talk about, and an ending, e.g. 'See you later.'

Group communication

Group communication is harder because it only works properly if everyone is able to be involved. In most groups there are people who speak a lot and others who speak rarely, if at all, because they feel uncomfortable speaking in front of a group of people or they are just not interested. Groups work best if there is a team leader who encourages everyone to have a say in turn, rather than everyone trying to speak at once.

Formal and informal communication

Formal communication tends to start with a greeting such as 'Good afternoon. How are you feeling today?' It can be used to show respect for others. Formal conversation is often used when a professional person, such as a health or social care worker, speaks to someone using a service. It is clear, correct and avoids misunderstanding. Communication with a manager is usually formal. A manager is usually more distant from those they manage so that if they need to, for example, issue a formal warning to someone, it is less awkward for both parties than if they are friends.

Informal communication (often used between people who know each other well, like friends and family) is more likely to start with 'Hi, how are you?' and allows for more variety according to the area someone lives in. For example, in some places it is common for people to call other people 'Love' even if they have only just met them. People usually communicate more informally with friends, including those they work closely with on a day-to-day basis.

Key terms

Formal – the use of conventional language

Informal – the use of more casual language

Just checking

1. What are three features of one-to-one communication?
2. What are three things that help group communication?
3. What is the difference between informal and formal communication? Which would you use with (i) a friend (ii) someone you have not met before but are trying to help in your job as a doctor's receptionist (iii) your manager (iv) a service user?

Forms of communication

This topic looks at different forms of communication. There are three main forms of communication, verbal, non-verbal and the written word. We can also use technology to communicate.

Verbal communication

Verbal communication uses words to present ideas, thoughts and feelings. Good verbal communication is the ability to both explain and present your ideas clearly through the spoken word, and to listen carefully to other people. This will involve using a variety of approaches and styles appropriate to the audience you are addressing. You will explore this further on page 13 and page 21.

Non–verbal communication

This refers to the messages we send out to express ideas and opinions without talking. This might be through the use of body language, facial expressions, gestures, tone of voice, touch or contact, signs, symbols, pictures, objects and other visual aids. It is very important to be able to recognise what a person's body language is saying, especially when as a health or social care worker you are dealing with someone who is in pain, worried or upset. You must also be able to understand the messages you send with your own body when working with other people.

Figure 1.2: The main elements involved in non-verbal communication.

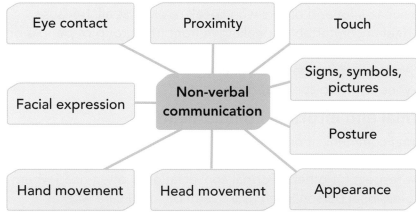

Body language – The way we sit or stand, which is called posture, can send messages. Slouching on a chair can show a lack of interest in what is going on and folded arms can suggest that you are feeling negative or defensive about a person or situation. Even the way we move can give out messages, e.g. shaking your head while someone else is talking might indicate that you disagree with them or waving your arms around can indicate you are excited.

Facial expression – We can often tell what someone is feeling by their eyes. Our eyes become wider when we are excited or happy, attracted to, or interested in someone. A smile shows we are happy and a frown shows we are annoyed.

Touch or contact – Touching another person can send messages of care, affection, power or sexual interest. It is important to think about the setting you are in and what you are trying to convey before touching a person in a health and social care environment. An arm around a child who is upset about something in hospital or a nursery can go a long way to making them feel better but a teenager might feel intimidated by such contact from an older person.

Signs, symbols and pictures – There are certain common signs or gestures that most people automatically recognise. For example, a wave of the hand can mean hello or goodbye and a thumbs up can mean that all is well. Pictures of all forms and objects also communicate messages; an X-ray and a model of a knee joint can more easily communicate to someone needing a knee replacement exactly what is involved.

Written communication

This is central to the work of any person providing a service in a health and social care environment when keeping records and in writing reports. Different types of communication need different styles of writing but all require **literacy skills**. A more formal style of writing is needed when recording information about a patient. It would be unacceptable to use text message abbreviations, such as 'l8er'. You will explore this further on page 20.

Technological aids

Technology is moving so quickly now that we have many electronic aids to help us communicate. For example, mobile phones can be used to make calls but we can also use them to send text messages and emails; and we have computers on which we can record, store and communicate information very quickly and efficiently over long distances. Some aids can turn small movements into written word and then into speech, such as the voice box most famously used by the scientist, Professor Stephen Hawking.

How could you communicate with other people if you did not have the use of your voice?

Key term

Literacy skills – the ability to be able to present the written word clearly and correctly and to be able to read the written word accurately

PLTS

This involves researching facts and generating ideas, so helping you to be an **independent enquirer** and a **creative thinker**.

 BTEC ## Assessment activity 1.1

Imagine you are working in a health centre on a work placement and you have been asked to produce some clear and easily understood information on a poster to help people who need technological aids understand how they work and how they can help them. Research a range of technological aids to communication and produce a poster showing how your favourite works. Include a diagram.

Grading tips

To achieve **P1** you need to clearly identify different forms of communication. To achieve **M1** you will need to work more independently and clearly explain and describe different forms of communication.

Just checking

1. Explain what is meant by verbal communication.
2. Give three examples of types of non-verbal communication.
3. Describe three examples when signs, symbols and pictures are useful forms of communication.

2. Understand barriers to communication

Figure 1.3: The people on the bus go 'Chatter, chatter, chatter...' but are they really listening properly to each other?

The people on the bus go 'chatter, chatter, chatter'

In this topic you will start to learn about barriers to effective communication, but in order to understand these you first need to understand the different elements that make up communication. This is called the communication cycle and is fundamental to our everyday lives.

This topic and the following four will help you to understand barriers to effective communication.

The communication cycle

In order to communicate you have to go through a process with another person. This process is called the communication cycle because the process goes round in a circle, as shown in figure 1.4.

Figure 1.4: The communication cycle

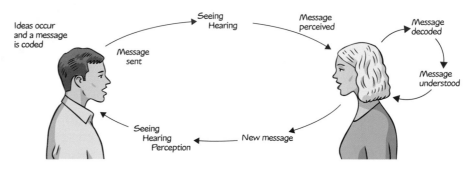

- **Ideas occur** – you think of something you want to communicate. Communication always has a purpose. It might be to pass on information or an idea, or to persuade someone to do something, or to entertain or inspire.

- **Message coded** – you think about how you are going to say what you are thinking and decide in what form the communication will be, for example, spoken word or sign language. You put it into this form in your head.

- **Message sent** – you send the message, for example speak or sign what you want to communicate.

- **Message received** – the other person senses that you have sent a message by, for example, hearing your words or seeing your signs.

- **Message decoded** – the other person has to interpret what you have communicated; this is known as decoding.

- **Message understood** – if you have communicated clearly and the other person has concentrated, and there are no barriers to communication, the other person understands your ideas. They show this by giving you feedback, i.e. by sending you a message back.

These stages of the communication cycle are shown as a list of bullet points rather than numbered because this process is repeated backwards and forwards as long as the conversation goes on. The sender of the message becomes the receiver of a message sent back, the receiver becomes the sender and so on. Each person continues the conversation because they have to check that they have understood what the other person meant. They do this by listening to what the person says and asking questions about it or putting it in their own words and repeating them back, so reflecting what has been said. A conversation can also be called an **interaction**.

Things that can go wrong

The person who has the first idea may not make the meaning clear and might assume that the other person is ready and willing to listen to them when they are not. They might also assume that the other person has heard what they said properly and has not been distracted by something else they are interested in. They might have used terms and language that the other person is unfamiliar with or might have started half way through a story assuming that they already knew the beginning. This can lead to the other person making assumptions as to what they meant, jumping to conclusions and so leading them to talk at cross purposes.

Key terms

Interaction – when someone or something has an effect on another

Appropriate – suitable or fitting for a particular purpose

BTEC Assessment activity 1.2 P3 M2

Imagine that you are working for a telephone helpline in the area of health and social care. Examples of these are NHS Direct or Childline. You are going to plan and carry out a one-to-one conversation on an issue of your choosing, and identify the communication skills you have used. It might be that a member of the public is ringing up to ask for advice during a flu epidemic. You can carry out your plan with a partner by giving them a script you have written and telling them which part they are reading. You will record the conversation and you will be assessed on the recording made and your written script.

You need to think about your tone of voice and using the communication cycle properly. Remember, this conversation is taking place on a phone so you cannot see each other.

Grading tips

At pass level you will need to give basic information and use listening skills to answer questions, using **appropriate** language. This will help you achieve P3. At merit level, you will need to plan the conversation independently with little guidance and give a realistic assessment of your own verbal skills during the conversation, suggesting ways you could improve next time.

PLTS

This activity will help you to be a **creative thinker** as you adapt your style or method of communication to make it suitable for use on the phone and the issue covered. You will be a **reflective learner** when you reflect on the effectiveness of your interaction.

Just checking

1. What are the six stages of the communication cycle?
2. How can someone check that they have understood something that has been said to them?
3. Describe three ways in which things can go wrong in the communication cycle.

Factors that affect communication

My life

Read all about it

Look at the newspaper article. What short term and long term effects do you think this will have on Abigail and how she communicates with other people?

Some things stop communication being as effective as it could be. People who work in a health or social care environment need to understand the barriers so they can overcome them. In this topic you will learn about some of these barriers.

Figure 1.5: How would being isolated affect how well you communicate?

CELLAR VICTIM RELEASED

ABIGAIL SMITH, 25, was today found alive in the dimly lit cellar she has been imprisoned in by her husband, Sam, 45, for 9 years. Sources say he was jealous of other men speaking to his wife so he kept her away from all other human contact.

It is very important to be able to communicate effectively in a health or social care setting. A service user will not be able to take part in a discussion about their care or planning their future if they do not understand what is being said. Equally, the person providing the service cannot help if they cannot find a way to understand what the service user is trying to ask for.

There are many factors that affect communication. They are:

- **Sensory deprivation** – when someone cannot receive or pass on information because they have an **impairment** to one or more of their senses, most commonly a visual or a hearing disability.
- **Foreign language** – when someone speaks a different language or uses sign language, they may not be able to make any sense of information they are being given by someone trying to help them if that person does not speak their language.
- **Jargon** – when a service provider uses technical language the service user may not understand. For example, the doctor may say that a patient needs bloods and an MRI scan. That can sound very frightening to someone who has been rushed into hospital. It is better if the doctor explains that they need to take some blood to do some simple tests and then explains what a MRI scan is. Understanding the facts can make something seem less scary.
- **Slang** – when a service user uses language that not everyone uses, such as saying they have a problem with their waterworks. This can mean their plumbing system but also means a problem going to the toilet. Sometimes it may be appropriate to use slang with your peers but in normal working with colleagues or service users you should avoid using any language that can be misunderstood or misinterpreted or that might cause offence.

Key terms

Deprivation – a lack of something

Impairment – a disability

Jargon – technical words used by a professional person as a short way of saying things that are hard for others to understand

Slang – the use of informal words and expressions that are not considered standard in the speaker's dialect or language

- **Dialect** – when people use different words for everyday objects or feelings depending on the area of a country they come from. In some areas of England people say 'innit' instead of 'isn't it' or 'summat' instead of 'something.' It may cause confusion if someone says, 'A've got a pain in me heed' instead of, 'I've got a headache'.

- **Acronyms** – when words are shortened to initials. There are lots of acronyms in health and social care and they can be very confusing. Sometimes people don't realise that not everyone knows what they mean and mistakes can be made or people can just feel left out if these terms are not familiar to them. A health care professional might say, "he has those tablets TDS" (which means three times a day). Or someone might say "you need to go to the CAB" (which means Citizen's Advice Bureau). This also relates to jargon.

- **Cultural differences** – when the same thing means different things in two cultures, communication can be difficult. For example, it is seen as polite and respectful to make eye contact when speaking to someone in Western culture but in other cultures, for example in East Asia, it can be seen as rude and defiant. You will learn more about this in Unit 6 Cultural diversity in health and social care.

- **Distress** – when someone is distressed, they might find it hard to communicate. They may not listen properly and so misinterpret or not understand what is being said. They might also be tearful or have difficulty speaking. See also emotional difficulties.

- **Emotional difficulties** – we all have emotional difficulties at times and become upset. You might have split up with your boyfriend or girlfriend or had an argument with someone or you may have had some bad news. The effect can be to not hear or understand what people are saying to you. This can lead to misunderstandings.

- **Health issues** – when you are feeling ill, you may not be able to communicate as effectively as when you are feeling well. This can affect your colleagues and service users. Similarly, people who are being cared for in hospital because of an illness may not be able to communicate in their normal way. Some long-term (chronic) illnesses such as Parkinson's disease or Multiple Sclerosis also affect an individual's ability to communicate and you need to be aware of this if you are working with these people. See also distress and disability.

- **Environmental problems** – when communication is affected by the environment that people find themselves in. For example, someone who does not see very well will struggle to read written information in a dimly lit room. A person who is in a wheelchair may find it impossible to communicate with the receptionist at the dentist's if the desk is too high and above the wheelchair user's head.

- **Misinterpretation of message** – when someone reads a person's body language wrongly. For example, someone with their arms folded and tapping their feet might be impatiently waiting for someone else who is late but you might look at them and assume they are cross with you. This can put you off asking for help.

Activity: Factors affecting communication

1. In pairs, choose two of the factors opposite and discuss the ways these could cause problems in a health and social care setting.

2. Four other factors that affect communication are differing humour, sarcasm, inappropriate behaviour and aggression. Think of an example where each of these could lead to a breakdown in communication at the reception desk of an optician.

Just checking

1. Why is it important for people who work in health and social care to understand barriers to communication?
2. Explain how cultural differences can affect communication.
3. How might emotional issues affect communication between a service user and a service provider?

More barriers to communication and ways to overcome them

Key terms

Aggression – behaviour that is unpleasant, frightening or intimidating

Assertion – behaviour that helps you communicate clearly and firmly

One of the barriers to communication is aggression. In this topic you will learn the difference between being aggressive and being assertive, and how to be assertive. You will also learn some verbal skills to use to check the understanding part of the communication cycle.

Aggression

Aggression is behaviour that is unpleasant, frightening or intimidating. It takes a variety of forms and can be physical, mental or verbal. It can cause physical pain or emotional harm to those it is directed at. It is caused by a range of factors, such as substance misuse, mental health, a personality problem, fear or an attempt to dominate someone else. People who are aggressive towards other people are often bullies.

Aggression is a form of communication in that it communicates a person's state of mind, such as annoyance. It is also a barrier to communication. Aggression is often emotion that is out of control and it can be destructive. When someone shouts at someone else, the other person can be afraid and will either shout back or shut the aggressive person out. If someone working in a health or social care environment is annoyed, frustrated or irritated (breathes quickly, shouts, has a clenched jaw and/or rigid body language) the person they are providing a service for may feel dominated, threatened and unable to respond. This will lead to a poorer service being offered due to the breakdown in effective communication.

Assertion

Assertion is the skill of being calm and firm but not aggressive in the way you communicate with others. It helps you to communicate your needs, feelings and thoughts in a clear confident way while taking into account the feelings of others and respecting their right to an opinion as well.

How to be assertive

You need to plan what you are going to say. Be polite, state the nature of the problem, how it affects you, how you feel about it and what you want to happen. Make it clear that you see the other person's point of view and be prepared to compromise if it leads to what you want. Control your emotions, such as anger or tearfulness and be calm and authoritative in your interactions with others. You need to be clear and prepared to defend your position and be able to say no. This won't cause offence if it is said firmly and calmly. Use questions such as, 'How can we solve this problem?' Use the 'broken record' technique where you just keep repeating your statement softly, calmly and persistently. At the same time, use body language that shows you are relaxed, e.g. make firm, direct eye contact with relaxed facial features and use open hand gestures.

Verbal skills to overcome barriers

When you use your verbal skills effectively, you can help overcome barriers that might be preventing effective communication. Some of the skills you need when communicating verbally, and assertively when need be, with service users are shown in the diagram. They are useful tools in the checking understanding (message understood) part of the communication cycle (pages 8–9).

- Paraphrasing means repeating back something a person has just said in a different way to make sure you have understood the message. For example, someone says, 'I have been sick since Sunday' and you respond by saying, 'You have been unwell for 4 days now then.'

- Closed questions are questions that can be answered with either a single word or short phrase, for example, 'Do you like sprouts?' could be answered, 'No' or, 'No, I can't stand them.' Closed questions give facts, are easy and quick to answer and keep control of the conversation. They are useful as an opening question, such as 'Are you feeling better?', for testing understanding, such as, 'So you want to go on the pill?' and for bringing a conversation to an end, such as, 'So that's your final decision?'

- Open questions are questions that give a longer answer, for example, 'Why don't you like sprouts?' might be answered by, 'I haven't liked the taste or smell of them since I was made to eat them all the time when I was a child…'. Open questions hand control of the conversation to the person you are speaking to. They ask the person to think and reflect, give opinions and feelings. They are useful as a follow-up to a closed question, to find out more, to help someone realise or face their problems and to show concern about them.

- Clarification means to make something clear and understandable. Summarising means to sum up what has been said in a short, clear way. Both of these will be explained in more detail in the topic on active listening (pages 18–19).

Did you know?

Aggressive words and behaviour adversely affect the rights and wellbeing of others. Think about that next time you are feeling annoyed with someone, especially someone close to you.

Activity: Aggressive vs assertive

In small groups agree on two different messages in a health or social care environment and produce a freeze frame to deliver the message to the other groups. Deliver one message in an aggressive way and the other in an assertive way. If you have access to a digital camera you can make a display of all the freeze frames as they are shown.

Figure 1.6: Verbal skills needed when communicating orally

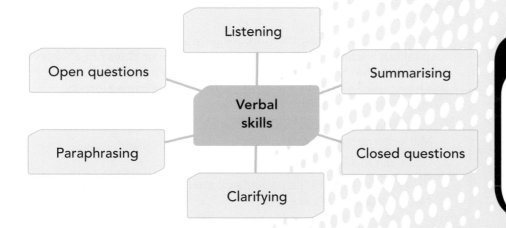

Just checking

1. Why is aggression a barrier to communication?
2. What is the difference between aggression and assertiveness?
3. Describe three techniques that are useful when checking understanding of something that has been said to you.

Overcoming communication barriers

You previously learned about many different barriers to communication (pages 10–13) and looked at some verbal skills. It is vital to be able to overcome these barriers if people are to receive the care they need. This topic is about how these barriers can be minimised or overcome.

Communication difficulties can isolate a person, making them feel cut off, so it is particularly important in a health or social care environment to overcome these difficulties. Barriers to communication can be minimised in the ways discussed below.

Adapting the environment

This can be done in a number of ways, such as improving lighting for those with sight impairments and reducing background noise for those with hearing impairments. Lifts can be installed with a voice giving information such as when the doors are opening and closing and which floor the lift is on for those who can't see. Ramps can be added, reception desks lowered and signs put lower down on walls, so that people with physical disabilities can access the people and information they need.

Understanding language needs and preferences

Service providers need to understand language needs and preferences of the people they are supporting. They may have to re-word messages so that they are in short, clear sentences, and avoid slang, jargon and dialect as much as possible. They explain details to people who cannot see and encourage them to touch things such as their face. They don't shout at those who cannot hear very well, but use normal, clear speech and make sure their face is visible. They employ a communicator or interpreter for spoken or signed language and show pictures or write messages, depending on what is best for the service user.

Figure 1.7: How do you feel when you can't hear yourself think?

Case study: Malik

Malik has not been in the UK long. He gets a job as a porter in a hospital but because his English is not very good he does not always understand what the other staff or patients have asked him to do. This has caused one or two arguments and he has come close to being sacked.

1. Suggest what Malik's employer can do to resolve this so that Malik can remain a porter.

2. What can Malik do to help himself?

3. How do you think (i) the patients (ii) staff (iii) Malik feels when communication fails like this?

Using individual preferred language

Most leaflets produced by public bodies such as the health service are now written in a variety of languages so that people who do not speak English can still access the information. If there is a member of staff who speaks the preferred language of a service user they will help translate. However, it is always important to ask a service user what their preferred language is for written and verbal communication.

Timing

It is important to pick the right time to communicate important information to a service user. If, for example, a doctor has just told a patient that they have a life threatening illness the patient needs time to take the information in. If the doctor tells them all about the treatment straight away the chances are that the patient will not really hear much of what is said because they are in shock. It may be better to make another appointment for when the patient has processed the information and is receptive to hearing additional information.

Electronic devices

There are many electronic devices that help overcome barriers to communication. These include:

- **mobile phones** – these are generally affordable and available to the population at large, making them more accessible than computers and far more cost-effective.They have many uses in health and social care. For example, they enable emergency response teams to co-ordinate their efforts, allow a surgical team to contact someone awaiting an organ transplant, gather and send information etc. They are especially important in health and social care in developing countries, where people may live several days' walk from the nearest doctor.

- **telephone amplifiers** – these are devices that amplify, or make louder, the ring tone of a phone so that people who are hard of hearing and maybe use a hearing aid can hear the phone more clearly. They also amplify the volume of the person speaking on the other end by up to 100%. Other devices on telephones include flashing lights so someone who is hard of hearing can see that the phone is ringing.

- **hearing loops** – a hearing loop system helps deaf people who use a hearing aid or loop listener hear sounds more clearly because it reduces or cuts out background noise. At home, for example, you could use a loop to hear sound from your television. You can also set up a loop with a microphone to help you hear conversations in noisy places. In the theatre, a loop can help you hear the show more clearly. A hearing impaired student can wear a loop and the teacher a microphone to help the student hear what the teacher says.

What ways can the environment be adapted to help people in a wheelchair?

Just checking

1. List three different ways of adapting the environment to help overcome barriers to communication.
2. Why is timing important when giving someone information?
3. Describe how an electronic device such as a mobile phone can help overcome barriers to communication.

Alternative forms of communication

My life

Can you hear me?

How can a care assistant communicate with someone who has a hearing impairment if the care assistant can't do sign language or the person can't understand it?

Figure 1.8: Some examples of British Sign Language

a) Wait

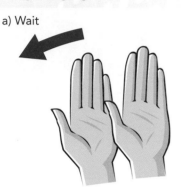

b) Go to see

c) Tell/say

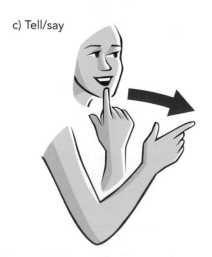

Sometimes it is not possible to overcome a barrier to communication so an alternative form of communication must be found. In this topic you will learn about alternatives such as sign language, lip reading and Makaton.

Sign language

Sign language is a language which instead of using sounds uses visual signs. These are made up of the shapes, positions and movement of the hands, arms or body and facial expressions to express a speaker's thoughts. Sign language is commonly used in communities which include the friends and families of deaf people as well as people who are deaf or hard of hearing themselves.

BTEC **Assessment activity 1.3**

Do some research on a British Sign Language (BSL) website, and try to contact a local BSL association, to help you to produce a leaflet to teach basic sign language to a work experience student going to work in a nursery with a child using BSL. In the leaflet explain why it is important to learn the basics even if the student cannot learn any more than that in the time available. Learn some BSL yourself and use it in a role play to show the rest of your tutor group the basics such as hello and goodbye.

Grading tips

This assessment activity will help you gain **P1** and **P2** by showing that you can identify a different form of communication to overcome barriers to communication. In the role play you will be able to show basic sign language skills. To achieve **M2** you will have worked more independently and be able to explain why it is important to make the effort to learn the basics in this situation. In order to achieve **D1** standard you will have used a range of primary and secondary sources of information to complete the task and will have been able to give an accurate evaluation of your basic sign language skills.

Lip reading

People with normal hearing subconsciously use information from the lips and face to help understand what is being said. Many people misunderstand deafness, thinking that if someone can't hear very well they are being rude or stupid, and this can leave a deaf person feeling very isolated, excluded from everyday activities and conversations, frustrated and lacking in confidence. Lip reading is a technique of interpreting the movements of a person's lips, face and tongue, along with information provided by any remaining hearing. It is used by someone who is deaf or hard of hearing. It is therefore important that you look directly at someone who is lip reading and stand in a well lit area, when speaking.

Makaton

Makaton is a method of communication using **signs** and **symbols** and is often used as a communication process for those with learning difficulties. It was first developed in the UK in the 1970s and is now used in over 40 countries around the world. Unlike BSL, Makaton uses speech as well as actions and symbols. It uses picture cards and ties in facial expressions with the word to make the word more easily recognised by those with learning difficulties.

Braille

The Braille system is a method that is widely used by blind people to read and write. Braille was devised in 1821 by Louis Braille, a Frenchman. Each Braille character is made up of six dot positions, arranged in a rectangle. A dot may be raised at any of the six positions to form sixty-four possible combinations and these raised dots are read by touch.

Technological aids

These have already been mentioned in an earlier topic as a way of overcoming barriers to communication (page 7). They are also alternative forms of communication.

Human aids

Human aids are people who help people communicate with each other. Examples are:

- **Interpreters** – people who communicate a conversation, whether it be spoken or signed, to someone in a different language they will understand. This is not easy because they not only have to interpret the words or signs but also have to find a way of expressing the meaning of the words clearly.

- **Translators** – people who change recorded information, such as the written word, into another language. Again, they have to convey the meaning as well as the words.

- **Signers** – people who can communicate using a sign language.

Key terms

Sign – a posted up notice giving a direction or command

Symbol – something such as an object, picture, written word, sound, or particular mark that represents something else

Activity: Signs, symbols and advocates

1. Do some research to find out the signs for (i) poison (ii) no entry (ii) no smoking (iv) fire exit (v) wet floor. Find at least five more common signs/symbols that most people will recognise which are used in a health or social care environment of your choosing. Produce an information leaflet for people who are new to the country and have not seen these signs before.

2. Find out what an advocate is then find all the different health and social care services that use advocates and research how they use them.

Just checking

1. What do we mean by the expression 'alternative forms of communication'?
2. Explain what Makaton is.
3. What is a human aid? Give three examples.

3. Be able to communicate effectively

In the next two topics you will start to learn more skills for effective communication. These include active listening, body language, facial expressions and eye contact. You have already looked at some of these at the beginning of this unit.

Skills for effective communication
Active listening and body language

Listening to people involves more than just hearing what they say. To listen well you need to be able to hear the words being spoken, thinking about what they mean, then thinking what to say back to the person. You can also show that you are listening and what you think about what is being said by your body language, facial expressions and eye contact. By yawning or looking at your notes when someone is talking you give the impression of being bored by what is being said. By shaking your head and frowning you are showing that you disagree with, or disapprove of, what they are saying.

The process of active listening involves:

* allowing the person talking time to explain and not interrupting
* giving encouragement by smiling, nodding and making encouraging remarks such as, 'That's interesting' and, 'Really?'
* asking questions for **clarification**, such as, 'Can you explain that again please?'
* showing **empathy** by making comments such as, 'That must be making life really hard for you'
* looking interested by maintaining eye contact and not looking at your watch
* not being distracted by anything else, such as an interruption on your mobile – switch it off or say you will ring back
* summarising to check that you have understood the other person. You can do this by saying, 'So what you mean is …?'

Key terms

Clarification – making something clear and understandable

Empathy – putting yourself in someone else's shoes by sharing and understanding someone else's emotions

Proximity – being near or close to someone or something

How can you tell that the people on the right are interested and listening carefully?

Activity: Listening to each other

Work in a group of three. Each person first needs to spend five minutes writing down some facts about themselves.

Number each person 1, 2 or 3. Person 1 tells person 2 about themselves. Person 2 listens carefully, and is not allowed to take any notes. Person 2 then repeats back to person 1 what they have remembered about what person 1 said. Person 3 is the observer and watches person 2 as they listen to person 1 and repeat what has been said.

Person 1 tells person 2 how well they have done in remembering what was said. Person 3 then reports back on how actively person 2 listened, referring to all the bullet points on page 18.

Repeat the whole process so that each of you takes on all three roles in turn.

Use of appropriate language

How would you feel if your tutor suddenly started using swear words while they were teaching you? Why would you feel like this? You adjust how you speak depending on who you are with and who is listening to you. Things that are said with a group of friends or at a family gathering might not be understood by others because we use different types of language in different situations. People even unconsciously change their use of dialect depending on who they are speaking to. A person's accent or dialect may become more pronounced when they are speaking to someone from their family or from the area they grew up in.

Tone of voice

If you talk to someone in a loud voice with a fixed tone the person you are speaking to will think you are angry with them. On the other hand, if you speak calmly and quietly with a varying tone the other person will think you are being friendly and kind. So it is important to remember that it is not just what you say, but also the way in which you say it, that matters.

Pace

If you speak really quickly and excitedly, the person listening to you will not be able to hear everything you say. If you keep hesitating or saying 'um' or 'er' it makes it harder for people to concentrate on what you are saying. If you speak at a steady pace, however, you will be able to deliver your message more clearly and the other person will be able to hear every word you say.

Proximity

The space around a person is called their personal space. In a formal situation, such as a doctor talking to a patient, the doctor does not sit close enough to the patient to invade their personal space. In an informal situation, people who are friends or intimate with each other will often sit closer to each other. People usually sit or stand so they are eye-to-eye if they are in a formal or aggressive situation. Sitting at an angle to each other creates a more relaxed, friendly and less formal feeling.

Just checking

1. State three ways you can show that you are actively listening to a person speaking by what you say in reply.
2. Give three ways you can tell someone is actively listening to you by their use of body language.
3. Explain how your pace and tone of voice can affect how the person you are speaking to understands what you are saying.

Effective communication

If you have not heard, or read, and understood a message properly it is impossible to make the best use of the information. This topic looks at the importance of the written word as a form of communication. It also looks at some situations that can arise in a health and social care environment which might lead to communication not being effective.

Effective communication, including active listening, can be hard work. People who work in health or social care environments tend to enjoy learning about other people and their lives. Things can go wrong, however, if:

* the context is wrong, e.g. the surroundings are unsuitable due to lack of privacy
* the service provider and service user are mismatched. Sometimes communication breaks down because of factors such as age, education level, gender and ethnic background
* a person withholds information because they fear being judged, for example, they have taken illegal drugs
* a person fears that confidentiality will be broken, even though this should never happen, for example, about their sexual orientation
* the service user thinks that the advice given is too vague and has not asked for clarification
* the subject matter is embarrassing, such as talking about sex or intimate body parts
* a person fears they are going to hear bad news so avoids going to a service provider until it is too late to help.

Activity: Doctor, Doctor

Read the following conversation:

Doctor: What can I do for you today?

Patient: I've got a pain.

Doctor: What sort of pain is it and where is it?

Patient: It's a shooting pain that goes right down my leg.

Doctor: So the pain is in your leg?

Patient: No, it is in my back but sometimes goes right down my leg.

Doctor: So the pain starts in your back and shoots down your leg?

Patient: Yes.

Doctor: I think you have got sciatica. I'll prescribe you some tablets to take three times a day. Come back and see me in a week if the pain does not improve.

1. Do you think the two people concerned have understood each other?

2. How did the doctor check he had understood the symptoms?

3. Why was it so important that the doctor understood clearly where the pain was and what sort of pain it was?

4. With a partner, role play a conversation between (i) a small child and a nursery nurse (ii) a deaf older person and a care assistant.

If health and social care workers do not develop good communication skills, the effectiveness of their work will be reduced and things can go wrong. This will not help service users to feel good about themselves and can lead to worse consequences. Remember, it is important to overcome problems such as those listed above, communicate effectively, including checking understanding, so that you get the best out of your interactions with colleagues and service users.

Written communication

Health and social care workers need to be able to communicate well with the written word. This could be by writing something themselves, such as a letter to refer a service user to a different service, a record of a person's condition and treatment or entitlement to a benefit, or a prescription. This means they need to be able to use different ways of presenting information, such as letters, memos, emails, reports or forms. They need to make their meaning absolutely clear and structure the information well and in an appropriate manner so that mistakes don't happen. It is also necessary to use grammar, spelling and punctuation correctly and writing should also be legible so that the person the information is intended for can actually read it.

It is also important that the language used is appropriate. You probably use text language every day on your mobile but you know not to use it when writing an essay or report. If you were emailing, or writing a letter to, your brother you might start it with the words 'Hi bro' but to someone to apply for a job you would start with either, 'Dear Sir or Madam' or, 'Dear Mr/Mrs …' Care professionals should also not use lots of technical words, acronyms or jargon if they are writing to someone who will not understand it.

They should read information provided by other care workers thoroughly. They need to be able to identify the main points and be able to find other information from a wide variety of sources. They also need ICT skills to update records and to access information.

Figure 1.9: What a mess

Different types of ~~form~~ communication will demand different styles of writing. If it is a formal piece of writing to another professional or to be used in court for e.g. it will need the correct ~~terminol~~ terminology whereas an informal look may not. You may not require full sentences to be used unless a longer more formal piece of writing merely noting in a report on a problem at work ambience, that writing should still contain

> ### Activity: Types of writing
>
> Think about all the different types of writing you use in a day. Draw up a table showing each type in one column and its uses in another column.

PLTS

When you are thinking about different types of communication, you are being an **independent enquirer**. When you think back about your interaction you are being a **reflective learner**.

Functional skills

When you write down what you think about your communication skills you are using **English** skills in writing

BTEC **Assessment activity 1.4**

1. Draw a mind map to present all the different forms of communication, the barriers to communication, the ways to overcome these barriers and the alternative methods of communication covered in this unit. Each branch should be in a different colour and the mind map should be clear and have only a few words on each large and smaller branch.

2. Take part in a group conversation using all the skills you have learned in this unit. As a group decide on a topic that interests you all, such as whether mobile phones should be allowed in school or college, and discuss it. The conversation will be recorded so you can all watch it back. You should each be aiming to join in equally, contribute but not aggressively, and be mindful of your verbal and non-verbal communication skills. When you watch it back you need to write down what you honestly thought of how well you used verbal and non-verbal skills to communicate effectively with the rest of the group.

Grading tips

Part 1 of the activity will help you achieve **P1** and **P2** by producing a mind map that has the basic facts on it. To achieve **M1** and **M2** you will need to work independently, using the facts from the book to identify all forms of communication, barriers and ways to overcome them.

In Part 2 of the activity you will need to show the use of appropriate verbal and body language during the group discussion and at merit level give a realistic assessment of your own verbal and non-verbal skills during the group discussion. To achieve **D1** you need to have used the communication cycle properly, being able to recognise the various parts of it as shown in the recording of the group discussion. You will also need to evaluate the strengths and weaknesses of the verbal and non-verbal skills you used and suggest ways you could do better in a future group discussion.

Just checking

1. Give five ways of presenting information.
2. How do health and social care workers use the written word?
3. Give three examples of situations where communication can break down and explain why this might happen in these situations.

Marge Cullen
Practice Nurse

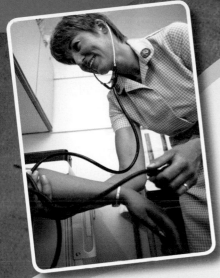

I am a practice nurse in a busy general practice. I work in a team which includes five doctors, two nurse practitioners, a health care assistant, two receptionists and a pharmacist. I have my own well equipped private room and I do tasks such as taking blood and urine samples and checking blood pressure. I also look after wounds, syringe ears, give immunisations and smear tests and many other similar tasks, as well as providing information.

Another task is to do annual health checks for people who have chronic (long-lasting or recurrent) conditions such as asthma and heart disease. This allows me to monitor the condition and gives the patient a chance to air any anxieties or discuss issues such as medication. I know I make it easier for some people to come and have embarrassing things done that they don't like asking a male doctor to do and I enjoy the fact that I am helping both the patients and relieving pressure on the doctors. I love my job because I enjoy meeting lots of different people and feeling that I am making a difference to them.

Think about it!

1. What have you learned about in this unit that would help you do a job such as this? Write a list of communication skills that will help Marge make the patients feel relaxed with her.

2. What are the barriers to communication that Marge refers to when she talks about some patients not wanting to see the doctor?

3. How do you think she overcomes these barriers?

4. Imagine you have been to college and have finished your training to be a nurse. Write a letter of application to a general practice for the post of practice nurse. Include the reasons why you think you could do the job, a description of your interpersonal skills and the evidence you have to show you have them. Do not include any practical skills as they will know you have those from your training.

Extension activity: Catching a bus

Sophie is 35 years old. She has been in a psychiatric hospital, after a complete mental breakdown, for fifteen years and is now preparing to live in the community. She has to learn how to catch a bus on her own again. Imagine she is coming to live in the area near your school and has to travel to a local town. You are her new care worker and are going to teach her how to cope with life outside the hospital. Remember that she will not know much about money and has only been on a bus a couple of times in the last two years, always accompanied by a care worker.

1. Sophie is not used to speaking to strangers. Write down what you would say to her.
2. Test out what you have written on another member of your group. Ask them to tell you honestly whether it would make sense if they were not used to catching buses.
3. Imagine how Sophie will be feeling about the experience of learning to travel to a nearby town by bus on her own. What are the barriers to communication for Sophie with (i) you (ii) the bus driver?
4. How can you help Sophie overcome each of these barriers?
5. Produce a reminder card for Sophie to have in her handbag, to refer to if she forgets what you have said to her.
6. How can you prepare her to cope when someone she has not met before sits on the seat next to her and tries to chat to her? To work out how you could do this think about a time when this has happened to you. Talk it over with a partner and role play the situation. Then write a list of practice opening lines to conversations that a stranger might use, such as, 'It's lovely weather, isn't it?' and then suggest what Sophie should say in response.

Assignment tips

- Whenever you visit any health or social care environment observe the care workers talking to service users. Make notes of three skills used and the effect on the service users.

- Make sure that before you take part in any interactions you plan them carefully. For both your one-to-one and group interaction produce plans that identify:

  - the skills you will use

  - where the interactions will take place

  - any resources you may need, such as a video camera for practising or in role play

  - any potential barriers to effective communication.

- Suggest any additional skills or factors that could improve communication if you were to repeat the interactions.

Credit value: 5

2 Individual rights in health and social care

Have you heard of the term 'individual rights'?

Have you ever considered what your individual rights are?

Have you ever witnessed a situation where someone's individual rights have not been considered?

This unit will help you to understand individual rights within the health and social care sectors.

If you have ever used any health or social care service, e.g. you have been a patient in hospital or at the dentist, you will have expected to be treated equally and with the same respect as in any other area of your life.

This unit provides an introduction to factors that contribute to a diverse and equal society, e.g. social, political and biological factors and the principles and values which underpin the support of individuals, e.g. ethical considerations and individual rights.

Learning outcomes

After completing this unit you should:

1. know factors that contribute to a diverse and equal society
2. understand the principles and values which underpin the support given to individuals.

Assessment and grading criteria

This table shows you what you must do in order to achieve a **pass**, **merit** or **distinction** grade, and where you can find activities in this book to help you.

To achieve a **pass** grade the evidence must show that you are able to:	To achieve a **merit** grade the evidence must show that, in addition to the pass criteria, you are able to:	To achieve a **distinction** grade the evidence must show that, in addition to the pass and merit criteria, you are able to:
P1 Identify factors that contribute to the equality of individuals in society [IE2, IE4, CT2, RL3, RL4, SM2, SM3, EP5] **Assessment activity 2.1(a), page 29** **Assessment activity 2.1(b), page 31** **Assessment activity 2.1(c), page 37**		
P2 Explain the individual rights of people who use services [IE2, CT2, RL3, RL4, SM2, SM3, EP5] **Assessment activity 2.2, page 39**		
P3 Explain the principles and values which underpin the support for individuals who use services [IE2, IE4, CT2, CT4, RL3, RL4, SM2, SM3, EP5] **Assessment activity 2.3, page 46**	**M1** Discuss the principles and values which underpin the support for individuals who use services **Assessment activity 2.3, page 46**	**D1** Assess how the principles and values which underpin health and social care relate to the promotion of the rights of individuals **Assessment activity 2.3, page 46**

How you will be assessed

For this unit you will be assessed by three assignments that will be marked by the staff at your centre. All of your assignments may be subject to sampling by your centre's External Verifier as part of Edexcel's ongoing quality assurance procedures.

- Your first assignment may involve producing a poster which identifies factors that contribute to equality and diversity in society. You will work on this across many weeks and topics until you have covered all the different factors (social, political and biological) covering the three factor areas in assessment activities 1(a), 1(b) and 1(c).

- Your second assignment may involve producing a short report which discusses the rights of the people who use, for example:

  a) your local health centre

  b) a centre for homeless people in the nearest city.

- Your third assignment may involve writing a magazine article for a local newspaper discussing and explaining the principles and values which underpin the support for the individuals who use the drop-in centre and including an evaluation of how these principles and values can be applied to the promotion of rights.

Ben, 16-year-old BTEC First Health and Social Care student and charity shop volunteer

This unit helped me to realise and appreciate that the world around me is made up of people who are all very different and that for everyone to get on well together we have to be more aware of people's individual rights.

It was really good finding out about everyone in my class when we were studying diversity; it was so interesting hearing about other people's lives and their experiences of equality and discrimination.

I hadn't really thought about ethics before doing this unit. I had heard the word before but I hadn't realised how important it is to approach life from a more person-centred viewpoint. Doing this unit has really opened up my eyes to the world around me.

In class we had lots of discussions about what our own values and principles are and we were able to compare these between ourselves and also discuss how our values might be right for working in a job in a health or social care setting. So this unit has really made me think about what sort of qualities I need to have to be a paramedic one day.

I work as a volunteer at a local charity shop on a Saturday and during school holidays. Completing Unit 2 has made me much more aware of people's differences and I think it has made me a far more patient and open minded person; I think this is a good quality to have.

Over to you!

- Have you ever considered your values and principles?
- Where do you live? Think about the diversity of the people who live in the area near you.

1. Know factors that contribute to a diverse and equal society

Key terms

Ethnicity – the way that people belong to a particular ethnic group, where people share the same culture and way of life

Gender – the social role of being male or female

Sexuality – a sense of a person's sexual and emotional attraction to others, e.g. heterosexual, homosexual and bisexual

Activity: Who are we?

Design a brief questionnaire to investigate how diverse your peer group is. Base your questions on the concepts in this topic.

Produce a display to show your results, this may include pie charts or graphs.

The focus of this topic is the social factors that contribute to a diverse and equal society which we are fortunate to live in. There are many social factors to consider which could include an individual's ethnicity, faith, gender, sexuality, age, family structure, social class and geographical location.

Social factors

Ethnicity

Ethnicity defines individuals and groups who have shared characteristics such as language, religion, dress, and origin. Ethnic groups in the United Kingdom include English, Welsh, Scottish, Indian, Irish, Pakistani and Chinese. Discrimination can happen when people consider the ethnic characteristics of other people as being inferior to their own.

Faith

There are many different faiths in the world and many people grow up following a particular faith. Faith gives people spiritual beliefs and it influences their cultural traditions and what they celebrate, e.g. Christians celebrating Christmas or Jewish people celebrating Passover. Discrimination can happen when people assume that their beliefs and practices based on their faith are the right ones and that everyone should believe in and do the same as them.

Culture

The language we speak, the diet we eat, our dress code, our behaviour and our lifestyle are all part of our culture. Our culture includes the things which make one group different and distinctive from another. It is a very important part of our identity, but people can be discriminated against because of the culture.

Gender

We are all born with a **gender**; we are classified at birth as either a male or female. Historically it was assumed that men were more important than women and that they should have more rights than women. The balance of equality between the genders has improved for example, more men now participate in activities such as child rearing, but there are still assumptions made about a person's gender that can lead to discrimination taking place.

Sexuality

We all have our own **sexuality**, and many people see their sexuality as a very important part of their identity and who they are.

Age

Age is an important factor in today's society; for example, you cannot drive until you are a certain age or vote or get married etc. People can be identified by their age (toddlers, teenagers, 'old people' etc.) and sometimes some age groups are seen as better than others or more able than others, and other age groups can be discriminated against, e.g. older people.

Family structure

People live in many different and varied families and friendship groups, e.g. being married, being single or co-habiting. Discrimination can happen when people think that one lifestyle is better than another. There are four kinds of family structure: nuclear, extended, lone-parent and reconstituted.

We live in a diverse society

BTEC Assessment activity 2.1(a) P1

Research and collate information and images about different social factors that contribute to a diverse and equal society. This information and the images will eventually contribute to a poster showing all the factors, after assessment activities 1(b) & 1(c). This activity will go part of the way towards meeting assessment criteria P1 which in turn meets learning outcome 1, you will need to complete 2.1(b) and 2.1(c) as well.

Grading tip

To meet P1 you are required to identify factors that contribute to a diverse and equal society. To identify means to establish the identity of something and this assessment criterion is not expecting you to do anything more than this, there is no need to include pieces of descriptive text.

PLTS

When you use different sources for your investigation and research into the different factors that contribute to a diverse and equal society you are developing your skills as an **independent enquirer** and **self-manager**.

Functional skills

ICT functional skills will be developed by using ICT systems to research and produce evidence for your assessment activity.

Social class

Social class is often linked to a person's income and the sort of job they do. People also differ in their lifestyles because of their jobs and the amount of money they have available – a few people have inherited wealth which means they do not even have to work. People may discriminate against other people because they are of a different social class to themselves.

Geographical location

People can be very proud of the area in which they live or were born. Different places follow their own unique customs, practices and beliefs but people who are not from their location may be seen as outsiders and not belonging. This can lead to people feeling uncomfortable when they are not in their own location and feeling discriminated against.

Just checking

1. What is meant by ethnicity?
2. What is the difference between someone's gender and someone's sexuality?
3. How might someone's social class affect their experience of life?

Political factors that contribute to a diverse society

The focus of this topic is the political factors that contribute to a diverse and equal society. There are many political factors to consider to get a clearer picture of what it is about us that contributes to the societies we live in. Political factors could be the Welfare State and the role of legislation and policies, and from these the delivery of health and social care services.

Legislation

There are many laws in the United Kingdom that help to create a fairer and non-discriminatory society, for example:

- The Sex Discrimination Act 1975 (amended in 1986)
- The Disability Discrimination Act 1995 (known as the DDA, updated 2005) and the Disability Rights Commission Act 1999
- The Equal Pay Act 1970 (amended in 1983)
- The Race Relations Act 1976 (amended in 2000)

We all have to keep to these laws to ensure a fairer and more equal society for everyone.

The Sex Discrimination Act 1975

This Act of Parliament has made it compulsory not to discriminate between men and women within the areas of employment, access to goods and facilities. The Act tries to provide equal opportunities for both men and women to get jobs and also equal promotions within their jobs.

The Disability Discrimination Act 1995 (updated 2005)

This Act of Parliament was designed to prevent discrimination taking place because of a person's disability. This could be in employment, access to services and transport and housing. This has affected many services which now must ensure that a person with a disability can

Case study: Penny, portage worker

'My name is Penny and I am a portage worker. I enjoy my job as I get to meet people from all backgrounds, ages, genders, classes and ethnicities. I like to work with different people as it keeps my job interesting and I get to learn about other people. My main role is with pre-school children who have developmental, learning or physical difficulties. In my work I try to help a child to develop by suggesting activities to do so that the child won't be too far behind when they start school.

I also work with other professionals which again is great because they come from different backgrounds and have different life experiences so it makes my job even more interesting.

'To be a portage worker you need to be open to other cultures and people's ideas of what is normal and right for them, you cannot think that what you believe and what you do is better than anyone else. You need to ensure you do not discriminate against anyone.'

What do you think – do you have the right qualities to be a portage worker?

access and use their service; they must not treat a person with a disability less favourably than a person who does not have a disability.

The Equal Pay Act 1970

This Act of Parliament has made it compulsory that employers do not discriminate between men and women in terms of their pay and working conditions. If the job being performed is of equal value then the pay should be equal, regardless of gender.

The Race Relations Act 1976

Race is about someone's skin colour, nationality, ethnic or national origins. This Act of Parliament has made it unlawful to discriminate because of someone's race in employment, housing or services.

Welfare State

The Welfare State was set up in 1945 (the NHS was set up in 1948 as part of this). The aim of the Welfare State was to eliminate what were known as the 'Five Evils' in post-war Britain: want, disease, ignorance, squalor and idleness. In order to put an end to 'disease, want and squalor' the National Health Service (NHS) and social services were started to give people free treatment when they needed help. These services abide by non-discriminatory practices to ensure all people – no matter what their ethnicity, faith, age, gender, culture, sexuality, family structure, geographical location or social class – receive equal access and treatment.

In 2000, the government introduced the Care Standards Act to improve the quality of social care.

Delivery of health and social care services

The delivery of health and social care services is directly influenced by certain quality standards that are referred to by the Care Quality Commission when inspecting all health and social care services. This is done to ensure that all services abide by the rules and meet the required standards. These quality standards come from the different legislation and policies.

Just checking

1. What is the Sex Discrimination Act 1975?
2. What is the Welfare State and when did it begin?
3. Which Act of Parliament makes it unlawful to discriminate because of a person's race?

PLTS

When you are researching and investigating the different political factors that contribute to a diverse and equal society you are being an **independent enquirer**.

When you are completing your plan for your poster and actually putting your poster together you are being a **creative thinker**.

Assessment activity 2.1(b)

P1

Research and collate information about different political factors that contribute to a diverse and equal society. This information and the images will contribute to a poster showing all the factors, after assessment activities 1(a) & 1(c) have been completed. This activity will go part of the way towards meeting assessment criteria **P1** which in turn meets learning outcome 1.

Grading tip

You can help to identify different political factors that contribute to a diverse and equal society through the use of a list and/or spider diagram. You should include very little descriptive text, but more than one word ideally. Do not be afraid of being more creative in presenting the factors you have identified rather than always using written text.

Equality and anti-discriminatory practice

Key term

Equality – everyone having the same chance as everyone else to obtain or achieve something

This topic looks at **equality** and anti-discriminatory practice. Ensuring equality is practised within health and social care settings is very important and is a vital care value within the sectors. By ensuring equality and non-discriminatory practice we can make sure that all service users receive the quality care each of them needs and deserves.

This topic and the following will help you to explore factors that contribute to a diverse and equal society.

Equality is a term that is relatively easy to understand; just think of the word 'equal' and this will help you to understand what it means. When something or someone is equal it is the same as something or someone else. A good example of this is in a race: when two runners cross the finish line at the same time it is a draw. The runners get equal place. They are equal; putting aside the runners' differences such as social class, ethnicity, culture or sexuality, there is equality.

Equality can also be looked at when we consider the chance everyone has to obtain or achieve something, e.g. access to a service within a health or social care setting that they may need. In this example, equality would mean everyone having the same chance to access the service – no matter who they are or where they come from.

Practitioners need to ensure that they understand and respect the individual differences of all service users in order to treat them equally, as people's differences could mean some people feel treated unequally compared with others because of their culture and background.

PLTS

Thinking about the diversity of the community around you develops your skills as a **reflective learner**.

Did you know?

It is unlawful to discriminate against people because of their gender, sexuality, age, disability, ethnicity and race.

Case study: Rachael, care assistant

'My name is Rachael and I am a care assistant. I work in a day-care centre and I provide care for those people who need help with their everyday activities. Each day I am involved with such activities as helping individuals with their meals, making refreshments and organising games and other creative and therapeutic activities, e.g. puzzles. Sometimes I help to organise a trip away from the centre – our most recent trip was to the theatre.

'In my everyday role I have to make sure I treat all the service users and my colleagues with equality and respect; I would say that I do not discriminate against anyone. I do this by, for example, always asking the people I support and work with what they would like to eat at meal times, as they always get a choice, and I ask them what activities they would like to be involved in during that day; nothing is compulsory – they can join in with what they like. I have to be a very good listener and sometimes need endless patience.'

Make a list of how Rachael ensures she does not discriminate against others and ensures equality.

Differences between people should be seen as a good thing, and **diversity** should be celebrated, but discrimination can result in a lack of equality between different people.

Non-discriminatory practice

When people discriminate unfairly against someone else they are being **prejudiced**. A service provider must be non-discriminatory in approach by ensuring they recognise and respond to the individual needs of service users.

When we care for people in the health and social care sectors, it is crucial to treat people as individuals by taking into account their different beliefs and abilities.

To prevent discrimination in the workplace and in society, organisations must do all they can to promote equality of opportunity ... this could be anything from ensuring that leaflets and information are provided in language appropriate to the area to making sure that there is adequate disabled parking in the supermarket car park. Most schools and colleges have codes of practice for behaviour to prevent bullying: this is also an example of promoting non-discriminatory practice. Organisations will also have codes of practice and policies to adhere to and will also be operating within the rule of the law.

Non-discriminatory practice should be promoted everywhere and by everyone. Service providers need to be 'actively' non-discriminatory in recognising and responding to the needs of their service users.

In return, people who use services also have a responsibility to treat the service providers in a non-discriminatory way; it is a two-way process of mutual understanding and respect.

There is legislation that promotes non-discriminatory practice and helps to protect people from discrimination. A good example is the **Sex Discrimination Act 1975**.

Activity: Ellen's day

Ellen works in a care home for older people; many of the service users are frail and require additional support. In the morning Ellen helps Betty with her personal care. Ellen knocks on the door to ask Betty's permission to enter her room. When in Betty's room, Ellen and Betty chat about how Betty has slept and how she is feeling this morning. Ellen asks Betty what she would like to wear today and when Betty has chosen, Ellen gets out her clothes ready. Ellen then offers Betty a shower, bath or a wash. Betty and Ellen discuss Betty's choice of breakfast and what she would like to do today.

With a colleague, discuss how Ellen's behaviour demonstrates respect and non-discriminatory practice towards Betty.

Key terms

Diversity – a wide range of views, culture, abilities and races among different people

Prejudice – having a bias against a person or group of people for reasons such as their age, social class, gender, race, religion, sexuality, ability, health, disability, dress or appearance

Sex Discrimination Act 1975 – prohibits discrimination because of an individual's gender in many areas, e.g. employment, education and provision of services

PLTS

When you consider how you treat other people in your everyday life, when you reflect on your values and principles of equality and anti-discriminatory practice you are developing your skills as a **reflective learner**.

Just checking

1. Why is it important to value diversity? Suggest how you can do this.
2. What does 'equality' mean?
3. Do you feel you have equality in your life?

Discriminatory practice

Figure 2.1: On the menu today

Key terms

Discrimination – to treat a person or group of people unfairly or differently from other persons or groups of people

Stereotyping – assuming something based on a fixed set of ideas

Labelling – identifying or describing someone with a label rather than as an individual. This term is linked to stereotyping

This topic will focus on **discrimination** and discriminatory practice. When discrimination happens it can have a very negative effect. When people discriminate they treat the individuals they are discriminating against differently from others. People can be discriminated against because of their social class, culture, ethnicity, race, gender, religion, sexuality or age. This topic will look at the different sorts of discrimination, discriminatory practice and non-discriminatory practice.

There are many types of possible discriminatory practices in health or social care settings, for example:

- **labelling** or **stereotyping** people, e.g. making assumptions
- being prejudiced
- avoiding people because they are different
- using negative body language towards people who are different
- not considering people's individual needs and preferences
- giving poor physical care because the needs of different people are ignored.

Forms of discrimination

There are many forms of discrimination that we should be aware of:

- devaluing, e.g. achievements not praised or being ignored, being unfairly criticised
- avoidance, e.g. not sitting next to someone
- verbal abuse, e.g. using language that puts the other person down
- physical abuse, e.g. assaulting a person
- neglect, e.g. ignoring a person's needs.

Stereotyping

When people say, "all young people like loud music" or "all old people like bingo" they are stereotyping these groups. You have probably had this experience yourself or may even think this sort of thing. Stereotyping can have a negative effect on people because it assumes that everyone in a certain group is the same and has the same needs. This is clearly not the case and thinking in stereotypes prevents you from being a good carer.

Prejudice

Prejudice means to judge someone without real knowledge or understanding even though that knowledge might be wrong. Sometimes people are prejudiced against others just because they are different, older, from another country, speak a different language or have a different faith. A person who is prejudiced against a group or person, tends to think they are superior and that their views and behaviour are right and others' are wrong. Once people develop prejudices against an individual or a group, they may be more likely to discriminate against them, particularly if they are in a position to make decisions about their health or welfare.

People who are homeless are often prejudiced against because people view them as irresponsible or drug addicts, for example. But people forget that people could be homeless for many reasons, as opposed to from choice, and this does not mean they are irresponsible or drug addicts.

The effects of discrimination

There are many different effects resulting from discrimination. All forms of discrimination will cause harm to people who use health or social care services, but some forms of discrimination can be very damaging and cause long-term, if not permanent, damage. Everyone has a different response to being discriminated against and what affects one person very badly may not affect another person in the same way. Such effects could include:

- injury – physical or emotional
- stress
- loss of confidence in own abilities
- depression
- anxiety
- anger
- aggression
- feelings of not being worth anything
- feeling devalued
- poor mental health
- poor self-concept
- feelings of not belonging.

These are all serious and could lead to an individual not making a full recovery from illness, or not wanting to participate in a full and active life.

Did you know?

Work-related stress costs society approximately £3.7 billion every year in the UK.

Do you subconsciously judge people based on their appearance or other factors?

Case study: Ageism

Colin is a 20-year-old carer and he has worked in the same nursing home for the past four years since leaving school. During his time at the nursing home, Colin has continued to study and has successfully achieved an NVQ at Level 3. He would really like to study for his assessor qualifications and he has discussed this with his manager. But his manager has indicated to Colin that he is too young to be considered for this as, despite his good work, he would most likely not have the respect of many of the care trainees because he is younger than them.

Discuss this case study in your group.

1. How should Colin react to this response from his manager?
2. Does ageism relate only to discrimination against older people?

Just checking

1. What are the four main different sorts of discrimination?
2. Identify four different effects of discrimination.
3. What does to stereotype mean?

Biological factors

Key term

Disability – a condition that restricts someone's ability to perform particular activities

Figure 2.2: Some examples of British Sign Language

a) Drink

b) What?

c) Month

Biological factors that contribute to a diverse and equal society are the focus of this topic. Learning **disabilities** and physical disabilities are examples of biological factors.

Learning disabilities

From the moment of your birth you start to learn – in order to survive and so you can develop into useful and successful adults. If you did not learn that putting a hand onto a stove or into a fire would burn you and cause serious injury or death, you may not survive. If you were not taught how to cross the road in a certain way, again you may not survive.

Learning takes place through both primary and secondary socialisation within our families, friendships and through going to school, college and university.

Everyone learns at different rates and speeds, but there is an acknowledged pattern and timescale by which children are expected to have learnt certain skills and acquired certain knowledge – both prior to starting school and then within the curriculum at school.

Learning disabilities come in many forms. Conditions such as dyslexia are well known about today and both children and adults who have this condition should be able to get the support they need. People with other conditions such as Down's syndrome may also have a learning disability.

Attitudes towards people with learning disabilities differ, and sometimes discrimination can take place against those people who have a learning disability. Legislation has been passed, e.g. the Disability Discrimination Act 1995, to try to ensure that this type of discrimination does not happen.

Activity: They are not normal...

You have been told by a care worker that people with learning difficulties are not allowed to leave the hospital where they are being cared for because "these people are not normal". These people using the hospital service have never been given a choice about their clothing or meals, as it is argued by the workers that giving them choices would only confuse them. The care worker also told you that these people are kept away from ''normal people'' so that they won't have to look at them or be scared by them.

1. Identify some examples of discrimination in this story.
2. Identify one example of stereotyping/labelling and explain how this stereotype or label contributes to discrimination.
3. Explain how the idea of 'normal people' is likely to result in discrimination.

Physical disabilities

Physical disability refers to any part of the human body which is not functioning properly and may prevent someone from participating in certain activities. Some physical disabilities do not necessitate the use of a wheelchair or other aid, e.g. arthritis of the hands, and may not be so obvious.

There are very many different physical disabilities but today people with a physical disability are far more likely to be treated equally and fairly than in the past. This is because of changing attitudes towards disability through awareness-raising campaigns and also legislation that makes it unlawful to discriminate against someone because of their disability, whatever it may be, e.g. the Disability Discrimination Act 1995.

BTEC Assessment activity 2.1(c) P1

Research and collate information about different biological factors that contribute to a diverse and equal society. This will go towards a poster showing all the factors that contribute in addition to 1(a) and 1(b). This activity will go part of the way towards meeting assessment criteria **P1** which in turn meets learning outcome 1.

Grading tip

When you 'research' you need to consider all the different and varied sources of information that are available to you based around the subject matter you are investigating. Good examples of research sources are:

- textbooks
- historical books – you may need to go to a library
- newspapers
- magazines
- journals
- newsletters
- web sites
- television programmes
- radio
- people – these may be people you know or professionals working in the area of your investigation.

It is a good idea to use as many different research sources as you can each time you carry out an investigation, as this will add quality to your evidence.

Case study: Counsellor

If a person has a long-term medical condition, a relationship breakdown, is suffering from stress or is coping with a disability, it may affect their health and well-being in a negative way. Using the skilled service of a counsellor may help to alleviate symptoms and conditions.

Counsellors provide time, attention and a safe environment to help people explore their feelings. This means that people are then more likely to be able to find their own way of making lifestyle changes to help them deal with their problems.

Counsellors work with people on a one-to-one basis or in couples, families or groups. Sessions can be face-to-face or via the phone or Internet.

1. Have you ever considered being a counsellor?
2. What qualities do you think you would need to do this job? Do you have these qualities?

Just checking

1. What does the term disability mean?
2. What is the Disability Discrimination Act 1995?
3. Name five sources you could use to carry out your investigation.

2. Understand principles and values

Key terms

Rights – something that a person can claim is due to them

Respect – a feeling or attitude of regard for somebody or something

Dignity – a calm and serious manner/style suitable for the situation and to treat someone with respect

This topic and the following four will help you to understand principles and values which underpin the support of individuals. This topic will look at the important area of individual **rights**. Whatever service we are using, we all have individual rights; we may not think about them most of the time, as we tend to only focus on our rights when they are being taken away from us or have actually been taken away. In previous topics you have looked at legislation that supports our individual rights.

Individual rights

To be respected

What is **respect**? This is when we value people as individuals who have life experience, and we listen to their views and opinions. We can show respect in the ways we address each other, our attitudes we display towards people and by maintaining their privacy and ensuring confidentiality.

To be treated as an individual

We are all individuals; even identical twins have their very own unique individuality. Everyone has a unique nature, character and personality that develop and grow through our different life experiences and though other factors such as culture, background, social class, age, ethnicity and gender. It is essential therefore in practice that we always treat different people as individuals and try to meet each individual's needs rather than making sweeping generalisations of needs (for example, 'All old people are the same…').

To be treated in a dignified way

What is meant by **dignity**? Dignity is a very important part of a person's life and an important aspect of being a service provider is to help people maintain their dignity so that they can keep their sense of self-respect. A good example of this is incontinence. Older people, particularly women, may be more prone to being incontinent (not being able to keep urine in their bladder between visits to the toilet). This condition can make sufferers feel ashamed and embarrassed and so it is important that health and social care workers reassure the service user to maintain the person's dignity.

To be treated equally and not discriminated against

It is an individual's right to be treated fairly and equally and not to be discriminated against because of social class, gender, sexuality, age, family structure, race, disability, religion, ethnicity and geographical location. Please refer to pages 28–9.

To be allowed privacy

Privacy means being free from intrusion or disturbance in your private life or affairs. Basic respect towards an individual, e.g. knocking on their bedroom door before entering, will make the person feel respected, in control and independent. A lack of privacy undermines an individuals' self-esteem and make them feel that they have lost their identity.

To be cared for in a way that meets our needs and takes account of preferences and choices

It is important that people's choices and preferences are maintained so that they can have as much independence as possible. This in turn supports self-esteem, empowerment and may have a positive effect on the individual's experience and recovery.

To be able to communicate using preferred methods

Good relationships can be formed through effective and appropriate communication. It will help to empower people who use services, as they will feel that their opinions, ideas and preferences are being valued and that they are respected as discussed in Unit 1.

To be allowed access to information about ourselves

It is very important that service users should be allowed access to any information that is held about them and their care. This can help the service user to make informed decisions about what choices they have; this could be a choice about their care or a choice like their diet and daily activities. This will raise a person's self-esteem and make them feel in control, empowered and that their individual rights are being respected.

To be safeguarded from danger and harm

Both service users and service providers have the right to a safe environment and to be protected from harm. There is legislation that supports this fundamental individual right. To ensure that this happens, institutions providing care must have a health and safety policy which spells out rules, regulations and necessary actions. These must be followed to keep staff and service users safe.

PLTS

If you discuss your thoughts about the rights of people who use services with your peers you are developing your skills as an **independent enquirer** and **team worker**.

Case study: Fusun

Fusun is 83 and lives at home but needs some personal care each day. She prefers to have a shower in the morning rather than at night before bed. She discussed this with her new support worker who agreed to change her daily routine to accommodate Fusun's needs and preferences.

1. How is this an example of individual rights?
2. How will this make Fusun feel?

BTEC

Assessment activity 2.2 **P2**

Write a short report which explains the rights of people who use your local health centre and also the rights of people who use a centre for homeless people. This activity will meet assessment criteria **P2** which in turn meets learning outcome 1 and learning outcome 2.

Grading tip

In the grading grid you have been asked to explain the rights of people who use services for **P2**. Explaining means making the information plain and clear, often with the use of relevant examples that could include personal experiences.

You have been asked to write a short report but you may also like to discuss with your peers and with your tutor your thoughts about the rights of people using the two services.

Just checking

1. What does 'dignity' mean?
2. What individual right do you consider to be the most important and why?
3. What choices do you have in your life?

Ethical considerations

Key term

Ethics – moral principles and philosophy

This topic will look at the interesting and very important issue of **ethics**. Ethics are moral codes that professionals must adhere to when working within health and social care. Ethical working includes respecting the basic principles and values that underpin practice. Ethics can involve facing moral dilemmas and questions, e.g. whether to prolong life against the wishes of a terminally ill person or to provide painful or degrading treatment in order to prolong life rather than to bring about a cure.

Social justice

Social justice refers to the concept of a society in which justice is achieved in every aspect of society, rather than merely the administration of law. Ethically speaking, all individuals should have social justice in their lives. Social justice is supported by practitioners and service providers adhering to the codes of practice and policies appropriate to their service.

A person–centred approach

This approach is particularly useful when considering the care of service users within health or social care sectors. The American psychologist Carl Rogers (1902–87) developed this humanistic, person-centred approach and stated: "at the heart of this approach is the basic trust in human beings and in the movement of every organism toward constructive fulfilment of its, his, or her possibilities".

A person-centred approach to care and support means that the service user is at the centre of the care and support they are receiving. This involves including them in any planning and decision-making about their life.

You can find out more by going to the website of the British Association for the Person-Centred Approach. To obtain a secure link to this website, see the Hotlinks section on page x.

Right to life

What is meant by a 'right to life?' It is a concept that describes a belief that a human being has an essential right to live, and particularly that a person has the right not to be killed by another human being. The concept of a right to life is central to debates on the issues of euthanasia, self defence, abortion, war and capital punishment.

This concept is very much an ethical dilemma and there are many debates about right-to-life situations which often involve health or social care practitioners.

Practitioners from the different faith and religious systems are often involved regarding ethical considerations, particularly right-to-life situations.

Activity: An ethical dilemma

- Euthanasia is the deliberate ending of a person's life, usually at his or her own request and with the intention of following the person's best interests.
- It comes in different forms and presents an ethical dilemma with moral difficulties for many professionals in the health and social care sectors.
- Euthanasia is illegal in Britain, but it is allowed in other countries, e.g. Switzerland.

There are many stories in the news and on the Internet about euthanasia and the different laws regarding ending your own life in different countries. Investigate the ethical issue of euthanasia; research the different opinions about this and consider your own thoughts and beliefs, which you should discuss with your peers.

PLTS

When you are investigating euthanasia you are developing your skills as an **independent enquirer** and **self-manager**.

Functional skills

When discussing your thoughts and beliefs about euthanasia you are developing your **English** functional skills.

Honesty

Honesty is an ethical consideration and a very important value and principle that should always be followed within health and social care practice. Honesty is an expectation of individuals receiving health or social care services. Can you remember a time when someone has been dishonest with you? Have you ever been dishonest? How did this make you feel? What was the result of the dishonesty? Honesty is always the best policy.

Empathy

Empathy means being able to put yourself in the same position as others, especially people using health or social care services. Empathy is conveyed by the way a care worker speaks to service users and the words they use. As a health or social care worker it is important to be able to empathise with people who use services, to see and feel things in the same way as them. However, this is not always easy as you might not have experienced what has happened to the person, which makes it hard to put yourself in their position.

Key terms

Empathy – identifying with and understanding another person's feelings and situation

Honesty – being trustworthy and truthful

Figure 2.3: Empathy is an essential ethical value

Just checking

1. What is meant by empathy?
2. What are ethics?
3. What is euthanasia?

Worker responsibilities

My life

Rise and shine

Nurse 'Morning Ben, wake up! It's time for breakfast!'

Ben 'Morning. What's for breakfast?'

Nurse 'Bacon sandwiches today.'

Ben 'But I don't eat bacon.'

Nurse 'You're not one of those vegetarians are you?'

Ben 'I am Jewish. I don't eat pork or bacon.'

Nurse 'I am sure a little won't do you any harm, Ben, and there's nothing else so you'll go hungry if you don't eat it.'

What are the nurse's responsibilities here?

Key terms

Equality of opportunity – having equal chances and opportunities no matter what your race, ethnicity, gender, age or sexuality

Responsibility – legally or morally obliged to be responsible to take care of something or someone and/or to carry out a duty

This topic covers the important area of how workers have **responsibilities** in the health and social care sectors which underpin the support of individual service users to ensure that individual rights are maintained.

Promotion of equality of opportunity

All people who use services have the right to **equality of opportunity** no matter what their ethnicity, race, gender, sexuality, age, religion and social class. You must ensure that you give all service users equality of opportunity and do not discriminate. Throughout your work you should actively promote equality of opportunity as a value and principle.

Provision of active support

Many people who use services may not feel confident enough in expressing their thoughts and feelings. In order to help them, you should use appropriate communication skills to encourage service users to express their thoughts and feelings and you should use active listening skills in this communication. You will need to demonstrate respect and value for the people you work with. This is active support.

Effective communication

If you do not communicate effectively and there are barriers to communication, the service user may have a bad experience and their recovery could be hindered. Effective communication is very important to ensure that service users are treated respectfully and have their individual needs and rights met. It is vital to actively listen to the service user. This will help to ensure effective communication and to support diversity.

Views and preferences

Professionals who work within a health or social care setting should always shape their practice by considering the views and preferences of people who use services. An individual's views and preferences may be based on a number of factors, e.g. their culture, which may shape their views on marriage, their diet preferences, how they would like personal care to be delivered, or which language they prefer to speak.

Accurate recording

Much health and social care work involves communicating with many people, from many different backgrounds and situations. This includes written communication, see p. 20, which relates to individuals' care needs and progress. It is essential that any information communicated is always carefully checked and recorded. Incorrect recording could be dangerous for a service user.

Storage and retrieval of information

Information and personal records about service users are kept electronically (computer) as well as manually (paperwork and files). Whichever way information is stored about a service user, the information should be filed correctly and securely to make sure it remains confidential. It is also important to make sure the information can be retrieved (found) when it is needed.

Did you know?

Active listening involves being interested, hearing, remembering and checking what you have understood with another person.

Case study: Medical receptionist

Being a medical receptionist is a very important job and it is classified as indirect care. Although medical receptionists provide a crucial service, they do not actually deliver the medical help that the service users come to the health centre for.

This job role includes having to handle confidential and private information about service users through handling their medical records and discussing their needs with other service providers. The job also entails making appointments, checking in patients and general administrative and clerical jobs, e.g. writing letters containing personal information about service users.

To do this job you need to have good interpersonal skills, particularly communication skills, as you will come across people from all walks of life and backgrounds, with different ethnicities and ages. You will be expected to effectively communicate via the telephone and email on a daily basis.

1. Think about your communication skills, do you think they would be good enough to be able to work as a medical receptionist?
2. If your answer is 'yes', why?
3. If your answer is 'no', why?
4. Compare your answer with your peers and discuss.

PLTS

When you are discussing your communication skills and the job of medical receptionist with your peers you are developing your skills as a **team worker**.

Functional skills

Discussions with your peers help to meet speaking and listening **English** functional skills.

Just checking

1. Name one piece of legislation that shapes a worker's responsibilities.
2. What does 'equality of opportunity' mean?
3. What does preference mean?

Responsibilities: confidentiality

Key term

Confidentiality – to be kept secret and to keep secure and private information about service users

This topic will focus on the important issue of **confidentiality**. Confidentiality is a key principle and value that must be considered in all areas of life and especially within the health and social care sectors. Lack of confidentiality could have many negative effects on service users and their families and friends. Health and social care workers have a responsibility to maintain confidentiality.

Confidentiality

Confidentiality is a very important right of all people who use health and social care services. Confidentiality is vital when working with service users within the health and social care sectors. It means keeping information about service users secure and private.

Workers should always ask a service user first if it is all right to let other people know information about them, e.g. the individual's date of birth. The exception to this rule is that information can be passed on when others have a right and a need to know it, e.g. other care workers may need to know important issues about the person or other professionals involved with their care may need to be kept up to date with information for their ongoing care.

Even when information about a person can be shared, as in the examples given above, the sharing of information should still preserve confidentiality and information should not be passed on to people who do not need it, e.g. friends or family members of the service user. Carelessly or unnecessarily breaking confidentiality is unacceptable practice as a health or social care worker.

Can you keep a secret?

Disclosure

As a health or social care worker, you should always ask an individual first if it is all right to let other people know things. It is wrong even to pass on the birth date of a person without that person's permission. **Disclosure** of information should only happen when the person agrees that it is all right to share the information.

Disclosure happens when certain people, e.g. other professionals, have a need to know about service users – they may need to be kept up to date with information.

If disclosure is not agreed then a breach of confidentiality has taken place, and this could have many negative effects on the service user as well as on the practitioner.

Breaching confidentiality

Breaking or breaching confidentiality is inappropriate behaviour and can have many negative consequences.

When it is necessary to breach confidentiality

Despite confidentiality being a very important principle and value and an individual right, it can be appropriate and necessary sometimes to breach confidentiality. A good example of this is in the situation where it is feared a service user might hurt themselves or others; another example is when someone is about to break the law or has already broken the law. Sometimes it is very important to pass on personal information to the appropriate colleague or authority e.g. the police. This can, however, cause tensions between an individual's rights and a worker's responsibilities; this is a very difficult dilemma, but one that must be addressed. Issues of disclosure can be particularly sensitive when dealing with the rights of children. Always discuss any concerns with your manager/tutor.

Legislation on confidentiality

Laws have been passed which protect people's rights to confidentiality. The most important is the Data Protection Act 1998, which covers both paper and electronic records.

The Data Protection Act 1998 provides you with the following rights:

- for you to be able to refuse to provide information
- that data held about you should be accurate and up to date
- that data held on you should not be kept longer than is necessary
- for you to know what information is held about you
- for you to see the information held about you and correct this information where necessary
- the right to confidentiality, that information held about you should not be accessible to unauthorised people.

Key term

Disclosure – to expose, to view or to reveal and to make known

Activity: Consequences

Here are some examples of breaching confidentiality. Read each of them and then discuss with your peers in class the possible consequences of this breach.

1. A social care worker passes on information about when a person's family are going to be away on their holiday to someone whose friend is in prison.

2. A health care worker tells someone about a person who lives on their street who has been mentally ill in the past but now has his illness under control.

3. A social worker tells someone about a person who has committed a crime involving children and who is about to be released from prison.

Did you know?

The Freedom of Information Act 2000 is also an Act of Parliament about confidentiality. It makes provision for the disclosure of information held by public authorities and to amend the Data Protection Act 1998.

Case study: I need her address

Chloe lives with her mum and younger sister Lily. Chloe's dad left her mum many years ago just after Lily was born and got into crime. He is now out of prison and wants to see Chloe and Lily. He does not know where they live, but he does know the school Chloe attends.

He goes to the school and asks the school receptionist, Sadie, for Chloe's address. He says it is very important that he knows her address as he has presents for Chloe and Lily. When Sadie tells him that she cannot give out details about any of the school children, he gets angry.

1. Why is it important that Sadie does not give out any information about Chloe?
2. Where in the school might there be information and personal details about Chloe?
3. What legislation directs Sadie's work?

Figure 2.4: What are the possible consequences of breaching confidentiality?

PLTS

When discussing together the consequences of the three examples of a breach of confidentiality in the activity you will be developing your skills as a **reflective learner**.

Functional skills

Completing the magazine article using ICT will work towards the development of **ICT** functional skills.

Just checking

1. What does disclosure mean?
2. Give one possible consequence for a service user if their personal information is not kept confidential.
3. Name one document about you that should be kept confidential.

 BTEC ## Assessment activity 2.3 **P3 M1 D1**

Write a magazine article which explains and discusses the principles and values that underpin the support for the individuals who use the drop-in centre (assessment activity 2.2), and evaluates how these principles and values can be applied to the promotion of rights. This activity will meet **P3**, **M1** and **D1**, which in turn meet learning outcome 2.

Grading tips

In the grading grid you have been asked to discuss the principles and values which underpin the support for individuals who use services for **M1**. Discussing something means examining by means of an argument and looking at different sides and points of view, either verbally or through the written word.

In the grading grid you have been asked to 'assess' how the principles and values which underpin health and social care can be applied to the promotion of the rights of individuals for **D1**. This means reviewing the information given and then forming a conclusion based on the evidence presented, often including your own thoughts supported by evidence and examples.

Jayne Dickson

Phlebotomist

I work alongside other health care workers, e.g. community nurses, GPs and hospital doctors, and am a lone worker in the community providing Phlebotomy services to housebound patients. Most of my patients are housebound due to age, infirmity, disability or having chemotherapy and so can't attend a clinic setting due to the infection risks. I am based in a community nurse clinic where I have my own desk and computer and I am one of two phlebotomists.

I am responsible for the timely and safe collection of blood samples from patients and the delivery of the samples to the laboratory at the local hospital. I am often the only person the patient might see for many days so I feel I also have

a big social and emotional responsibility too. To do my job you need to be professional, pay attention to detail, have a caring nature, a calm demeanour and be able to deal with difficult people who are either scared of needles and the procedure or very ill. You must treat each patient as an individual and with the utmost respect.

In a typical day I will get to the clinic in the morning and check my diary for any booked blood samples to be taken that morning. I also ensure I have time within my booked schedule for urgent blood tests that may present themselves during my day's work. I then check my car has all the equipment I need to be able to carry out the different blood samples. Once I have done all my visits and taken all my blood samples I take them to the laboratory at the local hospital and then I return to the clinic to complete my paperwork.

I really enjoy my work as a phlebotomist in the community. Visiting elderly, sick or lonely people in their own homes is very rewarding. When I have time I sit and chat with my patients and spend some time keeping them company. I really get to know them and their families and it is lovely to know that I make their lives easier by visiting them in their own homes rather than them having to struggle to the clinic.

Think about it!

1. Do you think Jayne has to consider confidentiality in her work?
2. How important do you think it is that she accurately records her patients' information and blood samples?
3. Do you think you have the qualities to be able to do this job?

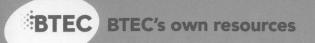
Extension activity: Thinking about values

In this unit you have learnt about the rights of individuals in society and what we can do to help promote equality of opportunity both in society and in the context of health and social care. This activity gives you the opportunity to do some "blue sky thinking" about laws you would like to see passed concerning an issue that you feel strongly about.

- Consider how values and principles in society could be improved to ensure that more people, more of the time, feel respected and not discriminated against.
- If you had the power to develop a new Act of Parliament to address this issue what would it include and what would it be called?
- Produce a persuasive rationale (justification) of your new Act of Parliament – what would it achieve? Would it improve health or social care practice?
- Do you think giving 16-year-olds the vote would help make our country a more equal and inclusive place to live?

Assignment tips

- A good way to ensure you can achieve a distinction grade for Unit 2 is to make sure you plan your assessment activities from the very beginning of the unit. This means you won't run out of time and the opportunity to complete **D1** .

- The assessment criteria do not have to be done in a specific order. So you may wish to do **P3**, **M1** and **D1** together, which makes sense as all three of these assessment criteria are based around learning outcome 2. **P1** and **P2** could be done in a different order as there are no connections between them.

- Remember you can only achieve a pass grade even if you do a wonderful poster and fantastic report to meet **P1** and **P2** and a really good discussion part for your magazine article to meet **P3** . You need to make sure you have plenty of time to complete the explanation and evaluation section of your magazine article to achieve a merit or distinction grade.

3 Individual needs in health and social care

Health and social care workers need to have knowledge, understanding and skills related to individual needs. This unit allows you to explore the influence of these needs on health and well-being and how they may be addressed to improve the health and well-being of an individual.

Knowledge of the everyday needs of individuals is fundamental to the study of health and social care. Organisations within the sector are working towards one single approach which aims to improve the outcomes for all individuals with health and social care needs. All health and social care professionals aim to apply principles and values which place the person using services at the heart of planning to meet their needs.

In this unit you will start by learning about the everyday needs of individuals and how these may change at different stages of life. You will have to consider both basic and higher level needs. You will then learn about the ways in which a range of factors influence needs and how they affect health and well-being.

Finally, you will gather relevant information from an individual and try to identify their specific health needs. You will consider ways in which these may be addressed and work with them to create a plan for improving their health and wellbeing.

This unit links with all other units from this qualification.

Learning outcomes

After completing this unit you should:

1. know everyday needs of individuals
2. understand factors that influence the health and needs of individuals
3. be able to plan to meet the health and wellbeing needs of an individual.

Assessment and grading criteria

This table shows you what you must do in order to achieve a **pass**, **merit** or **distinction** grade, and where you can find activities in this book to help you.

To achieve a **pass** grade the evidence must show that you are able to:	To achieve a **merit** grade the evidence must show that, in addition to the pass criteria, you are able to:	To achieve a **distinction** grade the evidence must show that, in addition to the pass and merit criteria, you are able to:
P1 Outline the everyday needs of individuals (IE1, IE2, RL3, SM2, SM3) **Assessment activity 3.1, page 57**		
P2 Explain factors which affect the everyday needs of individuals (IE1, IE2, RL3, SM2, SM3) **Assessment activity 3.2, page 63**		
P3 Carry out an assessment on the health and well-being of an individual (IE1, CT1, RL3, TW3, SM2, SM3, EP4) **Assessment activity 3.3, page 70**		
P4 Produce a plan for improving the health and wellbeing of an individual **Assessment activity 3.4, page 70**	**M1** Explain how the plan meets the health and wellbeing needs of the individual **Assessment activity 3.4, page 70**	**D1** Justify how the plan takes into account the individual's circumstances and preferences **Assessment activity 3.4, page 70**

How you will be assessed

This unit will be assessed either by a series of tasks relating to a common case study or through separate tasks based on the health needs of either fictional characters taken from TV or books, or real individuals, who could be your own extended family. An example of a scenario on which tasks could be based might be that a large health centre is being planned to provide a range of health and social care services for people in your local area or town. To make sure that the centre meets the needs of all the individuals in the community you might be asked to write a report to outline their everyday needs and the factors which can influence health and well-being.

You will also be asked to identify an individual, either real or fictional, and write a plan to support their health and well-being.

Zara, 16–year-old would-be social worker

I found this unit very useful as it taught me all about the basic needs of people of all ages. I hadn't really thought about us all having needs that were so basic that if they were not met we would die, compared with higher needs that make our lives better.

When I went on placement to a residential home for older people I found I had more patience with them than I would have done before doing this unit because I had thought about how I would want to be treated by others. I understood that being healthy is not just about being physically fit but is also about keeping our brains active, and looking after ourselves emotionally and socially. This meant I understood better why it was important to chat to the residents and play games such as bingo with them, encouraging them to join in even if they didn't really want to at first.

Writing the health plan also made me see that it is not so easy to give something up without support or tackle a task such as getting more exercise if someone has a job to do and family to look after.

To get the most out of this unit you need to keep imagining yourself in the position of whoever you are talking about or finding out about at the time. By thinking about how you would feel if you were in that person's position you will develop a better understanding of their needs and how they can be met.

Over to you!

- How do you think this unit will help you understand how you should support an individual in your care?
- What do you need to do to help others improve their own health and well-being?

1. Know everyday needs of individuals

Key term

Hierarchy – a list of things or people arranged in order

In this topic and the next two you will learn about people's everyday needs. You will explore Maslow's hierarchy of needs, which identifies our needs and which of them are most important. You will also learn what we mean by the terms health and well-being and how we have different needs at different stages of our life.

Importance of needs

Maslow's hierarchy

Psychologist Abraham Maslow (1908–1970) designed a **hierarchy** of needs in the 1930s. This is a pyramid of human needs with the most important at the bottom and the most complicated at the top. Maslow believed that basic physical needs such as food, drink, air to breathe, sleep and warmth must be met before people can grow and develop. People at different life stages have different views of their needs. For example, children left on their own may feel frightened and unsafe, even if their basic physical needs are met; but adults might be very happy to have some time to themselves to relax. Social needs include love, affection and friendship, which are very important to most of us. At the top of the pyramid is self-actualisation, which Maslow felt was the most important of all.

Figure 3.1: Maslow's hierarchy: How far from the bottom would you put yourself?

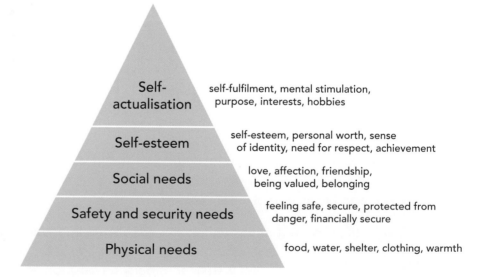

Self-actualisation	self-fulfilment, mental stimulation, purpose, interests, hobbies
Self-esteem	self-esteem, personal worth, sense of identity, need for respect, achievement
Social needs	love, affection, friendship, being valued, belonging
Safety and security needs	feeling safe, secure, protected from danger, financially secure
Physical needs	food, water, shelter, clothing, warmth

Failure to meet these needs

Failure to meet these needs can have serious consequences. People who live in dirty, cold accommodation with an unbalanced diet are less likely to feel safe and secure and are more likely to become ill. Similarly, people whose social needs are not met, and who lack love and

Activity: Maslow's hierarchy

1. Look at Maslow's hierarchy. Are all your basic needs being met? Are your safety and security needs being met? Write down where you feel you come at the moment, with level 1 being the bottom and level 5 being the top. You will not have to show anyone else, so be honest.

2. Write down all the different things that affect how you feel about yourself. Then write down how you feel about yourself overall at the moment, with 1 being feeling bad about yourself and 5 feeling very good. How does this level compare with the level you think you are on the pyramid?

3. Write a list of three things you are going to try to do to move up to at least the next level.

4. Why do you think that Maslow thought self-actualisation was the most important level of all?

affection, will find it harder to develop relationships with others and will have low **self-esteem**. They will be lacking in confidence and will be less likely to succeed in their education and in life generally.

Health and wellbeing

Health means different things to different people and a person's health can change from day to day. The word health comes from an old English word, meaning 'the state of being **hale**, **sound** or whole, in body, mind or soul'.

Well-being means the state of being healthy, happy, or **prosperous**, so health and well-being can be described in terms of how someone **functions** and feels, physically, mentally and socially and the way people feel about themselves and their lives.

The World Health Organization (WHO) is an agency of the United Nations that co-ordinates international **public health**. The WHO defines health and well-being as 'a state of complete physical, mental and social well-being and not merely the absence of disease or infirmity', a definition that was agreed by all during the first world Health Assembly and has not changed since then. Therefore health may be regarded as a balance of physical, mental and social aspects of life in a person.

Mental health

This refers to an individual's emotional and **psychological** well-being, which enables them to use their intellectual and emotional abilities to function in society and meet the ordinary demands of everyday life.

Key terms

Self-esteem – how highly we think about ourselves

Hale – free from infirmity or illness

Sound – free from defect, decay, damage, disease, injury; in good condition

Prosperous – having success, flourishing, well-off

Functions – performs, operates

Public health – the field of medicine concerned with safeguarding and improving the health of the community as a whole

Psychological – relating to, or arising from, the mind or emotions

Just checking

1. What do we mean by saying someone has a specific need? Give three examples.
2. Why are basic physical needs at the bottom of Maslow's pyramid?
3. What is the difference between health and well-being?

All our needs

This topic will introduce you to the physical, intellectual, emotional, social and spiritual needs which, if they are met, contribute to our overall health and well-being. They are commonly known as PIES.

Physical needs

Physical aspects are all the needs we have to keep our bodies working as well as they can. Even though everyone's bodies are different, there are certain needs we all share, such as good and nutritious food, clean water, shelter and an unpolluted environment to live in. We also need warmth, clothing, rest, exercise, sleep, safety, security and the facilities to maintain good personal hygiene. Our needs vary throughout our lives; for instance, older people may eat less than growing adolescents, but we all need food. Sometimes we take part in activities which can be harmful to us physically, such as taking drugs, smoking, drinking alcohol excessively or not taking enough exercise. These damage our bodies so that our physical needs are not met.

Intellectual needs

These are all the needs we have which develop and keep our brains working as well as possible. They include mental activity and stimulation to keep us motivated and interested, rather than bored. We need to continue with intellectual achievements and learning throughout our lives to keep our brains active. Children meet their intellectual needs by constantly exploring and questioning the world around them. You may be meeting your intellectual needs by doing this course or taking part in learning outside school or college.

Emotional needs

Everyone needs to be liked or even loved. Emotional needs are met when we experience things that make us feel happy and wanted and give us a positive **self-concept**, such as affection, good relationships, **fulfilment**, love and respect. Emotional needs change as we grow and develop. We need to be able to feel, express and recognise different emotions in order to cope with different situations that arise throughout our lives. Sometimes these emotions can be sad, such as grief after the death of a friend or relative, but this is all part of learning to live with a range of different emotions.

Social needs

These are the aspects of our life that enable us to develop and enjoy good relationships and friendships with others. These include opportunities to mix with others in an appropriate environment and to have access to leisure facilities and activities. It is important that

Key terms

Self-concept – a combination of how you see yourself and how you think others see you

Fulfilment – a feeling of satisfaction at having achieved something good

we have family and friends, and belong to groups or are part of a community, in order to have a sense of belonging and to feel that we are accepted. Think about a child who is bullied in the playground or through hurtful texting on a mobile phone. He or she will feel excluded and alone and not part of the community and will need support to overcome this difficult situation.

Activity: Stimulate your brain

1. Write a list of all the things you could do to stimulate your brain. Compare your list with a partner's and add any you didn't think of. Pick one that you would like to try. What is stopping you having a go at it?

2. One such activity is reading. Have a group discussion to find out who reads books regularly out of choice and who reads only when they are made to, such as in school/college. Decide who and what has influenced them to be like this.

Spiritual needs

Spirituality means different things to different people. It may include religion or what provides a sense of personal meaning throughout your life. Spiritual needs are needs based on our personal beliefs and are unique to each of us. They include hope, a quest for meaning and inner peace, a need to be valued and to receive help to cope with anxieties and fears; these needs are covered in detail in Unit 6.

Holistic definition of health

This is the definition of health based on a combination of physical, intellectual, emotional and social factors, i.e. looking at all parts of a person's health. This definition was based on Maslow's hierarchy. An example of someone with a **holistic** attitude to health is Paula Radcliffe, the British marathon runner. She keeps herself physically fit, eating a balanced diet and exercising. She learns about different training strategies and has written books (intellectual) and is happily married (emotional) with a family and lots of friends, meeting people all over the world as she trains and competes (social).

Just checking

1. List all the physical needs that you have had met today.
2. Why are friends important?
3. Explain spiritual needs in your own words: where do you think these belong in Maslow's hierarchy?

Key term

Holistic – looking at all the different needs of the client

What sort of approach do you have to your health and well-being?

55

Life stages

Key terms

Life stage – a distinct period of growth and development in the life span

Puberty – a normal phase of development caused by hormonal change, that occurs when a child's body changes into an adult body and readies for the possibility of reproduction, usually starting around 10–13 years

Hormones – chemical messengers present throughout the body

Menopause – the natural and permanent stopping of menstruation (periods), occurring usually between the ages of 45 and 55

Activity: Responding to life stages

1. Think about a receptionist in a health centre or a teaching assistant in a primary school. Why would they need to understand how people develop differently at different life stages?

2. What do these two jobs have in common?

Some needs are basic and we all have these needs, as shown in Maslow's hierarchy in the previous pages. However, others change throughout our lives. In this topic you will learn how needs change through the five **life stages**. There is more detail about the different life stages on pages 234–255 in Unit 8.

Needs in relation to life stages

Infants (0 to 3 years)

The needs specific to infants are: to be fed; to have everything done for them (such as their nappies changed); to have lots of sleep; to form attachment relationships (bonding) with their parents and other main carers; to have secure routines; and to have toys and books to help them learn and develop their gross and fine motor skills. Gross motor skills are those that help the infant control the larger muscles of the body, such as legs to crawl, stand and walk. Fine motor skills are those that control the smaller muscles, such as those in the fingers to hold an object or point.

Children (4 to 10 years)

At this stage, children are learning to be more independent so they need to have the opportunities to develop independence in all aspects of PIES needs: for example, in eating and drinking and in personal hygiene (cleaning their teeth, washing their hands etc.). They are further developing their motor skills and will be playing with more advanced toys. At school they will be developing intellectually, learning to read, write and use numbers in increasingly complex ways. Language also develops at this stage. School gives children the opportunity to meet their social needs and to interact with other children so they can learn social skills such as to share and make new friends.

Adolescents (11 to 18 years)

Most of you reading this book will be adolescents and you know that adolescence is one of the most difficult but exciting life stages for many individuals. It is when you are usually going through **puberty** and starting to change into an adult. Your reproductive organs start to function and changes in **hormone** levels mean that emotions can become confused and you may feel under a lot of stress. Friendship needs become particularly important as you form more intimate relationships associated with your sexual and emotional development. Adolescents need to feel a sense of belonging to groups and communities. You also need to eat well to cope with the physical changes in your body. During this time you will also need to learn skills to prepare for the world of work.

Adulthood (19 to 65 years)

Adulthood is the stage of life when most people start to feel that they understand and accept themselves and begin to feel more settled. Although we never stop learning new skills and acquiring knowledge, this happens more slowly for adults than for younger people. Adults tend to spend a lot of time making decisions, such as where to live, who to live with, whether to get married and have children, what job to do, when to retire – the list is endless. This is also the life stage when women usually go through the **menopause**.

In any age group the importance of different health needs changes with time but, because the different stages of adulthood are longer, adults have more varying needs. Health and social care workers need to understand these needs so they can help individuals using health or social care services.

Later adulthood (65+ years)

Inevitably, with age, people's bodies gradually change and start to wear out a little. They will have more needs as they get older, such as access to convenient health and leisure facilities, practical help as they become less mobile and support in times of distress. However, later adulthood can now be at least as long as early or middle adulthood and many people look forward to this stage of their lives. They can retire from work and their children have usually moved out so they can spend their days doing the things they have always wanted to do, provided they remain healthy and have saved for retirement.

Activity: Old?

1. Discuss with a partner what you mean when you say the word 'old'. How old does someone have to be before you call them old? Think about people you know, such as your tutors and family members. Do you think they are old?

2. Look at the people in the picture. They are all over 65. How do you think the word old makes them feel?

Do you think the people in the picture are old? Do you think *they* think they are old?

PLTS

In this activity you will need to be a **reflective learner** in order to think about and identify the skills needed to identify the PIES needs.

BTEC

Assessment activity 3.1   **P1**

Pick characters from television programmes that you watch and enjoy, or think of two individuals you know (these could be friends or family members), who are at different life stages. Write a report identifying their PIES needs and how they are being met.

Grading tip

This assessment task will help you gain **P1** if you show that you know the range of needs of your individual with reference to Maslow's hierarchy of needs.

Just checking

1. List three needs of children for each of the PIES.
2. Why is it important to meet new people as you get older?
3. Why do you think it is right to call people over 65 years of age older people rather than old or elderly?

Functional skills

By completing this activity you will have used your **English** skills to write your report.

2. Understand factors that influence the health and well-being of individuals

Key terms

Economic – to do with money

Lifestyle – a way of life or style of living that reflects the attitudes and values of a person or group

In this topic you will learn about socio-**economic** factors and physical factors that influence the health and well-being of individuals.

Socio-economic factors

These are the factors that affect how we live and work.

- **Social class:** this is the identification of social groupings based on power, wealth and influence and is covered in more detail in Unit 6. It may influence where you live, the education you receive and how you view yourself and those around you.

- **Employment:** a job allows you to use your expertise and develop new skills and knowledge, which is intellectually stimulating. It also provides you with an income, gives you an opportunity to socialise and gives your days a routine, thus giving you confidence and self-esteem.

- **Culture:** this is when a group of people have shared beliefs, values and customs and is covered in detail in Unit 6. Our culture influences the way we think, the food we eat, the people we mix with and even how we spend our leisure time.

- **Income:** this comes from earnings, or from other sources such as welfare benefits, pensions or investments, and has a major impact on our **lifestyle**.

An adequate income allows us to:

- afford leisure services

- pay our rent or mortgage

- afford the clothes we like to wear

- socialise with friends

- eat a balanced diet

- travel to make use of NHS and community health facilities

- heat our homes

- afford a car and holidays.

- **Living conditions:** if you don't have a warm, dry house with space for everyone, adequate ventilation and access to clean water, this clearly can have an effect on your health and well-being.

- **Education:** learning is something we do from birth. The amount and quality of education you receive will affect your health and

Think about it

Can employment ever have a negative effect on our life?

Activity: Socio-economic factors

Divide into three groups and take one of the socio-economic factors listed. Prepare a presentation on how these factors affect out PIES needs.

well-being, as it will determine your choice of jobs, your **employment prospects** and your income and standard of living. A good education will increase your status in society, make you feel good about yourself and give you a sense of security. For this reason, education is high up in Maslow's hierarchy of needs.

Physical factors

These factors include:

- **genetic inheritance:** we inherit genes from our parents which have different effects and make us unique, e.g. eye colour, height, sporting ability. Sometimes the genes are faulty and this is why some diseases or conditions are inherited, i.e. passed from one generation to another.

- **disability and health:** these will be covered later in this unit.

- **age:** a person's age can affect their health and needs as shown in the changing needs topic (pages 56–57).

- **environment:** we all need clean air and water and proper waste disposal facilities. For example, air **pollution** can cause and aggravate respiratory conditions and can irritate your eyes, nose and throat. Other sources of pollution are pesticides and herbicides on food, noise that can damage hearing, and even light. It is important to have access to fresh, clean water and good **sanitation** as bacteria in water can cause illness.

Key terms

Employment prospects – the chances of getting and keeping a job that pays well and has good opportunities for promotion

Pollution – damage to living organisms caused by human activities disturbing the environment

Sanitation – measures taken to protect public health, such as supplying clean water or efficient sewage disposal systems

Activity: Physical factors

Research each of the physical factors listed. Draw up a large mind map, with a different branch for each factor, to show key facts you have found. For example, the branch on genetic inheritance could include cystic fibrosis, haemophilia and Down's syndrome. It must show how each factor affects a person's health and needs.

Just checking

1. Explain what is meant by the term socio-economic.
2. Give three socio-economic factors and describe how each can affect a person's health and wellbeing needs.
3. Why do physical factors such as pollution influence health and wellbeing needs?

Further factors influencing health and wellbeing

My life

Lifestyle

Have you ever thought to yourself, 'This is the life' or, 'I could get used to this way of life.' What has made you feel like this?

Our lifestyle choices can affect our health and the way we feel about ourselves, and may mean that we are not able to take all the opportunities life has to offer. This topic looks at some of the factors that contribute to a healthy or unhealthy lifestyle and asks you to research the others.

Lifestyle factors

Personal hygiene

Personal hygiene could include areas such as cleaning teeth regularly (at least twice a day); taking a daily bath or shower; keeping nails clean and trimmed; and washing hair regularly.

Smoking

Smoking tobacco, usually in cigarettes, is legal. However, it is addictive and a major cause of ill health, preventable disease and death. All smoking material packaging now carry a government health warning and it is illegal in the UK to smoke indoors in a public place such as an office or pub.

Figure 3.2: The hazards of smoking

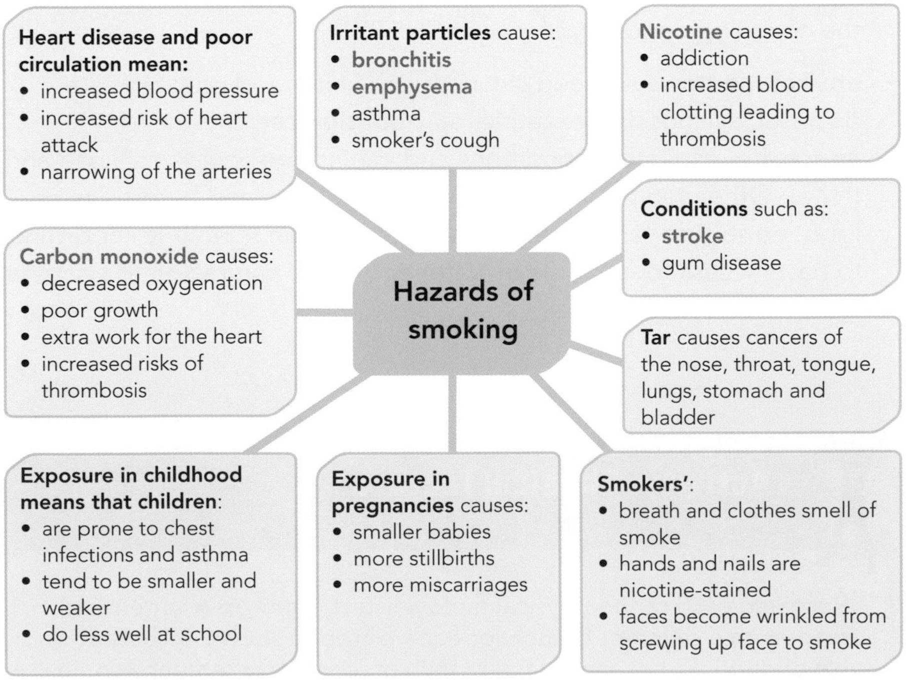
Hazards of smoking
Heart disease and poor circulation mean:
• increased blood pressure
• increased risk of heart attack
• narrowing of the arteries
Irritant particles cause:
• bronchitis
• emphysema
• asthma
• smoker's cough
Nicotine causes:
• addiction
• increased blood clotting leading to thrombosis
Conditions such as:
• stroke
• gum disease
Carbon monoxide causes:
• decreased oxygenation
• poor growth
• extra work for the heart
• increased risks of thrombosis
Tar causes cancers of the nose, throat, tongue, lungs, stomach and bladder
Exposure in childhood means that children:
• are prone to chest infections and asthma
• tend to be smaller and weaker
• do less well at school
Exposure in pregnancies causes:
• smaller babies
• more stillbirths
• more miscarriages
Smokers':
• breath and clothes smell of smoke
• hands and nails are nicotine-stained
• faces become wrinkled from screwing up face to smoke

Key terms

Nicotine – powerful, fast-acting and addictive drug

Carbon monoxide – a poisonous gas

Bronchitis – a chest infection

Emphysema – a chronic lung condition leading to severe shortage of breath, a dependency on oxygen, and death

Stroke – when part of the body is disabled due to a blood clot or a burst blood vessel in the brain

Did you know?

The NHS recommends that women consume no more than 14 units of alcohol a week, and men consume no more than 21 units. One small glass of wine is a unit, and a pint of lager is just over two units.

Alcohol and substance abuse

Consumption of alcohol is socially accepted in many cultures and can be pleasurable in moderation. However, alcohol is addictive and excessive drinking causes many illnesses and problems such as liver and brain damage. The NHS recommends limits to the amount of alcohol we drink each day or week, but many people do not realise how much they drink.

Substance abuse includes taking illegal drugs such as solvents, cannabis or ecstasy, or abusing prescription drugs. This can have profoundly damaging effects on your brain and body, such as loss of control of your actions, damage to organs such as the brain, liver and kidneys, and addiction.

Exercise

Exercise improves our **strength**, **stamina** and **suppleness** as well as our muscle and body tone. It also relieves stress, relaxes us, is enjoyable, gives us a chance to meet others and gives us personal satisfaction. Lack of exercise can lead to stiffening of the joints, poor stamina, strength and suppleness, obesity, stroke, coronary heart disease, poorly developed heart and skeletal muscles, heart attack, sluggish blood flow, osteoporosis and other conditions. Any of these mean our health and well-being suffer.

Figure 3.3: The benefits of exercise. Do you do enough?

- Personal satisfaction (from creative hobbies and pastimes)
- Stamina
- Suppleness
- Fun
- Muscle tone
- **Exercise**
- Relaxation
- Chance to meet others
- Body shape
- Relieves stress
- Strength

Sexual practices

A sexual relationship is an intimate physical relationship between two people which can help to keep an individual healthy and happy. However sexual intercourse without the use of any contraception may result in an unwanted pregnancy or a transmitted infection, both of which will affect the health and needs of the person involved.

Other lifestyle choices

These include, diet (covered in Unit 11), alcohol, substance abuse (the unsafe use of solvents and the taking of illicit or repeat-prescription drugs), stress (covered in Unit 1), working pattern, and social and community networks.

Activity: Lifestyle choices

1. Divide into groups. Each group should take one of the lifestyle choices listed above and research its short- and long-term effects.

2. Produce a PowerPoint® presentation which has at least eight slides; print off the slides with space for notes by each and be prepared to issue these and deliver your presentation to the rest of the class. Each member of the group must contribute and the rest of the class must make notes, to help them in their next assessment task.

Just checking

1. List five serious (a) short-term (b) long-term effects of smoking.
2. If you drink alcohol, why should you control the amount you drink?
3. List five benefits of exercise.

Look after yourself

Key terms

Infection – illness caused by bacteria, viruses or fungi, or by carriers such as animals or insects, and transmitted from person to person

Phobia – a debilitating and irrational fear of something (e.g. an activity such as going outside, or living creatures such as spiders)

Disease – a state in which the whole or parts of the body are not functioning properly, causing ill health

Illness – a state of poor health, sometimes referred to as ill-health

This topic looks at health factors that influence the health and needs of individuals, such as infection, injury, mental health or chronic disorders. These will have an impact on the socio-economic factors that contribute to your health and well-being.

Health factors

Infection

Infections are illnesses such as bronchitis that are spread by the passing of microorganisms between people; these could lead to the health factors listed below.

Infectious diseases or conditions may be easily managed and cured (such as a throat infection or cold), or they may be more serious (such as flu, bronchitis, pneumonia, meningitis, measles, eye infections, tuberculosis or HIV/AIDs), Having an infection may mean you have to take time away from education or employment or you are unable to participate in day to day family and social activities. Recovering from infectious illness can also take time.

Injury

An injury involves damage to body tissues or organs, perhaps as the result of an accident or physical attack. Some injuries can permanently affect your health; for example, a serious back injury may affect your mobility.

Mental health

Mental illness changes the way people think, feel or behave. About 1 in 4 people in the UK will suffer from a mental illness at some point in their lives, but there is a lot of prejudice and fear associated with this. It covers a range of conditions including depression (much worse than being upset), anxiety (much worse than being worried), obsessive compulsive disorder, **phobias**, bipolar disorder and schizophrenia. Mental illness can be brought on by stress, relationships, substance abuse, social isolation or exclusion, or economic deprivation. Many conditions can be controlled by prescribed medication or therapies such as counselling. It is always important to seek help.

Chronic disability or illness

- Chronic illness – is an illness or disease that is long term and for which there is treatment but no cure, such as asthma, diabetes or eczema.

Disabillity and **disease** affect our well-being in many ways. A disability or **illness** may affect physical fitness, restrict access to varied learning activities, cause emotional distress and reduce social opportunities, thus affecting health and well-being. It can also affect growth and physical development of the body; for example, a paralysed arm will lose muscle due to lack of use.

Disabilities may be physical, learning, acquired (e.g. after an accident), **congenital** (e.g. Down's syndrome), temporary (e.g. immobility after an accident) or permanent. Disabled people have to adapt their lifestyle to cope with many everyday situations that able-bodied people deal with automatically. Disability may also affect the development of new abilities and skills. Whatever the condition, the needs of a person with a disability include all those of an able-bodied person; however, people with disabilities have important additional needs, especially in relation to access to places and services. If these needs are met through the provision of an enabling environment, and person-centred care the impact of the disability or illness may be decreased.

Sensory loss is the loss or reduction of any of the senses (sight, hearing, taste, touch and smell). Loss of sight, for example, can cause emotional distress, make it impossible to do practical things without help, make access to intellectual stimulation harder and lead to feelings of isolation unless appropriate aids are provided.

Key term

Congenital – relating to a condition that is present at birth, as a result of heredity or environmental causes

PLTS

In this activity you should be a **self-manager** as you will need to concentrate on the task and use your time well. You will also need to be an **independent enquirer** to complete the research and a **reflective learner** to think about how the factors you have researched will affect the health and needs of an individual.

Activity: Difficulties and illnesses

Prepare an information booklet on either a range of emotional and behavioural difficulties or a range of mental illnesses and how they affect the health and needs of an individual. Don't forget that these apply right through the life stages. Include details of how these needs can be met and of any associations that exist to help individuals with these difficulties or illnesses.

Functional skills

In this activity you will use your **English** skills to read the information you need and write in an appropriate way. You will need **ICT** skills to research the information you need.

BTEC Assessment activity 3.2 P2

Think about the range of individuals you identified for assessment activity 3.1. Prepare a presentation with a handout identifying their PIES needs and the factors that affect those needs.

Grading tip

This assessment task will help you gain P2 if you produce a handout that represents an extended piece of writing and shows your understanding of socio-economic, physical, health and lifestyle factors which influence an individual's needs, as well as the potential effects of those factors on all areas of the individual's PIES development.

Just checking

1. Have you ever been injured? How did it affect your everyday life?
2. Identify three aspects of life that might be affected by a disability or illness.
3. How can mental illness affect a person's PIES needs?

3. Be able to plan to meet the health and wellbeing needs of an individual

The next three topics will give you the opportunity to take part in planning to meet the health and well-being needs of an individual. The needs might arise from their desire to improve their health in an area such as losing weight, improving personal hygiene routines, giving up smoking or managing a long term condition such as diabetes more effectively.

Everyday and health needs

When you produce a health plan, you will be thinking of the PIES (including spiritual) needs that you learnt about before. You will also need to consider the health needs listed on pages 62–63. This might include somebody with diabetes, asthma or other long term chronic illnesses such as emphysema.

Case study: Marie, Jonny and Colette

Marie is 58 years old and over the last few months she has noticed that she has put on weight. She used to weigh 53 kg but she now weighs 65 kg and feels very uncomfortable. Marie is certain that she needs to lose weight.

Jonny, her son, is 19. He drinks too much and he knows it. On Fridays and Saturdays, he goes out with his friends, comes home late and feels dreadful on Sundays and Mondays. He's also tried ecstasy a few times: it's great while it lasts, and easy to get hold of, but he's a bit worried that he might get used to taking it. He is pretty sure now that he needs to drink less and keep away from ecstasy.

Colette is 25. She has asthma and needs to have regular medication including using an inhaler. She sometimes forgets to take her inhalers with her and recently ended up in hospital after a severe asthma attack while she was out with friends. Colette knows that she must remember her medication.

1. In groups choose one of these individuals and brainstorm all the PIES needs that would be met if they carried out their plans. Don't forget, this is not just about physical health.

Assessment of general health and wellbeing

In order to plan to improve an individual's health, you need to assess what they think their needs are, so you can work together on the plan.

You could ask some simple questions about their background and lifestyle and find out why they want to make changes. You will need to ask about age and preferences. You will be working in a position of trust with your partner and it is important not to breach that trust.

Confidentiality

Service providers have lots of **confidential** information about service users. Imagine the huge amount of information a provider will have on someone who is older than you or is in some kind of residential care. This must be kept secure by service providers. The Data Protection Act 1998 protects people's rights to confidentiality, whether the data is stored on paper or electronically. When you use a questionnaire you must be very careful not to breach any rules of confidentiality.

Breaching or breaking confidentiality is inappropriate and can have many consequences, some of which are shown in the table below.

Table 3.1 Maintaining the confidentiality of information communicated by a service user is very important in health and social care

Consequence	Service user might be
Loss of trust	Less likely to say how he or she really feels or share a problem
Lower self-esteem	Likely to feel unvalued and as though they don't matter
Insecurity	Feeling their property and personal safety is threatened
Discrimination	Treated differently by others

There are times, however, when it is appropriate to breach confidentiality, for example, if service users are a risk to themselves or others, or if they have broken, or are about to break, the law. It is therefore inappropriate for a service provider to promise to keep everything confidential; they should explain that there will be times when it might be necessary to pass the information on to an appropriate colleague or authority. If you are in doubt at all you should always check with your manager/tutor.

Activity: Age, preferences and lifestyle

With a partner prepare a PowerPoint presentation to show how a person's age, preferences and lifestyle influence the plan for health and well being. You could look at the examples of Marie, Jonny and Colette (Case Study, page 64).

Key term

Confidential – confidential information should be kept secret. It has been entrusted only to the person to whom it has been communicated

Just checking

1. Why are age and preferences important when you start to carry out an assessment?
2. Why is confidentiality important when you are collecting information from or about an individual?

Assessing the needs

My life

How are you?

If you wanted to find out how healthy you are, what facts would you need to find out from your doctor? If you wanted to find out about the health of a large sample of people, how would you do this?

In this topic you will continue to learn about how to assess a person's needs so that a plan can be drawn up to meet these needs. More information on these measurements, and forms to carry them out, can be found in Unit 7 on pages 210–215.

Assessment of general health and wellbeing

A service provider needs to put together a complete description of a person's physical and mental condition, both past and present, before drawing up a care pathway. This is the individual's personal history and is very important in planning their care. To put together this personal history the service provider could:

- ask a person questions to gather details.
- gain information by observation. For example, you might be able to observe that the person gets out of breath easily when they run for the bus
- collect information such as the positive and negative aspects of a person's lifestyle, e.g. how many cigarettes they smoke, how much alcohol they drink or how much sleep they get each night
- take measurements of aspects that can actually be measured.

Physical and physiological measurements

Physical means to do with the body, so this includes measures such as height and weight. Physiological is to do with the normal functions of the body, so this means measures such as blood pressure, pulse or cholesterol levels.

Figure 3.4: Aspects of health that can be measured

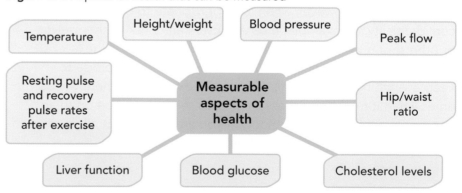

Body Mass Index (BMI)

This is a measure of the amount of fat in your body in relation to your height. BMI is worked out using the formula:

$$BMI = \frac{\text{Weight in kg}}{(\text{Height in m})^2}$$

People with BMIs between 19 and 22 appear to live the longest. BMI values are different for males and females, but table 3.2 gives general values for adults. You can find out more about this on the NHS or Department of Health website.

Table 3.2 BMIs for adults

Adult	Significance
Less than 18.5	Underweight
18.5–24.9	Healthy weight
25–29.9	Overweight
30+	Obese

Peak flow

This is a measure of the maximum **rate** (the expiratory flow rate), in litres per minute, at which air is expelled from the lungs when you breathe out as hard as possible. It is measured using a peak flow meter. Blowing into it, with your lips sealed firmly round the mouthpiece, causes a pointer to move to a certain point, so you can read off your peak flow on a scale. You do this three times and take the highest reading.

The most common reason for taking and recording peak flow readings is to monitor a person's asthma to make sure it is being kept under control by the prescribed medication. It can also be used to **diagnose** lung problems by comparing the reading to a chart of expected scores, based on age and gender: someone with a lung problem will have a lower score than is expected.

Blood pressure

Your blood provides all the organs of your body with the materials to stay healthy. Blood pressure is the pressure exerted by your blood against the walls of your arteries. It is measured in millimetres of mercury as two numbers and varies from person to person, but normal blood pressure at rest is anything up to 140/90. The top number is the systolic pressure, the maximum pressure in the arteries as the heart pumps blood out. The bottom number is diastolic pressure, the minimum blood pressure as the heart relaxes between beats.

High blood pressure is called *hypertension* and is a major problem as it can lead to a stroke or heart disease. Low blood pressure is called *hypotension* and is often normal for a particular person; in fact it can even lead to a prolonged life. However, it can lead to dizziness, or it may be the result of a more serious underlying problem such as Parkinson's disease.

Pulse rate

This measures how strongly your heart is beating. The force of the heart pumping blood around the arteries causes a pulsing sensation that can be felt. Pulse is measured in beats per minute. At rest, a healthy pulse in a young adult is around 70 beats per minute. If you exercise regularly your pulse should return to its resting rate in about 3 minutes.

Key terms

Rate – a measure of something compared with something else, such as litres per second or beats per minute

Diagnose – identify a medical condition

Activity: Taking measurements

1. Find pictures of instruments used to measure peak flow and blood pressure.

2. In your group, research (i) pulse rate (ii) resting pulse rate (iii) recovery pulse rate after exercise (iv) hip/waist ratio measurement (v) body fat composition (vi) cholesterol levels (vii) blood glucose levels (viii) how to measure all these accurately.

3. Put the pictures and information together in a form to be decided by the whole group, so that you all have information about everything. This information needs to be eye-catching and easy to understand.

Just checking

1. What is meant by assessing needs?
2. Name three ways of collecting information to put together a person's personal history.
3. Explain how to actually measure three different measures of health.

The best–laid plans

Key term

Targets – short- and longer-term challenges to help you meet your goal

This topic looks at ways to put together a health plan.

Planning
SMART targets

When you are drawing up a plan to improve health and well-being it is important to include **targets**, not only to motivate the person following the plan but also so progress made can be monitored.

Targets have to be SMART:

- **S**pecific – the target must be clearly stated, such as lose one kilo in weight in one week or take a 30 minute walk twice a week. This is clear and cannot be misunderstood or used as an excuse.
- **M**easurable – it is too vague to say 'eat more fruit': an amount must be stated, so you can prove that you have met the target.
- **A**chievable – the person must feel it is possible to achieve the target set, otherwise they will give up. Asking someone to give up smoking in a week or walk 3 miles each day for four days may not be achievable.
- **R**ealistic – the target set must be realistic; you must be able to do it. It is unrealistic to expect someone who is older and not very fit to run for 30 minutes a day to help lose weight but it is realistic to ask the same of a fit younger person.
- **T**ime-related – there should be a deadline for reaching the target so that progress can be assessed.

It is important that such a plan includes short-term targets, such as to lose 1 kilo in the first week. This is easy to think of doing, as it is only a short time and not a major thing to achieve. The longer term target might be to lose 10 kilos in six months; at first, this will seem a long way off and a lot of weight to lose. If you only set long-term targets, it is easy to say that you will start the diet next week and put it off. By breaking down the path to your final goal into smaller steps (short-term targets), the task seems less daunting and there is no excuse not to start straight away.

Action plan

The plan should start by stating the problem to be tackled. It should indicate what needs to be done to meet each target and by whom, and suggest alternatives in case these methods don't work. The plan should also outline any resources needed to meet the targets, so the cost of carrying out the plan can be budgeted for.

The plan then needs to be implemented, or carried out. Targets need to be monitored. This could be by you, the person following the plan; for example, you could write down everything you eat and drink each day to look at any mistakes you are making with your diet. Alternatively, it could be monitored by a health practitioner or a support group.

Monitor and review

By setting SMART targets you can monitor progress regularly and amend the plan if necessary to meet your longer-term targets and **goals**. Designing a plan is complicated because you are asking others to change how they do something they have often enjoyed doing, something about their lifestyle. People might not manage to change straight away so they might fail to reach a particular target or their final goal; it may be necessary to review the targets or even start all over again. If a target is not being met, choosing a different target may improve the chance of success. This may happen several times until someone succeeds in making the lifestyle change permanent: for example, someone who is overweight might start many diets before they manage to get to, and stay at, their goal weight.

The process of setting targets, reviewing them after a certain time has passed and then amending the plan with new targets, is called the planning cycle. This will help the person to make more progress towards their goal.

Summary of the features of a plan

These are:

- a statement outlining the health or well-being needs of the individual, based on an assessment of present health status through the use of physical measures of health and well-being. It may also include a summary of factors leading to these needs and the expected benefits of meeting these needs.
- SMART targets (short and long term)
- strategies to meet targets, with alternatives to overcome any difficulties that may arise
- regular monitoring and reviewing progress of targets
- strategies to maintain improvement in health and well-being.

Care plan for Ilsa Vinegars

Date	Need	Aim	Action	Evaluation
22/04/10	Ilsa has hearing loss and has new hearing aids. She needs to be able to communicate with those around her.	Ilsa to manage her own hearing aid including insertion, cleaning and checking batteries.	Jasmin to show Ilsa how to put her hearing aids in effectively and keep them clean and check the battery.	By 26/06 Ilsa will be managing her hearing aid and will be able to take part in conversations, listen to the radio and watch television.

This care plan shows how Ilsa's hearing can be improved by management of her new hearing aid.

You will be able to modify this plan for the assessment requirements for this unit. A sample plan is given at the end of the book on page 412.

Activity: Practice your planning skills

Look back at the case study on page 64 and think about how you would put together a care plan for one of the three individuals.

Think about it

If a tutor tells you that you have a year to do a piece of health and social care coursework, and gives you the title but no other guidance, what is likely to happen? You will probably spend quite a long time working out how to do it, doing a bit each week but mainly chatting to your friends, until the end of the year suddenly arrives. How would breaking the task down into smaller chunks, with deadlines for each part and guidelines on how to tackle each task, help you?

PLTS

When you are questions you will be an **independent enquirer**. When you think of ways to change things in the person's life you will be a **creative thinker**.

Functional skills

If you type up your plan you will gain functional skills in **ICT**.

Just checking

1. What does the phrase 'SMART targets' mean?
2. Why is it important to have short term as well as long term targets?
3. Why is it important to monitor and review targets?

BTEC Assessment activity 3.3   **P3**

Carry out an assessment of the health and wellbeing of an individual. This could be a friend or family member. You should consider factors such as BMI, mobility, fitness, mood/morale, self-esteem, risks to cardiovascular or respiratory health and find out information about their general health and well-being and lifestyle.

You could ask questions or take measurements in order to create your assessment.

Grading tips

- To achieve **P3** you need to interpret the results of any questioning or measurements and collate the information obtained systematically, for example through the use of tables, and charts.

- You could construct a simple questionnaire or plan some questions to ask during an interview to find out about your chosen individual's current health and well-being and lifestyle.

- If the individual has any chronic disorders such as allergies or asthma you should consider how these impact of everyday needs.

BTEC Assessment activity 3.4  **P4 M1 D1**

You will assess the health and well-being of an individual who you know very well, e.g. a friend or family member, who wants to make changes to their lifestyle (e.g. to reduce stress or give up smoking) or who has a long-term health condition (e.g. asthma or diabetes). Based on the assessment, you will produce a plan to improve the individual's health and well-being and justify your health improvement plan for the individual. You should gain permission from the individual and consult with your tutor before starting the assessment.

Grading tips

- For **P4**, obtain information from the individual using questioning and observation and by taking physical and physiological measurements. Based on the information obtained, produce a statement which summarises the individual's everyday health and well-being needs.
- The plan for **M1** could be presented using tables or other format useful to the individual. The plan should identify short-term, medium-term and long-term targets and identify the changes the individual will need to make to their lifestyle to achieve them.

- For **D1** you will need to give reasons to explain how the targets and lifestyle changes identified in the plan will improve the individual's health and well-being. You should also explain how the plan takes account of the individual's health at the start of the plan as well as age, lifestyle, preferences, etc. For example, the individual may prefer a sudden change or a more gradual change, e.g. slowly reducing the number of cigarettes smoked each day or stopping all together immediately. You should also describe possible difficulties the individual will have in keeping to the plan and suggest ways these could be overcome.

Julian Edmondson

Physiotherapist

I am a physiotherapist. I have my own private practice and treat a wide range of problems, from people with sports injuries to people who have problems with mobility. I assess a person's needs and draw up a treatment plan. This might include manipulating joints, showing people exercises they can do at home and then monitoring their progress at follow-up visits. These appointments also give the individual a chance to air any concerns. I need to have clinical competencies (i.e. technical skills specific to this job) and an extensive knowledge of the physiology of the human body. I also use skills such as report writing and those that enable me to communicate. I enjoy the fact that I am helping to relieve pain and improve the independence of my clients.

As well as making a real difference to people's lives I find the work very varied and interesting. It also helps to keep me fit and supple because it can be quite physically demanding at times. The downside of the job is when someone reaches a certain level of mobility and there is nothing else I can do to improve matters; it is very sad to see how unhappy some people are when they realise that this is the best they will ever be and it's a lot less than they used to have before, say, an accident or stroke.

I had to work hard to get this job. To become a physiotherapist you have to go to university to study for a physiotherapy degree approved by the Health Professions Council (HPC). Once I got my degree I became eligible for state registration and membership of the Chartered Society of Physiotherapy (CSP). I then successfully applied for a job in a hospital where I helped people who had been referred to the department I worked in by their doctors, and patients who had been admitted to hospital. After a number of years I set up my own private practice which I really enjoy. Although I miss working with a very wide range of other people, I enjoy the one-to-one work in a more peaceful and relaxed situation.

Think about it!

1. What have you learned about in this unit that would help you do a job such as this? Write a list of personal skills and qualities that help Julian to be a successful physiotherapist.

2. What are the needs of a person who has had a car accident and broken her leg badly?

3. How do you think Julian can help her meet these needs?

4. Imagine you are a physiotherapist and you have been asked to visit a woman in a residential care home. She has suffered a minor stroke and is having some co-ordination problems. She refuses to accept that there is anything wrong with her and will not follow the exercise plan you have devised for her. What could you do next to try to help her?

Extension activity: Making a health plan

Luciano is the manger of a restaurant. He drinks at least five units of alcohol in the restaurant every night and even on his night off. He often stays late after his customers have left, having a drink with his staff to relax before going upstairs to the apartment above the restaurant where he lives with his wife and two children. He is overweight, has high blood pressure and does not get enough exercise.

1. What are the risks to his health and well-being if he continues as he is?
2. What difficulties will Luciano face in trying to cut down on his drink, lose weight and get more exercise?
3. How could he overcome these difficulties?
4. Draw up a health plan to help Luciano improve his health and well-being.
   - Do a one-page plan for losing weight, another for reducing his alcohol consumption and one to get more exercise. At the top of each plan, identify the problem to be tackled.
   - When you are setting him short-, medium- and long-term targets to meet, remember that he works in the restaurant part of every day and each night except for one day a week.
   - Identify the benefits of meeting each target, in terms of PIES and health needs.
   - Include strategies to overcome any difficulties he may have in sticking to the plan.
   - Include some alternative strategies in case the first ones don't work for him.

Assignment tips

- Because of the sensitive nature of this unit it is important that you treat everything you hear seriously, sensitively and in confidence so that no-one either in or outside the group is offended or upset.

- It is very important that you ask permission of anyone you want to use for an assignment.

- Make sure that you keep well-organised notes when you are collecting information. Also record the date when you collected information and where you collected the information from.

- When drawing up a health plan, use a table with clearly headed columns so that you can check that you have included all you need: compare your headings with the bullet points in this unit, detailing the features of a good plan.

4 Ensuring safe environments in health and social care

Have you ever seen a hazard?

Have you ever felt at risk?

Have you ever been injured because the environment you were in was unsafe?

This unit will help you to understand the importance of ensuring safe environments in health and social care.

Any environment can be hazardous; it is up to the people who use the environment to be responsible for ensuring it is safe for everyone. This is supported by legislation and guidelines and practitioners who carry out risk assessments.

This unit provides an introduction to health and safety issues, legislation in health and social care, risk assessment and the actions that are necessary to minimise potential hazards and risks. It is important that you develop an understanding of hazards and risks, legislation and the use and process of risk assessment if you are considering working within a health or social care setting. This unit will give you the opportunity to plan and carry out your own risk assessment of an indoor space used for an everyday activity.

Learning outcomes

After completing this unit you should:

1. know potential hazards in health and social care environments
2. know the main principles of health and safety legislation applied to health and social care environments
3. understand risk assessment processes related to health and social care.

73

Assessment and grading criteria

This table shows you what you must do in order to achieve a **pass**, **merit** or **distinction** grade, and where you can find activities in this book to help you.

To achieve a **pass** grade the evidence must show that you are able to:	To achieve a **merit** grade the evidence must show that, in addition to the pass criteria, you are able to:	To achieve a **distinction** grade the evidence must show that, in addition to the pass and merit criteria, you are able to:
P1 Identify potential hazards that might arise in health and social care environments [IE3, CT4, RL5, TW1, TW2, SM3, SM5] **Assessment activity 4.1, page 79**		
P2 Outline the main features of current health and safety legislation as applied in health and social care [IE4, CT4, RL5, TW2, SM5] **Assessment activity 4.2, page 85**		
P3 Explain risk assessment processes in the context of everyday activities in health and social care [IE4, CT4, SM5, EP2] **Assessment activity 4.3, page 93**	**M1** Carry out a risk assessment of an indoor space used for an everyday activity **Assessment activity 4.4, page 94**	**D1** Discuss possible ways of reducing risk to users of the indoor space **Assessment activity 4.4, page 94**

How you will be assessed

For this unit you will be assessed by three assignments that will be marked by the staff at your centre. All of your assignments may be subject to sampling by your centre's External Verifier as part of Edexcel's ongoing quality assurance procedures.

- Your first assignment may involve the production of a poster identifying the potential hazards that might arise in health and social care environments.
- Your second assignment may involve the production of an information booklet outlining the main features of current health and safety legislation and guidelines as applied in health and social care.
- Your third assignment may involve the production of a report containing an explanation of risk assessment processes in the context of everyday activities in health and social care.

Michaela, 17–year-old BTEC First Health and Social Care learner and part–time care assistant

This unit made me realise that there is so much more to making sure an environment is safe than just having fire extinguishers available; there is a lot more to think about. I think it is important for everyone – no matter what job they do – to make sure they know about hazards and risks.

I found studying food safety and hygiene really interesting. It isn't something I have really considered before and it was quite scary to think how easy it is to give someone food poisoning. I think everyone should have to go on a food safety and hygiene course to reduce hazards and risks.

I also enjoyed doing some research on my college. I had to go around different areas looking for hazards and then suggesting what risk these could lead to and for whom. I actually carried out a risk assessment which was fun.

I didn't realise before that there are so many laws to try to reduce hazards and risks; I now know that every area of my life has some legislation that is in place to help protect me and make me safe.

When I go to work now I think about what I do and whether it may cause a hazard to others as it is my responsibility, as it is for everyone else, to ensure safe environments.

Over to you!

- Look around you, can you see any hazards?
- Have you or someone you know had an accident at work?

1. Know potential hazards in health and social care environments

Hazards

Hazards are around you all the time whether you are in your home, on the bus, playing in the park or eating out at a restaurant. This topic and the following one consider potential hazards in health and social care environments.

Rooms or outside recreational areas

Every room contains potential hazards which can then be a risk to the individuals who are using the room. Some rooms are more hazardous than others, e.g. a kitchen where hot liquid and food is prepared and handled or a garage where there may be chemicals and machinery that could potentially cause harm; in a hospital the rooms storing medicines/chemicals and sharp equipment are a particular hazard. A room may contain unsafe furnishings or inappropriate furnishings for the service user. The legislation relevant to these hazards is the Health and Safety at Work etc Act 1974.

It is important to think not just about indoor rooms but outdoor spaces too, i.e. outside recreational areas; these may also contain many potential hazards for individuals. Think about an outside recreational area that you know or have used and consider what potential hazards are there.

Toys

Many toys look safe enough, and they are supposed to be fun, but there have been some incidents where toys have caused injury and sometimes death. Toys which are purchased in the UK should conform to Toy Safety Regulations (1995).

Accidents do not always happen because the toy itself is unsafe but because the toy has been used inappropriately, e.g. used by a child who is too young to play with it safely. Old, worn-out and broken toys can also present hazards.

Everyone should ensure they follow these toy safety tips:

- make sure the toy is suitable for the age of the child
- check the toy for loose parts
- check the toy for sharp edges
- make sure children are supervised
- keep the toy and play area clean and hygienic.

Storage of chemicals

Within your home, school, college, workplace and other public places such as hospitals, there will be chemicals that could be dangerous if they are touched and/or swallowed, e.g. bleach. Everyone should ensure they follow these rules for the correct storage of chemicals:

- store in a safe place, especially if children are present, e.g. a locked cupboard
- chemicals should be stored in their original container and not transferred to another container that appears safe, e.g. a lemonade bottle
- containers must have safety lids and caps (these are the lids that have to be pushed and twisted off or they just click and won't work).

Control of infectious diseases

Infection can travel in body products and fluids, soil, animal fluids and waste and within food products.

One of the easiest and simplest ways to help prevent the spread of infectious diseases is for you to wash your hands correctly.

There is a procedure for correct hand washing and it is often displayed as a poster above sinks in public places and toilets – reminding people to wash their hands and to wash their hands properly (see page 88).

Fire

Fire and/or smoke can kill. Fire causes burns and smoke can choke; fire is a very serious hazard that could happen anywhere at any time. There are some fire precautions that you should be aware of to reduce the hazard:

- store flammable products appropriately
- do not overload electric sockets and appliances
- know where the fire extinguishers are stored and which type of extinguisher should be used for different sorts of fires and how to use them
- know where fire blankets are stored and how to use them
- know the fire evacuation procedure.

Activity: Wet, soap, wash and dry

Identify when you should wash your hands – produce a list and compare your list with your peers.

Remember

If you cannot control a fire, leave it, close the door behind you and move to a safe place and dial 999.

Just checking

1. What is a hazard?
2. What should you look for on a toy to check it is safe for children to play with?
3. How can chemicals be a hazard?

Activity: Hazards

1. Identify the hazards in the picture and suggest what can be done to reduce or eliminate these hazards
2. Identify what could happen to a person, i.e. 'the risk', if the hazard was not eliminated. Discuss this in your group.

Figure 4.1: What hazards can you see here?

Further potential hazards

Key terms

Eliminate – to get rid of something that is not wanted

Risk – the harm a hazard can do. The chance of suffering harm, loss, injury or danger

This topic looks at further hazards you might come across in health and social care environments. The more we all identify hazards and act appropriately to reduce or **eliminate** the hazard the less likely we are to be at risk of harm.

Equipment

All equipment and work surfaces should be kept clean to prevent the spread of infection.

Smaller items of equipment can be sterilised and some equipment is designed to be used only once and is then thrown away. Work surfaces should be regularly cleaned and disinfected. There are many products available today to keep surfaces clean and hygienic.

The inappropriate use of equipment is a potential hazard. There are many different kinds of equipment, such as machines used by professional staff in order to care for the service user; but if these are used inappropriately – or by the wrong person who doesn't know how to use the equipment properly and safely – it puts everyone at **risk**, and especially the service user.

Equipment also requires regular maintenance to remain effective and safe. Insufficient maintenance is a potential hazard and the Health and Safety at Work etc Act 1974 requires workplaces to ensure their equipment is safe and used appropriately.

Poor working conditions

If a workplace is in a poor state of repair and not in a good condition, e.g. there are unsafe furnishings, this could potentially produce hazards. Within a workplace whose responsibility is it to ensure the environment is safe? You will look at this in more detail on pages 86–87.

Building maintenance is a very important responsibility of the employer, as regulated by the Health and Safety at Work etc Act 1974, which also covers personal safety precautions.

Safety measures at work cover many areas; one of these areas is the lifting of service users. This is covered by the Manual Handling Operations Regulations 1992 which sets out the correct lifting technique that should be observed when lifting a service user in the workplace. Many employees within the health and social care sectors regularly have to lift people, some of whom may be frail and vulnerable. Poor lifting techniques have resulted in many thousands of people taking time off work and some have even had to take early retirement due to ongoing health problems, such as a bad back, which originated in poor lifting techniques.

Poor staff training

UK law requires employers to ensure the health and safety of their employees. Part of this requirement is that of staff training, e.g. fire

Remember

You should always lift with a straight back and bent knees.

safety policy. If there is no staff training or ineffective staff training this is a hazard which could potentially put people's lives at risk.

Figure 4.2: Do you know when to use the different types of fire extinguishers?

Water with additive

Foam

Powder

CO_2 gas

Radio transmissions

Much research has been carried out into the negative effects on the human body from radio transmissions. Being in close proximity to radio transmissions is a potential hazard and this is now regulated through the Health and Safety at Work etc Act 1974.

Pollution

Pollution comes in different forms, e.g. noise, air and water. Pollution in any form is a potential hazard, e.g. fumes may cause injury/disease to the human body. Noise pollution can damage hearing and a toxic chemical can pollute the water, soil or air. Pollution is regulated by the Control of Substances Hazardous to Health (COSHH) Regulations 2002. If hazardous waste is not disposed of correctly it could become a pollutant, e.g. a toxic chemical. Every health or social care workplace has regulations for the disposal of waste and all employees will be trained to ensure they know and understand the correct and safe disposal of waste at their workplace.

BTEC Assessment activity 4.1 P1

Design and produce two posters that identify potential hazards in two different health and social care environments. Examples might be a nursery or reception class, a nursing home or a day centre for older people, or those observed in your placement, or in a health and care environment you visit such as a health centre or a dental surgery.

Grading tip

For P1 you need to identify potential hazards which means you should name them and provide a brief comment about the hazard. Comments could relate to the abilities of the individuals using the health and social care environments.

Responsibilities for managing risk

Did you know?

The maximum penalties for breaching health and safety legislation are unlimited fines and up to two years in prison.

Health and safety failures currently cost Britain's employers up to £6.5 billion every year.

Key term

Employee – a person who is employed by someone else

Previous topics have looked at hazards and risks. While you are now aware that there are such things as hazards, and their associated risks in health and social care settings, we should question whose responsibility it is to ensure that these hazards are reduced or eliminated. On pages 90–91 you will look at the role of a Health and Safety Awareness Officer; but other people should also be involved and in this topic you will discover who they are.

Employers

Employers must ensure the following:

- that equipment is safe and in good working order

- the working environment does not put anyone at risk

- all necessary arrangements are in place to ensure the health and safety of all employees

- health and safety training is available and adequate

- a written safety policy is in place and accessible

- the workplace is kept in good condition

- the workplace does not emit toxic fumes or dust

- all protective equipment is available free of charge to anyone who needs it, e.g. gloves, uniforms, overalls and masks.

Employees

Employees must ensure the following:

- that they cooperate with their employer to carry out health and safety regulations in the workplace

- to communicate/report any dangerous situations (hazards) to the employer immediately

- not to tamper with or misuse equipment provided that meets health and safety regulations, e.g. fire extinguishers

- they take care of themselves and others around them who may be affected by what they do.

Service users

What about people who use health and social care services? This may include all of us at different times.

We all have the right to be in a safe environment and away from harm and we all have a duty to ensure safe environments.

So, as service users, people must also be aware of potential hazards and risks and, if any are noticed, they should tell a member of staff as soon as possible.

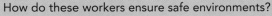

How do these workers ensure safe environments?

Case study: Abena

As a practice nurse I work at a general practice – I am the nurse you would see around at your medical centre/doctor's surgery; you might even come to see me for an appointment. I do lots of jobs in my role as a practice nurse, such as taking blood and urine samples, carrying out vaccinations and cervical smear tests. I also advise and provide information on health matters, e.g. contraception. It is my responsibility to ensure that where I work is a safe environment, not just for me but for all my work colleagues as well as those who come to the practice.

- How do you think Abena ensures that where she works is a safe environment?
- What sort of information will Abena need to provide?

PLTS

By reflecting back on your risk assessment you are being a **reflective learner** and developing your skills of reflection.

Just checking

1. Who is responsible for reporting a hazard in the workplace?
2. What should employees and employers ensure?
3. Apart from the employer and employee who else is responsible for ensuring a safe environment?

2. Know the main principles of health and safety legislation

Health and safety legislation is essential to ensure employers provide and employees work in a safe environment. This topic and the following topic look at the main features of health and safety legislation applied to health and social care environments.

Legislation and guidelines

There are many laws (also known as legislation) and regulations concerning health and safety:

- Health and Safety at Work etc Act (HASAW) 1974
- Food Safety Act 1990
- Food Safety (General Food Hygiene) Regulations 1995
- Manual Handling Operations Regulations 1992
- Reporting of Injuries, Diseases and Dangerous Occurrences Regulations (RIDDOR) 1995
- Control of Substances Hazardous to Health (COSHH) Regulations 2002
- Management of Health and Safety at Work Regulations 1999
- Data Protection Act 1998.

Health and Safety at Work etc Act (HASAW) 1974

This is a very important piece of health and safety legislation helping to safeguard and protect people. It is rather like an 'umbrella' covering all other health and safety legislation in the workplace.

Under this legislation employers must ensure the following is provided:

- a safe working environment
- information on health and safety
- health and safety policies and procedures
- risk assessments carried out on potential hazards.

Under this legislation as an employee you must:

- cooperate with your employer on health and safety issues
- take reasonable care of your own health and safety, as well as that of others
- not intentionally tamper/damage any health and safety equipment.

Reporting of Injuries, Diseases and Dangerous Occurences Regulations (RIDDOR) 1995

The Health and Safety Executive (HSE) requires all employers to report all accidents, diseases, dangerous occurrences and deaths to them.

A workplace should have an accident-reporting process in place to correctly document and record an accident or incident.

The completing of the report should be as detailed as possible – noting dates, times, venue, situation, witnesses and any treatment/action needed.

This report could form the basis of a risk assessment to ensure that measures are taken to reduce the risk of it happening again.

Manual Handling Operations Regulations 1992

The Health and Safety Executive (HSE) has produced guidelines to follow regarding safe manual handling techniques and procedures. This is necessary because injuries caused by poor lifting techniques result in thousands of lost days of work each year.

In a care environment the following is recommended for safe lifting:

- all staff should be trained in manual handling
- always plan a lift before you carry it out
- use the equipment that is available for the purpose
- never hurry or cut corners when lifting another person
- where possible have more than one person doing the lift
- practise the lift before doing it for real
- ensure you are wearing appropriate clothing.

Why is it important to lift correctly?

Case study: Wes

Wes was tired. He had just finished his first day's work experience at the local nursery and didn't realise children could be so exhausting even though it was enjoyable. He had finished tidying up with the staff and had his coat on ready to go home when the catering manager came out and asked him if he would help bring in a food delivery that had just arrived. Wes went straight outside and found some boxes waiting to be moved. He had seen a trolley but that seemed too much bother for just a few things so he bent over and picked up a couple of boxes of tinned tomatoes. He felt a nasty twinge in his side and his back, but kept on and managed to do three loads until the pain got too bad.

1. Think of at least three things that Wes should have done before he agreed to help.
2. Why is training in manual handling operations so important for workers in health and social care?
3. Look at the photograph in the margin of a careworker lifting a box using correct techniques. What do you think Wes did wrongly?

Just checking

1. What is legislation and why is it needed to guide health and safety in the workplace?
2. What does COSHH stand for?
3. Name one piece of legislation that requires the employer to report all accidents.

More legislation

In the previous topic you looked at some of the different legislation that supports and maintains standards of health and safety. In this topic you will cover specific examples of legislation covering particular hazards and health and safety case studies, to extend your knowledge of ensuring safe environments in health and social care.

Legislation and guidelines

Table 4.1 Legislation covering different hazards

Legislation	Health and Safety at Work etc (HASAW) Act 1974	Reporting of Injuries, Diseases and Dangerous Occurrences Regulations (RIDDOR) 1995	Control of Substances Hazardous to Health (COSHH) Regulations 2002	Manual Handling Operations Regulations 1992	Fire Precautions (Workplace) Regulations 1997
Hazard	Rooms and outdoor play areas that pose a risk Equipment in an unsafe condition Poor working conditions Poor staff training Unsafe furnishings Toys in an unsafe condition	Inadequate control of infectious diseases	Incorrect storage of chemicals Pollution of air and/or water	Incorrect lifting techniques and procedures	Fire

Management of Health and Safety at Work Regulations 1999

This regulation covers the way the duties laid down in legislation such as the Health and Safety at Work etc Act 1974 (HASAW) are actually managed in the workplace.

Each workplace setting within the health or social care sectors will have their own policies developed from the HASAW Act 1974.

Control of Substances Hazardous to Health (COSHH) Regulations 2002

Employers are required to ensure control over exposure to hazardous substances in the workplace.

Every workplace should have someone who is responsible for making sure the guidelines set down by COSHH regulations are carried out. This would cover, for example, the correct storage of chemicals:

- chemicals must be kept in the original containers supplied by the manufacturer
- substances must be stored in a safe place
- containers must have an appropriate safety cap/lid.

Discuss the hazard and risk associated with each of these symbols.

Food Safety Act 1990

This legislation lays down rules which apply to everyone involved in the production, storage, distribution or sale of food.

Food Safety (General Food Hygiene) Regulations 1995

This legislation covers the general requirements for the design, construction and operation of food premises. For more information on food safety see Unit 11.

Activity: Know your poison

Look at the symbols on the left used to indicate whether a substance is hazardous and what sort of hazard it is.

Match the following words to the correct symbol:

- toxic
- irritant
- corrosive
- oxidising agent
- flammable
- dust

BTEC Assessment activity 4.2 (P2)

Design and produce an information booklet outlining the main features of current health and safety legislation as applied in health and social care. In this activity you will need to investigate and research different current health and safety legislation relevant to different health and social care environments. The environment may be your workplace experience venue; it would be a good idea to ask for a copy of the workplace's health and safety policies, they should be easily accessible. Your information booklet can be in any format you choose; you may wish to produce it on a computer or by hand.

Grading tip

You need to 'outline' the main features of the legislation, policies and responsibilities for several of the relevant laws, regulations and policies so you should name them and then provide brief notes in your own words of how each applies in health and social care environments. Research using textbooks and the internet would be helpful and if possible, you could study the health and safety policy from a placement environment.

Functional skills

Reading and understanding a range of texts, e.g. symbols of hazardous substances, means you are developing your **English** functional skills.

Just checking

1. Name one health and safety law and give a brief outline.
2. What is the symbol used if the hazardous substance is toxic?
3. Why should chemicals be kept in their original container?

3. Understand risk assessment processes

Risks are related to hazards. For example, if the hazard is a trailing electrical lead, the risk is that someone could trip over it. This topic and the following four will help you to plan a risk assessment in a health or social care environment.

Identifying risks

There are many risks because of the hazards that are all around us. Some risks are more likely to occur, some less likely; likewise some risks are easier to control, some less so. Once we have identified a hazard we need to assess the risk this hazard may cause. Without thinking about it we carry out assessments on risk throughout our lives, e.g. when we go to cross the road (the road is the hazard) we assess the risk...are there any cars coming? Can I see around the corner enough to cross here? How fast are the cars moving? Is there a pedestrian crossing to use nearby? It's icy today so am I likely to slip when crossing the road?

Risk assessments are needed to minimise the risk. Once we have performed a risk assessment we can then manage the risk by either reducing it or eliminating the risk altogether, so helping to ensure a safe environment.

Risk assessment is covered on pages 92–93.

Estimating risks

Once we have identified the risk by spotting the hazard/s we then need to estimate the risk. What this really means is deciding on the 'likelihood' of something happening based on the hazard in front of us. Estimating the risk is usually done through the use of a scale of 1 to 5, where 1 means not very likely to happen and is a low risk up to 5 where it is very possible or likely that it will happen and a high risk. On the scale the number 3 is about in the middle and would indicate that there is a moderate chance of it happening.

We also need to decide, when we estimate the risk, who is at risk and think about the number of people at risk.

The fridge in the kitchen at home, the staff canteen kitchen, the hospital ward, the nursery school and the children's home kitchen may look innocent enough. It is an item of equipment we use all the time and we probably don't give much thought to its maintenance as long as it is working and our milk is cold! But a fridge that is not looked after or used properly is a hazard and it can produce many risks.

There is a correct way and an incorrect way of storing different foodstuffs in a fridge. If the food in the fridge is stored correctly then we are less at risk of suffering from food poisoning. However, if we disregard storage 'dos and don'ts' we are more likely to put ourselves

Did you know?

When cooling food down you should cool from 60°C to 21°C in a maximum of 2 hours and from 21°C to 5°C in a maximum of 4 hours to prevent harmful food poisoning bacteria from multiplying.

at risk of suffering from food poisoning, such as salmonella. Food poisoning is very unpleasant and is a condition that can prove fatal.

Controlling risks

When we control the risk we are deciding what to do to reduce or to eliminate the risk:

- to eliminate the risk of tripping over a ball left on the stairs we could remove the ball from the stairs and store it where it belongs, i.e. in a toy box
- to reduce the risk of people hurting themselves by slipping on a wet floor we could indicate the floor is slippery by placing 'slippery floor' warning signs on the wet floor and surrounding area
- to reduce the risk of spreading bacteria that can make us ill, we should always wash and dry our hands thoroughly before handling food and after going to the toilet.

Monitoring effectiveness of controls

So: you have identified the hazard and risk, estimated the extent of the risk and the likelihood of something happening on the scale of 1–5 and then you have put into place action to reduce or eliminate the risk. This is all good, but what else can you do? How could you be sure that the hazard will not return and that the extent of the risk will not increase in the future?

For example, you might have noticed that the fridge was dirty, overstocked, foodstuffs were stored incorrectly and the temperature control was set too high and not cold enough to store food safely. You then estimated that there was a high risk of food stored in the fridge becoming contaminated with food poisoning bacteria which could potentially make someone very ill. So you decided to empty, clean and re-stock the fridge correctly to reduce the risk. To try and make sure the hazard and risk did not return you would need to monitor the situation and encourage other people to work towards keeping the risk low in future. You could place clear written instructions about safe fridge practice on the front of the fridge.

Often monitoring how the risk is being controlled is carried out by a person with these specific responsibilities at work, e.g. a Health and Safety Officer, see page 91.

Record keeping

Whether it is a risk assessment document, health and safety policy documents or the work place accident record book, regular and accurate record keeping regarding hazards, risks and reviews should be kept at all workplaces.

When you are next at a workplace setting, ask the practitioner what record keeping process they follow, what records they have, and how often their records are reviewed and updated?

Activity: What's in your fridge?

You have been asked to produce an educational poster to show people how the food in their fridge should be stored correctly so as to reduce the risk of food poisoning.

The following foodstuffs are to be stored in the fridge and should be included in your poster: raw red meat, cooked red meat, raw poultry, fresh fish, bread, butter, milk, fruit juice, cheese, cabbage, carrots, salad leaves, tomatoes, yoghurt, ham, salami, strawberries, grapes, left-over lasagne, salad dressing, eggs.

Just checking

1. What is the difference between a hazard and a risk?
2. What is salmonella?
3. On which shelf in a fridge should you store raw red meat?

Risks associated with everyday activities

You have already looked at what hazards and risks are and how we can **estimate** the risk as being very likely or less likely. In this topic we will look at the risks associated with everyday activities.

Everyday activities

There are many activities that we may do every day that can be associated with risks. We do not constantly think about the associated risks when carrying out an activity, e.g. cooking, it is often the case that we mainly think about the associated risks when an accident has happened to us or one of our loved ones.

Personal care

We all carry out personal care activities every day; this may be to ourselves or to someone else, e.g. a family member. When you use the bath or shower you are at risk of slipping, there is a risk that you might be allergic to a personal hygiene product or you could cut yourself whilst shaving.

Mobility and travel

When you drive a car, walk on the street, ride on the bus or train or fly on a plane you are mobile and travelling; sometimes not far from home and sometimes further afield. There are many risks associated with being mobile and travelling. You must wear your seatbelt in a car otherwise you may be seriously injured or killed in an accident. When you fly long distances e.g. to Australia, you are more at risk of developing a very serious condition called Deep Vein Thrombosis (DVT). Travelling to countries around the world puts us at risk of contracting diseases uncommon in the UK e.g. Malaria, to reduce the risk you are encouraged to get protected by vaccinations and other medications.

Work or education

The increased use of computers at work or in school/college increases associated risks, e.g. Repetitive Strain Injury (RSI). In science labs in school/college you are at risk because of the dangerous chemicals and equipment that you may be using and of course anywhere may

Figure 4.3: Do you always follow these steps to good hand washing?

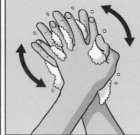

have slippery floors. For example, if it's raining outside and everyone is walking inside with wet shoes, boots and umbrellas, the floor will soon become a hazard.

Hobbies/leisure

We all enjoy having a hobby and doing things we love in our leisure time, but many hobbies and leisure pursuits can put us at risk. Extreme/adrenaline sports are often associated with being very risky e.g. scuba diving, sky diving and rock climbing. Horse riding is a sport done by many people of all ages and every year there are examples in the news of how risky this activity can be, with reports of people being left paralysed after a fall or worse still killed. Other activities such as going to the gym or running can also be risky – using a piece of weight lifting equipment incorrectly in the gym or running on the side of a road wearing inadequate visibility clothes could put you at risk of an accident. Enjoying a walk in the countryside/fell walking is also associated with risk e.g. do you have the right walking shoes on to protect your ankles and knees, do you have warm and waterproof clothing with you in case the weather turns cold and wet?

Reassessing the risk

Reassessments need to be carried out regularly; this is often the responsibility of a health and safety officer within the workplace. Reassessments are carried out to ensure that any risks which have been eliminated or reduced stay that way and do not return.

The role of a Health and Safety Awareness Officer will be covered in the next section.

Case study: Scarlett

Scarlett is a nursery school assistant and a mum of one of the children at the nursery school. There are lots of different rules and policies governing health and safety practices at the nursery school. Scarlett has recently noticed another member of staff not washing her hands after cleaning the toilets and then going straight into the kitchen to prepare the children's break-time snacks.

1. What risks is this member of staff taking by not washing her hands – to herself and others?
2. What should Scarlett do?

Just checking

1. How do you control a risk?
2. How long should you wash your hands for?
3. What are bacteria?

Functional skills

By taking part in informal discussions and exchanges about how to control, monitor and reassess a risk you will develop your functional skills in **English** – speaking and listening.

Activity: Hazards and risks

Scenario 1

A chair in a hospital out-patients department waiting room has a broken leg.

Scenario 2

The drain outside the nursing home is blocked and overflowing with dirty water.

Answer the following questions for scenario 1 and 2.

1. What is the nature of the hazard?
2. What is the risk on a scale of 1–5?
3. What could be done to control the risk?
4. How could this be monitored?
5. How often should it be monitored and reassessed?

Controlling, monitoring and reassessing risks

Key terms

Consent – to give permission, to allow what someone wishes

Guidance – advising and guiding

In this topic you will look further into how risks are controlled, monitored and reassessed by investigating the work of a Health and Safety Awareness Officer and the role this person plays in helping us to ensure safe environments.

Health and Safety Awareness Officer

A Health and Safety Awareness Officer (HSAO) is not a health and safety inspector; they do not have powers to enter a work premises without the agreement of the workplace beforehand; everything must be done with **consent**.

Health and Safety Inspectors have the right to enter any workplace without necessarily giving notice. An inspector would expect to look at a specific issue associated with the workplace, the work activities, the management of health and safety and to check that people are complying with health and safety law.

Health and safety law relating to work activities is actually enforced by inspectors from the Health and Safety Executive (HSE) or by inspectors from your local authority.

There is lots of information available for workplaces about health and safety and the work of inspectors and awareness officers on the HSE website so everyone should know what health and safety inspectors and awareness officers do to ensure safe environments. To obtain a secure link to this website, see the Hotlinks sections on page x.

Care workers

This unit is all about your responsibility as a care worker to play your part in creating a safe environment for the service users and families you are working with, yourself and your colleagues. Each day you will be aware of any hazards and the risks they pose and ensure that all controls to minimise the risks are taken. For example, you may notice there are ants in the kitchen: you will report that hazard and your employer should ensure steps are taken to get rid of them.

Workplace health and safety officer

Every workplace should have a nominated person who has health and safety responsibilities. This person would carry out risk assessments, monitor the risk and reassess the risk and work with all the people at the workplace to raise awareness of hazards and risks.

The following information is from a typical example of a job specification for a health and safety officer at a school:

Knowledge and experience

• A sound understanding of the main Health and Safety Regulations, including COSHH

- Relevant qualifications and/or experience in the relevant aspects of Health and Safety

Skills and abilities

- Ability to identify work priorities and manage own workload

- Ability to act on own initiative, dealing with any unexpected problems that arise

- Ability to demonstrate good interpersonal skills in communication

- Ability to identify potential risks and implement appropriate control measures

- Ability to work within and apply all school policies, such as health and safety

Personal qualities

- Ability to demonstrate reliability, discretion and self-motivation

- Ability to work under pressure

- Willingness to participate in further training and development opportunities

- Willingness to maintain confidentiality on all school matters

- Ability to communicate information to learners and staff

What knowledge and experience, skills and abilities, and personal qualities do you have that would make you suitable for this job role? What skills would you still need to develop?

Case study: Chris, Health and Safety Officer

'I am a health and safety officer at a community centre in my local town. I did not ever plan to be a health and safety officer when I was at school; it sort of just developed over the years. When I was working in a factory many years ago I saw someone have a terrible accident which left them in a wheelchair. There were hazards at the factory, but no one really took any responsibility for them and because of that someone got hurt. After that I got involved in health and safety at work and took some courses in health and safety.

'The community centre I work at is used for all sorts of clubs and activities and it is my responsibility to ensure the environment is a safe one. I carry out regular risk assessments; I then control the risks identified, monitor and regularly reassess the risks.

'It is an interesting job and satisfying because I feel like I am carrying out a very important role in my community.'

1. How does Chris ensure the community centre is a safe environment?

2. What sort of hazards/risks would Chris come across?

Just checking

1. What does a Health and Safety Officer do at work?

2. Name one quality needed to be a Health and Safety Officer.

3. Do you have to take any qualifications to be a Health and Safety Officer?

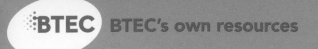
Risk assessment in the workplace

Key terms

Risk assessment – examining something that could cause harm and then deciding whether enough precautions have been taken to prevent injury

HSE – Health and Safety Executive regulates health and safety in the workplace

Code of Practice – set of standards of conduct for workers and employers

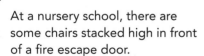

Activity: Fire!

At a nursery school, there are some chairs stacked high in front of a fire escape door.

- What is the hazard?
- What is the risk? (type of injury that could result if harm occurs)
- Type of people affected?
- Level of risk? (high, medium, low or 1–5 scale)
- Current control measures in place?
- Future control measures needed?
- Person responsible?
- Review date?

Over the previous few topics we have looked at different hazards and risks and considered information about why we carry out **risk assessment**, how we carry it out and who does it. Remember that a risk assessment is carried out to analyse a risk so that this risk can then be managed by either reducing it or removing it altogether. In this topic you are actually going to carry out your own risk assessment of an indoor space used for an everyday activity.

Assessing risks in the workplace

The Health and Safety Executive (**HSE**) suggests the following five-point process to assess risks in the workplace.

- **Look for hazards** – look around your work environment and consider what you might think is a hazard. Make sure you write this down.

- **Who might be at risk?** Consider the people who may be harmed because of this hazard; you think about everyone who uses the work environment and in what capacity.

- **Evaluate the risk coming from the hazard** – consider whether it is possible to reduce the risk. Will the risk have to be controlled? For example, when a risk cannot be removed its severity could be reduced from a high risk to a low risk.

- **Record the findings** – on a risk assessment form, there should be a risk assessment form in every place of work. These forms may be different at different places of work, but they should all contain the following sections: the hazard/type of injury that could result/type of people and number affected/risk level (high, medium, low or 1–5 scale)/current control measures in place/further control measures required/person responsible for actions required/review date.

- **Review the assessment** – hazards and risks do not go away once you have written them on the form; they need to be reassessed regularly.

Health and safety in the workplace

Regulating health and safety in the workplace is the responsibility of both the Health and Safety Commission (HSC) and the Health and Safety Executive (HSE).

The HSE works in a supportive role to the HSC, ensuring that the health and safety of people at work is maintained and people are not put at risk while they are at work.

Employers are advised about what they need to do via **Codes of Practice** for their workplace.

Employers can be prosecuted by the HSE if they fail to ensure the health and safety of people who access the place of work; this could be both the employees and other people using the premises, such as customers or patients.

Figure 4.4: A risk assessment is necessary in all workplaces

Day Unit, A Hospital							
RISK ASSESSMENT							
Hazard – task/ activity with potential to cause harm	Type of injury that could result if harm occurs	Type of people and number affected	Risk level (low, medium, high)	Current control measures in place	Further control measures required	Person responsible for implementation of further measures required and date to implement	Date to review assessment (annual review unless task changes/alters)
Wheelchairs blocking fire exits	Unable to evacuate ward quickly – may result in people being trapped	All staff, service users and visitors to the Day Unit	H	Storage provided away from fire exits	Folding wheelchairs for safer storage	Health and safety officer; unit manager	
Meals kept aside on work surface for clients absent from ward	Food poisoning	Service users	H	All meals should be sent back to the kitchens and fresh meals prepared when clients return to the ward	Fridge needed to store food safely	Health and safety officer; unit manager	
Lack of sufficient hoists and equipment	Lifting injuries	Staff	H		Maintenance book needed to ensure equipment is regularly checked	Staff in charge of each shift	

Assessment activity 4.3 **P3**

 PLTS

When you are carrying out your risk assessment you will be developing your **independent enquirer, self-manager** and **reflective learner** skills.

Write a report which explains risk assessment processes in the context of everyday activities in health and social care.

Grading tip

Remember, explaining something means you have to use examples and give your opinion (always supporting your thoughts with evidence). An explanation is more than just a description. **P3**

Case study: Jodie

As a care worker at a local residential care home for older people, Jodie is required to make the tea and coffee for her work colleagues, the service users and their visitors. The kitchen is downstairs in the basement and the lounge is upstairs on the ground floor.

While she was carrying a tray of hot drinks up the stairs for morning coffee break, Jodie slipped on a piece of loose carpet and fell to the bottom of the staircase, suffering multiple injuries.

As she fell the hot drinks splashed over her bare arms and face, and her fall caused her to break an ankle and fracture a wrist.

Jodie was taken to hospital where she had the ankle put into a cast and then she had to take four months off work to recover.

1. What could have been done to make sure this accident didn't take place?
2. What legislation would this refer to?
3. Who was responsible for Jodie's accident?
4. Produce a risk assessment for this scenario.

Functional skills

When taking part in formal or informal discussions about legislation and the case studies you are developing your speaking and listening **English** functional skills.

PLTS

When you are discussing the case studies in this topic you are developing your **independent enquirer** skills.

Just checking

1. What is a risk assessment?
2. Whose responsibility is it to carry out a risk assessment at work?
3. What does the Health and Safety Commission (HSC) do?

 Assessment activity 4.4

Carry out a risk assessment of an indoor space used for an everyday activity.

Discuss possible ways of reducing risk to users of the indoor space. You will need the help of your tutor to organise this. You will need to think about issues of confidentiality and consent when carrying out your risk assessment. You could refer to the headings on the form on page 93 to help you when planning.

Grading tip

Remember you cannot do this assessment activity until you have completed assessment activity 4.3 (page 94). To achieve **M1** you need to carry out your risk assessment in an everyday indoor environment, e.g. classroom, kitchen or bathroom and concentrate on the risks associated with the key activities of that place. To achieve **D1** you need to discuss ways of reducing the risks when carrying out the key activities.

Bob Smyth
Environmental Health Practitioner

I work in a team of three other environmental health practitioners (EHPs) and I am employed by the local authority. My role is to help maintain and safeguard standards relating to people's health and wellbeing, by ensuring that people have a better quality of life and that the society they live in is a healthy one. There are many areas of work as an EHP, such as food hygiene and nutrition, workplace health and safety, housing conditions, air/noise pollution control, contaminated land, industrial waste, communicable diseases and animal health. As an EHP you may be a specialist in one of the areas above or you can be a generalist across many of them.

In a typical day I am given a list of organisations to visit and inspect. I do this unannounced, meaning that the organisations do not know I am coming, as this is the only way we can be sure that real food hygiene and safety practices are taking place. I then complete all my paperwork for that visit and I keep a computer record too. Sometimes I am involved with food complaints made by the general public about restaurants or other food outlets. I have also investigated cases of infectious diseases and I have sometimes needed to take food samples to send off for specialist testing. Sometimes I am involved in initiating legal proceedings and giving evidence in court too.

I really enjoy my work and contributing to a very important role in public health and safety. I get to meet lots of people and there is much variety in my daily work. It is never boring but sometimes my work is not very pleasant, e.g. visiting dirty and unhygenic buildings.

Think about it!

1. What areas have you covered in this unit that would provide you with the background knowledge and skills used by an Environmental Health Practitioner? Write a list and discuss with your peers.

2. What further knowledge and skills might you need to develop for this role?

3. How would you deal with premises that you inspect which are very unhygenic and unsafe? How would you deal with the employer/owner? What skills would you need? Write a list and compare your thoughts with your peers.

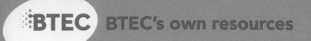
Extension activity: Making a health plan

- Consider a hazard at your school/college and get a team of your peers together to carry out a risk assessment on this hazard. You will then communicate your findings to the health and safety officer/committee with your 'persuasive' plan of action to remedy this risk.
- This could be done each term as a way of being involved with the health and safety of your school or college.
- Remember that by doing the planning, the risk assessment and then putting together a persuasive action plan, you are continually developing your PLTS, especially your independent enquirer, self-manager and reflective learner skills.

edexcel

Assignment tips

- A good way to ensure you can achieve a distinction grade for Unit 4 is to make sure you plan your assessment activities from the very beginning of the unit; that way you won't run out of time and the opportunity to complete **M1** and **D1**.

- Research for this unit could involve visits to different health and social care environments so that you become familiar with how the abilities of individuals can differ at different ages and in different care contexts. If included in your programme, use work experience to observe the practices of care workers that reduce risks. Discuss your observations from visits and placements in class before you complete the assessment activities.

- The assessment activity for **P3**, **M1** and **D1** should be completed at the same time but it would be helpful if the whole activity is carried out only after you have spent some time in a placement or have visited health and social care environment used by individuals of differing abilities, e.g. young children, frail older adults or adults with learning disabilities.

- For **D1** consider how you will discuss possible ways of reducing risk to users of the indoor space. Consider holding a discussion group with your peers and teacher to achieve **D1**. Your teacher could complete and sign an observation/witness statement that you had covered this assessment criteria in enough depth and breadth to be awarded **D1**.

5 Vocational experience in a health or social care setting

If you are reading this unit, then you are interested in becoming a health or social care professional. A career in health or social care can be hard work, but it will never be boring. You will find that every day is different and every individual you work with is unique; no two people are exactly the same. Going on work experience as part of this unit will give you valuable insights into the working life of health and social care professionals, and enable you to see some of the roles and responsibilities undertaken.

This unit is designed to complement the 60 hours of work experience which you will have to complete in order to successfully achieve Unit 5. The unit will take you through a series of questions which you may wish to ask about work experience and also provides you with answers. The unit will also encourage you to think about your own skills and abilities and record your progress during your period of work experience. Enjoy your work experience and remember, the more you put into it, the more you will get out of it.

Learning outcomes

After completing this unit you should:

1. be able to complete the application process for a period of work experience in a health or social care setting

2. be able to complete a period of work experience in a health or social care setting

3. be able to demonstrate interpersonal skills in a health or social care setting

4. be able to reflect on own performance in a health or social care setting.

Assessment and grading criteria

This table shows you what you must do in order to achieve a **pass**, **merit** or **distinction** grade, and where you can find activities in this book to help you.

To achieve a **pass** grade the evidence must show that you are able to:	To achieve a **merit** grade the evidence must show that, in addition to the pass criteria, you are able to:	To achieve a **distinction** grade the evidence must show that, in addition to the pass and merit criteria, you are able to:
P1 Complete an appropriate letter of application, with an attached CV, to a local health and social care setting [IE2, CT4, SM3] **Assessment activity 5.1, page 109**		
P2 Plan appropriately for an interview relating to work in health and social care [RL2, RL3, EP2] **Assessment activity 5.2, page 117**	**M1** Demonstrate appropriate interview skills **Assessment activity 5.2, page 117**	**D1** Assess the strengths and weaknesses of your interview skills **Assessment activity 5.2, page 117**
P3 Carry out a period of work experience, using relevant skills, in a health or social care setting [RL2, RL3, TW1, TW3, TW4, TW5, SM5, SM6, SM7, EP2] **Assessment activity 5.3, page 135**	**M2** Discuss your overall performance, during the period of work experience **Assessment activity 5.3, page 135** **Assessment activity 5.4, page 135**	**D2** Produce an action plan to show how you could have improved your work experience performance **Assessment activity 5.3, page 135** **Assessment activity 5.4, page 135**
P4 Demonstrate appropriate interpersonal skills in a health or social care setting [RL2, RL3, TW1, TW3, TW4, TW5, SM5, SM6, SM7, EP2] **Assessment activity 5.3, page 135**	**M3** Discuss own interpersonal skills used in a health or social care setting	
P5 Complete a reflective log-book during your period of work experience in a health or social care setting [RL2, RL3, SM3, SM5, SM6, SM7, EP2] **Assessment activity 5.4, page 135**		

How you will be assessed

You will be assessed by means of an internal assignment which will be designed and marked by the staff at your centre. It may be sampled by your centre's External Verifier as part of Edexcel's ongoing quality assurance procedures. The assignment is designed to show your understanding of the unit outcomes. These relate to what you should be able to do after completing this unit.

Your assessment could be in the form of:

- presentations
- case studies
- practical tasks
- written assignments.

Rosa, 17–year-old working in a residential home for older people

This unit really helped me to decide that I wanted to work in health and social care. The work is different every day and you get to meet such interesting people. I particularly enjoyed working with older people, which surprised me; I thought that I wouldn't but they have so many interesting stories to tell. It made me appreciate my grandparents a bit more too so I'm not so impatient when my granddad repeats things. Although the other parts of the unit were interesting and helpful, the best part was the 60 hours actually on work experience. I learned so much and was able to practise my interpersonal skills when I worked as part of the team.

I am so glad that I learned the correct way to produce a CV and write a letter of application; both of these helped me when I applied for my current post at the residence. I also found the practice interview useful; I felt so much more confident when I went for the real thing. I remembered what I learned about posture and positive eye contact and also about taking notes with me.

Over to you!

- What are you most looking forward to on your work experience?
- What interpersonal skills do you think you will need to work in health and social care?

Interpersonal skills in a health or social care setting are fully integrated within this unit and are also discussed in detail in Unit 1. When you go on work experience you will demonstrate your interpersonal skills which you require for the assessment of this unit.

1. Complete the application process for a period of work experience

Key terms

Health care assistant – someone who works with nurses in a hospital or nursing home and delivers basic nursing support such as assisting with food, bathing, care of the skin and hair

Social care assistant – someone who works in a residential setting or day centre and provides support for individuals who are not ill, but find movement or daily living difficult

Statutory – provision which has been put in place by Act of Parliament

Private – support which is funded either through payment of fees or through an insurance company

Voluntary – support which is provided by organisations funded through public donations

Did you know?

Many people who are now health or social care professionals began their careers by going on work experience as part of a BTEC course in Health and Social Care.

What would you like to become when you have finished your course: a nurse, a **health care assistant**, a **social care assistant**? This topic will help you explore some of the reasons why work experience is so important, as you explore your future in health and social care. You need to think about this before you apply for work experience in a health and social care setting.

Where should I go on work experience?

There are many different types of individuals who use health and social care services and these services could be **statutory**, **voluntary** or run as a **private** institution (see Unit 10 for further information, pages 326 to 327). This means that you will find that there is a wide range of possibilities for work experience but it is more likely that you will be able to find work experience in: a nursery or play group, nursing or residential home for older people, a local day centre for older people or people with learning disabilities or residential accommodation for people with learning disabilities. All of these will give you rich experiences to work with. Some of these are described in more detail on pages 120 to 125.

Good reasons for going on work experience

Your work experience will provide you with opportunities to observe professionals at first hand and to gain an understanding of the roles and responsibilities they undertake every day. This might be exciting things like going with children on a playgroup picnic or it might be more ordinary things, like sweeping floors and making lots of cups of tea or sitting quietly and chatting to an elderly service user. All these things would be part of a career in health and social care.

You will also be able to learn more about team working, which is a vital element of all health and social care careers whatever path you decide to take. You will put this and other essential interpersonal skills, such as communication, into practice every day.

You will have the opportunity to consider a range of health and social care possibilities, sometimes through the work experience itself or through listening to the experiences of your friends.

You will gain the satisfaction of knowing that you are making a worthwhile contribution to society and to the lives of people around you. But above all you will find out whether or not a career in health and social care is really for you.

Activity: Reasons why

Choose two reasons for going on work experience and the setting you would like to work in and write a short paragraph describing each of them in detail. You can include this information in the letter of application which you will be sending to your work experience.

What type of work experience would you like to do? What do you want to find out?

Case study: Ben and Lucy

Ben and Lucy are both learners on the BTEC First Diploma in Health and Social Care and have been on work experience at a training centre for people with learning disabilities. Lucy had not really wanted to go on work experience, but was persuaded by her tutor. Ben has really enjoyed his time at the training centre and has decided to apply for a job at the centre now that he has finished his course. The manager remembered Ben's positive approach and has offered him an interview.

Lucy did not enjoy her time at the training centre; she could never find enough to do. Lucy completed all of the tasks she was given, but did not ask if there was anything else she could do. Consequently the staff presumed that Lucy did not want to be helpful and left her to sit and read magazines once she had finished her set tasks. Lucy was never confident in speaking to the people who attended the training centre, but because she never discussed this with either her tutor or her work experience supervisor, Lucy never received the support that she needed.

1. How has Ben's work experience helped him to choose which career path to take?
2. How could Lucy have improved her experience at the setting?
3. How could the staff at the training centre have supported Lucy more effectively?

PLTS

Thinking about your reasons for going on work experience will help you to be an **independent enquirer** when you generate ideas and to explore possibilities as a **reflective thinker**.

Functional skills

Writing your descriptive paragraphs will help you to improve your **English** skills in writing.

Remember

Your supervisor's report from your work experience can be used as supporting evidence if you wish to progress onto the BTEC National Diploma in Health and Social Care in addition to the required grades. Your report will also provide you with evidence of your suitability for a career in health and social care, so it is up to you to do your best.

Just checking

1. Name two good reasons for going on work experience.
2. How will a positive report from work experience help you with future career plans?
3. What skills could you practise on work experience?

How do I find out about work experience?

Work experience is a great opportunity for you to begin to explore the world of work that interests you. If you take the time and give it some real thought, you will be surprised at what you might find. There are several ways in which you might find out about suitable places for your work experience. Wherever you go, the following questions and answers will help you to decide if this is the right choice for you.

Choosing your work experience

Can I get there?

If there is no regular bus or other means of transport between your home and the setting, then the answer is probably no.

Will the travel time mean that I can return home in time to complete my course work?

If you will not arrive home until after 6.30pm then the answer is probably no.

Do I think that the setting will enable me to learn more about working in health and social care?

The answer here should be yes!

Speaking to your tutor

Your tutor will have a lot of experience and knowledge about the types of work experience settings which you will be able to attend. **Remember,** not every setting is able to take learners who are under 18 years old; this may be due to the types of individuals within the setting. Other settings may be experiencing staffing difficulties or have some other reason why they cannot accept a learner at a particular time. Other placements may be unwilling to take a learner because the last one did not behave well and they are reluctant to take another. This is why it so important for you to try your best wherever you go, because you may affect the future of others as well as your own.

Speaking to friends/former learners

You may choose to ask friends about their experiences at a certain place – especially if they have already been to a setting you are interested in. Remember, that your experience will be very different simply because you are a different person. Listen to what they have to tell you but keep an open mind and take a positive approach.

Looking in local newspapers

Local newspapers often have several jobs pages; often different types of jobs appear on certain days every week, for example, health and social care on Wednesdays and clerical work on Fridays. Your centre library may take the local newspaper, but if not, your local public library will. You could buy your own paper, but make sure to find out which day is the one that you want. You should work with a friend on the course and highlight suitable advertisements. Settings which offer training may be more willing to take learners on work placement. When you have found a potential work setting, type in the address on an Internet search engine to have a more in-depth look at the details of the setting. You could find out its exact location, the types of support provided and decide whether you would really like to complete your work experience in a similar setting.

Figure 5.1: Do either of these jobs appeal to you?

Nursery Assistant – Oxfield Nursery

A great opportunity to join a new day care centre part-time. Previous Nursery experience is desirable; applicants must have experience of working with all ages within a childcare setting. An enhanced CRB check will be essential for this role. You will need to be qualified to NVQ Level 3 or equivalent.

Some of your responsibilities will include:

- ensuring the children are cared for in a happy, safe and stimulating environment
- working as part of a team.

Please contact the HR Department at Oxfield for more information on 01855 789987.

CARE ASSISTANT – CATSEA RESIDENTIAL DAY CARE CENTRE

Help us provide emotional support, skills training and personal supervision for people at our residential day care centre.

Your responsibilities will include:

- assisting residents with daily living activities
- promoting socialisation and interaction among residents
- ensuring that the facility is maintained and that the basic services are provided.

Please submit a CV and covering letter to Catsea Residential Centre, Catsea, CS56 7UJ.

Activity: Using the library

Visit your centre library and find out the answer to the following question:

What other publications could help you find a suitable work experience, in addition to newspapers?

Just checking

1. Why should you look in a local newspaper for ideas about work experience?
2. Why should you discuss your ideas about work experience with your tutor?
3. Give one reason why a setting may not take a learner on work experience.

Application procedures after the search

This topic will discuss the procedures you follow after you have decided where you want to go.

Three ways of finding out

1. Conducting an online search

The Internet is a useful tool for searching for suitable work experience settings. Many settings have their own web pages but remember, they are designed to attract potential residents, customers and their relatives, rather than providing you with all you need to know about suitability as a work experience setting. You can also log on to the Social Care Inspectorate website to read the reports from recent inspections. These reports are a matter of public record, which means that anyone can read them. The following checklist will be useful in helping you to decide about the usefulness of any website which you may access:

- Is the type of setting made clear?
- Is the support provided made clear?
- What does the setting actually tell you about how the average day is organised for the people who use the service?
- What types of staff are employed in the setting?

2. Visiting a local Job Centre

Every town and city has a Job Centre; large towns and cities may have several. All of them are designed to support people in finding suitable employment.

Inside the Job Centre you will find computer terminals where you can look up different available jobs. Pay rates are also displayed; sometimes these are given as an hourly rate and sometimes as a yearly salary. All of the staff are well trained and experienced in dealing with different people and do their very best to help everyone who comes in. If you are going to visit a Job Centre, you should either contact them

Activity: Visiting a Job Centre

Find out where your nearest Job Centre is and make arrangements for a visit. Remember to take a notepad and pen with you to record information. Most people who attend are looking for employment and will not wish to be disturbed so be polite at all times. Remember to thank the staff at the centre for allowing you to visit.

Discuss your findings with your tutor.

yourself, asking permission and explaining your reasons, or ask your tutor if they would arrange this; perhaps you could visit as a group at a time convenient for the staff at the Job Centre.

3. Visiting an employment agency

Another way of locating a suitable work experience is to visit an employment agency; usually these agencies specialise in particular types of employment. You could look in a directory, for example the Yellow Pages, to find a suitable agency. Remember that an agency will be very busy dealing with clients who are seeking employment, but they may allow you to look at the jobs on offer if you look smart and are polite. This type of agency would also be useful when you are looking for employment after you have completed your studies. Most employment agencies also have their own websites and so you could look at this first before arranging for a visit.

Remember to inform the agency that you are not currently seeking employment but looking for ideas with regard to work experience.

Application procedures

Once you have found a work experience role you wish to apply for you should check to see how the setting would like to receive an application. There are a number of ways to do this.

Telephone contact

You may need to phone to ask for an application form, to express interest in the role or find out how to apply.

Application form

You may be asked to fill in an application form for a role. When you fill in an application form you should remember the following:

- complete all sections on the form
- follow all instructions on the form carefully (should you use block capitals for personal details or use only black pen?)
- be careful to write clearly and not to make any mistakes
- make sure you answer all questions fully and appropriately (you may find it useful to take two copies of the form and use the first one as a practice).

Application letters (covering letter) and CVs

You may need to write a letter of application and a CV. A letter of application is a formal letter written in a business style, to apply either for a job or a voluntary position (see pages 106–107). A Curriculum Vitae (CV) is a list of your education, employment, skills and relevant personal qualities sent to potential employers as additional information (see pages 108–109).

Think about it

How should you dress for a visit to either a Job Centre or an employment agency?

PLTS

When you are researching potential work placements, you are being an **independent enquirer**.

Functional skills

When you are speaking to staff at Job Centres and employment agencies you are using the **English** skills of selecting the appropriate method of communication for different audiences.

Just checking

1. What is one difference between a Job Centre and an employment agency?
2. Name two places where you could find the details of an employment agency.
3. Where could you find a copy of a professional magazine or journal?
4. What should you remember when completing an application form?

Applying for a place on work experience: application letters

Preparing to go on work experience involves more than just making a couple of phone calls. There are lots of issues to consider, but everything you do to prepare now will be useful as you progress in your studies or into work. This section will help you to write a letter of application (also known as a covering letter).

Writing a letter of application

As part of your assessment for the unit, you will have to write a letter applying for work experience at a local health or social care setting.

Activity: The right way to write

Look at the two letters of application on pages 106 and 107. Which is the most suitable to send to a work experience setting?

What are your reasons for your choice?

Why is it important that your letter gives the right impression of you as a potential candidate for work experience at the setting?

Figure 5.2: Letter of application 1

> Lucy James
> 56 Random Avenue
> Catsea
> CS22 9YH
>
> Ms J Smithson
> Redbridge Residence
> 19 Alison Road
> Catsea
> CS21 7DG
>
> 9th September 2010
>
> **Re: Work Experience at Redbridge Residence**
>
> Dear Ms Smithson
>
> I am currently a learner on the BTEC First Diploma in Health and Social Care at the Catsea Sixth Form College. As part of my studies, I am required to complete a minimum of sixty hours of work experience in a health or social care setting. I am interested in learning more about supporting older people in a residential setting as I would like to work in this area when I have completed my studies. I understand from my tutor that you have previously provided learners from the course with experience at your setting and I would be really grateful if you would consider allowing me to complete my work experience at the Redbridge Residence.
>
> I am an enthusiastic and caring individual with excellent communication skills and I enjoy working as part of a team. I currently volunteer on Saturdays at a drop-in centre for older adults at the Mountainside Community Centre which has given me experience of working in a similar setting.
>
> I attach a stamped addressed envelope for your reply and enclose my current CV. If you would like more information about the course or a reference, my tutor Rachel Smith will be pleased to provide this.
>
> Thank you for taking the time to read my letter.
>
> Yours sincerely,
>
> *Lucy James*
>
> Lucy James

In your letter, you should include all of the following:

- your name
- your address
- the name of your course of study and centre (school or college)
- the name of your tutor or work experience supervisor
- your reasons for going on work experience
- your reasons for choosing that particular setting
- thank the person for taking the time to read the letter
- your name at the end of the letter, do not just sign it as your signature may be unclear.

Did you know?

Many letters to work experience settings are never read by the right person; here are some of the reasons:

- the letter was too long
- some of the important details were missing
- the letter never arrived because the address was incorrect.

Figure 5.3: Letter of application 2

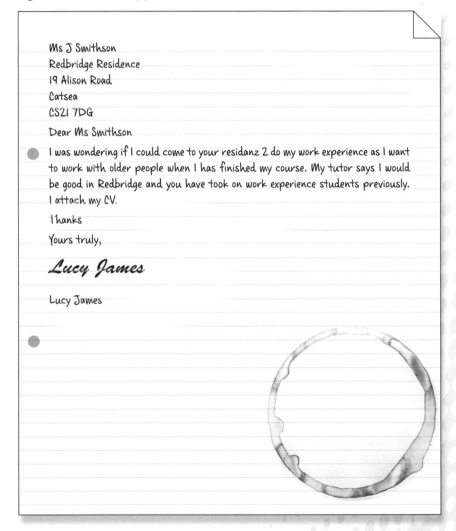

Ms J Smithson
Redbridge Residence
19 Alison Road
Catsea
CS21 7DG

Dear Ms Smithson

I was wondering if I could come to your residanz 2 do my work experience as I want to work with older people when I has finished my course. My tutor says I would be good in Redbridge and you have took on work experience students previously. I attach my CV.

Thanks

Yours truly,

Lucy James

Lucy James

Your letter should not be more than one page in length. The person reading the letter will be very busy and also you will be including a Curriculum Vitae (CV) containing relevant information. Your letter should be polite and formal, i.e. not over-friendly; you are applying for a work role and not planning a holiday with friends. You should write the letter on a computer and print it out as this gives a more professional appearance. Ask your tutor to check it over before you send it.

Just checking

1. List three points which should be included in your application letter.
2. Why should you ask your tutor to check your letter before you send it to the setting?
3. Name one thing which could prevent your letter being read by the manager of your chosen setting.

Applying for a place on work experience: the CV

My life

What's in your CV?

Have you ever written a CV? Cover up the list below and list all the things which you think should be in a CV.

Activity: The best CV

Look at the two CVs on these pages. Which is the most suitable to send to a work experience setting? What are your reasons for your choice? How would you improve these CVs?

To support your covering letter you will also need to produce a CV which lists your education, employment, skills and relevant personal qualities and can be sent to potential employers as additional information. This section will help you to do this.

Writing a CV

As part of your assessment for the unit, you will have to write a CV for when you apply for work experience at a local health or social care setting. Your CV must include all of the following details:

- your name
- your contact details (including email address and mobile number)
- your education and qualifications (including dates)
- employment (including dates)
- skills which you have for the role
- relevant personal qualities
- any other important relevant information, e.g. a driving licence or first aid qualification.

Figure 5.4: What do you think about this CV?

Curriculum Vitae

Elizabeth Simmons: age 17; DOB 19th November 1994
South Willows Comprehensive School 2005-2010
West Newtown Sixth Form College 2010-present

Qualifications:	GCSE English	C
	GCSE maths	D
	GCSE Single science	D
	GCSE Art	B

Currantly studying BTEC First Health and Social Care

Other Qualifications:
Duke of Edinburgh Bronze and 25 m swimming
First Aid

Work experience: local supermarket

Hobbies: eating pizza
Hanging out with friends

References: Grandma Simmons 01777222969
Neighbour Mr Jones 0875623561

Figure 5.5: What do you think about this CV?

CURRICULUM VITAE

PERSONAL DETAILS

Name: Elizabeth Simmons
Date of Birth: 19/11/1994
Address: 19 Wayward Road, Newtown NP48 6HH
Telephone: 01667 878889

EDUCATION

2005–2010: South Willows Comprehensive School
2010–present: West Newtown Sixth Form College

QUALIFICATIONS

GCSE English (C); GCSE Maths (C); GCSE Single Science (D); GCSE Art (B)
BTEC First Diploma Health and Social Care; result pending
First Aid qualification

OTHER AWARDS

Duke of Edinburgh Bronze Award

WORK HISTORY

2008–present: Shelf Stacker Fresco supermarket
2006–present: Baby sitting for a seven year old boy twice a week

HOBBIES

Tennis
Reading crime novels

REFERENCES

Ms E Darcy, Course Tutor, West Newtown Sixth Form College 01569 554774
Mr Richards, Manager, Fresco supermarket 01569 874321

Just checking

1. Name three points which should be included in your CV.
2. Why should you ask someone else to look at the CV before sending it?
3. Name one thing on a CV which could mean you are not considered for a job.
4. Why should you word process the CV?

BTEC ## Assessment activity 5.1

Write a letter of application, with an attached CV, to a local health and social care setting. Show the letter and CV to your tutor and discuss where it may be improved.

Grading tip: P1

Use the checklists on pages 107 and 108 to ensure that your letter and CV include all of the correct details. To achieve P1 you will need to show you have researched the requirements for the post you wish to apply for.

 PLTS

By thinking about your letter you are being an **independent enquirer**, by giving it a good layout you are being a **creative thinker** and by checking the content you are being a **self-manager**.

Preparing for your interview: practicalities

When you have applied for a role you will hope to be invited to an interview. You may receive a letter or a phone call inviting you for interview and you have to respond appropriately. Preparing for the interview is almost as important as the interview itself and can make all the difference as to whether you get the job. This topic will help you think about all the things you need to do to get ready for that important occasion.

Your interview

As part of your assessment for this unit you will have to prepare for an interview at your potential work setting. Good preparation will mean that you are more confident on the day. Here are some points to help you:

Telephone skills

You may receive a reply from the setting in answer to your application letter, asking you to contact the setting by telephone to confirm your attendance at the interview. You should speak clearly, answer any questions and be polite. You may wish to practise speaking on the telephone first, in order to build up your confidence.

Letter of acceptance

If you receive a letter asking you to attend for interview you will need to reply, to confirm that you are coming on the day and at the time stated. As with the letter of application, this should be a polite and formal letter – typed or word processed.

Knowledge of the setting

Before you attend the interview, you should find out as much as you can about the setting, such as the type of support offered, in order to show interest. You may be asked what you know about the setting when you go for your interview, and having some knowledge of what happens there will demonstrate your enthusiasm and motivation. Note down the name of the manager from the letter and remember it for your interview.

Transport and being punctual

Arriving on time for your interview is really important; first impressions do count. You will be more confident about arriving on time if you find out about transport well before the interview date. You can check online or visit your local bus station to find out the times for the appropriate bus. Write them down and remind yourself of them, so that

Remember

First impressions do count, so prepare well and you will do well at your interview. The manager at the setting has probably interviewed a lot of people; he or she will not be surprised if you are nervous and will make allowances for this.

Did you know?

A good interview can lead to you being considered for work in the setting after you have completed your studies.

you do not panic on the day. One way of making sure that you arrive on time is to do a practice run with a friend or relative, to discover exactly how long the journey takes. This means that you can arrive without rushing, and feeling as confident as possible. You should arrive for your interview punctually and it is good practice to arrive about 15 minutes before the start time.

Worries and concerns

Is there anything about the interview which especially worries or concerns you? Think about your interview for the course you are on when you succeeded in gaining a place; try to think of the positive points from that interview to boost your confidence. Write down any worries and concerns and discuss them with your tutor. Perhaps you need to increase your knowledge about the setting, or find out about transport; whatever your worries are, your tutor can help. Many worries are due to lack of preparation, so getting ready in plenty of time will increase your confidence.

Making an action plan

Here are some of the things you might want to put in an action plan to help you prepare for interview:

- get a good night's sleep so you are rested and relaxed
- make sure you have thought about what you are going to wear and the clothes are clean and ready
- have a list of questions ready to ask
- prepare some answers to questions they might ask you
- know your travel plans and get up in good time to be punctual
- have breakfast before you leave in the morning
- take some money with you
- make sure your mobile phone is charged and that you have the contact details with you.

You will probably think of other points that are particular to your own circumstances.

Activity: Preparing for interview

Produce an action plan of your preparations for the interview and discuss these with your tutor.

PLTS

When you are finding out about the setting in preparation for your interview, you are being an **independent enquirer**.

Think about it

You are nearly at your destination and the bus breaks down. What do you do?

Just checking

1. Why should you find out about the setting before your interview?
2. Why should you discuss any worries or concerns with your tutor before the interview?
3. Why should you check the transport details before the day of your interview?

A professional appearance

Without realising it, we often judge people by what they wear and how they do their hair, make up, even what jewellery they are wearing! This topic will look closely at how appearances matter.

Appearance

Appearances do count and part of your preparation for interview should be to ensure that you look as professional as possible. How you dress for an evening out with friends is probably very different to the way you dress for class. In the same way, dressing for an interview is also different to how you might dress to go shopping. Now is not the time to try out that new green hair tint or acquire one more piercing. The important thing is to give the impression that you are serious about the interview and about working in that particular setting. If you take this approach you are more likely to behave in a professional way which will help you through the interview process. You will feel confident and are more likely to enjoy the whole experience. Here are a few hints to help you:

Dressing to impress

There is no need to spend a lot of money on your interview outfit, you will probably find that you have all of the right clothes already; it is just a case of putting them together.

- Plain styles are best, no tops with slogans or pictures.

- Head coverings are fine if they are part of your religious or cultural routine.

- Trousers or skirts are fine for girls as long as they are smart; shorts are not appropriate.

- Keep make-up and jewellery to a minimum to give a more professional appearance.

- Wear shoes or boots that you can walk in and make sure they are clean, freshly polished and not scuffed.

- Keep hair off the face if possible and wash it that morning.

- Make sure what you wear is comfortable as well as smart; your interview could last at least half an hour, followed by a tour of the setting.

Who is dressed appropriately for an interview and who is not?

PLTS

When you are discussing your ideas with two other people, you are being a **reflective learner** by inviting feedback and reflecting upon this.

Think about it

Why is it important to wear clothes and shoes that you are comfortable in at your interview?

Activity: Dressed for success?

Look at the pictures of people dressed for interview, check them against the list on page 112 and decide who is dressed appropriately and who is not. Discuss your ideas with two other people; did they agree with you?

Just checking

1. Why should you not dress in party clothes for your interview?
2. What would be incorrect about wearing shorts for your interview?
3. How could getting up late on the day of your interview affect your appearance?

Demonstrate interpersonal skills

My life

It's not what you say, it's the way that you say it!

Make a list of non-verbal and verbal communication skills you will use in an interview.

Remember

Interpersonal and communication skills are covered in Unit 1. Read these carefully as you will need to show these skills when being assessed for this unit.

'Don't you speak to me like that!' Have you ever heard those words? Was it the actual words which caused offence, or perhaps the tone of voice and the facial expression? How well do you communicate? This topic will help you think about your important **interpersonal** and communication skills needed for an interview and the work place. You will need these during your interview, but also during your work experience. You can find more information in Unit 1.

Figure 5.6: How can you show each of these skills in an interview?

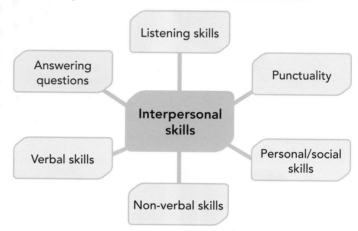

Key terms

Interpersonal skills – skills we use when interacting and communicating with others

Slang – words which are considered less polite or not correct in formal situations

Case study: Natalie and Kylie

Natalie and Kylie were preparing for their interviews at the Helping Hands training centre. Natalie had practised her interview with her tutor and also taken part in a role play with Kylie. She made good eye contact and used a polite, clear tone of voice. Occasionally Natalie used **slang** when she was speaking, something her tutor had warned her about. Kylie was very confident; she had been on work experience before and she had practised with Natalie, but she saw no reason to take part in the role play or to discuss her preparations with her tutor. Both learners attended their interviews with varying success. Natalie used good eye contact, shook the hand of the interviewer, sat down and answered all questions politely and clearly. She did use a slang expression once, but apologised quickly and moved on. Kylie felt that the interviewer was asking too many questions and became cross. Unfortunately, this was expressed in her tone of voice as she spoke sharply which the interviewer took to be rude. The interviewer then became annoyed, folded her arms and stared crossly at Kylie. Kylie couldn't wait to leave the interview and went home in tears.

1. How did Natalie deal with her one mistake?

2. How could Kylie have been better prepared?

Your use of interpersonal skills will support you at interview and also when you are in the setting. Speech should be clear and free of slang or jargon; eye contact should be confident without staring; **verbal skills** are also important – this is the way that you say things which often has as much effect as the words you use. A polite, friendly tone, pitched so that the listener can clearly hear you, will always be acceptable. Good **listening skills** are also important, it is so easy to misinterpret when you only partially hear something. **Body language** as non-verbal communication is important, for example if you fold your arms, you can look defensive, which can make the other person cross or nervous. An open posture invites a more friendly response. In addition, the use of staring could be seen as a method of control and can appear threatening. Your use of communication skills can encourage others to respond appropriately. If you get a poor response, consider your own communication, and ask yourself, how good was it?

The interviewer only knows what they have read in your CV and application letter; they will be observing you to assess your skills in addition to listening to your answers. Good use of your skills will enable the interviewer to develop a rapport with the interviewee so that they are more prepared to discuss topics. The interviewer will be hoping that you can show evidence of an ability to encourage users of the service to interact with you and develop professional relationships.

Key terms

Verbal skills – the way we speak, for example, tone, pitch and the speed of our words

Body language – our posture, position of our arms when speaking, use of gestures, eye contact, facial expression

Listening skills – listening carefully, concentrating on what is said

Remember

How you say something does matter: communicating in an interview is very different to communicating with your friends and family. Practise your skills to improve them.

Activity: Practice makes perfect

Take part in a practice interview with your tutor or a friend; check your performance against the following check list.

- Was my speech clear?
- Did I use a polite but friendly tone?
- Did I use appropriate words and phrases (no slang)?
- Did I make positive eye contact without staring?
- Was my body language suitable?
- Did I listen carefully and answer questions correctly?

Write down what you did well and what you need to practise.

Did you know?

Good interpersonal skills at interview can often be a deciding factor in the decision to accept you.

Just checking

1. What are interpersonal skills?
2. Why should you not use slang at an interview?
3. Why is it important to listen carefully at an interview?

Preparing for the interview

This topic will help you to think about what an interviewer might ask you and what you might like to know about the work experience placement from the interviewer.

Procedures

Before you go to an interview you should think about the types of questions you might be asked; this means you will be more prepared with good answers for questions they might ask you. When you arrive you will usually be asked to wait and then the interviewer will come to meet you. You might be interviewed by several people or just one person. When the interview starts, the interviewer might ask if you found the place easily, or how you are, in order to make you feel more relaxed before they start asking the 'serious' questions. Try to answer all of the questions, think about what you are saying and remember to sound motivated and interested throughout the interview.

Your turn to ask the questions

When you attend your interview it is natural that you will also want to ask some questions. Having questions prepared will help to show the interviewer that you are interested in the work of the setting and that you would like to learn more. Your interpersonal skills will be on show here: make eye contact without staring, hold onto your notes and sit back in your chair without slouching. Speak clearly and politely; no one will mind if you are nervous, they will understand. Asking some of your own questions will help you to feel more in control of the situation.

Questions about the placement and setting will be all about the kind of care and support or activity that happens in the setting. For example, you can find out why people might use the service, what their needs are, and how many people attend or live there.

Figure 5.7: What sort of questions would you ask?

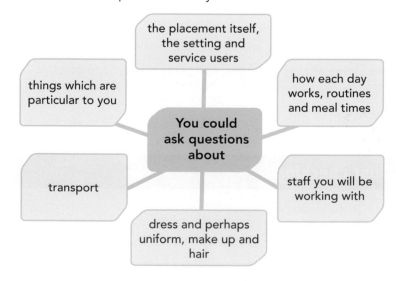

Questions about the working day cover the pattern to each day, times of starting, for example, and finishing. Be careful about asking too much about breaks and lunch, they may think that's all you are interested in!

You may want to know about your fellow workers, how many staff there are, even something about their qualifications, or if you will have a supervisor or someone specially assigned to work with you.

Questions about appearance cover what you should wear and what you should not wear at work. You might need to find out about the right kind of shoes to wear, suitable hairstyles (does long hair need to be tied back, for example?), acceptable make up and jewellery.

You may want to ask about different ways to get to the setting (what buses or trains are there?)

There might be more questions to ask, ones that are particular to you (you might have a regular doctor's appointment you can't change, for example, at a particular time).

How did your interview go?

After your interview, think about how well it went. You will probably get a sense of this during the time with your interviewer. Look at your interview plan and consider if you met all your objectives. What could you have done differently? What went well? This reflection on your actions is covered further on pp. 126–127 and is important for your assessment.

Just checking

1. Give two points to remember when thinking of questions to ask at interview.
2. Who should you check your questions with before the interview?
3. What could you do if there is not time to ask questions at the interview?

PLTS

When you are reviewing your interview skills and producing an action plan, you will be using your skills as a **reflective learner**.

BTEC   Assessment activity 5.2

1. Produce your own notes to show you have planned for an interview relating to a specific work experience placement **P1**. This should include how you will check the arrangements for the interview beforehand, e.g. using the telephone, how you will get to your placement, what you will wear for the interview, what questions you may be asked and how you might answer them and the ways in which you can show interest during the interview.

2. Attend the interview and obtain a signed witness testimony from the interviewer to confirm that you demonstrated appropriate interview skills **M1**. The interviewer may be a manager or supervisor in your placement. If your placement does not interview students before they go on placement, then the interviewer will be your tutor or another professional who will interview you as if for a placement.

3. After the interview, write a report that assesses the strengths and weaknesses of your interview **D1**. Use the comments made by the interviewer during the interview any feedback given afterwards to help you assess your interview skills.

Grading tips

- When planning your interview **P1**, consider the questions you may be asked and what questions you could ask during the interview to show interest. In groups with your peers construct some appropriate questions and role play interviews to practice your interview skills **M1**. If possible, view a video of the role plays and discuss the strengths and weaknesses you demonstrated in class **D1**. Consider your body language, your verbal skills and how well you communicated your answers to questions when evaluating your interview skills and use the learning from these activities to help you with **M1** and **D1**.

2. Be able to complete a period of work experience

Activity: Following instructions

In order to complete tasks, it is essential that you are able to follow instructions. With a partner, scope out a scenario where one of you in a work experience setting fails to follow instructions and what the implications of this might be for:

a) the service user(s)

b) colleagues

You can decide what the setting might be and the scenario to fit in with your own and your partner's interests.

In this topic you will explore some of the skills you need to demonstrate while you are on work experience. By developing these skills you will begin to achieve what it takes to work in the exciting and challenging sector of health and social care.

Work experience skills in health and social care

Timely reporting of incidents and accidents

Many of the individuals who attend or reside in a health and social care setting are vulnerable for a variety of reasons. For example, they may have reduced mobility or balance which might make them more likely to have an accident. It is your duty as a member of the team to report accidents or incidents straight away. If the accident is your fault in some way, apologise; remember that failing to report this could mean that you have failed in your duty of care.

Using your initiative

Sometimes on work experience you may find a problem to solve or some time to fill if there has been a change in the plans for your time. For example, you may have had to stay at the day centre with service users rather than going on a trip as your place on the coach might have been filled by someone else. Think of how you could fill the time purposefully. You might lead a group in a new activity: do you have particular skills which you haven't been able to use? But do ask before you take things into your own hands!

Taking positive criticism

Most criticism is given in order to help, so take criticism or advice in the spirit in which it is intended. You are learning the skills of reflection in this unit, apply them to what has been said and think objectively about what the person is hoping to achieve. If you are unhappy speak to your tutor or to your work experience mentor. If you do not understand the reason for the criticism do ask politely. But don't brood or become upset: all of us make mistakes.

Awareness of safety issues for you and others

When you are on work experience, you have a legal responsibility to be aware of your own and others' safety. This means that you conduct all tasks in a manner which does not place yourself and others at risk. For example, clearing away equipment, laundry and crockery rather than leaving them out as hazards for individuals; ensuring that doors are closed and locked where necessary.

Understanding the limits of your role

While you are on work experience, it is important to remember that you are there as a learner and not employed as a member of staff. You need to be clear about what you can or can't do, and what is outside the limits of your role as a learner. Your tutor will provide you with a list, for example, assisting with personal hygiene needs or preparing meals. You should never give advice to users of the service unless you have been specifically asked to by a member of staff and have their permission. An example could be the administration of medication or taking a vulnerable user of the service for a walk without a member of staff. Remember that limits are there to safeguard you and also to safeguard the vulnerable users of the service.

Completing all tasks

It is really important that you complete all tasks which are assigned to you. If you leave tasks partially completed other people, members of staff or fellow learners, will have to finish them. This will mean that they have additional work to do. It will also give the impression that you are unprofessional. Non-completion of tasks may also mean that users of the service are left feeling uncomfortable or unsupported. Some tasks such as tidying away after an activity are essential in order to maintain the wellbeing of the setting and prevent accidents.

Team working

Team work is essential in health and social care in order to ensure that everyone receives the support they need. Working closely with others, discussing tasks and following procedures which have been designed to comply with the legislation, will ensure the best of care and support for the vulnerable users of the service.

Interaction with people who use the services

Interaction demonstrates your interest and will enable you to develop a rapport with service users. Remember to be polite, speak clearly and be prepared to listen; often people are most appreciative of a learner who takes the time to sit and interact. Do remember not to gossip about members of staff or other users of the service.

A professional approach

Remember that one of the purposes of your work experience is to provide you with an insight into the role of the health and social care professional and to gain an understanding of a professional approach. To take a professional approach means to act responsibly, showing consideration for all users of the service and performing all tasks to the best of your ability, asking for help if you need it. It also means dressing appropriately, being punctual and following procedures and policies in order to provide the highest standard of care and support.

PLTS

Team working is a key personal, learning and thinking skill. You will be able to provide lots of evidence of your skills as a **team worker** in your time on work experience.

Key term

Interaction – communicating with different people

Just checking

1. What do you mean by a professional approach?
2. Why is interacting appropriately with service users and colleagues important on work experience?
3. How does not exceeding the limits of your role in work experience relate to your duty of care?

Carrying out work experience

Would you like to work in an early years setting?

The next three topics will explore three different settings which you might visit. There are case studies with questions which all refer to the interpersonal skills you will need to demonstrate during your work experience.

Working in an early years setting

There are many different types of early years setting – nursery classes in a school, nurseries run in the workplace, you may even have a nursery at your college. The purpose of this sort of early years setting is to provide a caring, stimulating and supportive environment for children before they are ready to go to school. There are many different people who may use a day nursery for their children; you may have some interaction with these individuals, but the main part of what you will be doing is working with children. Depending on the age group of the children, the type of care will vary from play and a variety of activities, such as music and stories and singing, to the beginnings of formal learning. Nursery settings also vary in times for different children and, depending on their circumstances, some children may come all day and some just for the morning.

You will always have a mentor on hand to help and advise you, but it will be helpful to observe carefully what the other staff do. Remember, too, that the safety of each child is very important, so if you are not sure about anything at all, including the appropriateness of an activity, just ask.

The right choice

- Do you like new challenges every day?
- Would you enjoy working with children?
- Do you have lots of patience or could you become more patient than you are?
- Do you enjoy a variety of games and activities?
- Do you have plenty of energy?
- Do you enjoy practical games like playing with sand or play dough?
- Do you enjoy getting a bit messy with paint or water or sand?
- Do you have a good sense of humour?

If you can answer yes to all of these questions, then this could be the right choice of work experience for you.

Case study: Saima's first day

Saima arrived at the Little Acorns Day Nursery for her work experience. The door was opened by Sally, who had recently qualified as an early years worker and was now employed at the nursery. 'Welcome to Little Acorns,' she said, 'please sign the book and I will show you where to put your coat and bag'. Saima was taken through to the pre-school room which was where the children from 3 to 5 years played. It was very noisy; one child was singing and banging a drum, one child was not settling well and crying for her mother, two children were playing with bricks and knocking them over. 'Don't worry,' said Sally, 'it all settles down soon.'

The **Head of Room** came in and introduced herself to Saima. 'My name is Julia and I will be your **supervisor**' she said, 'please ask me any questions, and tell me if you have any course work to complete so that I can help you.' Saima was advised to join in with the children's activities in order to get to know them. She found that they were happy to play with her because of her gentle and friendly approach. By the end of her first day, Saima found that she had settled in and was enjoying herself though she was a bit tired! When she was told it was time to go home, Saima remembered her tutor's advice and asked if there was anything else that she could do to help before she left. Her supervisor was impressed with this and made a note to add this to Saima's end of **placement report**. Saima found that she had a lot to write in her **reflective log-book** when she arrived home.

Saima did her best to learn the names of the children and also the routines of the setting as soon as she could, which helped her to feel more like a member of the team. Saima enjoyed her work experience but felt that she would prefer to move on to the BTEC National Diploma in Health and Social Care at the end of her course, so that she could achieve her ambition to become an adult nurse.

1. Look at the skills checklist on p. 134. Identify three skills that Saima demonstrated.
2. Which of these skills would you have found easiest and which one hardest?

Activity: Working in the nursery

Can you think of the tasks you might be asked to undertake in a day nursery? Make a list and then go to the library and find a book on working with young children. Check your list against the descriptions of the nursery day in your chosen text book.

Remember

The main purpose of your work experience is for you to learn, so listen to the staff and ask questions when they are not too busy to answer you.

Did you know?

One of the best ways of learning is to observe others, so take every opportunity to observe the staff as they interact and work with the children.

Key terms

Head of Room – day nurseries may be divided into separate rooms to provide support for children in the different age groups. The overall supervisor for each room is known as the Head of Room

Supervisor – a qualified member of staff who will support you during your work experience and contribute to your report

Placement report – at the end of your period of work experience, the setting will complete a report on your overall performance

Reflective log-book – whilst you are on work experience you will complete a reflective log-book of your progress

Just checking

1. What do you mean by a professional approach?
2. Why is interacting appropriately with service users and colleagues important on work experience?
3. How does not exceeding the limits of your role in work experience relate to your duty of care?

Work experience: residential support for older people

Key terms

Activities of daily living – these include activities like eating and drinking, personal hygiene, sleeping, recreation, walking

Physical disability – for example conditions such as arthritis which affects the joints and may worsen in older age

Be prepared to join in with different activities!

Perhaps you have older relatives or neighbours who live in your community. What about those who need more support? Where do you think those people live? This topic will explore the support provided for older people who are no longer able to live completely independently.

Residential care

As people grow older there may come a time when they are not able to live at home or they may decide that they do not want to live independently. They might need to live somewhere where they can still have a good quality of life but with a bit more help with **activities of daily living**. They might have a **physical disability**, such as trouble with walking, or they may have some kind of dementia, such as Alzheimer's disease. Or, following the death of a partner, they might feel alone and want to live somewhere with more company and support.

Whatever the reason, many residential settings provide older people with a warm and supportive community, where they can live in comfort. Residents are often able to bring their own furniture, photos and books – areas of their life which are important to them.

They will have support staff to help with meals, with baths or showers, and to ensure a safe environment. There are also often different activities happening during the day, organised by the residents and staff, which can be lots of fun and quite energetic – so be prepared for variety in your work experience.

The right choice

Here is a checklist which will help you to decide whether residential care could be the choice for you:

* Do you like new challenges every day?
* Would you like to work with older people?
* Do you have patience or could you become more patient than you are?
* Are you able to empathise with people?
* Do you enjoy seeing people making progress?
* Do you enjoy practical tasks?
* Do you have a good sense of humour?

If you can answer yes to all of these questions, then this could be the choice of work experience for you.

Case study: Rashid

Rashid, a learner on the BTEC First Diploma in Health and Social Care, had been on work experience for two weeks. Rashid had so far enjoyed his placement at the Red Bridge Residence; he loved to sit and chat with the older residents and was happy to undertake any tasks he was given. Rashid particularly enjoyed working with Jean, the activity coordinator, encouraging the residents to participate in games, musical sessions and activities to stimulate their memories.

One morning, Jean telephoned the residence to say that she was ill and could not come to work. Rashid volunteered to take the session; he decided to organise a quiz, using a DVD from Jean's cupboard. The residents were fond of Rashid and did their very best to join in, with the exception of Mrs Smith who fell asleep half way through the session. Rashid did not attempt to wake her as he recognised her right to sit back if she wished to. Rashid also gave out cups of tea, and helped those who could not reach their drinks because of their arthritis.

Rashid's supervisor was impressed with his inventiveness and wrote this down on his end of placement report. After Rashid completed his work experience at the Red Bridge Residence he was told that he would be welcome to apply for work there when he had completed his course.

1. What skills would Rashid be using when he was chatting with the residents?
2. How did Rashid 'think on his feet'? What skill does this show?

Did you know?

A lot of adult nursing involves working with older people, so if adult nursing is your ambition, then this type of work experience could be right for you.

Key term

Activity coordinator – many residential settings employ an activity coordinator to encourage individuals to participate in activities which stimulate thinking and encourage physical movement

PLTS

When you are researching the two conditions in the activity, you are being an **independent enquirer** by analysing and evaluating information and judging its relevance and value.

Activity: Conditions needing support

Use the Internet to research two conditions which could indicate a need for residential support in older age. Use this information to help you understand why some older people can no longer live by themselves.

Just checking

1. Give two reasons why an individual may live in a residential setting.
2. What are activities of daily living?
3. Name two tasks which you might be asked to do in a residential setting.

Work experience: the training centre

Key terms

Social work assistant – someone who works with a social worker, providing support for individuals and families

Nursing assistant – someone who works with registered nurses as a support

'Valuing people now' – a government policy which states the ways in which individuals with a learning disability should be included in society and treated equally

Training centres will usually help people with learning disabilities to develop knowledge and skills for both life and employment. What life skills do you have? Can you catch a bus on your own, iron your clothes and manage your money? There are many skills which may be taught at a training centre.

Working with individuals who have learning disabilities

Some people are born with a learning disability, which means that their learning ability may not have developed at the same rate as their physical abilities. Many people with learning disabilities are talented and able, but may need support in particular areas in order to live independently. A training centre for people with learning disabilities is a supported environment which helps people to develop skills and knowledge both for life and for employment. If your ambition is to be a **social work assistant**, an occupational therapy assistant or a **nursing assistant** with individuals who have learning disabilities, then a period of work experience at a training centre could be right for you. You will come across a wide range of professionals in this setting and may find it stimulating, challenging and interesting.

Did you know?

The government policy **'Valuing people now'** is intended to ensure that people with learning disabilities are treated with respect and dignity.

Is this the type of setting you would like to work in?

The right choice

Here is a checklist which will help you to decide whether this could be the choice for you:

- Do you like new challenges every day?
- Would you like to work with people from different age groups?
- Do you like to think on your feet?
- Do you enjoy seeing people making progress?
- Do you enjoy practical tasks?
- Do you have a good sense of humour?

If you can answer yes to all of these questions, then this could be the choice of work experience for you.

Remember

Some of the people at the centre will be older than you and should be treated with respect at all times.

Case study: Tracy

The Rainways Training Centre provides support and training for individuals with learning disabilities. The ages of the people who attend range from 19 to 65 years old. The centre regularly provides work experience for learners on the BTEC First Diploma in Health and Social Care and enjoys a good relationship with several local schools and colleges.

Tracy was a learner on work experience at the centre, and had been there for three weeks. She was involved in supporting the tutors in delivering a variety of sessions which have included how to make lunch, how to write a letter, how to join the library and how to iron clothes. Tracy had formed good relationships with many of the people who attended the centre and was enjoying her work experience at the centre. Her supervisor was pleased with Tracy as she used her initiative and worked hard.

On Thursday one member of staff was ill and the manager asked Tracy if she could go with another member of staff to escort Jeremy, who attended the Thursday club, to his bus stop. Jeremy had challenging behaviour as part of his learning disabilities and both Tracy and the member of staff had to encourage him to stay on the pavement rather than running into the road. Once Jeremy was on the bus, the member of staff rang his mum so that she could meet him at the other bus stop. Tracy found the experience challenging but interesting, recognising that she had helped to support Jeremy in becoming more independent. Every day was different at the centre and Tracy never knew what to expect when she walked through the door at 8.30am. Tracy decided to apply for work at the centre when she had completed her studies. She had become part of the team through her own efforts, and was sad when her period of work experience ended.

1. What skills did Tracy have which made her suitable for work in a training centre?
2. How did Tracy support Jeremy's independence and travel skills?
3. What skills did Tracy show when supporting Jeremy's independence and travel skills?

Think about it

Do you have the same qualities as Tracy? Could you work in a training centre?

Just checking

1. What is 'Valuing people now'?
2. Why is independence important for all individuals?
3. What skills would you need to promote independence?

4. Be able to reflect on own performance

Reflection is what you see when you look at yourself in a mirror. In health and social care, reflective skills give you the opportunity to think about what happened on a typical day, and why. This topic and the topics following will help you to reflect on your time at work experience.

Figure 5.8: The reflective cycle

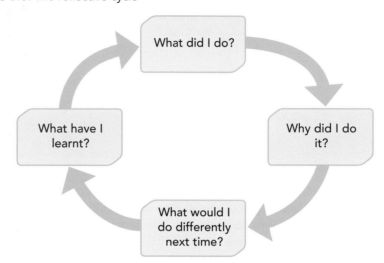

Some of your course work will consist of **description**; in other words you will be saying what something is, how it looks or how it works. For example you could be describing your work experience, the type of setting, how many staff are employed or the type of support it provides. When you complete your application letter you will be describing yourself; when you give your reasons for applying, you may have reflected on why you would like a placement there. A good description provides the reader or the listener with a picture in words and demonstrates your knowledge of a particular subject. When you are on work experience, you may be expected to describe an incident, providing a member of staff with the facts, so that appropriate action may be taken. All of these are valuable skills but, to become an effective professional, you will need to take your skills a step further and learn to reflect. You may already be using this skill without realising it; for example when you think about the reasons for events and incidents. 'Why was Cara annoyed when I didn't answer her?', 'Why did that party work better than the one before?'

Reflection

Reflection involves looking at events which have happened and considering why they occurred, in order to learn from the experience. If something worked well, reflection can help you repeat your success; it can enable you to consider how things can be further improved. Reflection can also help you to understand why tasks on work experience are carried out in a particular order. For example, why does the nursery day begin with the same song every morning? Might it be that young children need the security of a consistent **routine**? You will be reflecting on your personal achievements, including what you learnt and what your next career steps might be.

The good practice checklist for reflection

- What was good about the event/day?
- What was not so good?
- What have I achieved?
- What have I learned?
- What could I learn in the future?
- Can I link what I have seen or done with something I have already learned?
- What might I do differently next time?

If you apply the good practice checklist to all parts of your course, you will find that reflection becomes a natural part of your thinking process. Reflection will not only help you to improve but also to recognise your strengths and how to continue with these.

Activity: Reflection 2

Write down the name of a film which you like and why you like it.

Write down the name of a film which you don't like and why not.

Reflect upon what makes one film enjoyable and the other less so.

Did you know?

Many health and social care professionals use reflection as part of their professional development profiles, to enable them to see where skills may need upgrading.

Case study: Mrs Shah

Mrs Shah is a manager of a Day Care Centre for older people who live in the local area. She is a good and efficient manager who understands her duties well. One day a visitor to the centre asked if she could volunteer as a helper. Mrs Shah said that she was welcome to do this once her CRB check had been completed and the visitor agreed. The visitor became a volunteer and worked extremely hard, helping wherever she could and becoming a trusted member of the team. One day the volunteer asked if she could take one of the group members for a walk to the shops; because she was busy, Mrs Shah said yes, even though a qualified member of staff should also have been present. While they were on their way to the shops the older person fell over and, because there was only a volunteer present, dealing with the accident took longer and the lady became distressed.

1. When Mrs Shah got home at the end of the day, she reflected upon the incident and the circumstances which surrounded it.
2. What conclusions do you think Mrs Shah came to when she was reflecting upon the incident?
3. Have you ever had a bad day like this? What could you learn from it?

PLTS

Reflective practitioner: when you are reflecting upon your day, you are beginning to see events from more than one perspective.

Just checking

1. Name two benefits of reflecting on your experiences.
2. Why can reflection improve your effectiveness as a professional?
3. How could reflection help you with other units of the course?

Why do I have to complete a work experience reflective log-book?

Writing a reflective log-book is an essential part of your course for this unit. In this topic you will explore some ways of making the best of your reflective log-book and how it can benefit your work placement and possibly your career in health and social care.

As part of your assessment for the unit you are required to complete a reflective log-book of your work experience. Some famous people in history have written diaries; some to record important events, others to record their thoughts and feelings. For example, Anne Frank – who was a young Jewish girl during World War Two – wrote of her experiences, thoughts and feelings when she and the rest of her family were in hiding. Other people use diaries to record birthdays and other important dates. All diaries are useful whatever you write in them. Your reflective log-book is intended to support you in recording your progress on work experience and the development of skills and understanding of your role as a member of the health or social care team. You can look back and see your progress; you can also record your feelings, worries and successes in the setting of your choice.

Good reasons to write a work experience reflective log-book

- It is an essential part of your assessment for the unit.

- It will help you to reflect on your own achievements.

- It will help you to organise your thoughts and feelings about work experience.

- It will help you to record your knowledge and skills gained, e.g. what activities you undertook, increased confidence.

- It will provide you with information to include when applying for a place on a more advanced course.

- It will provide you with evidence of relevant experience when you are applying for employment in health and social care.

- It will help you to understand your strengths and weaknesses, e.g. how well did you use your initiative, follow instructions, use interpersonal skills?

- It can provide you with information for including in course work.

- It will help you to record your reflections and build on them.

- It will encourage you to complete reports more accurately when working in health and social care.

Activity: Keeping an up-to-date reflective log-book

Write down all the details of everything that happened on one day two weeks ago. Now write down everything which you can remember about what happened yesterday. Which item contains the most details? Writing your reflective log-book regularly will make it more accurate and of more use to you.

Case study: Saleem's reflective log-book

Saleem had just begun his work experience at the Acorn Training Centre and was having a busy day. He understood the reasons for writing in his reflective log-book and fully intended to keep up-to-date with this. However, he had actually not started writing his reflective log-book when he was at the end of his first week at the centre. There was always so much else to do: meeting friends after placement, visiting family and completing other course work. All of these things were important and necessary; but the reflective log-book still had to be written and time was moving on. Saleem had asked his supervisor for permission to write his reflective log-book during the working day and had been told that he could. His supervisor did express surprise at his delay, but knew that Saleem really needed to get on with it.

Unfortunately the day became very busy. Two members of the group had a fight and staff had to intervene, one individual was ill and had to be taken home and then, when the afternoon film was being shown, a ball from the nearby school hit a window and broke it. Saleem, who was now trying to write his reflective log-book, had to come and clear away the glass, leaving him no time to work, because it was then time to serve drinks before everyone went home. That evening Saleem had to write up his reflective log-book, trying desperately to remember the events of the day and also the rest of the days he had been at the centre.

1. When should Saleem have begun writing in his reflective log-book?

2. Should he really have been writing his reflective log-book at the setting?

3. What could affect the accuracy of Saleem's reflective log-book?

Just checking

1. Name three reasons for writing a work experience reflective log-book.
2. Name two reasons for keeping your reflective log-book up-to-date.
3. Where should you be writing your work experience reflective log-book?

What should I write in my work experience reflective log-book?

Writing in your reflective log-book

Writing in your reflective log-book will help you to remember what you did on work experience, how the support routines are carried out over the day and the tasks you have to perform on each day of your work experience. If you read through what you have written, it will remind you of what you have to do on your next visit. It will also help you to work out what not to do! Here are a few items which you might record in your reflective log-book, but you may think of many more.

The good log-book checklist

- the type of setting
- how the setting is funded (private, statutory or voluntary)
- professionals who come into the setting, for example therapists, hairdressers, opticians
- the daily routine
- any particular tasks which you have been given to do
- the interpersonal skills your used, e.g. verbal and non verbal communication, listening skills
- any special occasions such as a trip to the shops, a trip to a theme park or zoo
- the general organisation of the setting
- the needs of the individuals who either live there or attend
- how these needs are met by the staff
- types of staff and qualifications/personal attributes required to work there
- are there any more learners from your course or another centre?
- activities which you have taken part in
- dress codes for the staff and yourself, including special requirements for the setting
- evidence of at least two policies, for example, fire prevention or health and safety.

Key term

Attendee – someone who attends a session but does not live there

Figure 5.9: An example Work Experience Log Book

Work Experience Log Book

Monday 1st February 2010

I arrived at the Redbridge Residence for older people this morning for my first day on work experience. I felt really nervous because I didn't know what to expect. On my first day breakfast was over when I arrived, but that was because I missed my bus and didn't get there until 10am. The manager said that I should be on time in future. I felt cross at the time but now I realise that being late means that other people have to do my tasks as well as their own. It's all about team work really, we learned about that in class. I was worried that I might do something wrong or break something expensive. In fact the day went really well and everyone was friendly. I remembered what my tutor told me and found out where the fire exits were and what happened if the fire alarm went.

Monday 8th February 2010

I spent most of the day chatting to the residents and joining in with a game of bingo. I also laid tables and cleared away the dishes. The manager said that bingo helps to keep the residents' brains active. It certainly kept my brain working; one resident kept insisting that she had the right numbers when she didn't. I was asked to sit and help her. I am enjoying my time here, the residents always seem pleased to see me and they have such interesting stories to tell. I am beginning to understand the need for routines in a setting like this. For one thing it makes sure that everything is done and all the residents receive the support they need. The other reason is that it gives the residents a sense of security which is important. I really enjoyed today.

Did you know?

You will be able to use at least some of the information in the checklist for assessments in other parts of your course. Gathering information now will save you time later.

Functional skills

Completing your reflective log-book will demonstrate your ability to produce documents using your **English** skills.

Activity: Log-book

1. Look back at the good log-book checklist and think about how many of them are included in Figure 5.9.

2. Find out about two policies in your centre; you could begin with fire prevention.

Just checking

1. How can writing down routines help you to remember them?
2. Why should you not ask residents or attendees for information?
3. Why should you ask your supervisor about any information you require?
4. Why would an optician visit a day centre for older people?
5. Why would a hairdresser visit a day centre for older people?

Why do they do it like that?

If you just record the facts about work experience, you will only have completed half a task. The real benefit of keeping a log-book comes from reflecting on what happens and learning why it happened.

Reflecting to understand

Here are some suggestions to help you to start to reflect on what you have seen.

When you record events and facts ask yourself the following questions. Why? What for? Where? How? When? For example:

- Why did that child smile at me?

- Why does dirty laundry have to go in the bag and not on the floor?

- Why does punctuality matter in the day centre?

- Why should I remember that Mrs Khan doesn't like sugar in her tea?

- Why did I get it wrong this time when I got it right last time, what was different?

If you cannot answer your own questions, ask your supervisor or your tutor. Reflecting, thinking about events and facts, and the reasons for things being done in a particular way, helps us to learn and improve our performance. If you write the questions and the answers in your reflective log-book, you will learn from this.

As part of your assessment for the unit, you will need to reflect upon your overall performance. You will need to consider and write about the following points:

- How effective are my interpersonal skills, my tone of voice, my body language, use of language?

- How well do I follow instructions and complete the tasks I am given?

- How well do I receive constructive criticism?

- Am I a good team worker?

- Have I learned the routines of the setting?

- Am I punctual?

- What have I learned?

- Has my confidence increased?

- What are my strengths and what are my weaknesses?

Activity: Reflecting on your own performance

Think about something you did really well: a meal you cooked, a piece of coursework you wrote, a task you did at your part-time job. Write down why it worked well, and what you could have done to make it even better.

Did you know?

Reflecting on your own performance will help you to celebrate success as you gain skills and confidence on your work experience.

Case study: Millie

Millie had just arrived home from her first day at work experience at the Red Panda Day Nursery. It had been a busy day and Millie hardly had time to think. She had been asked to work in the baby room; which had not been her first choice, she had wanted to work with the 3- and 4-year-old children. There were six babies in the room who all seemed to want feeding at the same time and, when it was lunchtime, Millie was asked to clear up the soft play area and wipe the surfaces where the children had spilled juice earlier. It wasn't her favourite job, but Millie recognised that it was all part of the nursery day. Millie also mopped up a spillage on the floor with the same cloth and was sharply told not to do that again.

Millie made a mental note to ask why she had to use different cloths for surfaces and floors. Later that day Millie asked the head of room about the incident, who explained the need to prevent the spread of infection by following rules of hygiene. When it was time for the children to go home, Millie wanted to open the door to the parents but was told that the door must be opened by a member of the nursery staff, to reassure the parents. Again, Millie wondered why, but later realised that parents may need to enquire about their children's well-being when they arrived after a busy day at work.

1. What did Millie learn that should be written in her reflective log-book?

2. What reflections can she make on her day?

3. What could Millie have learnt from working in an area which was not her first choice?

Just checking

1. Name two things which you should include in your reflective log-book.
2. Why should you only write about real events in your reflective log-book?
3. Why do you need to reflect on how you deal with criticism and correction?
4. Why are good team skills important in a health or social care setting?

Ready for the real thing!

This topic will help you prepare for final assessment for this important unit. What have you learned?

Skills

There are many skills you will gain during your work experience (discussed on pp. 118–119) and in your reflective log-book you should show how you have done the following things:

- Punctuality: how did you make sure you were on time? Were you ever late?

- Regular attendance – you should attend your work experience placement regularly.

- Timely reporting of incidents and accidents – were there any while you were on your work placement? If yes, what happened?

- Ability to follow instructions – think about what you did if an instruction was unclear.

- Responding to positive criticism.

- Team working.

- Completing all tasks.

- Understand a duty of care. In a health and social care setting you must remember that you are responsible for people using health and social care services and you have a duty to prevent them from harm.

- Awareness of your own and other people's safety.

- Understand the limits of your own role.

- Interact with people who use services – including staff and other adults.

- Demonstrating a professional approach.

Putting a folder together

Some learners like to put all their work experience material together in a folder. This makes it easier for your tutor to mark but also means that you have everything in one place if you have to take it to another work experience placement or job interview. You would include:

- letter of application

- your CV

- evidence of planning, e.g. bus timetables, notes to take to interview, any notes made during the interview

- reflective log-book, report and action plan

- end of work experience report from your supervisor.

Assessment activity 5.3

Carry out a period of placement to a total of at least 60 hours in a health or social care setting and submit a log of the hours spent in placement each day that is signed by your placement-based supervisor (**P3**). Demonstrate appropriate interpersonal skills throughout the time spent in placement (**P4**).

Grading tips

To meet **P3** you must receive a positive report by the end of your placement. This should be evidenced in a written report, usually in a form provided by your tutor. However, it will be your responsibility to ensure that your workplace supervisor completes the form and signs it before you leave the placement and that you submit it to your tutor as evidence for **P3**.

Remember that a positive attitude and the effort you make when in placement can help make it a rewarding and enjoyable experience. To confirm you have met **P4**, ensure that your ability to use appropriate interpersonal skills is also specifically confirmed in writing by your workplace supervisor either in the placement report form or in a separate witness testimony.

Assessment activity 5.4

Maintain a log book of your experiences during your health and social care placement that is reflective. This could be in the form of notes you make systematically at the end of each day in placement about daily routines, your own contributions to activities in the placement, what you learned, the skills you used, including your interpersonal skills. To meet the reflective aspect of **P5** you will also need to include notes about new knowledge you have acquired, what

you have learned about yourself and how you have developed over the duration of the placement. In addition, your log book will need to discuss how well you think you performed overall in the placement (**M2**) and specifically discuss the interpersonal skills you used in placement (**M3**). For **D2** you should draw up a plan to show how you could improve your performance in a future placement.

Grading tips

When making entries in your reflective logbook for **P5**, always be honest and include comments about both good and less positive experiences each day, giving reasons why your performance was as it was, for example:
- 'I worked well as a team member because I tried to support other and volunteered to do extra tasks if needed.'
- 'I found working in a nursery much harder that I though and sometime I did not have as much patience as I should have.'

- 'I was surprised at how much I enjoyed working with people who have learning disabilities; today I learned how to support someone in a cooking session.'

To achieve **M2** you will need to discuss in a report how you have performed over the whole period spent in the placement. Discussions with your tutor and peers will help you with this.

By completing **M2** you should be have identified the aspects of your placement experience that were less strong and your action plan for **D2** should identify how you will make these improvements.

 PLTS

When you are reflecting upon your performance on work experience, you will be a **reflective thinker**, evaluating your skills in order to improve them.

Functional skills

If you type up your action plan you will be using functional skills in **English** (writing) and **ICT**.

Figure 5.10 Action plan for work experience

Area for improvement	Action	Time	Achieved
Interacting with users of the service	Contribute more to class discussion	3rd March	Yes
Time management	Set targets for home tasks	15th March	Not completely, targets reset for 4th April
Use of initiative	Volunteer to be team leader in group task	6th April	Yes but I still need more practice
Following instructions	Listen carefully in class/check if I don't understand the message	5th April	I am improving but will write instructions down as my memory could be better
Punctuality	Buy new alarm clock	3rd March	Yes, have been on time for all classes this week

Recognising your successes

At the end of your work experience, read your log-book, think about your time at the setting and answer the following questions; if you are honest, you will be able to recognise your successes and understand where you may need to develop:

- What do you know about the setting, and the support it offers, that you did not know before?

- Why is this knowledge of benefit to you?

- How could you use this knowledge in other parts of your course?

- How effective were your interview skills? Which skills were good and which needed developing? Give an example of both and state your reasons.

- How well did you complete your log-book? Were you reflective or descriptive? Give your reasons.

- How pleased are you with your overall performance on work experience? What were the positive points? What are your reasons for your judgements?

- Were there any negative aspects to your performance? What are your reasons for your judgements?

- Read through your answers and use them to produce an action plan. Show this to your tutor and ask him/her if they agree with your points.

Just checking

1. Why do you think employers prefer applicants who have had some experience?
2. How many hours of work experience do you need to complete?
3. Why would you complete an action plan at the end of your work experience?

Hannah Oliver
Care Assistant

I am a support assistant in a residential setting for young adults with learning difficulties and challenging behaviour. I work a variety of shifts; from 7.30 am to 4.30 pm, or from 4.30 pm to 10 pm. Some members of staff work nights but I only do that occasionally if someone is ill or during holiday periods. I am involved in the planning of support for individuals within the setting and also providing personal care for those people who cannot do this for themselves. I not only need practical support skills, I need patience, empathy and a sense of fun.

The residence is home for twelve individuals and I have to respect their right to be themselves. We go on trips, have parties, play games and eat together just like any other family. I enjoy the challenge of every day being different; sometimes I have to manage difficult situations but the skills I have learned through observing experienced staff enable me to cope. I find that the more effort I make to ensure that the residents have all of their needs met, the more rewarding the job becomes. I particularly enjoy celebrating the festivals and special days with our residents. We are a multicultural group and we have learned about each other's customs and beliefs; we have a celebration most weeks, two sometimes! The best thing about my job is that I am increasing the quality of life for the residents and contributing to the life of the family here at the residence.

Think about it!

1. What are some of the needs of the residents?
2. What can Hannah do to meet these needs?
3. Give three factors she would need to remember when meeting these needs.

Extension activity: Where are the glasses?

Mrs James is an older lady who attends the Firs Day Centre three times a week. Mrs James has mild memory loss but enjoys the centre and looks forward to coming. She is brought by her daughter who usually stays and enjoys a cup of tea before going off to work at a local day nursery. One day the daughter wakes up late and rushes to her mother's house, hurries her out and drives quickly to the day centre. Unfortunately she forgets to pick up her mother's coat and Mrs James arrives at the centre flustered, cold without her coat and missing her reading glasses which were in the pocket of the coat. Now Mrs James has forgotten that her daughter was in a hurry; she cannot find her reading glasses and accuses one of the other ladies of taking them. The other lady becomes upset and both ladies begin to complain loudly about each other. The rest of the ladies begin to take sides in the argument and everyone becomes very upset.

Note: read through the information given at least twice before starting on the questions and remember to be objective – do not make judgements about any of the characters.

1. How do you think that the staff should deal with this situation?
2. What do you think were the real reasons for the situation?
3. How could the staff help to ensure that it did not arise again?
4. Produce a list of suggestions for relatives of individuals, such as Mrs James, who have memory loss to try to prevent similar situations occurring. (Remember to consider the needs of the relatives, older people and staff at the centre.)

edexcel ▦

Assignment tips

- Find out as much as you can about your work experience setting before you begin.

- Prepare well for your interview by producing a plan of action.

- Complete your reflective log-book during your time of work experience; don't leave it all until the end.

- Remember to follow the reflective cycle on page 126 and the reflective checklist on page 127 when writing up your experiences in your log.

- Link information learned in class with information and skills learned on work experience.

- Learn the routines of the setting as quickly as possible to build up your confidence and efficiency; this will improve your overall performance.

- Use constructive criticism to help you to improve your overall performance.

- Produce an action plan for future development at the end of your work experience.

- Make sure that you fully understand the requirements for the higher grades if you wish to achieve these.

- Use your end of work experience report to produce action points for your development plan.

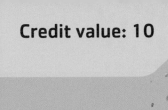

Credit value: 10

6 Cultural diversity in health and social care

This unit aims to introduce you to the wide range of beliefs held by individuals within our society. It will help you to understand and value the ways in which we are different. You will learn what is meant by cultural diversity and about the beliefs of individuals from a wide range of different religious and secular backgrounds. The unit covers the beliefs and practices of different cultural groups and the factors that influence equality of opportunity within our society. The understanding you will gain can be used to help promote equality of opportunity for service users in health and social care environments if you move on to a career in this area of work.

The unit will then lead on to the rights of individuals and the role and responsibilities of service providers in upholding these rights. You will also learn about legislation, conventions, regulations, codes of practice and charters that support this work. In a multicultural society like Britain it is important that workers in the health and social care sectors recognise, understand and respect its diversity. Britain's diversity has major implications for the provision of quality service.

This specialist unit will provide useful preparation for work in the health and social care sectors and a good understanding for those of you who intend to progress on to the BTEC National Diploma in Health and/or Social Care or the BTEC National in Children's Care, Learning and Development.

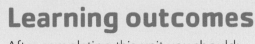

Learning outcomes

After completing this unit you should:

1. know the diversity of individuals in society
2. understand beliefs and practices in different religious or secular groups
3. understand factors that influence the equality of opportunity for individuals in society
4. know the role of legislation, codes of practice and charters in promoting diversity.

Assessment and grading criteria

This table shows you what you must do in order to achieve a **pass**, **merit** or **distinction** grade and where you can find activities in this book to help you.

To achieve a **pass** grade the evidence must show that you are able to:	To achieve a **merit** grade the evidence must show that, in addition to the pass criteria, you are able to:	To achieve a **distinction** grade the evidence must show that, in addition to the pass and merit criteria, you are able to:
P1 Identify social, cultural and political factors that create diversity within society (IE1, CT2, TW1, EP1, EP5) **Assessment activity 6.1, page 147**		
P2 Explain the beliefs and practices of individuals from two contrasting religious or secular groups (IE1, CT2, TW1, EP1, EP5) **Assessment activity 6.2, page 157**	**M1** Compare the similarities and differences in the practices and beliefs of individuals from two contrasting religious or secular groups **Assessment activity 6.2, page 157**	
P3 Explain factors that may influence the equality of opportunity for individuals (CT2, RL1, RL5, SM3) **Assessment activity 6.3, page 169**	**M2** Discuss how discriminatory practice can be avoided **Assessment activity 6.3, page 169**	**D1** Assess the possible effects of discrimination on the physical, intellectual, emotional and social health/well-being of individuals **Assessment activity 6.3, page 169**
P4 Outline one piece of relevant legislation and one code of practice or charter for a chosen health or social care environment that aims to promote diversity (IE3, IE4, RL1, RL5, SM3, CT2, EP1, EP5) **Assessment activity 6.4, page 182**	**M3** Describe how the legislation and code of practice or charter promotes diversity **Assessment activity 6.4, page 182**	**D2** Assess the effectiveness of the chosen legislation and code of practice or charter in promoting diversity **Assessment activity 6.4, page 182**

How you will be assessed

This is an internally assessed unit and you will be assessed on a series of assessment tasks that show your understanding of diversity in Britain and the implications of that diversity for health and social care workers.

- For the first task you should show understanding of the social and political factors that make people different from each other and the beliefs and practice of individuals from two contrasting religious/secular groups.

- Secondly, you must demonstrate understanding of factors that may influence equality of opportunity, and issues of discrimination.

- The third task expects you to show understanding of the rights of individuals, one piece of relevant legislation and one code of practice or charter and how these support individual rights.

Syed, an aspiring nurse

My ambition is to be a nurse and this unit has opened my eyes to just how many different beliefs are held by groups of people in Britain. I'd learnt about some of them in RS but hadn't covered cultures such as Rastafarians. It also horrified me to learn how badly discrimination can affect people receiving health or social care. I had not realised the full implications. When I went on placement to a care home I met an older person who was a Sikh. It was really interesting to chat to him about his beliefs and how well respected he felt himself to be by the care workers. He said that being treated like this made other residents realise that this was the right way to behave towards him and so he felt properly at home now – able to live there feeling a valued member of the group. It made me realise how important it is to treat people properly and not judge them just because they have different practices from me.

To get the most out of this unit you have to be really honest with yourself about your attitude and behaviour to people who have different beliefs from yourself. By doing this you are being a reflective learner and will be able to recognise how to treat others better, now and in the future. You won't have met people from most of the different cultures that live in Britain but will meet more when you get a job and mix with other adults. Even if your job is not in health and social care what you learn in this unit will help you in all aspects of day-to-day life.

Over to you?

- How do you treat people who have different beliefs from you?

- Is there anyone in your health and social care group with a different set of beliefs and way of life from you? What could you find out from them?

- How can you change to become a successful health or social care worker?

1. Know the diversity of individuals in society

Key terms

Multicultural – multi means many. Multicultural means many different cultures and groups in one area

Diversity – the ways in which people are different from each other. Key differences include gender, age, social class, disability, sexuality

Many years ago Britain was thought of as being 'white', because the majority of people who lived here had a skin colour that was white although 'white' people can trace their backgrounds to different peoples and cultures such as Romans, Germans, Anglo-Saxons and Danes. We now live in a culture where the term **multicultural** is more appropriate. Our modern society is now multicultural as you can see whenever you walk down most streets or watch television. This is to do with much more than the colour of people's skins or their religion. In this topic you will start to learn about the **diversity** of individuals in society. It looks at ethnicity and the difference between religious and secular beliefs.

Figure 6.1: How does the group to which a person belongs influence their beliefs and identity?

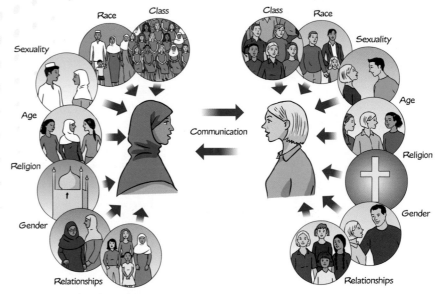

Social, cultural and political diversity

Diversity means a variety or range of differences. To value diversity means to respect and value the cultures and beliefs of other people. If we are unwilling to accept that other people's beliefs and cultures may be different from ours, and so dismiss and ignore them, we will not be able to learn about them and so understand them.

As a worker in health and social care you will get to know the people you work with and should not make any assumptions about them. You will be open to other people's life experiences and differences, and will value their diversity. You will form good relationships with your colleagues and the people who use services. A team of service providers who have different interests and skills is more likely to be able to tackle the range of tasks when helping an individual, and the team will enjoy working together.

There are three main types of diversity: social, cultural and political. Social diversity is to do with each of us being an individual and how we interact with each other, depending on our personal beliefs in day-to-day life. Cultural diversity is similar, but the way in which we interact with each other depends on our particular culture. Politics is a process by which groups of people make decisions which have power over people. Political diversity refers to the range of different beliefs held by various political groups. Political diversity is social diversity but with the addition of power.

Ethnicity

Ethnicity refers to the fact that someone belongs to a particular ethnic group. An ethnic group is a group of people who share the same way of life and **culture**, which is sometimes linked to their **beliefs**. Ethnicity used to be referred to as race and discrimination against a person with a particular ethnic background is sometimes still referred to as racism. You may have been asked when you enrolled in college to fill in part of the enrolment form which asks you to state your own ethnicity: this is the ethnic group you perceive yourself to belong to. Asking this question is good practice and is used by organisations to monitor diversity in their institutions.

Religious and secular beliefs

A **religion** is a set of beliefs which is based on the idea of a sacred being; for example, Christians believe in God. **Secular** beliefs, however, have no connection to religion or a place of worship. A secular belief is connected to natural laws of logic and reason. In a secular state, e.g. Australia, there is no national religion – all religions are equal. You will learn more about religious and secular beliefs later in this unit.

Key terms

Ethnicity – being part of a group sharing the same way of life and culture

Culture – a set of beliefs, language, styles of dress, ways of cooking, religion, ways of behaving and so on shared by a particular group of people

Beliefs – strongly held opinions stored in the subconscious mind

Religion – a set of beliefs based on the idea of a sacred being

Secular – something that has no connection to any religion or place of worship

Activity: What does it mean?

1. Draw a mind map, flow diagram or other appropriate diagram based on the key terms showing how they all fit together.
2. One example of a culture is that belonging to travellers. Find out what travellers believe in after researching in the library or the Internet. Remember, someone in your school or group might be a traveller so be sensitive to their feelings.
3. What problems might arise due to their way of life when a person of your age needs to use health or social care services?
4. How does your local authority overcome these problems?

Just checking

1. What is meant by diversity? Name five ways in which people may be different from each other.
2. Why is it important to value diversity when you work in health or social care?
3. What is the difference between (i) political and social diversity (ii) religious and secular beliefs?

More diverse factors

Key term

Social class – a group of people who share a common place in society

Did you know?

National Statistics Online show that the gap between the earnings of men and women is still growing. In 2008 this gap was 17.1% for comparable jobs. The largest gap is in the South East and the smallest was in Northern Ireland.

Others examples of social and political diversity are due to social class, gender and sexuality. All these are factors that affect how people feel about themselves and their health and well-being, and affect how they are treated by others.

Social class

Social class is to do with the status that an individual has in society. This is based mainly on occupation, wealth and lifestyle. The traditional British class system is divided into three layers: working class, middle class and upper class. The higher up the class system a person belongs, the more power and influence they tend to have. There are more people who are working class than middle class and more people who are middle class than upper class. Upper class people tend to be those with inherited wealth and include some of Britain's oldest and titled families. The middle class includes industrialists, professionals, business people and shop owners, people who tend to wear a suit to work, and the working class includes agricultural and factory workers, people who work with their hands.

Due to the ever-increasing variety of jobs the class system has over the years become more complicated and since 2001 has been divided into eight classes, according to occupation. Even this is not totally clear. Someone who is, for example, an assembly line worker, might win the lottery and become a millionaire but this alone does not automatically make them upper class. Social class affects health and well-being as a person in a lower class is less likely to have the same opportunities in life as those in a higher social class, as they have poorer employment prospects and a lower income.

Gender

Traditionally women were expected to stay at home and look after the house and family. Women were not allowed to vote on equal terms with men until 1928. As the years have passed changes have happened that have made men and women much more equal, including legislation that makes it illegal to discriminate against someone due to their gender. Despite this, women still tend to hold fewer of the more highly paid jobs and are less likely to be promoted, especially in the more highly paid professions. Even women who are highly paid are still usually expected to run the house and support the family as well.

Sexuality

Sexuality refers to a person's sexual behaviour and choice of partner. Most people are heterosexual, i.e. attracted to someone of the opposite sex; a minority are homosexual, i.e. attracted to someone of the same sex; and some are bisexual, attracted to both sexes. Until 1967 homosexuality was illegal in the UK (until 1980 in Scotland), and the homosexual age of consent was lowered from 21 to 18 in 1994

Activity: Rights of women

1. Do some research to find out how the rights of women have changed since the start of the nineteenth century. Draw a timeline to show key events.

2. Now think about jobs in the health and social care sector. When you go to the hospital are the (i) nurses (ii) doctors mainly men or women? What about your dentist, GP and optician? Think about other jobs in this sector. Are they men or women? Compare your thoughts with those of the rest of your group.

3. Discuss whether you think there are some jobs that are better done by women than men and vice versa. Explain why you think this.

and to 16 in the year 2000. This is the same age of consent as that for people in heterosexual relationships. The Civil Partnership Act 2004 gave them, and civil partners who live together but are not married, many of the same rights as married partners, such as tax benefits, joint property rights, next-of-kin status and shared parenting responsibility. However, many gay rights campaigners see this as a 'second best' status and are still fighting for the right to 'full marriage'.

Even though homosexuality is very much more accepted these days there are still those who are homophobic because their culture says this is wrong. Some people struggle with their homosexual feelings, possibly hiding them for years and even marrying someone of the opposite sex, but this affects their health and well-being and they may feel very confused, isolated and afraid of rejection by their family and friends.

Case study: Steven

Steven is homosexual but has hidden his true feelings all his life. He is 45 years old, has a wife, two children and a very well paid job as a doctor. Lately he has become more and more unsettled and has met a man in a gay bar he feels he could be happy with. He thinks his wife suspects something is wrong but he is afraid to tell her because he does not want to break the family up. He is worried that he will lose his children's love and his parents' respect and that his colleagues and patients will be unhappy working with and being treated by a gay man.

1. In a group discuss Steven's predicament. What do you think he should do? What do you think the effects will be on his health and well-being if he admits his true feelings? What is likely to happen to his health and well-being if he keeps the secret hidden away?

2. Role-play the situation when he tells his wife and family and then his work colleagues.

Just checking

1. What is meant by the term social class?

2. How does gender affect a woman's employment prospects?

3. How does a person's sexuality affect their health and well-being?

Friends and family

In this topic you will learn about three more factors that contribute to diversity, namely family structure, age and disability. All of these aspects are changing as our society changes. Families are becoming more and more complicated, as on average people are living longer and people with disabilities are much more accepted as valuable members of society than in the past.

Age

Two hundred years ago, if you lived beyond the age of 50, you were considered to be old and to have lived a long life. In January 2009 the BBC reported that today's life expectancy in the UK is 77 years for men and 82 years for women. More people are living longer because of advances in medical science and greater health awareness, so the population of the UK is increasing – with more older people in our society than ever before. When people retire from full-time employment they should have many years of life to look forward to and our society today contains many active and healthy older people.

Family structure

A family is a social group made up of people who are related to each other by birth, marriage or adoption. Being part of a family shows others that those people are connected in some way. We can classify four different types of family:

The extended family

This consists of three or even four generations of one family who either live together, or very near each other, and have very regular contact with each other. The advantages of such a family are a strong support network for help when, for example, parents work, someone is sick, parents want to go out or someone need errands run. They also support each other financially and help the development of children.

The nuclear family

This includes two parents (who may be married or **cohabiting**) and their children. This is a more common family structure than the extended family in Britain. Although all the members may not live near other generations of the family they still stay in close contact via the phone, visits or email.

The lone-parent family

This family has one parent, maybe because of divorce, separation, being widowed or never having had a relationship with the other parent. It is more usually the mother the children live with.

The reconstituted family

In this type of family individuals with children develop a relationship with another person who may or may not have children from a previous relationship. They may go on to have children together. The family therefore has at least one step-parent.

Disabilities

People with disabilities have to adapt their lifestyles to cope with everyday situations that able-bodied people deal with automatically. A disability may affect both mental and physical fitness, restrict access to varied learning activities, cause emotional distress and remove some social opportunities. It may also affect the growth and physical development of the body: for example, a paralysed arm will lose muscle due to lack of use. Disability can also affect the development of new abilities and skills, as well as emotional development.

Whatever the condition a person has, their needs include all those of an able-bodied person, but they have important additional needs, especially in relation to access to both places and services. If these are met through the provision of an enabling environment, by families, friends and health and social care services giving the help needed to maintain independence, the impact of the disability may be decreased.

Figure 6.2: What is disability?

Physical, where part of body does not work properly

Permanent

Temporary

Acquired after an accident or illness

Disabilities

Congenital, i.e. born with it

Sensory, affecting senses such as hearing or sight

Mental, such as disorders of the brain or learning difficulties

Just checking

1. How does the type of family we live in affect diversity? Explain this with reference to the four types of family.
2. How has life expectancy changed over the last two hundred years?
3. What are some different types of disability?

PLTS

By completing this task well you will have done some research to be an **independent enquirer** and been a **creative thinker** to create the display.

Functional skills

By using **ICT** and the student book for research you will have selected and used a variety of sources of information independently to find information.

 Assessment activity 6.1 **P1**

BTEC

Imagine you are a teacher and you have been asked by the head teacher to update the school displays on diversity in society. Produce a display showing and explaining the factors that lead to social, cultural and political diversity in our society and which make people different from each other. Remember, religion is only one small part of this.

Grading tips

You will need to identify cultural, social and political factors that create diversity within society to achieve **P1**.

2. Understand beliefs and practices in different religious or secular groups

Key term

Eternity – an endless amount of time

One of the main differences in our society and across the world is in the beliefs we hold. These might be religious or secular. There is a wide range of these beliefs and this topic and the following four will help you to understand beliefs and practices in different religious or secular groups. These include festivals and holy days, food, dress, symbols, forms of worship and health or medical beliefs. This topic looks at Christians and Hindus.

Christians

Beliefs – Christians believe in God. Christianity began in the Middle East over 2000 years ago from the teachings of Jesus Christ. Christians believe that Jesus Christ lived a humble and selfless life, died to save humanity by taking our sins with him and rose from the dead. God is the trinity of the Father, Son (Jesus) and Holy Spirit which can inspire us to better things. Christians believe that when they die they will join God in the kingdom of heaven for **eternity** and in life they follow the teachings of Jesus and the Ten Commandments, which they believe were given to Moses by God.

Festivals and holy days – The main Christian day is Sunday, which is seen as a day of rest. However, fewer and fewer people observe this and many shops are now open on Sundays. Christians celebrate many festivals, the main one is Easter, in Spring, which celebrates the death and resurrection of Jesus. Chocolate eggs are given as a symbol of new life. Another major festival is Christmas on 25 December when they celebrate Jesus' birthday. On Christmas Day they give presents and eat a family Christmas dinner.

Food – Some Christians choose to fast or give up a food or drink they enjoy for the 40 days of Lent which come before Easter. Some Roman Catholics do not eat meat on Friday but choose to eat fish.

Dress – For those ordained into the Christian church as priests, nuns or monks, there are specific clothes related to their calling.

Symbols – The main symbol of the Christian faith is the cross, on which Jesus was crucified. The holy book is the Bible; the Old Testament (shared with the Jewish faith and with stories from the Prophets) and the New Testament, which tells the story of Jesus' birth, life, death and resurrection, and contains his teachings.

Forms of worship – Christians worship on a Sunday by going to church and taking part in a variety of services, at which they sing hymns of praise and pray to God. People may be baptised, usually as babies, by having a cross made of water drawn on their forehead to welcome them into the Christian faith. A further service is Holy Communion although not all Christians take part in this. Those who have been

Figure 6.3: What do they believe in?

confirmed can be blessed and eat a wafer of bread to represent Christ's body and drink communion wine to represent his blood.

Christians have no specific health or medical beliefs although they may have personal beliefs which affect their care.

Hindus

Beliefs – Hinduism is a religion that started before 3000 BCE. Hindus believe in a supreme power called Brahman. They believe Brahman is in everything and that his power can be seen in different gods and goddesses. They also believe in reincarnation and that everything living has a soul (atman). When a person dies the atman moves into another living thing, which could be a person, plant or animal. This can only be broken when someone becomes good enough to become part of Brahman. Hindus call Hinduism Sanatan Dharma, which means 'eternal truths.'

Festivals and holy days – The best known Hindu festival is Divali (Diwali), the festival of lights which celebrates New Year at the end of October or beginning of November and the victory of good over evil. Hindus decorate their homes and public places with lights, set off fireworks to scare off evil, give presents and share meals.

Food – Most Hindus are vegetarian and those that do eat meat will not eat beef as the cow is considered to be sacred. Many will also not eat pork, fish or food that contains eggs and Hindus do not drink alcohol or smoke.

Dress – There are no strict dress requirements for men but Hindu women wear a sari. Some Hindus worship wearing the sacred thread (over the left shoulder and hanging to the right hip).

Symbols – A variety of Hindu symbols are used in art, sacred objects and ritual. They usually signify Hindu concepts or the gods or goddesses themselves. They include the Om made up of three Sanskrit letters: aa, au and ma, which, when combined make the sound Aum or Om; the colour of saffron; and the Swastika which symbolises the eternal nature of the Brahman.

Forms of worship – Hindus worship in a temple or shrine and read their holy books, the Vedas. Hindu worship is more an individual act rather than a communal one, as it involves making personal offerings to the deities (gods). Family members often worship together as the majority of Hindu homes have a shrine where offerings are made and prayers said. Worshippers repeat the names of their favourite gods and goddesses, and repeat mantras. Water, fruit, flowers and incense are offered to these gods.

Health/medical beliefs – Males have a responsibility to look after females and may not leave females in the presence of an unfamiliar male. Hospitals therefore need to provide same-sex caregivers. Family members – especially elders – have a strong influence on who will make treatment decisions.

Activity: Christianity

There are many strands or types of Christianity. Research them and produce a leaflet that explains these different strands simply to people who are not Christian.

Include the Ten Commandments, facts about the Bible and whether all strands of Christianity say the Lord's Prayer.

Just checking

1. What is the main belief of (i) Christianity (ii) Hinduism?
2. Which of these groups worships in a temple or at home? What might they do at their shrines?
3. What are the main (i) similarities (ii) differences between Christianity and Hinduism?

Are you a believer?

In this topic you will learn about atheists and Buddhists. It is important to value diversity in order to promote equality of opportunity for all service users.

Atheists

Most people think that atheism involves not believing in God but atheists actually believe that God does not or cannot exist because of their knowledge of the world and different religions. Atheism is an example of a secular belief. They celebrate events such as weddings but do not follow a particular religion in the celebrations, adapting the ceremony to centre more on the people involved.

Agnostics

Whereas an atheist does not believe in the existence of any god, an agnostic is someone who is not sure whether God exists or not.

Buddhism

Beliefs – Buddhists believe that life is one long cycle, the *samsar*, which consists of birth, life, death and rebirth. After death a person's soul is reborn in a new body and the only way to break the cycle is to reach enlightenment or *nirvana*, the end of everything that is not perfect like greed, hatred, suffering and ignorance. Buddhism is a tradition that focuses on personal spiritual development. Buddhists strive for a deep insight into the true nature of life and do not worship gods or deities. The Buddha is not a god but was simply a human being, called Siddhartha Gautama, who was born into royalty but left his privileged life to find enlightenment when he saw the suffering of others. Buddha means 'Awakened One'. There are various forms of Buddhism, each of which believes in different routes to reach enlightenment but there is very little friction between the different groups.

Festivals and holy days – The most important Buddhist festival is Wesak (or Buddha Day) which is held on the first day of the full moon in May or June. On this day the Buddha is meant to have been born, gained enlightenment and passed away, all in different years. They celebrate by giving presents, sharing a meal and going to a service.

Food – Buddhists are strict vegetarians because they are opposed to causing harm to any living creature.

Dress – Some Buddhist monks wear a red, yellow or saffron (orange) robe.

Symbols – The wheel (*Chakra*) is one of the most important Buddhist symbols, as it represents the teachings of the Buddha.

Forms of worship – Buddhists worship in a temple or monastery. They often meditate as well.

Health/medical beliefs – Since prayer is part of the healing and cleansing process, prayer and meditation are important to enable medications and other medical treatments to assist with healing. Some holy days include fasting from dawn to dusk but considerations are allowed for the frail and elderly for whom fasting could create problems. Terminal illness may be seen as a unique opportunity to reflect on life's ultimate meaning, and the meaning of one's relationship with the world. Therefore, it is important that medication does not interfere with consciousness.

What other Buddhist symbols are there?

Activity: Census

Every ten years the government sends a questionnaire to every household in the UK. The information it gathers is for the Census, a summary of the details of who lives where and other information, such as their age at the time. In 1801 there were just five questions with one being about whether anyone is blind, deaf, dumb, an imbecile or a lunatic. Such expressions are now considered to be very offensive and have been removed. However the proposed 2011 census form will be much longer (about 32 pages) covering a range of issues, such as which religion you follow and what your ethnicity is, with categories ranging from Arab to Irish Traveller to choose from. Householders will also be asked to give details of any overnight visitors in their property on census night and anyone refusing this information could be prosecuted and fined.

1. Why do you think the government wants to know (i) what religion people follow (ii) details of overnight visitors?

2. Do you think the census is an invasion of privacy or a useful tool to promote diversity?

3. In your group share ideas and do some research to find out the different ways in which the government uses the information generated by the census. The information in the census is only available to the public after 100 years, to protect people's privacy and personal data.

4. In your group, use the information you have collected to produce a PowerPoint® presentation to explain how the census helps to promote diversity.

Just checking

1. Explain why atheism is a secular belief.
2. How can being a Buddhist affect a person needing medical treatment?
3. What do Buddhists believe in?

As God is my witness?

Key terms

Moral principle – the principles of right and wrong that are accepted by an individual or a social group

Evangelistic – very enthusiastic and forceful delivery of religious message

In this topic you will learn about Humanists and Jehovah's Witnesses.

Humanists

Humanists live according to **moral principles** based on reason and respect for others. They believe that this world and this life is all we have and that it should be as happy as possible. Their beliefs have only been recognised for about the last hundred years. Humanists accept the theory of evolution as opposed to beliefs such as those of some Christians (Creationists) who believe that God created the world in seven days. They do not believe in God and as such can be considered to be atheists. The feeling of Humanists is that to believe in God is to contradict our knowledge of, for example, science and goes against common sense. However, they are very anti-discriminatory and believe that everyone has the right to believe what they want, so it is acceptable to have a number of religions as long as no-one is forced into believing in one. Humanists are therefore also a secular group and, like atheists, adapt any celebrations – such as for the birth of a child – to centre more on the people included rather than any religious belief.

Jehovah's Witnesses

Beliefs – They believe that since Christ proclaimed that his kingdom was not part of the world, and refused to accept a temporal crown, they too must keep separate from the world and refrain from political involvement. Jehovah's Witnesses are members of a Christian-based religious movement probably best known for their door-to-door **evangelistic** work.

Festivals and holy days – The most important religious event of the year for Jehovah's Witnesses is the commemoration of the Memorial of Christ's Death, which takes place on the anniversary of the Last Supper, calculated according to the lunar calendar in use in Christ's time. They believe that this is the only observance commanded by Christ. Witnesses do not celebrate Christmas or Easter because they believe that these festivals are based on (or massively contaminated by) pagan customs and religions. They point out that Jesus did not ask his followers to mark his birthday. Witnesses do not celebrate birthdays or other secular festivals that originate in other religions.

Food and dress – They have no strict food or dress requirements.

Symbols – Jehovah's Witnesses reject the cross, the usual Christian symbol, because they believe that Jesus died on a stake. The one symbol that is used to represent the Jehovah's Witnesses is the watchtower.

Forms of worship – Jehovah's Witnesses have no professional clergy. All baptised members are considered ordained ministers and take on the missionary work of telling outsiders about Witness beliefs. Witnesses are trained from their youth to work as part-time missionaries for the whole of their lives. Witnesses believe that the first-century Christian congregation was primarily a preaching organisation, and they try to follow that example. Most Witnesses attend the Kingdom Hall closest to their home. Often, several congregations share a single Kingdom Hall by alternating meeting times. Religion occupies much of the time of each Witness. They attend meetings regularly, and read and study their faith intensely, both on their own and in home groups.

Health/medical beliefs – Jehovah's Witnesses refuse blood transfusions, including autologous transfusions in which a person has their own blood stored to be used later in a medical procedure. Strict Jehovah's Witnesses would rather die or let a family member die than accept a blood transfusion as the New Testament commands to abstain from blood.

Case study: Ruth's work

Ann teaches in a school. One of her sixth-form students is Ruth, who keeps falling asleep in class and is not interested in any activities such as trips to universities. Ruth's friends eventually tell Ann that the reason for this is because she spends every evening knocking on doors to promote the word of the Jehovah's Witnesses and then does her homework late at night. She cannot go on any trips because her parents expect her to work full time as a missionary for their beliefs.

1. What do you think Ann should do about this situation?

2. Discuss your ideas in a full class discussion. Think carefully about the possible outcomes of any suggested solutions. When you have all reached an agreement role-play the solution.

3. Do some research to find out what the watchtower symbol looks like.

Just checking

1. Explain what you understand about the theory of evolution.
2. How can Humanists not believe in God but not object to people who are not Humanists following a religion?
3. Why do Jehovah's Witnesses not believe in blood transfusions? What are the possible consequences when a Jehovah's Witness needs an operation?

What a festival!

Key terms

Atonement – amends made for an injury or wrong

Circumcision – male circumcision is the removal of some or all of the foreskin from the penis

Did you know?

- During World War Two the Nazis organised the mass persecution and extermination of the Jewish population in Europe in concentration and death camps. The most infamous camp is Auschwitz near Krakow where 1.1 million people died (90% of whom were Jewish). In total 6 million Jews were murdered in the Holocaust in an attempt to destroy Judaism.

- Kosher means killing an animal in such a way that its blood drains away completely, as the Jewish Bible **commands** Jews not to eat blood. The meat is then soaked and salted to complete the process called koshering.

Three more groups are Jews, Rastafarians and Pagans.

Judaism

Beliefs – Judaism began in the Middle East over 3,500 years ago. Jews believe that God created the world and everything in it, and follow the Ten Commandments just as Christians do. Judaism was founded by Moses. The Jewish Bible is known as the Tenakh. Jews believe that God appointed the Jews to be his chosen people in order to set an example of holiness and ethical behaviour to the world.

Festivals and holy days – Judaism has a number of festivals and holy days, including *Pesach* (Passover), which lasts for eight days and is celebrated in spring with a special meal called the *Seder*. It reminds Jews that their ancestors were once slaves in Egypt and that God helped them to flee from slavery. Other important holy days are *Yom Kippur*, the Day of **Atonement**, and *Hashannah*, the Jewish New Year. Shabbat (Sabbath) is the weekly holy day, which lasts from sunset on Friday evening to Saturday night.

Food – To celebrate the Shabbat Jews eat bread called *challah*, made in the shape of a plait, and drink wine. Meat must be killed and prepared in a special way, so Jewish people buy their meat and other foods from specialist kosher shops and butchers. They do not eat pork, rabbit or shellfish and they have different sets of utensils, one to use with meat and one with milk, because meat and milk foods are never prepared or eaten together.

Dress – Orthodox Jewish men wear *Tefillin*, which are cubic black leather boxes with leather straps, on their head and their arm during weekday morning prayers. Orthodox Jewish men always cover their heads by wearing a skullcap known in Hebrew as a *kippah* or in Yiddish as a *yarmulke*.

Symbols – The Star of David is the best known symbol of Judaism. The Menorah is another symbol and is a seven-branched candle stick

Forms of worship – the Jewish Bible is made up of the Torah (Five books of Moses), the books of the Prophets and holy writings. Jewish people worship in the synagogue and their spiritual leaders are called Rabbis.

Health/medical beliefs – The *Brit Milah* (**circumcision** ceremony) is an important initiation rite for young Jewish boys.

Rastafarians

Beliefs – Rastafari is a movement of black people, founded in the 1930s in Jamaica. Rastafarians worship a single God, they believe that Africa is the birthplace of mankind and that the Emperor Haile Selassie, crowned King of Ethiopia in 1930, was a living God. They believe that black people are the chosen people of God, the genuine Israelites, but that they have been suppressed through slavery. Many Rastafarians believe that following their **repatriation** to Africa black people will become rulers of the world, resulting in the suppression of white people. They believe that Ethiopia is their homeland and that one day they will return there to live in freedom.

Festivals and holy days – Rastafarians celebrate a number of holy days, such as Ethiopian New Year's Day (11 September).The history of Ethiopia is remembered, and its importance acknowledged through Biblical passages and prayer. A Nyabinghi session, which is the traditional music of the Rastafari religion and which includes drumming and chanting, is also held to mark the occasion. They also celebrate significant dates such as 2 November, the Crowning of Emperor Haile Selassie.

Food – Rastas have a deep respect for nature and because vegetables are of the earth they are predominantly vegetarian though some may eat fish (but not shell fish).

Activity: Bob Marley

Bob Marley was a Rastafarian. Find a picture of him and the lyrics of some of his songs. Make a display using the photo and the lyrics to show how reggae music protests and celebrates the beliefs of Rastas.

Pagans

Beliefs – Paganism includes several spiritual movements that are based on a respect for nature and the need to preserve the environment, many of which came about before our major religions. They also believe in the equality of the sexes. Paganism encompasses a diverse community with some groups concentrating on specific traditions, practices or elements such as ecology, witchcraft, Celtic traditions or certain gods. Wiccans, Druids, Shamans, Sacred Ecologists, Odinists and Heathens all make up aspects of the Pagan community.

Pagans do not have any special requirements for food, dress, health or medical beliefs, although some are vegetarians and they may take herbal medicines.

Worship – Pagans prefer to worship their gods and goddesses, and celebrate the seasons, outdoors, such as a clearing in the woods. Most of their rituals celebrate the four elements (fire, water, earth and wind) and they chant, sing and dance to try to contact the divine world that surrounds them. They do not worship the devil or use black magic.

Key term

Repatriation – return to one's country

Emperor Haile Selassie, who inspired Nelson Mandela and Martin Luther King

Activities

Rastafarians

1. Carry out some more research into Rastafarians. Include details about (i) food, (ii) dress, (iii) symbols, (iv) health/medical beliefs and (v) forms of worship. Use the information to produce a PowerPoint® presentation.

The Pagan community

2. Produce a set of fact cards, one for each of the groups mentioned as part of the Pagan community.

Just checking

1. What do Jews believe?
2. Who was Haile Selassie?
3. Why do Pagans prefer not to worship in buildings?

Muslims and Sikhs

The last two religious groups covered in this unit are Muslims and Sikhs. In this topic you will learn about their beliefs and practices.

Muslims

Beliefs – Islam is the religion of Muslim people. Muslims are guided by the Five Pillars of Islam. These are:

- belief that Allah is the only God and that Mohammed is his prophet
- prayers must be said five times a day
- people should undertake the Hajj (pilgrimage)
- fasting must take place during the month of Ramadan
- muslims must behave charitably.

The Holy Book of Islam is called the Qur'an. Muslims also believe that there are prophets, or special messengers and Ibrahim (Abraham) and Mohammed are prophets.

They believe in the day of judgment when the life of every person will be assessed. Muslims believe in angels and also in predestination, as Allah has already decided what will happen in the world, although this does not stop humans making free choices.

Forms of worship – at midday each Friday Muslims go to the mosque to worship with other Muslims. They use prayer mats and they must face in the direction of Mecca, wherever they are in the world. Religious practices include the Five Pillars of Islam, which are five duties that unite Muslims into a community. Most Muslims (about 87%) belong to the Sunni denomination and some to the Shi'a (about 13%).

Festivals and holy days – The two main festivals set down in Islamic law are Eid-ul-Fitr and Eid-ul-Adha. The first of these marks the end of a month of fasting called Ramadan during which Muslims do not eat or drink during the hours of daylight, and the second marks the end of Hajj, the annual pilgrimage to Mecca.

Food – Muslims do not drink alcohol or eat pork. Meat should be *halal* that is, animals and fish must be slaughtered in a particular way. Ramadan is the month of fasting where food and drink may not be taken between sunrise and sunset.

Dress – many Muslim men and women adhere to a dress code which includes covering the body shape in loose garments. Woman sometimes choose to cover their head.

Symbols – the crescent is a common symbol in Islam and the colour green is also very common. Much of the traditional artworks (mosaics for example) are highly patterned or decorated. However, it is forbidden to represent living things in art.

Health beliefs – cleanliness and personal hygiene are both very important in Islam. Face, hands, feet and sometimes hair must be washed and shoes removed both before praying and entering a mosque. The left hand is considered unclean and is not used for eating.

Why is Mecca so important for Muslims?

Sikhs

Beliefs – Sikhism has only existed for about 500 years. Sikhs believe there is only one God and think religion should be practised by living in the world and coping with life's everyday problems, by leading a moral life. They follow the teaching of ten **Gurus** about the unity of God, equality of men and women, belief in **reincarnation** and meditation, leading to their union with God. Guru Nanak was the founder of Sikhism and the tenth Guru, Gobind Singh, created a new order of Sikhs called Khalsa.

Festivals and holy days – some of the many festivals are Vaisakhi, the New Year festival held in April, and Divali (Diwali) the festival of lights. But they celebrate this for a different reason from the Hindus; the Sikh Divali is the anniversary of the release from imprisonment of the sixth Guru, so it symbolises freedom. The main day for Sikhs to go to worship is Sunday but this is because it is a day when most of them do not work, rather than for religious reasons.

Food – Sikhs eat meat as long as the animal has not been killed in a Jewish or Muslim way. Some do not eat pork and others do not eat beef; therefore food served in the place of worship is vegetarian, so all can eat it. Sikhs are not meant to smoke or drink alcohol.

Dress – The Khalsa wear the 5Ks of Sikhism, which are: *Kesh* (uncut bodily hair – men wear their hair tied up in a turban), *Kanga* (a small wooden comb worn in the hair), *Kara* (a steel bracelet worn on the wrist), *Kaccha* (cotton shorts, worn underneath clothes) and *Kirpan* (a ceremonial steel sword).

Symbols – The special Sikh sign is made up of several images: the *Khanda* (which is a double-edged sword representing the belief in one God), the *Chakkar* (like the Kara it is a circle representing God without beginning or end and reminding Sikhs to remain within the rule of God) and two crossed *kirpans* (representing spiritual authority and political power).

Key terms

Guru – a personal spiritual teacher

Reincarnation – rebirth of the soul in another body

Did you know?

The dates of Sikh festivals have traditionally been defined using a lunar calendar, with the result that the festivals were not on the same Western date each year. Recently a new calendar has been introduced to fix this problem by lining up with the Western calendar so that Sikh festival dates are the same each year.

Unfortunately not all Sikh organisations approve of this calendar, with the result that there are now several dates for most festivals, depending on the calendar you choose.

Just checking

1. What is Ramadan?
2. Why do Sikhs celebrate Divali?
3. Name two differences between the food requirements of Muslims and Sikhs

Functional skills

You will use the **ICT** functional skills of presenting information in ways that are fit for purpose and audience in this task.

PLTS

Organising your time and work load to meet the deadline for the presentation helps you to be a **self-manager**.

BTEC Assessment activity 6.2

You work in a training hospital and have been asked to run a training session for the nurses to help them understand the beliefs and practices of two contrasting religious or secular groups. This is to help them understand better how to treat patients who are members of these groups so they have equality of opportunity to access health care. Produce a presentation and some teaching notes to accompany it.

Grading tips

In order to achieve **P2** you need to explain the beliefs and practices of the two groups you have chosen. To improve to merit level **M1** you need to compare the similarities and differences in the practices and beliefs of the two groups. This means you have to be more analytical than if you just want to pass.

3. Understand factors that influence the equality of opportunity

Key term

Equality – the idea of equal treatment and respect

While you have been learning about the various religious and secular groups covered in the last few topics you will have noticed that some of the groups state that they believe in the equality of the sexes. In this topic and the following five you are going to look at a range of factors including religious beliefs that influence the equality of opportunity for individuals in society.

Equal opportunity is promoted with the intention of providing an environment in which people are not excluded from the activities of society, such as education, employment, or health care, on the basis of things they cannot change. Some of these things are shown below. Equal opportunity practices include measures taken by organisations to ensure fairness and **equality** in the employment process.

The factors that influence the equality of opportunity for individuals in society include:

- ethnicity
- religious beliefs
- social class
- gender
- sexuality
- age
- family structure
- disabilities.

It is very important in a health and social care environment for workers to understand these factors and how they can affect their care of service users. A care practitioner needs to acknowledge an individual's personal beliefs even if they do not share those beliefs. For example, if a hospital patient is Jewish and needs to eat kosher food it is only right that the hospital should serve him kosher food while he is in hospital. This will help him feel that his Jewish identity has been acknowledged rather than ignored, so improving his feeling of self worth and hopefully aiding his recovery. This gives him a more equal opportunity to access the care he needs.

Similarly, if an individual needs to pray at a certain time of day the service provider needs to allow them the time and space to do so. If someone is not able to pray their state of mind will mean that there is less chance of treatment being successful – because a person's intellectual and emotional needs must be met as well as their physical needs in order to make a full recovery. The exception to this would be if emergency treatment was required immediately to save the person's life.

Case study: Sanjay

Sanjay is a student at the high school and on non-uniform day he wears his turban to school. He becomes very upset when another student touches his turban and is taken to see his Head of Year because he is inconsolable and says the other boy has deeply offended him.

1. Why do you think Sanjay is so upset?
2. What do you think the Head of Year should say to (i) Sanjay and (ii) the other boy?
3. How could the significance of the turban affect a Sikh if he is rushed to hospital after an accident?

Unfair treatment

People are sometimes treated unfairly because of their differences. Factors such as age and gender can influence the equality of opportunity in employment. For example, there have been incidences when an older person with more experience is passed over for promotion in favour of a younger colleague. It has also been claimed that some candidates for jobs have been less successful because of their 'ethnic' surnames – race discrimination has applied because their qualifications are the same as those of the other candidates.

Case study: Shamma

Shamma is a Muslim and applies for a job as a nursery nurse. She has children of her own, has the right qualifications and is a very kind and caring woman. She wears a burkha to the interview. She is not given the job and is told it is because her appearance will frighten the children, as the only part of her body they can see is her eyes. She is offended by this and says the decision is unfair. She takes the nursery manager to an industrial tribunal but does not win her case.

1. Explain why Shamma has worn her burkha to the interview.
2. What do you think of the decisions made in this situation? Discuss this in a small group and be prepared to share your views with the rest of the class.

Just checking

1. What is meant by the term 'equal opportunities'?
2. Why is it important that health and social care workers understand the factors that influence equality of opportunities for individuals?
3. Give an example of when people are treated unfairly because of their differences.

Discriminatory practice

Key terms

Discrimination – treat a person or group differently from others

Prejudice – an unreasonable feeling against a person or group of people

Stereotype – a fixed idea or assumption about an individual or group of people

In this topic you will learn about discriminatory practice. There are four different forms of discrimination, namely: unfair, direct, indirect and positive discrimination. You will also learn about prejudice, stereotyping and labelling.

Discrimination and prejudice

There are several kinds of **discrimination**. Someone might have a **prejudice** (a bias) against a person or a group of people for reasons such as age, gender, race, ethnicity, social class, religious beliefs, secular beliefs, family structure, sexuality, ability, health, disability, address, dress or appearance. They might then discriminate against that person or group and treat them differently.

There are four different forms of discrimination:

- Unfair discrimination is when a person is treated unfairly in comparison with somebody else. One example of such behaviour is if someone is not being considered seriously for a job because they are older than another candidate, despite having the same qualifications and experience.

- Direct discrimination is when someone is rude, hostile or offensive to someone or treats them less favourably because they see them as being different: for example, when someone who is overweight is called names at school. This form of discrimination is easy to prove because it is heard or witnessed by other people.

- Indirect discrimination is the setting of criteria, rules or conditions which exclude or disadvantage groups of people. In employment, this might involve setting a condition which is not necessary for the job, e.g. saying English has to be the mother tongue when the job is for a night-watchman who doesn't have to speak to anyone. Employment tribunals often look out for this type of discrimination as it is very important that it is avoided.

- Positive discrimination is when a decision is made in a person's favour for the exact reason that there is something different about them: for example, advertising for a person who has red hair and fair skin because it is to play the part of the sister of someone who has these characteristics. Sometimes it is done less openly, such as when a service has few people from an ethnic minority at a senior level, so they appoint someone from an ethnic minority although they have interviewed a cross-section of people.

Stereotyping and labelling

People discriminate against others, knowingly or unknowingly, by making assumptions about them i.e. by **stereotyping** and labelling them.

Figure 6.4: Typical teenage stereotypes

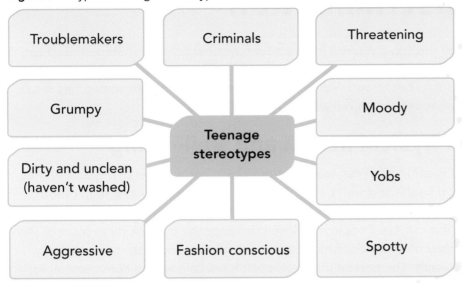

One example is when someone meets a mother pushing her teenage son in a wheelchair and speaks to the mother over the head of her son, talking about him as though he isn't there. That person has subconsciously labelled the son as someone who has mental problems and cannot speak for himself, i.e. labelled him as 'less able,' just because he is in a wheelchair.

Another example of this is when people talk to older people slowly, loudly and patronisingly because they assume they are deaf and are intellectually less able. This is stereotypical behaviour. Other examples are when it is assumed that male dancers are homosexual or that people from certain parts of the country are not very bright.

When groups of people are labelled as though they are all the same they lose their identity and assumptions are made about them. Some may even decide to behave as expected, feeling that they are not valued. For example, a student has friends at school who play truant. She is seen with them in school so the teacher accuses her of truanting as well. When this has happened a few times she might decide that she might as well truant as no-one believes her anyway. This is a self-fulfilling prophecy.

There has been an advert on the television where a woman drops her purse when a teenager walking with a group of friends bumps into her. He has piercings and a skinhead haircut. The young man bends down to pick up the purse, hands it straight back to the woman and apologises for bumping into her. She looks surprised. The viewers are meant to assume that he will steal it because he was in a group and looked different, so being **judgemental**.

Case study: Discrimination?

Freda is a dietitian and she lives with Shaun, who is a hospital porter. They are brother and sister. He has mild Down's Syndrome and is more than capable of doing the job. He is popular with the other staff and patients alike. He decides to apply for the head porter's job and is interviewed. However, despite having a really good interview, he does not get the job and one of the other porters, who he gets on well with, says to him that he knew he wouldn't get it because people like Shaun are lucky to get a job in the first place.

1. Why do you think Shaun didn't get the job?

2. How do you think this comment will affect Shaun?

3. Freda says this is because the person who conducted the interview had stereotyped Shaun. Do you agree with her? What label does she think he has been given?

4. What advice would you give Shaun?

Key term

Judgemental – making decisions or forming opinions on the basis of something such as appearance, without proper evidence, and being too critical

Just checking

1. What are the four types of discrimination?
2. Give an example of when you think it might be fair to discriminate in favour of a particular group.
3. What is the difference between stereotyping and labelling?

The effects of discrimination

In this topic you will learn about how being discriminated against can affect all aspects of a person's physical, intellectual, emotional and social health and well-being. This discrimination can sometimes result in abuse, which will also be referred to in this topic.

Physical health and well-being

Discrimination can lead to stress which has a range of physical effects on health and well being. These include sleeplessness, high blood pressure, ulcers, heart disease, headaches, diarrhoea, tension, eczema and asthma. People may lose their appetite or drink more alcohol than they normally do, which can have adverse effects on their physical health. The person might also self-harm as a way of communicating distress. Ultimately discrimination could lead to injury and death.

Intellectual health and well-being

Discrimination can cause anxiety and depression, which can cause someone to be distracted, lose concentration and interest in things they used to enjoy. It can also cause paranoia, a sense of not feeling safe and living in fear of others. Another effect of discrimination can be a feeling of not being worth anything, as well as a loss of confidence in a person's own abilities. All of these can lead to poor mental health.

Emotional health and well-being

Discrimination can cause nervous feelings, such as butterflies, as well as irritability, and can ultimately lead to depression (see below) and a nervous breakdown. It can give a person a feeling of low self-worth. A person in a hospital might be so emotionally upset and low by feeling discriminated against that they might not respond to treatment as well as they could have done otherwise.

Social health and well-being

A social effect of discrimination can be the person becoming withdrawn and not wanting to be with other people. Such a person may lose a sense of who she or he is. This can lead to social isolation, for example, when a child feels that the other children don't like her because of her looks, she may not want to go outside at playtime.

Depression

One result of discrimination can be depression, a complex medical condition which can include physical symptoms such as slower movement or speech, an increase or decrease in appetite and so weight, constipation and changes in the menstrual cycle and in sleep patterns. Social symptoms include a change in the way a person interacts with others, including avoiding contact with others and

Case study: Shamina

Shamina has a slight stammer which becomes worse when she is feeling nervous. She has been the victim of bullying by a group of girls in her year group at school, which started as teasing but has led to name calling as the bullies like it that they can make her stammer worse by doing this. Eventually they decide it will be fun to take this further and send her some nasty text messages. Shamina used to love school but now starts to invent illnesses so she can stay at home instead of facing the bullies at school. This encourages the bullies to send more text messages and messages over the Internet when she is not in school and this escalates into full scale cyber bullying

1. What effect will this have on Shamina's physical, intellectual, emotional and social needs?

2. How could Shamina deal with the situation?

3. Suggest the possible consequences of Shamina taking this action.

Activity

1. Using the information on pages 162–3, design and make a leaflet informing people about the different forms of abuse, the symptoms and who to go to for support, protection and advice. You will need to do some research to find more information to help you do this.

2. Find a recent case of discrimination which has led to abuse which has made the headlines. Research the facts about it on the Internet and in a group discuss (i) the effects of abuse on the person (ii) how you think the services concerned could have done things differently and better.

difficulties in home and family life, and psychological symptoms such as feeling tearful, guilty and intolerant of others, suicidal thoughts or thoughts of harming others, and feelings of hopelessness and helplessness.

Abuse

Discrimination can also lead to abuse. This can happen at all ages and happens against males or females, including disabled and older people.

There are several different forms of abuse:

- physical abuse, when someone is physically assaulted in some way

- sexual abuse, when someone interferes with a person's body in a sexual and unwanted way

- verbal abuse, when someone assaults a person verbally, such as insulting them and calling them names

- neglect, when a person is ignored or not given the help they need

- exclusion, when someone is stopped from getting help or is deliberately isolated

- avoidance, when someone deliberately avoids contact with another person

- devaluing, when someone ignores a person's ideas and opinions or denies him something others are allowed, so making him feel less valued.

Just as it is inappropriate for the service user to abuse the provider, so it is also inappropriate for a service provider to fail to protect a service user from abuse. The exception to this is when someone does not understand what they are doing, such as in the case of some mental illnesses.

Key term

Abuse – treating someone wrongly, harmfully or inappropriately

Just checking

1. List at least 5 physical effects of discrimination

2. Give an example of a possible (i) physical (ii) intellectual (iii) emotional and (iv) social effect on a person in a rehabilitation unit following a stroke who feels he is being discriminated against by a physiotherapist and becomes depressed.

3. Give an example of a possible (i) physical (ii) intellectual (iii) emotional and (iv) social effect on a child who is from a family of travellers, attending a new school and feels he is being discriminated against by other students.

Be non-discriminatory

Key term

Inappropriate – unsuitable

Discriminatory practice removes the service user's rights and can make it very hard for them to voice an opinion. To stop discriminatory practice from happening in health and social care environments, organisations should promote equality of opportunity by having relevant policies and procedures in place. This topic looks at non-discriminatory practice as the responsibility of both individual carers and the institution they work in, with both colleagues and service users.

Inappropriate behaviour

Discriminatory practice includes **inappropriate** behaviour which we all have a duty to challenge. All service providers have a responsibility to behave appropriately but, as care workers, they also have the right to be treated properly themselves. This is why zero tolerance posters now appear in places such as hospital reception desks, school offices and other public places.

Individual worker's responsibilities

When they join a health or social care service, each worker is provided with a handbook or the equivalent that contains policies and procedures for them to follow so that they know the right way to behave at work. Health and social care workers are expected to meet the needs of the individual service user by providing a service of equal quality but which meets their personal needs. This is not the same as everyone receiving the same service. For example, everyone should be able to register with a doctor but a sick person will take up more of the doctor's time.

Figure 6.5: Why should care workers always stay calm?

Did you know?

The European Court of Human Rights was set up in 1959 in Strasbourg, France. It has been sitting full time since 1998. The building is shaped like a ship and has large expanses of glass, designed to emphasise the accessibility of justice to all. It most often rules on the right of an individual to a fair trial.

Case study: David and Anna

David is a new care assistant in a residential home. He notices that another care assistant, Anna, who has worked there a long time, often speaks more severely to any resident who is different from her. She says things such as, 'I suppose I'll have to ask Cook to make sure she uses kosher meat for your meal, but it will make extra work for her' or, 'I don't see why I should let you have your meal at a different time just because you have to pray.' David doesn't think this is right and is worried about the effect on his working relationship with Anna if he says anything about it to her.

1. What would you do if you were David?
2. Explain what Anna's responsibilities are towards all the residents.
3. Role-play two different ways of dealing with the situation with two other students.

Working with colleagues

People often become good friends with people they work with but you won't always get on with everyone. Carers have a duty to challenge any discriminatory practice; it might be that the person concerned is not even aware of what they are doing and a quiet word can put it right. This might be difficult if the person is a friend and you might still need to take the matter further. There are several ways in which inappropriate behaviour can be challenged.

Step 1: Challenge the person yourself.

To do this you need to be assertive (see Unit 1). Ask to speak to the person and explain the problem but be aware that they will also have their story to tell. Ask another impartial or objective person to be present as a witness. State your case firmly but quietly and if they apologise or you come to an agreement then the matter is over. This is the best way because it is constructive and the person concerned does not get into trouble with anyone else. If they will not accept that they have acted inappropriately move to step 2.

Step 2: Follow the complaints procedure as stated in writing by law in every organisation or agency in any of the sectors.

This may mean filling in a form or getting someone to speak or write on your behalf (an advocate) if you are unable to do so; someone more senior than the service provider you are complaining about may then interview you. If you are still not satisfied by the outcome or result of this move to step 3.

Step 3: Take your appeal to the law.

Check the relevant legislation, and take your case to the European Court of Human Rights if necessary. If you have a case someone will help you pursue this but it's likely that you wil need legal advice: an organisation like the Citizen's Advice Bureau will help. There is more detail about the relevant legislation on page 179.

Working with service users

Carers must take responsibility and work with service users without discriminating against them. This can be done, for example, by allowing service users full input to their care, providing items such as translation facilities, making sure that service users have food that meets their dietary requirements and religious needs and essentially treating them with dignity and respect. Person-centred care is the essential key to a good working relationship between service users and their family and those who are caring and supporting them.

Just checking

1. How are individual workers usually informed of the way they are expected to behave?
2. What should a worker do if they see another worker displaying discriminatory behaviour?
3. What are the three steps that can be taken to challenge inappropriate behaviour?

Beyond the individual

Activity: Reflective practice tool

1. Think about a lesson or an educational visit you have enjoyed recently. Draw up a table with columns headed: Lesson or visit, what worked well, what did not work, what will I do differently next time?

2. Complete the table, thinking about the learning you took part in. This table is an example of a reflective practice tool.

3. Devise your own reflective practice tool for a receptionist at your doctor's surgery to use. Imagine some encounters he or she has with a variety of service users, in different moods, asking for prescriptions, appointments and help with a variety of problems. Think about how he or she might respond and enter some of them on your reflective practice tool.

In this topic you will continue to learn how health and social care organisations try to promote equality of opportunity by looking at non-discriminatory practice as the responsibility of the institution they work in, when working with both colleagues and service users.

Institutional responsibilities

It is the responsibility of the institution or organisation to make sure that service users and service providers feel safe and protected, so they can receive the help they need in the most supportive environment possible. The employer must therefore make sure that all employees follow non-discriminatory practices by putting in place policies and other procedures and making sure they are being used. Employers must also make sure that care workers treat service providers with respect. You will learn more about policies, legislation, codes of practice and charters later in this unit.

Reflective practice

Reflective practice is about learning from experience and is an important strategy for health and social care institutions to continue the professional development of their employees and improve the quality of care. It involves thinking about and critically analysing actions with the goal of improving professional practice. You will learn about this and its role in your choice of career in Unit 5.

Professional Development

Employers have to make sure that workers receive continued professional development (CPD) so that they keep up to date not only with new theories, treatments, procedures etc. but also anti-discriminatory practice. Methods of undertaking CPD include the following:

Induction

When someone starts a new job or moves to a new department they take part in an induction session or course. This introduces them formally to the workplace and teaches them all the policies, procedures and codes of practice that they need to follow in that particular place of work.

Mentoring

A person new to a job might be assigned a mentor. This is a trusted worker who can show them what to do and help them if they have any problems.

Work–based learning

This takes place when someone learns knowledge and skills while based in their workplace rather than in a school or college. For instance, you might have been on a period of work experience from school, or on a visit to a workplace, and will have learned aspects of the jobs that you would not have learned in a classroom. Another example would be someone working full time in a workplace as an apprentice who is taught the job as he goes along, by others in the workplace and also maybe by a trainer or tutor coming into the workplace. A surgeon will also learn new operating techniques and procedures by assisting and watching another surgeon use them.

Courses/qualifications

Employees can also develop their skills and knowledge by going on courses. Many one-day courses give the participants a certificate of attendance to prove they have completed the course. Longer courses might lead to the participant being assessed in some way to meet a required standard and, if they have done well enough they will gain a qualification. Health and social care workers are also expected to continue to learn and improve their practice after they have started the job so will be sent on courses as and when appropriate. This may be run in-house (within their own workplace) or by other professional bodies and organisations.

Sources of information for professional development

These include the induction, training courses, qualifications, work-based learning and mentors mentioned above. Other sources of information include:

- other colleagues in the same or similar service provider
- professional bodies which are organisations, usually non-profit making, that exist to further a particular profession. They maintain and enforce standards of training and ethics in their professions so protect both the public interest and the interests of the professionals
- Sector Skills Councils (SSCs) which are independent organisations developed by employers in industry. They work together to improve service provision. They are employer-led and involve trade unions and professional bodies. SSCs were set up by the government to tackle the skills and productivity needs of their sector throughout the UK
- professional journals and magazines containing articles on all aspects of that profession, as well as adverts for jobs and resources. Examples are *Nursery World* for nursery nurses and the GTC magazine for tutors.

Just checking

1. Why does the institution have responsibility for making sure employees follow anti-discriminatory practice?
2. Name three different types of CPD that employers can provide to make sure their employees follow good practice.
3. List five possible sources of information on professional development.

Materials and media

The communication and visual materials you use when working with service users should be varied to accommodate all preferences. The media also has a responsibility to promote non-discriminatory practice.

Materials

These materials include equipment, activities, visual displays, and toys and books that provide positive images of gender and race, all of which should avoid stereotyping.

- Equipment: for example, in a rehabilitation unit for people who have suffered brain injuries such as a stroke, equipment should cover a whole range of household jobs, and the patients, regardless of gender, should be encouraged to use it all. It might be that there is a washing machine and an iron and men as well as women should be taught how to use them, so that they do not learn, or relearn, stereotypical behaviour. There should equally be tools to use such as a hammer and nails, and again, people of both sexes should be encouraged to use them.

- Activities: these can include celebrating different religious festivals in a youth centre, depending on the various religions of the young people attending the group, so that when it is Ramadan, for example, they are all told what happens, and get the chance to try different foods.

- Visual displays: these need to show positive images and avoid stereotypes so a display in a day care centre could have pictures showing older people who are actively doing things like ballroom dancing and cycling. The displays should also celebrate the achievements of the different service users, so it might be that photographs are on display to show these achievements.

- Toys and books that provide positive images of gender and race: both sexes should be encouraged to play with all toys, such as the toy tea set. Books can show pictures of, for example, female tractor drivers and male nurses, and people who are from a variety of ethnicities and cultures.

The role of the media

The media include books, leaflets, newspapers, magazines, radio, television and the Internet. The media are excellent at passing on information very quickly to the rest of the world. They are very powerful in portraying images of particular groups.

- Books: these can be biased because they contain the author's or editor's opinions.

- Leaflets: many leaflets are very factual, designed to deliver a message about, for example, a certain illness, but their choice of words and pictures can also be very influential.

- Newspapers: millions of people read newspapers every day and they may influence us, with the headlines and the pictures they use.

- Magazines: these can influence, for example, young girls to think they have to be thin to be attractive because so many of the models they picture are very thin. More serious magazines may cover issues such as conservation issues and politics, but again it has to be remembered that the articles often contain the writers' opinions.

- Television and radio: television news tries to give a non-biased view of the stories covered and does it very well. Other programmes, such as documentaries, can stereotype issues positively or negatively and can influence viewers' opinions on a subject.

- Internet: Anyone can have a website so not all information on the Internet is factual. The website writers could be stating their opinions rather than facts, and even worse, could be pretending to be someone they are not.

BTEC Assessment activity 6.3

P3 M2 D1

Imagine you are a nursery manager and you have been asked to deliver a workshop on equal opportunities and non-discriminatory practice for all the staff, in a way that is different and interesting but makes the points clearly. Do this by:

1. drawing a comic strip that identifies and describes the factors that influence the equality of opportunity for individuals in society. Explain it to your group so your tutor can write a witness statement to say how you successfully explained it. Then write an explanation of the comic strip to go with it in your assessment folder.

2. producing a story board that outlines discriminatory practice, how it can be avoided and the effects on health and well-being. Talk your group through the ideas on your story board and then write a written report explaining your storyboard step-by-step to go in your assessment folder. For **D1**, include an assessment of the effects of discriminatory practice on an individual's physical, intellectual, emotional and social health and well-being.

Grading tips

By drawing the comic strip and explaining the factors you can achieve **P3**. By discussing how the discriminatory practice can be avoided you may be awarded **M2** and, if you assess the effects of these practices on a person's physical, intellectual, emotional and social health and well-being, you may gain **D1**. For **D1** you might find it helpful to review individual needs in Unit 3 on page 54.

Just checking

1. Suggest an activity that can be used in a nursery to encourage boys and girls not to be stereotyped.
2. Give an example of how books can influence children by showing stereotypes.
3. What are the dangers of books, magazines and the Internet?

Activity: Fact and suggestion

Collect articles from two different sources on the same item of news. How do they compare? Do they give the same impression? Highlight any actual facts in one colour and any suggestions in another colour.

Collect two articles about a health and social care issue, such as the latest claims as to whether a particular food is good for you or not. Again, highlight the facts and suggestions in different colours.

1. How does the difference in the way different papers portray a story make you feel?

2. Do the papers try to influence your feelings about a subject? Explain how they do it.

3. In a group discuss examples of where it is very wrong to mislead people by portraying a story with either a positive or negative slant.

PLTS

Using a comic strip and story board to present your information will involve you using your skills as a **creative thinker**. If you organise your time properly and meet the deadline you will have been a good **self-manager**.

Functional skills

If you produce either of the items using a computer you will have presented information that is fit for purpose and audience for the **ICT** functional skill and used speaking and listening for the **English** functional skill.

4. Know the role of legislation, codes of practice and charters

It is not possible to understand what rights means without also learning about responsibilities. In this topic you will learn what is meant by rights and responsibilities and begin to understand the rights of individuals in health and social care environments. The rights you will learn about are the right to be respected, treated equally and not discriminated against, treated as an individual and treated in a dignified way.

Rights and responsibilities

A **right** is something that a person feels is due to them, something that person feels is fitting for them to do. A **responsibility** is a burden of obligation. People have the right to have their own beliefs and lifestyles but no one has the right to damage the quality of other people's lives. This means that rights often come with responsibilities towards other people.

The easiest way to understand this is to consider a specific example. An adult has the right to drink alcohol, even though there is a danger of it damaging their health and shortening their life. However, the drinker might have a responsibility not to do anything that shortens his life because he has family responsibilities and he also has the legal responsibility not to drive while under the influence of alcohol so that he does not put other lives at risk.

Right to be respected

Respect for a person is of the utmost importance. This means to show consideration or regard or courtesy for someone and treat them properly. Even if a person has been convicted of a serious crime they should still be treated with respect. However, the service provider also has the right to be respected and, except in the case of someone who is mentally ill and unable to understand they are doing wrong, the service provider has the right to tell the service user that he is being disrespectful if he, for example, calls her names.

Right to be treated equally and not discriminated against

Equality means everyone having the same chance as everyone else to obtain or achieve something, for example access to a service they need.

Think about someone being cared for in a residential home. If the carer does not respect their views, and does not take them into account when helping the person, that individual will feel unhappy and have low self-esteem, which will affect their health and well-being and their growth and development. We should value and learn from these differences rather than treat people differently and discriminate against them because of their differences.

Treated as an individual

Everyone should receive a service of equal quality that meets his or her personal needs. This is not the same as everyone receiving the same service. Treating people as individuals, taking into account their different beliefs, abilities, etc. is crucial to caring for others. A service provider needs to acknowledge an individual's personal beliefs even if he or she does not share those beliefs. For example, if Manny is Jewish and only eats kosher food at home it is only right that he is given kosher meat whether he is in a care home or in hospital. This will make him feel that his identity has been valued and will hopefully help his sense of well-being and so aid rehabilitation or recovery. It is important that people have control of their own lives and workers in all care sectors aim to help people develop or maintain their independence.

Dignity

Another important aspect of being a service provider is to help people maintain their **dignity** so that they keep their self-respect. For example, a child at primary school who accidentally wets himself will be embarrassed if it is pointed out to everyone else. A good nursery teacher will simply take the child somewhere private, reassure him and get his clothes sorted out. This allows the child to maintain his dignity rather than feeling ashamed.

Key term

Dignity – feeling worthy of respect

Activity: Respecting the client

With a partner, write two scripts for a conversation between an occupational therapist, who helps people to overcome difficulties that arise after, for example, a stroke, and a client who is struggling to learn to walk again. The first one should ignore the rights of the service user to respect, equality, dignity and being treated as an individual. The second one should show how the occupational therapist would really treat the individual.

1. Describe the possible negative consequences for the service user of the first conversation.
2. Describe the possible positive effects on the service user of the second conversation.

Just checking

1. What is the difference between a right and a responsibility? Use an example of each in your explanation.
2. Explain why being given a service that meets your individual needs is not the same as you receiving the same service as everyone else.
3. How does being treated with respect give us dignity?

Feeling safe

Key term

Confidential – information that is secret. It has been entrusted to only the person to whom it has been communicated

Activity: Breaching confidentiality

Explain the possible consequences of the following breaches of confidentiality in each of the following situations.

1. A worker passes on information about when a person's family are going to be away on holiday to someone whose boyfriend is in prison but doesn't say that the 21 year-old son will be at home on his own.

2. A worker tells someone about a person who lives near him who has been mentally ill but now has the illness completely under control.

Individuals in health and social care environments also have the right to confidentiality. This includes the right to be allowed privacy, to be protected from danger and harm and allowed access to information about themselves.

Confidentiality

Health and social care workers have lots of information about people who use services. Think about the information your doctor has about you. This includes facts such as your full name, address, telephone number, date of birth and details of any illnesses, injections and treatments you have had. It also includes information you might have shared with him or her in conversation, such as worries about your weight, or an embarrassing problem, information about issues such as contraception, or even information about your family or friends. The information will vary depending on which service provider you are using but each will know a lot of **confidential** information about you. Imagine, therefore, the huge amount of information a service provider has. This information must be kept secure by health and social care workers unless there is a child protection concern.

Breaching or breaking confidentiality is inappropriate behaviour and can have many consequences; some of these are shown in the table below.

Table 6.1: Possible consequences of breaching confidentiality

Consequence	Service user might be:
Loss of trust	Less likely to say how they really feel or share a problem
Lower self-esteem	Likely to feel unvalued and as though they don't matter
At risk	Feeling their property and personal safety threatened
Loss of professional reputation	Feeling the provider is unprofessional
Law breaking	Likely to sue the provider
Discrimination	Treated differently by others

Privacy

In order to have dignity a person often needs privacy. Privacy means being free from intrusion or disturbance in your private life or affairs. For example, a person who can no longer look after himself and is in a residential care home will feel very upset if the carers walk into his room whenever they want to without knocking first. Having been used to the privacy of his own home for many years, the constant disturbance and lack of privacy will undermine his self-esteem and could make him feel he has lost his identity as an independent person in control of himself and his own actions.

Protected from danger and harm

Health and safety issues affect both service providers and users. Both have the right to be in a safe environment away from harm and there is considerable legislation around this issue. It is now part of a worker's daily routine to assess the safety of all situations.

There are times when it is appropriate to breach confidentiality in order to protect someone from danger and harm. Examples of this include if service users are at risk because they might harm themselves in some way; if they are a risk to the safety of others; or if they have broken, or are about to break, the law. Another example is when a care worker has to bring a manager up to date about a service user's situation as they may need to make a decision that affects that service user's care. It would therefore be inappropriate behaviour for a care worker to promise to keep everything confidential; they should explain that it might be necessary on occasions to pass the information on to an appropriate colleague or authority. For example, if there is a child protection concern a health or social care worker will need to be alerted.

Allowed access to information about themselves

The Data Protection Act 1998 includes giving individuals the right to be allowed access to information about themselves. This can reassure a service user, if they can see, for example, that nothing about their health is being kept a secret from them.

Did you know?

Privacy law is concerned with the protection and preservation of the privacy rights of individuals. More and more, governments and other public as well as private organisations collect large amounts of personal information about individuals for a variety of purposes. The law of privacy says what type of information may be collected and how this information may be used.

Figure 6.6: Data Protection Act 1998

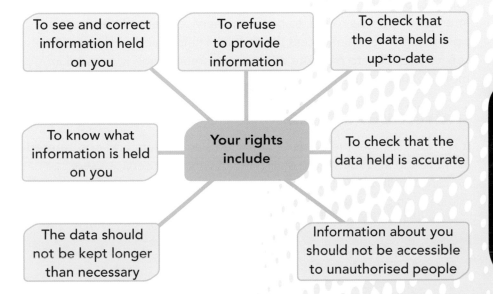

- To see and correct information held on you
- To refuse to provide information
- To check that the data held is up-to-date
- To know what information is held on you
- **Your rights include**
- To check that the data held is accurate
- The data should not be kept longer than necessary
- Information about you should not be accessible to unauthorised people

Just checking

1. Why is it so important for a service user to maintain confidentiality?
2. What does privacy mean?
3. How can keeping something confidential help protect an individual from danger and harm?

It's your choice

Key terms

Independence – freedom from the control and influence of others and from the need for their support; the ability to make your own decisions

Self-esteem – how a person feels about themselves and their abilities

Empower – enable someone to make decisions for themselves and take control of their lives

The individual rights covered in this unit include the right to be able to use their preferred methods of communication and language. It explores individuals being cared for in a way that meets the needs of service users, takes into account their choices, and protects them.

Choice

It is important that people have choice in their lives so they can maintain as much **independence** as possible. A person should be allowed access to their own personal information. For example, someone with a life-threatening illness should be given all the information so that they can make decisions about their own treatment. They might have a choice of undergoing treatment that will give them a few more months of life to spend with their family, but which could make them feel very ill during those extra months, or they might decide to choose not to receive the treatment and have a better quality of life for the short time they have left. Similarly, if a person wants to live on their own but has a disability they should have the choice to live in a residential home or live in their own home with carers going to help them each day. Giving a person as much choice and control over their lives as possible increases **self-esteem**.

Communicate using their preferred methods of communication and language

Service providers should communicate effectively with service users so that relationships can be formed to **empower** the users to feel that their opinions about their care are valued, that they are respected and that they can take part in decisions that affect their own care. It is therefore important that service users are allowed to communicate using their preferred method. For example, if someone is used to using British Sign Language then the service should find someone who can use BSL. Similarly, if someone does not speak English a translator or interpreter must be found, to cause the service user as little stress as possible and help him access the required help quickly. The need for service providers to promote effective communication is covered in more detail in Unit 1.

Individual rights

It is important that the rights of individuals are understood and catered for in health and social care environments and that service users can be cared for in a way that meets their needs, takes into account their choices and protects them.

Individual rights include being:

- respected
- treated equally and not discriminated against
- treated as an individual
- treated in a dignified way
- allowed privacy
- protected from danger and harm
- allowed access to information about themselves
- able to use their preferred methods of communication and language
- cared for in a way that meets their needs, takes into account their choices and protects them.

Responsibilities

Employers

It is the responsibility of employers to make sure their employees understand and protect the rights of individuals in their care, by producing codes of practice and other such guidelines. Employers must also make sure that employees follow the rules and that the employees have their rights met, by both the employer and the service users.

Employees

It is the responsibility of employees to make sure they acknowledge an individual's rights and care for them in a way that meets their needs, takes into account their choices and protects them. If they do this the employer will know that they can trust workers to do their jobs properly.

Activity: Emma's illness

Emma is 23 years old and yesterday she collapsed, breaking her leg as she fell. She was rushed into hospital with appendicitis, where they operated to remove her appendix and set her leg in plaster. She was very upset when she came round from the operation because she is a dancer and singer and will miss an important audition for a lead part in a pantomime. Emma is self employed and will not be able to earn her living while she is out of action, and is worried about paying her rent on the flat she shares with Georgina and Tiffany.

Look at the list showing an individual's rights. Describe how the nurses will treat Emma to help her recover while she is in hospital. Remember she has rights and physical, intellectual, emotional and social needs.

PLTS

You will use the skills of being a **reflective learner** and **creative thinker** by thinking about, and imagining, Emma's experience in the hospital and will be a **self-manager** by organising yourself so you complete and hand in the task in time.

Functional skills

When you read the information in the book and write in such a way as to communicate your ideas effectively, you are using **English** functional skills.

Just checking

1. Why is it important for service users to have some choice in their lives?
2. Give an example of how being able to communicate in a person's preferred way helps them to recover better.
3. What are (i) employers (ii) employees responsible for when looking after the rights of service users?

Know the role of legislation

Health and social care workers must protect and allow for the rights of individuals through their behaviour, attitudes and work. They are therefore provided with guidelines, which come in five main forms: conventions, legislation, codes of practice, policies and procedures to follow. This topic starts to look at the roles and impact of some of the conventions, legislation and regulations in health and social care environments.

Conventions

A convention is a set of agreed or generally accepted standards or norms, often taking the form of a custom. In simple terms it is an agreement as to how things will happen in a certain situation. For example, when people greet each other in a formal situation they will shake hands. An agreement between countries to obey the same law is known as a convention.

Legislation

Certain types of rules or customs may become law and legislation is introduced to make sure the convention happens. Legislation is a set of laws, as passed by Parliament. One example is the law that says we drive on the left-hand side of the road in the UK. If laws are broken, the person or service breaking them can be charged with a crime.

Regulations

Regulation means controlling behaviour by rules or restrictions. Regulations can be considered to be restrictions which lead to some sort of sanction, such as a fine, if they are broken.

European Convention on Human Rights and Fundamental Freedoms 1950

This convention granted:

- respect for human rights, such as liberty
- freedom from slavery, torture or forced labour
- the right to marry and have a family
- the right to life
- freedom of thought, religion and speech
- the right to a fair trial.

Mental Health Act 1983

The Act is designed to:

- protect individuals suffering from mental health problems
- protect society from individuals behaving dangerously as a result of their mental health problems.

It does this by allowing individuals to be **detained** in hospital against their will if they are mentally ill, or in prison if they have committed a crime.

The impact of this Act is to severely restrict an individual's freedom, to keep the community safe.

The Convention on the Rights of the Child 1989

This Convention aims to:

- provide the care and protection for children under the age of 18, whatever setting they live in, that adults do not need.

It says that:

- the child's best interests should be at the heart of the decision-making process concerning children
- the child should not be discriminated against
- the child should have freedom of speech
- the child has a right to survive and develop.

The Children Act 1989

This Act:

- provides children with the right to be protected from 'significant harm' whether from their parents or someone else
- puts into place minimum standards and regular inspections for nurseries and residential schools
- gives rights to children who have been cared for by social services to become independent and have access to information about their personal histories
- makes the rights of children paramount.

Race Relations (Amendment) Act 2000

This Act:

- gives public authorities a statutory general duty to promote race equality.

It aims to:

- make promoting race equality central to the way public authorities work; this includes schools
- eliminate unlawful racial discrimination
- promote equality of opportunity and good relations between people of different racial groups
- make schools improve the educational experience for all children, in particular those belonging to minority ethnic groups.

Activity: Legislation

Draw a mind map of the legislation covered so far on a large piece of paper

1. Which do you feel has had the most impact on the rights of individuals and why?
2. Do some more research into the Act or law you have just identified to find some more interesting facts to add to the brief detail given here.

Just checking

1. What do we mean by legislation?
2. What are the main points of the European Convention of Human Rights?
3. What is the dilemma that exists in the Mental Health Act 1983?

More Acts

This topic covers brief details of more conventions, legislation and regulations, namely the Disability Discrimination Act 1995 (extended 2005), Human Rights Act 1998, Data Protection Act 1998, Nursing and Residential Care Homes Regulations 1984 (amended 2002) and the Children Act 2004.

Figure 6.7: Why are inspections valuable?

Disability Discrimination Act 1995 (updated 2005)

This Act is designed to:

- ensure the rights of people with disabilities with regard to employment, access to education and transport, housing, goods, facilities and services

- make sure that disabled people are not discriminated against by service providers

- make sure service providers provide access for disabled people by making reasonable adjustments, such as adding a ramp or lift.

The 1998 Act was significantly extended and updated by the Disability Discrimination Act 2005 which gives disabled people rights in the areas of employment, education, access to goods, facilities and services, buying or renting land or property and the functions of public bodies.

Human Rights Act 1998

This Act:

- builds on the European Convention of Human Rights by taking it further

- **abolished** the death penalty in UK law

- makes it unlawful for any public body to break the convention

- requires UK judges to take account of the European Court of Human Rights in Strasbourg.

Data Protection Act 1998

This Act deals with how information about any living person is used (more details earlier in this unit – see page 173).

Nursing and Residential Care Homes Regulations 1984 (amended 2002)

These regulations:

- control the setting up and running of care homes

- inform homes of the procedures they must follow to ensure a safe environment

- require all homes to register with the local authority

- ensure that homes have enough staff to cater for the number of service users

- ensure residents have access to bathroom facilities, their own room and privacy

- require that all homes can produce a list of details of all their residents and all staff who work at the home at any one time.

The Children Act 2004

This Act:

- builds on the Children Act 1989 by setting out a new framework focused on the needs of the child, much of which came from the National Society for the Prevention of Cruelty to Children (NSPCC)

- organises agencies so that they all work together efficiently to benefit children

- makes sure children in care are educated as well as children living with their own families.

Key term

Abolish – get rid of

Activity: Acts, conventions and regulations

1. Add the details from this topic to the mind map you started at the end of the last topic.

2. What sort of person are all the Acts, conventions and regulations aimed at?

3. How useful do you think each of the Acts is?

4. Do some research to find out about any more recent legislation, such as the Care Standards Act 2000, and add it to your mind map.

Just checking

1. What is important about the Disability Discrimination Act 1995?

2. What did the Data Protection Act 1998 do for our rights?

3. Why are the Residential Care Homes Regulations 1984 (amended 2002) considered to be such an important piece of legislation?

More guidance

This last topic looks at charters, organisation policies, procedures and codes of practice. Some examples are the General Social Care Council/ Care Council for Wales/Northern Ireland Social Care Council codes of practice for social care workers and employers.

Charters

A charter is set out by the government and informs service users of their rights and what they can expect from **statutory** services. The NHS has a charter called 'Your Guide to the NHS' which was published in 2001. This charter:

- gives a clear guide to a patient's rights and responsibilities, and the national standards and services people can expect from the NHS now and in the future

- explains a patient's rights now and in the future under the NHS Plan. For example, from 2002 if an operation is cancelled on the day of surgery the hospital will have to offer another date within the next 28 days or pay for the treatment within this time in the hospital of the patient's choice

- underlines the responsibilities patients have towards the NHS as well as making clear the commitment the NHS has to its patients.

Many health centres and other organisations have charters to give service users information such as when they are open, how to complain etc.

Organisation policies

A policy is different from a code of practice in that it tells a service provider how to deal with a particular situation in his or her own workplace. Every service has its own policies, which depend on its specific needs and situation. Service providers have policies that cover areas such as positive promotion of human rights, work practices, staff development and training, quality issues and confidentiality.

Procedures

A procedure is a list of steps for a service provider to follow to complete a particular task in a certain way and is based on the value base. One example of a procedure that a nurse may follow is for a bed bath. The details will be set down so that, when followed correctly, the patient suffers as little embarrassment as possible.

Code of professional practice

All **professional bodies** and services should have a code of practice, sometimes called a code of conduct, which offers guidelines for people who work in that body or service to follow. An example of this, shown below, is an extract from the Nursing and Midwifery Council's Code of Practice:

Key term

Professional bodies – organisations that set standards for, and look after the interests of, their members, who all do one type of job. One example in the health sector is the Royal College of Nursing

Figure 6.8: Extract from the Nursing and Midwifery Council's Code of Practice

Code of Professional Conduct

As a registered nurse, midwife or health visitor, you are personally accountable for your practice. In caring for patients and clients, you must:

- respect the patient or client as an individual
- protect confidential information
- co-operate with others in the team
- maintain your professional knowledge and competence
- be trustworthy
- act to identify and minimise risk to patients and clients.

These are the shared values of all the United Kingdom health care regulatory bodies.

Any code of practice advises service providers on how to behave, not only to promote the individual rights of the service users, but also to protect themselves. It will also set out the standards of practice and conduct to be followed by those who work in the sectors.

General Social Care Council (GSCC)

The GSCC and similar bodies which exist for the rest of the United Kingdom (Care Council for Wales, Northern Ireland Social Care Council and the Scottish Social Care Council) were all set up on 1 October 2001 under legislation to regulate the social care profession:

- Care Standards Act 2000 in England and Wales
- Health and Personal Social Services Act 2001 in Northern Ireland
- Regulation of Care (Scotland) Act 2001 in Scotland.

They have codes of practice, policies etc. for social care workers and employers in a wide variety of formats such as Microsoft Word , PDF versions, foreign languages, large print, easy read, pictorial, Makaton and audio.

Case study: Colin

Colin is a personal trainer who helps people to get fit. He has decided to have a change of direction in his professional life by working with disabled children.

Colin gets a loan from the bank and starts to plan his own day care centre for disabled children where he can help them to get fitter and healthier.

1. Look at all the pieces of legislation and guidance covered in the last six pages. Which will affect Colin's plans? Draw up a table, with the title of the Act, Convention or Regulations in one column, and what he needs to do to comply with each one in the other column. For example, the Disability Discrimination Act 1995 means he will need to add a wheelchair ramp, among other things.

2. Draw up some floor plans for Colin's day care centre.

3. Think of a name and design a logo for the day care centre.

PLTS

This assessment task will help you to be an **independent enquirer**, **creative thinker**, **reflective learner** and **self-manager**. If you are allowed by your teacher to work in a group to share information you will also be able to practise being a **team worker** and an **effective participator**.

Functional skills

You will read, compare, select and understand texts and use them to gather information and write to communicate information, ideas and opinions effectively and persuasively, for **English** functional skills.

Just checking

1. What is a charter? Name an example.
2. How is a policy different from a code of practice?
3. Name the four Social Care Councils for the UK.

BTEC Assessment activity 6.4

Download a copy of a GSCC code of practice. Choose one piece of legislation that is relevant to social care. Look at your local authority's website and find out how they use the legislation and the code of practice.

Design and make a leaflet that shows how the legislation and code of practice supports the rights of the individual and so promotes diversity in your local area.

Write a report on the legislation and code of practice. In the report you need to:

- explain how well the legislation and code of practice promote diversity in your area
- describe how the legislation and code of practice promote diversity
- assess how effective the legislation and code of practice are in promoting diversity within your local social services.

Grading tips

In order to gain **P4** you need to write the report to go with the leaflet. If you complete the review you will move on to **M3** and the assessment will help you achieve **D2**.

Sheona Makin
Occupational therapist

I am an occupational therapist. My job is to help people learn to live as independent a life as possible when they have developed difficulties. They may have been born with a condition which causes problems, may have had an accident or illness or become less able due to ageing or as the result of a lifestyle. A patient might have been referred to me because, for example, he has had a brain injury or a stroke and has lost the use of part of his body.

At my first consultation with a patient I assess his condition and produce a report called a needs assessment. This summarises the patient's needs and includes an action plan. It identifies a series of steps the person needs to achieve to regain as much independence as possible. I then make a series of appointments to see my patient to work with, and advise, him so that he learns, for example, how to dress and wash himself with his disability. During this process I have to gain his trust and motivate him to overcome his difficulties as far as is possible.

Think about it!

1. What are the personal qualities an occupational therapist needs to be successful?
2. The most important initial obstacle to overcome is to gain the patient's trust. How could Sheona go about doing this?
3. This job involves, for example, patients being in a state of undress with the occupational therapist. What difficulties will Sheona have to tackle if the patient is (i) a Muslim (ii) a Sikh?
4. A patient recovering from a brain injury is finding it hard to come to terms with his disability. Some people he thought were his friends before the brain injury have not been in contact since his condition changed and he is very hurt by this. What could you say to make him feel better?
5. The same patient found his family to be very supportive while he was in hospital and rehabilitation but now he is back at home, his 12-year-old son has treated him with such hostility that the patient feels abused. What sort of abuse is this and how can Sheona advise him to cope with the situation?

Extension activity

Asif is 49 years old and has just lost his job as manager of a section in social services. He has never been out of work before and is very depressed about this. The situation is worse because he suspects he was made redundant because his recently appointed boss might be racist. Asif thinks this because of comments his boss made about Muslims' jobs in this country when he thought Asif could not hear. Asif was born and educated in the UK and got his manager's job through hard work and study. He is anxious and depressed, feeling he is letting his family down and that he will never get another job. He starts to get headaches and, unknown to him, his blood pressure has risen. Asif is worried about how he will support his son, who has just started university, and becomes very withdrawn and reluctant to go out. He is claiming benefits but is very unhappy about having to do so.

1. What do you think Asif should do about his suspicions of his boss?
2. What is worrying Asif so much about the situation he finds himself in?
3. What effect is (i) Asif's redundancy and (ii) feeling that he is being discriminated against having on his health and well-being?
4. What can his wife and son do to help Asif in this stressful situation?
5. If his boss *has* been racist, how does this affect Asif's rights?
6. What are his employer's responsibilities towards Asif?
7. What legislation exists to protect Asif?

Assignment tips

- You can carry out any plans and investigations in small groups but you must remember that any final evidence presented for assessment must have been produced by you as an individual.

- The BBC website has a very useful section for researching the beliefs and practices of different religious groups. To obtain a secure link to this website, see the Hotlinks section on page x.

- Other useful resources for understanding the issues covered in this unit include newspapers, magazines and television soap operas.

- Organise a trip to a place of worship that is different from one you might be familiar with.

- Having different speakers, for example, from the Citizen's Advice Bureau or a law firm which can give further information and understanding on legislation or discrimination, may help you to explore these complex areas.

Credit value: 10

7 Anatomy and physiology for health and social care

This unit is designed to enable you to develop a knowledge and understanding of the way the body works, the systems within the body and the processes that are necessary to keep us alive. This unit also provides an introduction to the organisation of the body and the major organ systems, and how the systems work together in order to help the body to function healthily. In addition you will learn about routine measurements that are made on service users in health and social care settings, and why they are carried out. Finally you will investigate the potential malfunction of body systems and the care service users receive when this occurs.

Learning outcomes

After completing this unit you should:

- know the organisation of the human body
- understand the structure, function and interrelationship of major body systems
- be able to carry out routine measurements and observations of body systems
- know the effects of malfunctions on body systems
- know routine care given to individuals with body malfunctions.

Assessment and grading criteria

This table shows you what you must do in order to achieve a **pass**, **merit** or **distinction** grade, and where you can find activities in this book to help you.

To achieve a **pass** grade the evidence must show that you are able to:	To achieve a **merit** grade the evidence must show that, in addition to the pass criteria, you are able to:	To achieve a **distinction** grade the evidence must show that, in addition to the pass and merit criteria, you are able to:
P1 Identify the organisation of the human body and the position of the main body organs (IE2, IE3, SM2, SM3, SM5) **Assessment activity 7.1, page 191**		
P2 Illustrate the structure and function of two major body systems and how they interrelate (IE2, IE3, CT1, CT5, CT6, SM2, SM3, SM5) **Assessment activity 7.2, page 209**	**M1** Discuss, for each system, how its structure helps it to carry out its functions **Assessment activity 7.2, page 209**	**D1** Explain how systems interrelate to maintain homeostasis **Assessment activity 7.2, page 209**
P3 Carry out routine measurements and observations used to monitor the two body systems (IE2, IE3, RL2, RL3, TW1, TW2, TW4, TW5, TW6, SM2, SM3, SM5, EP1, EP4, EP5) **Assessment activity 7.3, page 215**		
P4 Outline a common malfunction in each of the two body systems (IE2, IE3, RL2, RL3, TW1, TW2, TW3, TW4, TW5, TW6, SM2, SM3, SM5, SM6, EP1, EP3, EP5) **Assessment activity 7.4, page 223**	**M2** Describe how the presence of the malfunction might affect routine measurements and observations of each body system **Assessment activity 7.4, page 223**	
P5 Identify potential risk factors for each of the two malfunctions (IE2, IE4, SM2, SM3, SM5) **Assessment activity 7.5, page 225**		
P6 Identify the routine care given for each malfunction (IE2, IE3, RL2, RL3, TW1, TW2, TW4, TW5, TW6, SM2, SM3, SM5, EP1, EP4, EP5) **Assessment activity 7.6, page 228**	**M3** Describe the routine care for each malfunction **Assessment activity 7.6, page 228**	**D2** Explain how the routine care given for each malfunction affects the body systems **Assessment activity 7.6, page 228**

How you will be assessed

This unit will be assessed by an internal assignment that will be written and marked by the staff at your centre. The assignment is designed to allow you to show your knowledge and understanding of the unit outcomes. These relate to what you should be able to do after completing this unit.

Your assessment could be in the form of:

- presentations
- case studies
- practical tasks with witness statements
- written assignments.

James, Health and Social Care learner

I have really enjoyed this unit because eventually I'd like to work with the Ambulance Service. Learning about anatomy and physiology helped me when I was on my first placement at a nursing and residential home because I could understand a bit about what was wrong with some of the residents. It was much easier to see the reasons why some of the treatments were being given and the staff I was working with were really good about explaining things when I asked them. They also explained how important it is to observe the residents as you can tell a lot about how they are just by looking at them and talking to them.

At college we took lots of measurements with our tutor's help and got the chance to get used to using all of the equipment. Some people thought it was difficult to take pulses because they weren't always feeling in the right place on the wrist. It was useful using paperwork to practise recording the results we got so we could check that we were doing it right.

I was allowed to observe lots of care being given on placement and it was good to see the care that every service user received to help relieve the symptoms of a complaint or make them better. Every service user was treated like a person and the measurements and observations recorded meant that progress could be monitored and treatment and care changed if necessary. If my Nan needed care I'd like her to go to a home like the one where I did my placement. I think she'd be happy there.

Over to you!

- In this unit you will be studying the structure and functions of eight body systems. See if you can identify the eight systems and what each one does.

- When you have done this, try and identify one malfunction that could affect each system.

1. Know the organisation of the human body

Activity: Your inheritance

What colour are your hair and eyes? How tall are you? Do you resemble other members of your family? Think about your parents, grandparents and brothers and sisters. Who is alike in looks and behaviour, and who is very different? Can you work out what each of your relatives has inherited from the others?

Key term

Permeable – allowing gases or liquids to pass through

Walking, studying, playing sport; even watching the TV or chatting on Facebook… your body has to carry out many activities every day so that you can do everything you need to do. You are not aware of many of the things that it does as it all happens automatically. However, every part of the body needs to be working so that you can do all the things you need to do.

Organisation

Cells

The human body is made up of millions of tiny cells that can only be seen under a microscope. They vary in size and shape and have different functions, but every cell in the body has three features in common:

- the cell membrane, which is the outer covering of the cell
- the nucleus, which controls the cell's activities
- cytoplasm, a fluid-like material.

One of the substances in the nucleus is DNA. This is the material that provides all the information about your genetic make-up that you have inherited from your parents and grandparents. This will determine things like the colour of your eyes and hair and will influence how tall you will be.

As an embryo grows in the uterus, its new cells will develop differently depending on what part of the body they will become and what functions they will perform. For example, some will become muscle cells and others will become nerve cells. This means that they will look and act very differently. It doesn't matter what function each cell has, they all need oxygen and food in the form of glucose so that they can release the energy they need.

Figure 7.1: A single cell from the human body

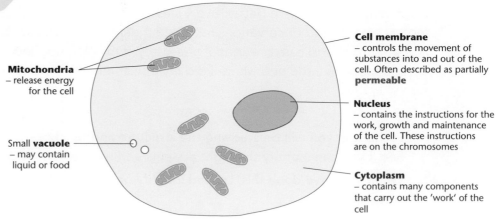

Mitochondria – release energy for the cell

Small **vacuole** – may contain liquid or food

Cell membrane – controls the movement of substances into and out of the cell. Often described as partially **permeable**

Nucleus – contains the instructions for the work, growth and maintenance of the cell. These instructions are on the chromosomes

Cytoplasm – contains many components that carry out the 'work' of the cell

Figure 7.2: Different cells develop and carry out different tasks

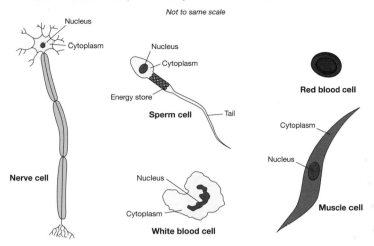

Tissues

Cells group together to form **tissues**. A tissue is a group of cells of the same structure that perform the same function. An example is skin tissue, which is made up of lots of skin cells. They all work together to provide a waterproof protective covering for the internal organs of the body. Another example is heart muscle, which is strong enough to beat for a whole lifetime.

Organs

Organs are made up of different tissues that work together to carry out a particular function. An example is the heart, which is made up of different types of tissue. The heart muscle pumps blood round the body, but it has its own system of blood vessels too: arteries to deliver oxygen and nutrients to the muscle, and veins to remove carbon dioxide from it. There may be several different organs in one whole body system.

Systems

A system is made up of different tissues and organs working together to perform a specific function in the body. The organs of the digestive system include the oesophagus, stomach, liver, pancreas and large and small intestines; the organs of the excretory system include the kidneys, two ureters, a bladder and a urethra.

Many of the organ systems need to work together to help the body perform effectively.

Just checking

1. What is the difference between a cell and a tissue?
2. As a group, research the structure and function of different body cells. You could each research one different type of cell. The diagrams above should start you off. Make sure that you have included as many of the different structures in each cell as you can. When you have done this, pool your research results and create a large poster with diagrams as a quick reference guide.

Key term

Tissues – a distinct type of material made up of specialised cells which have specific roles in the body

Did you know?

The skin is the largest organ in the body, providing waterproof protection to all the organs and systems. The liver is the largest internal organ in the body.

Activity: Organs and systems

Make a list of as many organs or organ systems as you can. Then get together with two or three classmates and see how many you come up with. If you have been able to identify different organs, see if you can decide which systems they belong to.

Location of organs: is your heart in the right place?

The body has evolved to do all the things we need it to do. Each organ has its own place in the body and usually everyone's heart, lungs, stomach and brain are in the same place.

Figure 7.3: The location of organs in the body

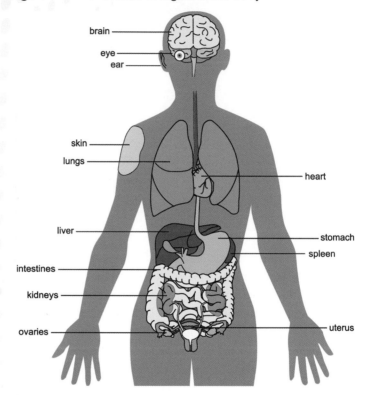

If you think about what the organs are made up of, you will realise that many of them are quite soft and need to be protected from damage. The most important ones are protected by parts of the skeleton: the brain is protected by the skull, and the heart and lungs by the ribcage and other bones.

Table 7.1 The organs of the body, their system and functions

Organ	System and Function
Skin	Acts as waterproof protection, organ for sense of touch. Helps us to cool down through perspiration.
Heart	Cardiovascular or circulatory system – maintains oxygen supply Pumps blood round the body delivering oxygen to the cells and removing carbon dioxide.
Lungs	Respiratory system – maintains oxygen supply Tiny air sacs at the end of the passageways in the lungs allow oxygen that is breathed in to enter the blood stream and carbon dioxide to leave the bloodstream so it can be breathed out.
Brain	Nervous system – receives information from the environment The brain sits inside the skull, which protects it.
Eyes	Nervous system There are two eyes either side of the front of the skull. They lie in the orbits – bony sockets that protect them.

Ears	Nervous system There are two ears, one on each side of the skull. The outer ear is the only part of the ear that is visible.
Stomach	Digestive system – digests food materials in the body This is in the upper part of the abdomen.
Pancreas	Digestive and endocrine systems The pancreas is situated on the left side of the abdominal cavity just below the stomach.
Intestines	Digestive system There are small and large intestines. They are in the lower part of the abdomen below the stomach.
Liver	Digestive system Situated on the right side of the abdomen next to the stomach.
Kidneys	Excretory or renal system – eliminates waste products from the body There are two kidneys, one each side of the spine at the back of the abdomen.
Bladder	Excretory or renal system The urinary bladder is situated in the pelvis behind the pubic bone, which protects it from damage.
Ovaries and testes	The reproductive system – enables men and women to reproduce Women have two ovaries in the pelvis, one on each side of the uterus. Men have two testes, situated in the scrotum behind the penis.
Uterus	The reproductive system The uterus is in the pelvic cavity (below the abdominal cavity) in women. The bladder lies in front of it and the large intestine behind it.

BTEC Assessment activity 7.1

Produce a set of annotated diagrams, identifying the location of the main organs and tissues in the body.

To achieve **P1**, you need to show your understanding of how the body is organised. You must explain what cells, tissues, organs and systems are. In addition, you need to take some time to learn where the main organs are. You have already done an activity where you have drawn organs onto a body shape. Draw another body shape and draw the main organs in the right place. The organs you should be able to locate are listed in Table 7.1.

Grading tip

To help you learn and understand where the organs are located, work with a partner and describe the position of the different organs to each other.

PLTS

This involves reviewing work that you have already completed and testing what you have learned, which will help you to develop skills as a **reflective learner**. You will also have the chance to work with other people to develop your ability as a **team worker**. The presentation of your completed work as a clearly annotated diagram will show that you are becoming a **creative thinker**.

Functional skills

If you decide to complete this activity as an annotated diagram, you should make sure that you check your **English** carefully, including spelling, grammar and punctuation. You might want to complete any writing using **ICT** skills so that you can make corrections, or write the labels in pencil first.

Just checking

1. Which system is the skin a part of? Why is it part of this system?
2. What is the function of the ovaries and testes?
3. Look back at the information on cells and find out how the red blood cell is adapted to carrying oxygen.

2. Understand the structure, function and interrelationship of major body systems

Key term

Cardio – to do with the heart

The cardiovascular system

Most people would say that the **cardio**vascular or circulatory system is one of the most important systems in the body because without it we cannot survive. The two main roles of this system are:

- to maintain oxygen supply to all parts of the body and to help get rid of carbon dioxide (a waste product)
- to transport materials such as glucose to the cells

The heart

The heart is about the size of an adult fist. It is made up of specialised cardiac muscle and is known as a double pump because each side of the heart works separately – the right side pumps blood from the heart to the lungs and the left side pumps blood from the lungs via the heart to the rest of the body. It has four chambers: two upper atria and two lower ventricles. It also has special valves that make sure the blood always pumps in the right direction. The muscle of the heart is specialised because it needs to be strong enough to beat every day for the whole of a human lifespan. The heart also has its own pacemaker (the sino-atrial node), which sends electrical impulses to make sure the heart maintains a regular heartbeat.

The blood

Plasma is the liquid part of the blood and different types of blood cells are suspended in it. Red blood cells or erythrocytes contain haemoglobin, a protein that carries oxygen and makes the cells red. White blood cells or leucocytes help to fight infection. Platelets or thrombocytes are fragments of blood cells that produce enzymes that help with blood clotting.

Blood vessels

Blood has to deliver oxygen to all parts of the body so it needs an efficient transport system in which to do this. This transport system is a bit like a road system with different sized vessels. There are three different types of vessels – arteries, veins and capillaries.

Figure 7.4: The circulatory system

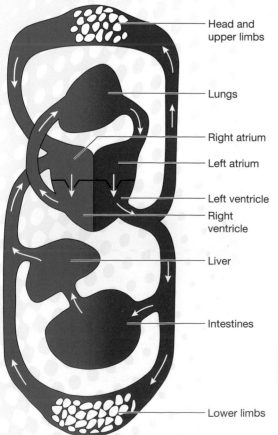

Head and upper limbs

Lungs

Right atrium

Left atrium

Left ventricle

Right ventricle

Liver

Intestines

Lower limbs

Table 7.2 Different types of blood vessels

Arteries	Usually carry oxygen rich blood away from the heart
Veins	Usually carry carbon dioxide rich blood to the heart
Capillaries	These are so small that only one red blood cell at a time can pass through them. The thinness of the walls means that it is easy for oxygen and nutrients to move out of them and waste products such as carbon dioxide to move into them.

Figure 7.5: The heart is a double pump and has to last a lifetime

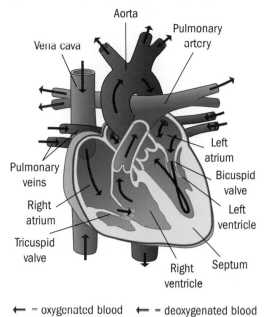

← = oxygenated blood   ← = deoxygenated blood

Blood circulation

Carbon dioxide rich blood arrives in the right atrium of the heart and is pushed into the right ventricle, which pushes the blood into the pulmonary artery. It goes to the lungs where gas exchange takes place. Carbon dioxide leaves the blood and moves into the lungs and oxygen leaves the lungs and moves into the blood. The blood is now oxygen rich and travels back to the heart and through the left atrium and left ventricle. The ventricle forces blood into the aorta, which takes the blood to all parts of the body. The oxygen is delivered to the cells and carbon dioxide is collected from the cells and taken back to the heart for the whole process to start again.

In some people the electrical conduction of the heart doesn't work properly and the heart beats too slowly, too quickly or irregularly. This can reduce the quality of someone's life or may even be life-threatening. In such cases, a battery-operated artificial pacemaker can be inserted under the skin of the patient. It is about the size of a matchbox and is set to maintain the heartbeat at a regular rate. About 25,000 people in the UK have pacemakers fitted every year.

Just checking

1. Explain what the different types of blood cells do.
2. Describe the journey of one red blood cell, arriving at the entrance to the right atrium and completing a whole circuit around the body.
3. Find out more about the different parts of the heart such as the atria, ventricles, valves and the 'pacemaker' (the sino-atrial node).

Major body systems 2

The main function of the respiratory system is to maintain the supply of oxygen in the body and to remove the waste carbon dioxide. It is rather like the way a car engine works: it is filled up with petrol which mixes with air to start the engine and the exhaust fumes are the waste product. Oxygen and food are the body's fuel and carbon dioxide is the waste that needs to be removed from the body.

The respiratory system

Air is breathed in through the mouth and nose where it is warmed and moistened. The nose is lined with cilia – microscopic hair-like structures that help to filter the air and prevent the entry of dust and debris into the respiratory organs. The air passes down the throat and through the larynx and trachea. The trachea branches into two bronchi and one bronchus goes to each lung; each bronchus branches into bronchioles (smaller air passageways) which end in sacs called alveoli.

Figure 7.6: The respiratory system

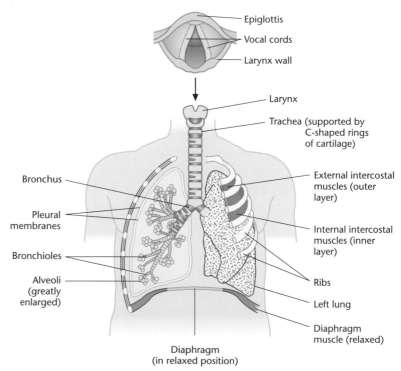

Two important structures in the respiratory system are the larynx and lungs.

The larynx

The larynx is the structure between the throat and the trachea. It has two very important functions. At the top of the larynx there is a small leaf-shaped flap of cartilage called the epiglottis that closes over the entrance to the larynx to stop you choking when you swallow food.

There are also two membranes in the larynx called the vocal cords. These vibrate as air passes over them and this produces the sound that enables us to speak.

The lungs

There are two lungs in the body: these work to provide us with the oxygen we need and to remove the carbon dioxide that we create as waste in the body. They are made up of a network of tubes that look a bit like a tree in winter. At the end of the smallest tubes are the alveoli where gas exchange takes place. There are about 300 million alveoli in your lungs.

Gaseous exchange takes place by a process called **diffusion**. In the alveoli there is a high concentration of oxygen and a low concentration of carbon dioxide. In the capillaries there is a high concentration of carbon dioxide and a low concentration of oxygen. The process of diffusion allows the oxygen to move out of the alveoli and into the capillaries and the carbon dioxide to move out of the capillaries into the alveoli.

Figure 7.7: Gaseous exchange in the alveoli

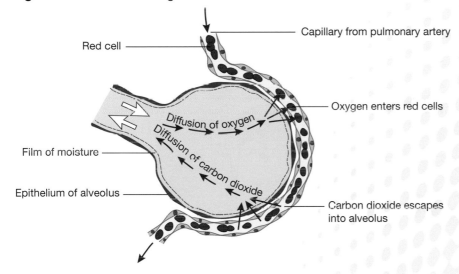

Red cell
Capillary from pulmonary artery
Oxygen enters red cells
Diffusion of oxygen
Diffusion of carbon dioxide
Film of moisture
Epithelium of alveolus
Carbon dioxide escapes into alveolus

The mechanism of breathing

During breathing, the chest moves as the lungs inflate and deflate; a number of things happen to allow this. During breathing in, or inhalation, the **intercostal** muscles, which are between the ribs, pull the ribcage upwards and outwards. The diaphragm, which is a sheet of muscle separating the chest and the abdomen, flattens and the lungs inflate. During breathing out, or exhalation, the reverse happens – the lungs deflate, the diaphragm lifts into a dome shape and the intercostal muscles pull the ribcage downwards and inwards.

Key terms

Gaseous exchange – when the body takes in oxygen and gets rid of (expels) carbon dioxide

Diffusion – the net movement of molecules from an area of high concentration to an area of low concentration

Intercostal – between the ribs

Just checking

1. Find out how many litres of air the lungs can hold.
2. Find out what percentages of oxygen and carbon dioxide there are in inhaled and exhaled air.
3. Revise what you have learned in this section about respiration. Using diagrams, explain the mechanism of respiration.

Major body systems 3

Your nervous system is divided into two parts: the central and the peripheral nervous system. The central nervous system is made up of the brain and the spinal cord. The peripheral nervous system is all the nerve fibres that connect to the central nervous system. Both systems receive information from the environment about what is happening to the body, which they process and respond to by sending messages to the nerve cells.

The nervous system

The brain

The brain is the control centre for the body. It receives and interprets impulses from sense receptors in the body and sends impulses to make muscles and glands work. The brain co-ordinates the body's movements and allows it to function efficiently. It controls feeding, sleeping, temperature regulation and salt and water balance in the body. It stores information in the memory and deals with emotional and intellectual processes.

Figure 7.8: The brain

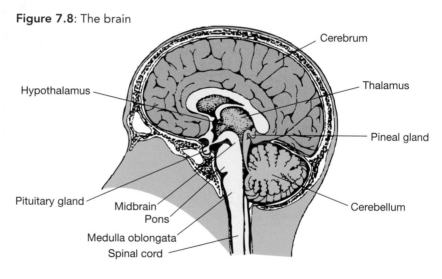

Table 7.3 The four main parts of the brain

The **brain stem** (midbrain, pons and medulla oblongata)	Controls involuntary reflex actions
The **cerebellum**	Maintains posture and co-ordinates movement. It receives messages from the cerebrum and muscles and joints
The **diencephalon** (includes the thalamus and hypothalamus)	Controls homeostatic mechanisms and the autonomic nervous system
The **cerebrum**	The largest part of the brain, divided into three areas that control movement, interpret sensory impulses and control thought, memory, emotions and personality traits

The brain acts like a control centre for the rest of the body, detecting changes and responding to them.

The spinal cord is a long cylindrical organ that runs inside the vertebrae. The spinal canal has a central cavity containing cerebrospinal fluid. Thirty one pairs of nerves branch off the cord to provide nerve supply to the whole of the body.

Nerves

Nerves are made up of nerve cells or neurones. They vary in structure according to where they are or what they do, but all cells have a cell body containing the nucleus.

If you touch a hot radiator, a message will go to your brain and you will know that the radiator is hot: you have a receptor at the end of every sensory neurone which transmits a message to your brain about what you are feeling.

The ends of your motor neurones are attached to muscles so when the impulse sent from a sensory neurone is translated by a motor neurone, you will move your hand away if the radiator is too hot.

The autonomic nervous system

The autonomic nervous system works without us being aware of it. It is responsible for many processes that happen all the time, such as maintaining homeostasis and blood pressure. There are two parts to the autonomic nervous system – the sympathetic and parasympathetic nervous systems.

In an emergency the sympathetic nervous system takes over, influenced by the action of adrenaline. The result of this is raised heartbeat and breathing, sweating and a dry mouth. This is known as the 'fight, fright or flight' response.

The parasympathetic nervous system is the system that is in control most of the time when we are relaxed. It slows heart rate and breathing and helps us to digest food after a meal.

The sympathetic and parasympathetic nervous systems are the two parts of the autonomic nervous system that keep the body working without us being aware of it.

Did you know?

Some nerve cells are longer than any other cells in the body. One nerve may stretch from your brain almost to the end of your spinal cord. Another reaches from there down to your foot. It is thought that there could be as many as 1,000,000,000,000 neurones in the body.

Figure 7.9: Different types of nerve cells

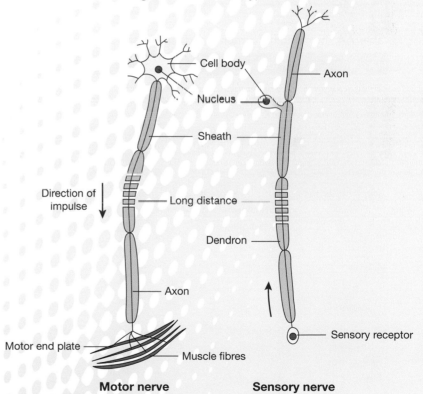

Motor nerve **Sensory nerve**

Just checking

1. Which part of your brain allows you to remember what happened yesterday?
2. Explain to a fellow learner what the reflex arc is and how sensory and motor neurones behave in response to a stimulus.

Major body systems 4

This topic will look at the role of the endocrine and digestive systems.

The endocrine system

The endocrine system produces chemical messengers called hormones: these are released directly into the bloodstream by glands and have various roles in the body.

Adrenaline

Adrenaline is secreted in times of emergency or stress and produces specific reactions in the body:

- stored glycogen in the liver is converted into glucose to provide energy
- the rate and depth of breathing, and the heart rate, increase
- blood is diverted to the brain and muscles from other parts of the body.

Once the emergency is over adrenaline stops being secreted and the body returns to normal, though people may shake for some time afterwards.

Table 7.4 The different hormones and their roles

Organ	Hormone	Process
Pituitary gland	Trophic hormones Somatotrophic (growth) hormones Prolactin Luteinising hormone (LH) Follicle stimulating hormone (FSH)	Stimulates production of hormones from other glands. Stimulates growth of long bones in limbs Stimulates milk production Triggers ovulation, controls menstrual cycle and sex hormones from testes Controls menstrual cycle, starts ripening of ova, assists in control of sperm production
Hypothalamus	Hormone releasing factors Anti-diuretic hormone (ADH) Oxytocin	Stimulates pituitary gland to produce hormones Controls water balance Helps uterine contraction in childbirth and stimulates the let-down reflex for breast feeding
Thyroid gland	Thyroxine	Controls rate of body processes, controls heat and energy production from food, controls growth and development of the nervous system
Pancreas	Insulin	Controls blood sugar
Adrenal glands – situated above the kidneys	Adrenaline Cortisol Aldosterone Androgens	Controls emergency action, response to stress Controls conversion of fats, proteins and carbohydrates to glucose Acts on the kidneys to control salt and water balance Stimulates male sex hormones and characteristics (beard growth, deepening of voice, muscle development)
Testes	Testosterone	Controls sperm production and growth and development of male features at puberty (e.g. beard growth)
Ovaries	Progesterone Oestrogen Placental hormones (pregnancy)	Helps control normal progress of pregnancy. Interacts with FSH, LH and oestrogen to control the menstrual cycle Controls the development of female features at puberty. Interacts with FSH, LH and progesterone to control menstrual cycle Controls normal progress of pregnancy. Oestrogen and progesterone start milk production

The digestive system

Digestion includes four processes: ingestion, digestion, absorption and elimination.

Ingestion and digestion

Digestion begins in the mouth: the teeth cut and grind food into small particles that can be swallowed in the saliva, carbohydrates start to break down. Food moves down the oesophagus to the stomach. Muscles along the whole of the digestive tract automatically to push food onwards. This is known as peristalsis.

After about five hours in the stomach, the mixture of food and enzymes, moves into the small intestine. Here, digestion continues over the next four hours (roughly). Carbohydrates are broken down into glucose, proteins into amino acids and fats are **emulsified**.

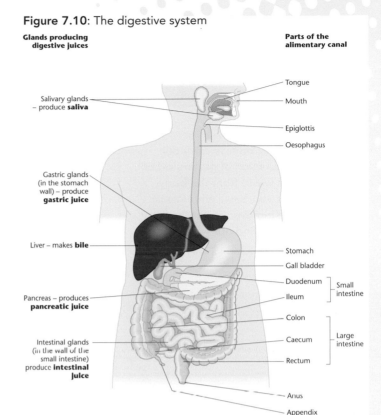

Figure 7.10: The digestive system

Table 7.5 Enzymes and their role in digestion

Mouth	Salivary amylase	Starts to break down carbohydrates
Stomach	Hydrochloric acid	Kills bacteria and converts pepsinogen to pepsin
	Pepsin	Begins digestion of protein
	Rennin	Curdles milk
	Intrinsic factor	Helps body to absorb Vitamin B12
Small intestine	In pancreatic juice: Amylase	Converts starch to maltose
	Lipase	Converts fats to fatty acids
	Trypsin and chymotrypsin	Converts proteins to peptides
	In intestinal juice:	
	Maltase	Converts maltose to glucose
	Sucrase	Converts sucrose into glucose and fructose
	Lactase	Converts lactose into glucose and galactose
	Peptidases	Converts peptides into amino acids
From the liver	Bile	Emulsifies fats

Absorption and elimination

In the small intestine, nutrients can be absorbed through the gut wall and into the blood. After about seven to nine hours, food that has not been digested moves into the large intestine. Water is absorbed into the body, leaving behind faeces, a semi-solid mass that is eventually eliminated at the end of the digestive tract, via the anus.

Key term

Emulsify – to disperse the particles of one liquid evenly in another

Did you know?

Adrenaline may help to suppress pain in an emergency (though not usually for very long). Other effects of adrenaline include heightened senses, dry mouth, pale face and clammy hands.

Just checking

1. Draw an outline of the body and position all the endocrine glands on it.
2. Identify the organs of the digestive system and explain their functions.

Major body systems 5

The body carries out chemical processes known as metabolism. During metabolism waste products are produced: carbon dioxide, water and urea. These cannot be used and may be harmful to the body. The excretory system filters waste products from the blood and eliminates them from the body.

The excretory system

The main part of the excretory system is the renal system. This consists of:

- two kidneys – bean-shaped structures which lie either side of the vertebral column and are about the size of an adult fist. The right kidney is slightly lower than the left kidney, to make room for the liver which is on the right side of the body

- two ureters – tubes about 3 mm in diameter and 25-30 cm long that carry urine from the kidneys to the bladder

- one bladder – a muscular bag that collects urine. It can hold about 500 ml of urine and is situated in the pelvic cavity

- one urethra – a tube leading from the bladder to the outside of the body through which urine is expelled. The male urethra is 18–20 cm long; this is much longer than the female urethra, which is only 4–6 cm long

Figure 7.11: The renal system

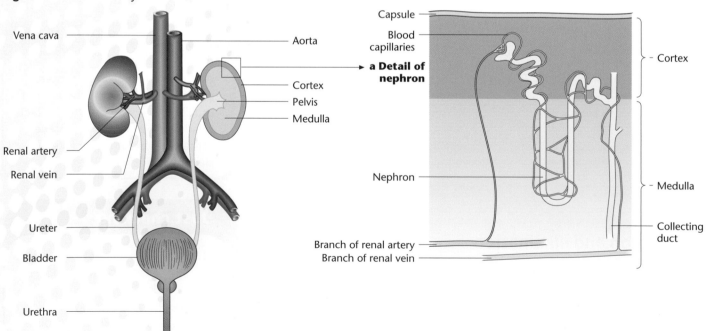

Each kidney is supplied with blood by a renal artery, which branches off the aorta (the main artery of the body). Filtered blood is returned to the vena cava, the main vein of the body, via a renal vein.

In each kidney there are about one million nephrons which filter the blood, reabsorbing the useful materials such as glucose, amino acids, salts and water and getting rid of products such as urea (the waste product of the breakdown of proteins).

Water content of the body is controlled by anti-**diuretic** hormone or ADH. If there is not enough water in the body, ADH is secreted and this stops water being excreted from the body. If there is too much water in the body, ADH is not secreted and excess water will be excreted from the body.

The kidneys also regulate the chemical composition of body fluid (e.g. sodium chloride, potassium and calcium) and regulate the acid balance of the body. About 150–180 litres of fluid are processed by the kidneys every day and about 1.5 litres of urine are manufactured.

The skin

The skin is involved in the removal of waste from the body: excess water, salt, urea and uric acid are excreted via the sweat glands. It is also involved in temperature control, through blood circulation, through sweat glands, the fatty layer that helps keep you warm and the little hairs that cover your skin.

Did you know?

The skin and eyes were the first organs to be transplanted successfully, but the kidney was the first internal organ to be transplanted. This is because humans have two kidneys but can live normally with just one. The first successful kidney transplant was carried out in America in 1954 when 23 year old Ronald Herrick donated one of his kidneys to his twin brother Richard, who was dying of kidney disease. Richard went on to live for another 8 years and Ronald was still alive in 2010.

Key term

Diuretic – increasing the flow of urine

Figure 7.12 The structure of the skin

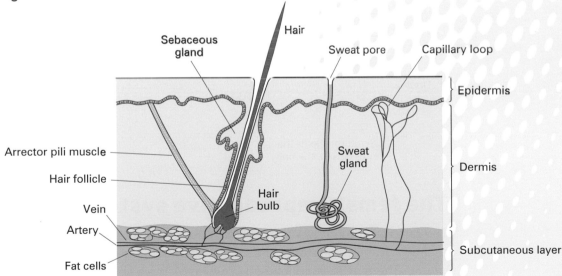

Just checking

1. What is urine made up of?
2. There are three different parts of the kidney. Find out what they are and explain what each does.
3. Name 3 ways in which the skin can help control your temperature

Major body systems 6

Reproduction involves the manufacture of specialised sex cells called ova or eggs in the female and sperm in the male. These cells are called gametes and when one of each join together a cell called a zygote is formed. It contains a full set of chromosomes – half each from the mother and father. After 40 weeks of pregnancy, this zygote becomes a baby.

The male reproductive system

The male reproductive system is made up of the penis and the testes suspended in the scrotum. The testes are situated outside the body because the best temperature for sperm production is slightly lower than body temperature. The testes produce sperm and testosterone. During sexual arousal, the penis fills with blood and becomes erect. At the point of ejaculation, the epididymis, the vas deferens (the sperm sac) and the muscles at the base of the penis contract strongly and semen, a fluid containing the sperm, is released from the tip of the penis. Men can continue to produce sperm well into old age.

Figure 7.13: The male reproductive system, side view

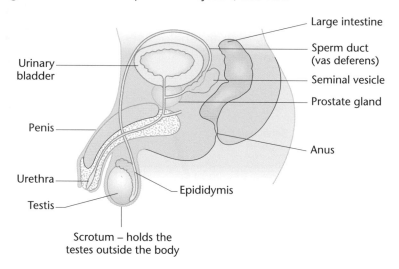

The female reproductive system

The female reproductive system is made up of two fallopian tubes and two ovaries, the uterus and cervix (neck of the uterus) and the vagina. The ovaries produce eggs or ova. Men are able to continue producing sperm during their lifetime, but when a baby girl is born she already has all the eggs that she will produce – about 400. One egg (or ovum) will be released each month from around the age of 12 (when menstruation begins) until the menopause, around the age of 50. The fallopian tubes transport the released egg to the uterus and it is usually in these tubes that the egg is fertilised. The uterus is a small muscular sac situated behind the pubic bone; during pregnancy it enlarges to accommodate the baby carried and nourished inside.

Figure 7.14: The female reproductive system, side view

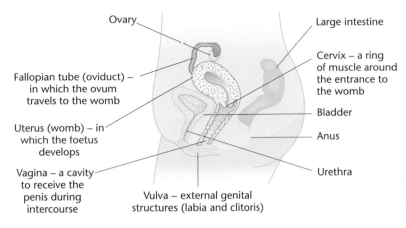

- Ovary
- Fallopian tube (oviduct) – in which the ovum travels to the womb
- Uterus (womb) – in which the foetus develops
- Vagina – a cavity to receive the penis during intercourse
- Vulva – external genital structures (labia and clitoris)
- Large intestine
- Cervix – a ring of muscle around the entrance to the womb
- Bladder
- Anus
- Urethra

Table 7.6 Male and female sex cells

Sperm	Egg
Very small – 1/500 mm	Very large – 1/10 mm
Nucleus contains half of the male's chromosomes	Nucleus contains half of the female's chromosomes
Cytoplasm contains lots of mitochondria to provide energy	Cytoplasm contains lots of nutrients for embryo development
Can move on their own	Cannot move on their own
Several hundred million produced every day from puberty onwards	Present at birth and released about every four weeks from puberty to menopause
Each ejaculation contains 200–400 million sperm	Only one egg released every four weeks

The menstrual cycle

During approximately the first five days of the menstrual cycle, the lining of the uterus is shed. This is commonly known as a period.

Follicle stimulating hormone (FSH) stimulates an egg to mature in the ovary. Oestrogen is produced and this stimulates the uterus to start building its lining. The high levels of oestrogen also cause FSH to stop being produced and luteinising hormone (LH) to be secreted. The LH causes an egg to be produced in the ovary (ovulation) and a corpus luteum is produced. This is essential for establishing and maintaining pregnancy.

If a fertilised egg has not appeared in the uterus by day 24 of the cycle, the corpus luteum dies and the lining of the uterus breaks down and is shed as a period.

What happens if an egg is fertilised?

If the egg is fertilised, the corpus luteum remains active for about three months, producing oestrogen and progesterone. By this stage of the pregnancy, the placenta will have formed: this will produce these hormones for the remainder of the pregnancy and will provide nourishment to the embryo. The hormones ensure that the lining of the uterus continues to develop and stops production of FSH so that no more eggs are produced. High hormone levels also stimulate the development of breast tissue in preparation for milk production. Just before birth, the pituitary gland is stimulated to produce prolactin and oxytocin, two more hormones. Prolactin triggers the production of breast milk and oxytocin starts labour.

Did you know?

- Men remain fertile throughout their adult life but women are only fertile until they are about 50 years old.

- A normal human pregnancy lasts 40 weeks.

Just checking

1. Produce a table of hormones that are secreted during the menstrual cycle. Explain when in the cycle each is produced and what effects they have on the female reproductive system.

2. Research what happens during pregnancy and produce a timeline of the main points of development of the foetus.

Major body systems 7

My life

Move it!

As you have learned, the skeleton has 206 bones. In small groups see how many bones you can name. Do you know the formal and more commonly used names for some of them? (Hint: the scapula is also called the shoulder blade.)

The musculoskeletal system is the body system that controls movement and coordination. The human body contains 206 bones and more than 600 muscles.

The musculoskeletal system

The skeleton

The skeleton provides the bony framework of the body and without it humans would not have a shape. It has several functions, which include:

- allowing the body to move with the muscles

- protecting some of the vital organs of the body such as the brain and heart

- producing new blood cells in the bone marrow of some bones

- producing calcium, which helps with blood clotting and muscle contraction.

Figure 7.15: The skeleton

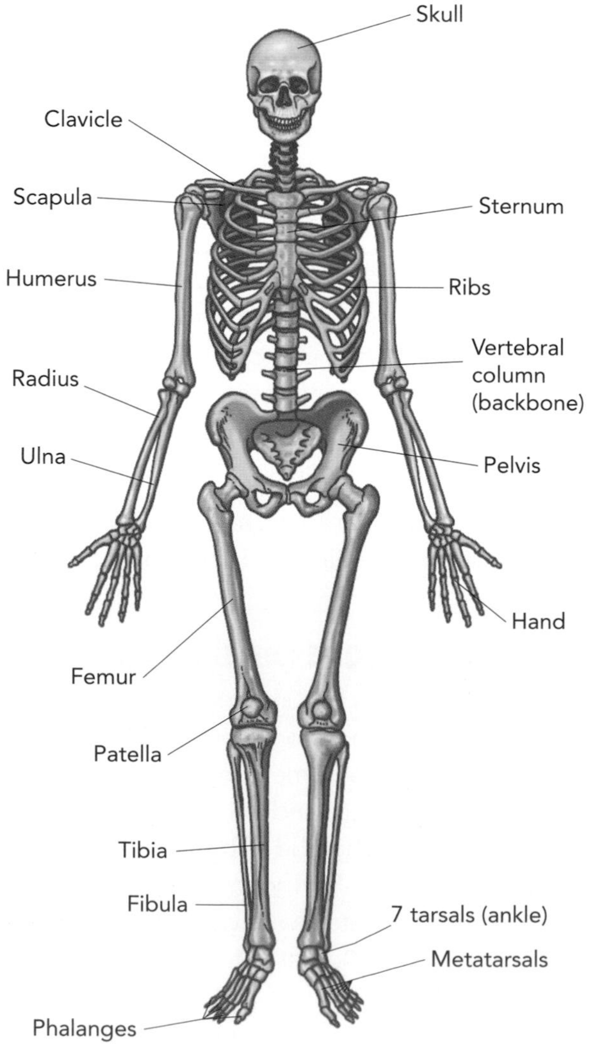

Did you know?

While the adult skeleton contains 206 bones, an infant's skeleton has about 300 bones. As a child grows, some bones fuse together, e.g. in the skull which at birth consists of eight separate cranial bones.

There are two parts to the skeleton – the axial and appendicular skeletons. The axial skeleton consists of the skull, vertebrae and ribcage. The skull consists of 22 separate bones which are fused together to protect the brain, eyes and ears. It sits on the vertebrae or backbone. The 33 vertebrae protect the spinal cord. They are separated from each other by pads of cartilage which act as shock absorbers. The back muscles attach to the vertebrae. The ribcage consists of 12 pairs of ribs and protects the heart and lungs.

The appendicular skeleton consists of the bones of the arms and legs, the shoulder girdle which attaches the arms to the vertebrae, and the hip girdle that connect the legs to the vertebrae. The pelvic girdle helps to protect the reproductive organs, and is strong enough to support the body's weight.

Joints and ligaments

Joints are where two bones meet. There are three types of joint:

- immoveable (fixed), such as the skull bones
- slightly moveable, such as the vertebrae of the spine
- freely moveable, such as the hip and knee joints.

Ligaments are strong elastic structures made of a protein substance. They hold bones together at a joint.

Bones cannot move by themselves. They need the action of muscles to allow movement.

Muscles

As well as different types of joints, the body contains different types of muscle. Cardiac muscle is specialised tissue found only in the heart (see the section on the cardiovascular system) and smooth muscle is found in the intestines, uterus and blood vessels. The muscle tissue that is involved in the movement of the body is striped or striated muscle. This tissue is so-called because when viewed under a microscope it looks striped.

Muscles are attached to bones by fibrous tissue called tendons. When a muscle contracts, it pulls on the bone and moves the joint. Muscles can only work by contracting, which is why they need to work in pairs. Muscles are always slightly contracted so that they are ready for movement. This is known as muscle tone.

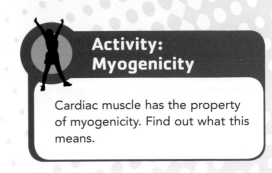

Activity: Myogenicity

Cardiac muscle has the property of myogenicity. Find out what this means.

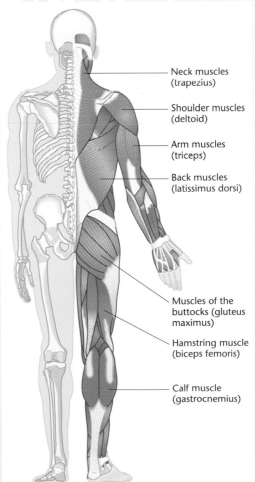

Figure 7.16: Some of the main skeletal muscles

- Neck muscles (trapezius)
- Shoulder muscles (deltoid)
- Arm muscles (triceps)
- Back muscles (latissimus dorsi)
- Muscles of the buttocks (gluteus maximus)
- Hamstring muscle (biceps femoris)
- Calf muscle (gastrocnemius)

Just checking

1. Find out what the following parts of the skeleton are:

sutures	the axis	the femur
the humerus	the clavicle	the patella
the atlas	the tibia	the ulna

   Then label them on a diagram of the skeleton.

2. Move different parts of your body and identify as many joints as you can. Then carry out some research to find out what types of joints they are and how they move.

Interrelationships between body systems 1

Different body systems work together to make sure that the body functions efficiently as a whole, with the brain working as a control centre. Homeostasis is the process by which the body maintains a stable environment in which cells, tissues and systems can function. If there is a change in the body, these processes can stop, slow down, or speed up. Many activities that take place in the body are controlled by homeostatic mechanisms, including body temperature, blood pressure and oxygen supply.

Negative feedback works rather like the central heating system of a building. A thermostat will be set to the desired temperature. If the temperature falls below this, the thermostat will detect this change and send a message to the boiler to switch on. The heating comes on and the building warms up. When it has reached the temperature set by the thermostat, the boiler gets a message to switch off. The heating will switch on again when the temperature drops below the thermostat

Figure 7.17 The body has different processes to maintain a stable environment in which cells can work

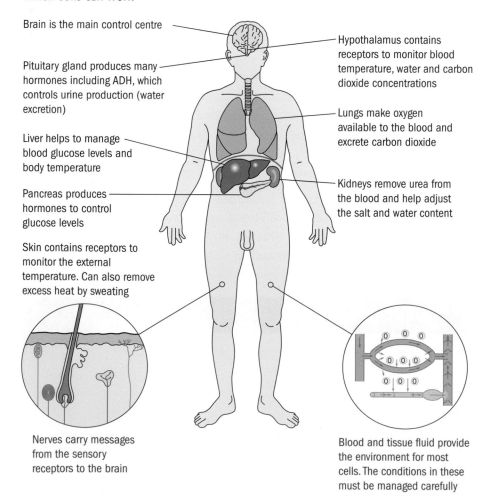

Brain is the main control centre

Hypothalamus contains receptors to monitor blood temperature, water and carbon dioxide concentrations

Pituitary gland produces many hormones including ADH, which controls urine production (water excretion)

Lungs make oxygen available to the blood and excrete carbon dioxide

Liver helps to manage blood glucose levels and body temperature

Pancreas produces hormones to control glucose levels

Kidneys remove urea from the blood and help adjust the salt and water content

Skin contains receptors to monitor the external temperature. Can also remove excess heat by sweating

Nerves carry messages from the sensory receptors to the brain

Blood and tissue fluid provide the environment for most cells. The conditions in these must be managed carefully

Activity: Homeostasis

Homeostasis comes from two Latin words. Can you find out what they are and what they mean?

Negative feedback is a mechanism used to detect and correct changes in the body. How does this relate to homeostasis?

setting. Homeostasis relies on feedback like this from the body in order to keep the internal environment constant. One example of how the body maintains a stable environment is through ADH. See page 201 for a description of how ADH functions.

Maintenance of body temperature

You may have heard of explorers such as Bear Grylls and Ray Mears. They both go to some of the hottest and coldest places on the planet, but how do they manage to survive? People who live in these areas adapt to survive, for example the Inuit people who live in the Canadian Arctic and subartic areas. Many of the body's processes work best at a constant temperature of about 37°C, so the body can make changes to ensure that this is maintained. Often, these changes are made at the expense of what are known as peripheral areas (like the limbs): you may have cold hands and feet or skin, but your internal organs will be warm and functioning normally. Receptors in the skin will detect when you are too hot or cold, and will send a message to your brain. The temperature control centre in the brain will then react to the message, telling your body systems to respond to help you to cool down or warm up. The body systems working together to maintain temperature control are the excretory system, the nervous system and the skin.

Blood pressure

The blood pressure is measured in millimetres of mercury and normal blood pressure should be approx 120/80mmHg. The higher figure (120) shows the systolic pressure – the pressure in the vessels when the heart is contracting and pushing the blood out. The lower figure (80) shows the diastolic pressure – the pressure in the vessels when the heart is filling.

Certain factors can change the blood pressure and a rise in blood pressure, e.g. due to stress. Receptors in major arteries such as the aorta and carotid arteries in the neck detect a rise in blood pressure and send a message to the medulla in the brain. Messages are then sent out to slow the heart rate and widen the arteries, which will lower the blood pressure. In this instance, the systems working together are the nervous system and the cardiovascular system.

Just checking

1. The concept of homeostasis and negative feedback can be quite difficult to understand. Working in pairs, read through this section and then, with your books closed, try to explain to each other what negative feedback is. You can use a pen and paper if this helps.
2. Why is it important that homeostatic mechanisms are present in the body? What would happen if body temperature continued to rise because there was no mechanism to stop it?

Interrelationships between body systems 2

Activity: Respiration

Carry out some research to find out how the breathing centre in the brain controls the rate and depth of breathing.

Oxygen supply

The respiratory system is responsible for maintaining oxygen supply in the body. The medulla in the brain contains clusters of neurones that represent the respiratory centre. One cluster is responsible for inspiration (breathing in) and one for expiration (breathing out). In the brain there are two regions concerned with respiration. One changes the depth of breathing and the other the rate of breathing.

There are receptors in the aorta and the carotid arteries in the neck that are sensitive to chemical changes in the blood, especially oxygen and carbon dioxide levels. If they detect a rise in carbon dioxide, they send a message to the brain telling it to increase the rate and depth of breathing. When carbon dioxide levels fall, the depth and rate of breathing will return to normal. Here there are three systems working together: the nervous system, the cardiovascular system and the respiratory system.

Figure 7.18: The effect of insulin on rising blood sugar

What happens?

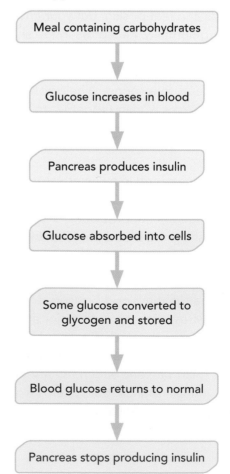

Blood glucose

Cells need glucose to function and this glucose must be supplied at a steady rate. Normally humans eat three meals a day, at intervals, so there must be a type of homeostatic mechanism at work to keep the glucose supply constant.

From the flow chart in Figure 7.18, you should be able to see that the nervous system is working with the digestive system and the endocrine system to maintain steady blood glucose levels.

Assessment activity 7.2

 P2 M1 D1

Illustrate the structure and function of two of the major body systems through the use of diagrams and show how they interrelate to perform a function in the body **P2**.

To achieve **M1**, write a report explaining how the structure of the two systems you have chosen helps them to carry out their functions. You should by now have covered all of the major body systems included in this chapter; you can choose from any of them, but the cardiovascular and respiratory systems interrelate well.

To achieve **D1**, in your report you need to be able to explain how systems work together to maintain homeostasis. You should choose the same systems as those you wrote in **P2**.
Remember, however, that you will probably need to include more than two systems in your explanation.

Grading tip

You should find this task easier to complete if you think carefully about which body systems you choose to study in greater detail, as this will help you to meet **D1** more easily. The respiratory and cardiovascular systems interrelate well. As your starting point, think about what both systems do and why they depend on each other to perform those tasks. How easy would it be for the body to work efficiently if one of the systems did not do what it is supposed to do? Which other system is also involved?

PLTS

When you plan and carry out research, you will develop skills as an **independent enquirer**. As a **creative thinker**, you will be generating your own ideas about how you want to complete the task and connecting your ideas to make a well constructed and logical piece of written work. As you learn to manage your time so that you can set goals and meet them you will develop skills as a **self-manager**.

Functional skills

In this assessment you will need to produce labelled diagrams that will help to explain the structure and functions of the two systems you choose to describe. You may wish to use diagrams from websites, but you must label them yourself. This will help you to develop **ICT** skills. You will also be able to work on your **English** skills when writing your report. Check your grammar, punctuation and spelling carefully.

Just checking

1. Explain to a partner how the nervous system helps regulate oxygen supply. Use diagrams if that helps.
2. Which systems work together to help regulate blood sugar?
3. Where is the pancreas and what does it do?

3. Be able to carry out routine measurements and observations of the body

Observations

A lot of information can be gained by simply observing a service user. This can be very important and is particularly of relevance if a carer is working with the same service users on a regular basis. The better you get to know your clients, the more able you will be to observe small changes in their condition.

Skin colour and texture

The colour and texture of skin can provide a lot of information to care workers (see diagram on page 201).

Table 7.7 Skin symptoms and conditions

Observation	Possible reason
Pale clammy skin	Shock or haemorrhage
A blue tinge, especially round the lips or the fingernails	Lack of oxygen, possible heart problems
Flushed pink skin	Fever
Dry, flaky, itchy skin	Eczema, dermatitis
Reddened skin with silvery, scaly patches	Psoriasis
Congested skin with spots and blackheads	Acne

Evidence of sweat

Sweating is a normal part of temperature control in humans and helps to reduce body temperature. Sweat is released onto the skin where it evaporates and cools the body. There are many causes of sweating, including infections (such as flu) and fear. In addition, some people will have a cold sweat during a heart attack and people with diabetes may sweat if their blood glucose level becomes too low.

Temperature on touch

Touching someone's skin can give you information about its temperature, and this may provide clues about a service user's condition. Someone who feels very hot to the touch may have a temperature which might indicate an infection, whereas someone who is cold to the touch may have hypothermia or poor blood circulation, especially if the hands and feet are cold.

Activity: Symptoms

Find out the symptoms of the following:

- vitiligo
- melanoma
- eczema

Abnormal breathing rates and rhythms

Many medical conditions that affect the blood or the lungs can increase the breathing rate and may cause breathlessness. It is important to listen and observe as you take other routine measurements, as you may hear wheezing, which can be a sign of asthma or an allergy. You may also notice bubbling, gasping or grunting.

Examples of conditions that can cause abnormal breathing rates are:

- anaemia
- heart problems
- fractured ribs
- damage to the brain
- pneumonia

Thirst

If you notice that someone is drinking a lot of fluids or is complaining that they are thirsty, it is possible that they are dehydrated and need to replace lost fluid in the body. Excessive thirst is also a symptom of diabetes, so this should always be reported and investigated.

Coughing

Coughing is a method of removing sputum, dust, debris or a foreign body from the respiratory system. The two basic types of cough are chesty and dry. Chesty coughs usually produce phlegm or sputum, but not always. A dry cough is irritating but does not produce sputum. Chesty coughs can be productive or non-productive. In both, mucus or sputum is present but a person with a productive cough will be able to move some of it whereas a person with a non-productive cough will not.

Coughing can be a symptom of different disorders or diseases. Some coughs are temporary and accompany a cold but others are longer lasting and may produce sputum.

Thick green or yellowish sputum is often a sign of a chest infection such as bronchitis or pneumonia. Blood in the sputum can indicate tuberculosis.

Think about it

Think about your breathing. Can you identify times when you find it more difficult to breathe or need to breathe faster? Why do you think this is? If you get out of breath when you exercise, how long does it take you to recover?

Activity: Diseases and disorders

Research the diseases and disorders given in the activity on p. 210 and find out their signs and symptoms, especially the ways in which they affect breathing rate and rhythm. Make a table of your findings.

Just checking

1. Identify three different skin symptoms and what they might indicate.
2. What are productive and non-productive coughs?
3. What might blood in the sputum indicate?

Routine measurements and observations of the body

When people are feeling ill, it may not be clear what is wrong with them. Taking measurements helps health professionals to diagnose and treat any condition that is present, and will help to establish which measurements are within normal ranges and which are higher or lower than expected.

Routine physiological measurements

Pulse rate

Taking someone's pulse is a non-invasive way of measuring their heart rate; pulse rate is recorded in beats per minute. The rate, strength and rhythm are all important as a fast pulse rate can indicate fever, fright or bleeding and a slow pulse rate can indicate heart problems, a brain injury or even the fact that a person is very fit and active. The pulse is usually taken where an artery crosses a bone and the most common place to take the pulse is at the wrist just below the thumb.

Did you know?

The pulse can also be taken in the neck, in the groin, at the temple and on the upper surface of the foot.

Activity: Taking pulses

In pairs, practise taking each other's pulse. You need to make sure that you find the right place on the wrist and that you use your middle finger to take it. Count the number of beats in 30 seconds and multiply your result by two to get the number of beats per minute. Try taking it at different times of the day, or after a meal or some exercise, and note any differences.

Taking pulse rates

Blood pressure

The blood pressure is the pressure that is exerted on the walls of the arteries by the blood. It is measured in mm of mercury and is recorded as two numbers, one on top of the other. The top (systolic) measurement is the pressure on the arteries while the heart is beating and the lower (diastolic) is while the heart is resting.

Blood pressure is normally measured by a sphygmomanometer, which is battery or electrically operated. A cuff containing a rubber bladder is placed round the upper arm at the level of the heart and is inflated, which blocks off blood supply to the arm. A valve is then slowly released and the cuff deflates, allowing blood to flow again. Once the machine has recorded the data, the results are shown on a display screen. Often the pulse will be displayed as well.

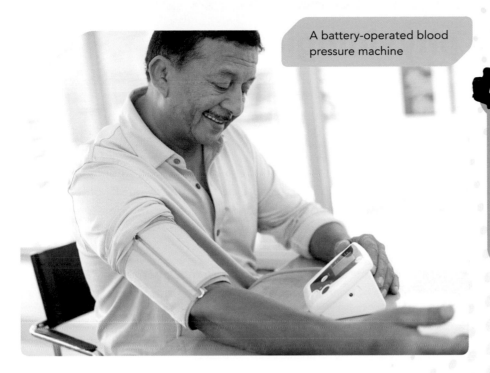

A battery-operated blood pressure machine

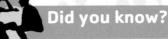

Did you know?

Yoga and massage can often be used to reduce blood pressure. Stroking pets, such as cats and dogs, has also been proven to lower blood pressure and dogs are often taken to visit people in hospital for this reason.

Breathing rate

The simplest method of measuring breathing rate is to watch a service user's chest rise and fall and count the number of times this happens in a minute. (Alternatively, you can watch for half a minute and double this number.) You can do this at the same time as the pulse is being taken as the service user is usually unaware and does not change their breathing rate. The breathing rate can change if patients know it is being monitored. As with the pulse, staff should observe the type and rhythm of breathing as this can often indicate an underlying problem.

Peak flow

Peak flow measurement is a method of measuring lung function. It measures the speed of an exhalation which gives an indication of how wide the bronchial tubes are. It is used particularly by asthmatics. A peak flow meter is used to take readings. The service user places the mouthpiece in their mouth and blows as hard and fast into the meter as possible. The measurement taken shows the air flow in the lungs and is measured in litres per minute. Usually three measurements are taken and the highest of the three is recorded. Peak flow may be taken before and after treatment to monitor the condition of the lungs.

A peak flow meter

Just checking

1. In how many places on the body can you take a pulse?
2. What conditions might be caused by raised blood pressure?
3. How would you measure a service user's respiration rate?

Further routine physiological measurements

Body temperature

Body temperature needs to be kept within quite narrow limits so that all the body's processes work properly. However, people can experience variations in temperature during the day and women experience a rise in temperature during ovulation. Temperature is taken with a thermometer. There are different types of thermometer that can be used:

- ear thermometers – take a temperature measurement by an infra red beam in the ear canal – not always very accurate

- LCD strip – can be placed on the forehead and the liquid crystal display strip will show the temperature – not very accurate but will show a rise in temperature

- electronic digital thermometers – have a digital readout to display the temperature – probably the most accurate but will vary according to the manufacturer.

Activity: Thermometers

Obtain some different types of thermometer and try them out with a partner. Try using them after you have had hot and cold drinks to see if there is a difference. Which type of thermometer do you think is easiest to use and most accurate?

Blood glucose testing before a meal

Blood glucose levels

Most people with diabetes have their own blood glucose monitor and record their results themselves. A strip is placed in the machine and a drop of blood is dripped onto it. The machine then displays the result. There are new machines on the market today that allow blood glucose measurements to be taken without needing to pierce the skin.

Expected range of measurements

At the beginning of this section it was explained that it is important to take and record measurements so that health care staff have a set of baseline observations; these are usually a person's normal measurements. When something happens in the body that changes these measurements, staff can identify what the changes are and this could help them to diagnose any problems. The table on the next page shows the normal expected ranges of different measurements.

Table 7.8 Ranges of measurements

Measurement	Normal range
Pulse	60–80 bpm
Blood pressure	110/75 mmHg (young person) 140/90 mmHg (older person)
Breathing rate	8–17 breaths per minute
Peak flow	500–700 litres per min (men) 380–500 litres per min (women)
Body temperature	36.5–37.2°C
Blood glucose level	5–8 mmol glucose per litre of blood

BTEC Assessment Activity 7.3 (P3)

Use measuring equipment to take routine measurements and observations on a partner. You could take one set of observations when your partner is sitting quietly in a chair and another set after he or she has taken some exercise or after a sports session. Use the charts at the back of this book to record your observations. How accurate do you think you were when taking the measurements? Can you draw any conclusions from your results?

To achieve (P3) you need to present your results systematically (in tables and charts) and explain what steps were taken to ensure safe working practices. You should obtain a witness testimony from your tutor to support the accuracy of your measurements and that you followed safe practice when taking the measurements.

Grading tip

Take some time to practise with all of the equipment before you start. It is important to be familiar with the equipment you are going to use so that you reduce the chance of making errors when you do the real thing. You should also practise recording the results so that anyone else reading them will be able to see clearly what you have recorded.

PLTS

This task will give you the opportunity to develop skills as an **independent enquirer** by taking responsibility for choosing the equipment you will use. As a **reflective learner** you will be reflecting on what you did and the results you got. Working with a partner will enable you to develop skills as a **team worker** and planning your work within a time scale will help you to become a **self-manager**. Planning your work and collaborating with your partner will help you to become an **effective participator**.

Functional skills

This activity will give you the chance to improve **Maths** skills as you will need to record all of the measurements you have taken in the correct format.

Just checking

1. Why is it important for measurements to be accurate?
2. Why is it important for measurements to be recorded clearly and accurately?

Considerations when carrying out routine measurements

Health, safety and accuracy considerations

Although the focus of caring is the protection and care of service users and patients, it is also important to maintain your own health and safety and that of your colleagues and the relatives and friends of those you look after. You may not be able to work if you have had an accident because of faulty equipment, and if any of your actions are reckless or careless, you could be held responsible for harm to others.

Accuracy of equipment

It is very important that measurements are taken accurately: inaccurate data could lead to delays in diagnosis and treatment for the patient. The equipment used must be in good working order, well-maintained and tested regularly. Batteries should be checked to ensure that they have not run down. If possible, the same piece of equipment should be used on the client each time measurements are taken.

If the equipment being used is electrically operated, care must be taken to ensure the safety of clients and carers. Care workers must check all monitoring devices for faulty wires, malfunction, and loose or faulty plugs and sockets. If a piece of equipment is faulty, it should be reported immediately verbally and in writing – there may be special forms or a book for this. It must be taken out of use, labelled stating the nature of the breakdown, and then repaired by the appropriate people. Most pieces of equipment have instruction booklets and these should be used only for that specific piece of equipment.

Peak flow meters should be replaced approximately every two years to ensure accuracy of measurement. Ideally, clients should have their own meter to use, but if this is not possible the mouthpieces should be disinfected after use or disposable mouthpieces should be used.

Duplicating readings

It may be necessary to duplicate readings to ensure accuracy; for instance, two people might take the same measurements on a service user. Some measurements will need to be repeated on a regular basis to ensure that no problems are developing. For instance, it is normal to take the patient's temperature hourly during a blood transfusion, because raised temperature is often one of the first signs of a reaction to the blood being given. As far as possible, the same equipment should be used when taking duplicate or repeated measurements, because there may be differences in the results from different pieces of equipment.

Safety and wellbeing of the individual during measurements

Health care workers have a responsibility to ensure that no harm comes to service users while they are being cared for. Some service users may be nervous and others may want to make sure that they are receiving appropriate treatment. Care workers should always make sure that they explain what they are going to do, and why, before they start to take measurements or provide care. This is part of what is known as informed consent: the client needs to know the facts so that they can agree to what is happening to them.

In terms of taking measurements, care workers need to ensure not just the accuracy of equipment, but its safety too. Glass thermometers containing mercury used to be used to take temperatures, and were placed under the patient's tongue. This type of thermometer was taken out of use because of the risk of the patient biting and breaking it and also because of the danger of being exposed to mercury, which is a poisonous metal. Some people feel discomfort when their blood pressure is measured as the cuff inflates and tightens around the arm, so it is important to ensure that the cuff is positioned correctly and the measurement is taken as quickly and efficiently as possible. The main direct risk to service users, other than those mentioned above, is when taking peak flow. Forced exhalations into the meter may cause some clients to experience an asthmatic attack.

Infection control

If a service user is ill, the last thing they need is to be made more ill by a failure to follow infection control procedures. You must always wash your hands and/or use sanitising gel before starting work, if you have been out of the work area for a break or to use the toilet, between each service user you attend to, before handling food and if you are in contact with any body fluids. You should always ensure that gloves and aprons are used if necessary and you must work according to the policy in your place of work.

All equipment should be cleaned and disinfected thoroughly before and after use. The cuff of a blood pressure machine should be wiped with an alcohol wipe between each service user. Thermometers must be sterilised before and after use in an antiseptic solution; they should never be washed in hot water as this can cause them to break. Ear thermometers should always be used with disposable probe covers to prevent the risk of infection. Electrical or battery operated equipment must not be submerged in water or any other liquid at any time.

Just checking

1. Why is it important to check for accuracy when you take routine measurements?
2. Give three reasons why measurements might be inaccurate. What consequences could this have?

4. Know the effects of malfunctions on body systems

A problem before or during birth or a malfunction later in life can mean that body systems don't work at all or stop working as efficiently as they should. This can result in a disability or disorder that can limit someone's life and be very painful. When this happens the quality of a person's life may be quite poor as several body systems may be affected.

Heart attack

The heart muscle needs a constant supply of oxygen, which is carried to it by the coronary arteries. This is because it beats 100,000 times a day, 35 million times a year and 2.5 billion times in a lifetime. Normally the arteries are in good condition and the blood flows smoothly. However, if there is a build up of fatty material in the arteries, they become narrower. When this happens the flow of blood slows down and less oxygen reaches the heart muscle. People can then suffer chest pains known as angina. If a coronary artery becomes completely blocked, the heart muscle beyond the blockage stops receiving oxygen and some of the heart muscle dies. This is known as a heart attack and symptoms can include chest pain or discomfort (angina), shortness of breath and pain in one or both arms, the left shoulder, neck, jaw or back. The severity of symptoms will depend on how advanced the heart disease is, but if enough of the heart muscle cells die, the heart will stop beating altogether and the sufferer might die.

Your chances of developing heart disease will be influenced by factors such as what you have inherited from your parents and grandparents and what your lifestyle is like. If members of your family have suffered from heart disease then you will be more likely to suffer. Age and gender both have an effect as well: men are more likely to suffer heart disease

Figure 7.19: The events leading to a heart attack

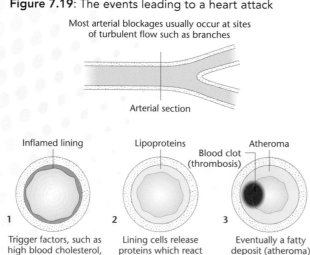

Most arterial blockages usually occur at sites of turbulent flow such as branches

Arterial section

Inflamed lining

Lipoproteins

Blood clot (thrombosis)

Atheroma

1 Trigger factors, such as high blood cholesterol, result in inflammation of the lining

2 Lining cells release proteins which react with the cholesterol and other fats and are deposited on the lining

3 Eventually a fatty deposit (atheroma) forms – sometimes a blood clot may form

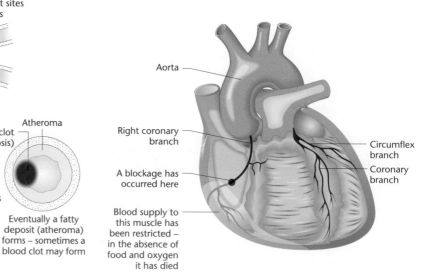

Aorta

Right coronary branch

A blockage has occurred here

Blood supply to this muscle has been restricted – in the absence of food and oxygen it has died

Circumflex branch

Coronary branch

than women although the risk to women increases after the menopause. People with diabetes and some ethnic groups are more susceptible too.

Stroke

A stroke can occur when a blood vessel in the brain becomes blocked or bursts. The part of the brain beyond the affected vessel cannot receive oxygen and dies – as the heart muscle dies during a heart attack. Depending on where in the brain this occurs, sufferers can experience loss of movement and speech difficulties. If the blockage occurs in the left side of the brain, the right side of the body is usually affected; if the blockage is in the right side of the brain, the left side of the body is usually affected. Speech might be affected if the blockage occurs in the left side of the brain where the speech centre is.

High blood pressure

Your chances of having a stroke are increased if you have high blood pressure, which can be caused by too much salt in the diet or a stressful lifestyle. Reducing the amount of salt in the diet can help to control blood pressure; currently the recommended daily allowance for salt intake is 6 g a day (about one teaspoonful). It can be difficult to know how much salt you consume every day as so much is hidden – especially in processed foods – so it is important to read food labels carefully if you are trying to reduce your salt intake.

Stroke symptoms include the following:

- sudden numbness or weakness of the face, arms or legs, especially on one side of the body
- confusion – trouble speaking or understanding
- difficulty in seeing with one or both eyes
- dizziness, loss of balance or coordination
- sudden severe headache with no known cause.

Did you know?

Coronary heart disease (CHD) is a preventable disease that kills more than 70,000 people in England every year. Roughly 2 million people suffer from angina and 110,000 people have a heart attack annually. CHD is the biggest killer in the country. The government is committed to reducing the death rate from coronary heart disease and stroke and related diseases in people under 75 by at least 40% (to 83.8 deaths per 100,000 population) by 2010.

Source: Department of Health

Just checking

1. Go to the NHS website and find out what Act F.A.S.T. is by taking part in the interactive test. Then visit the Stroke Association website and find out more about the signs and symptoms of stroke and how a stroke is treated. Produce a leaflet that could be used to inform the general public about strokes and what they can do to help prevent them. To obtain a secure link to these websites, see the Hotlinks section on p. x.
2. Carry out some research to find out how much salt there is in processed foods such as breakfast cereals, bacon, sausages and potato crisps.

Case study: Stephen

Stephen Boyd is 44 years old and works as a lorry driver delivering chilled foods to a large supermarket chain. This means that he spends a lot of time on the road and eats a lot of fast food like pork pies, sausage rolls, sandwiches and crisps when he is away from home. He likes to play football for a local over 40s team, but recently he has been away so much that he hasn't had time to play or go to the training nights.

Last week when he woke up and tried to get out of bed, the right side of his body was numb and heavy and he couldn't stand up. When he tried to tell his wife Jo that something was wrong, he couldn't speak clearly. Jo rang for an ambulance and Stephen was admitted to the local hospital. He was told that he had had a stroke.

What do you think might have helped to cause Stephen's stroke?

The effects of malfunctions on body systems

Asthma

Asthma is a condition that affects the airways of the lungs. It usually happens because of an allergy and this causes the airways to become narrower as the muscles around their walls tighten. It is hard to breathe and sticky phlegm is produced. Symptoms can include coughing, wheezing, shortness of breath and tightness in the chest. It can affect anyone of any age.

Infections and environmental factors are the main risk factors for sufferers of asthma. Common triggers include cigarette smoke and other fumes, and allergies to pollen, dust and animals.

Lung function in people with asthma is monitored by taking peak flow readings. This can give an indication of how successful treatment is, or it could be an indicator of how the body responds to differences in air quality or allergens such as pollen, animals or dust.

Treatment for asthma includes preventers and relievers. Relievers relax the muscles surrounding the airways and relieve symptoms, whereas preventers help to control swelling in the airways and help to prevent sensitivity to triggers. Relievers are usually blue in colour and preventers are brown, red or orange.

Emphysema

Emphysema is a chronic lung condition which causes difficulty in breathing. It is caused by gradual damage to the lung structure. The alveoli gradually lose their elasticity and it becomes very difficult to exhale. The body does not receive enough oxygen and the sufferer is unable to exhale carbon dioxide. Sufferers are constantly battling to breathe and get tired very quickly.

The risk factors for emphysema are smoking and living in an environment that has high levels of air pollution. It is more common in urban than rural areas and in people who work in dusty environments. Men tend to suffer more than women.

Sufferers are advised to stop smoking and to use oxygen to help with their breathing. Infections need to be treated promptly with antibiotics to prevent further chest complications.

Chronic bronchitis

Bronchitis is inflammation of the bronchioles of the lungs. Bronchitis can be **acute** and get better relatively quickly, but **chronic** bronchitis will not get better although some of the symptoms can be relieved. Continued coughing will produce mucus or phlegm and eventually the bronchioles will become scarred, which makes them floppy and narrow. This results in shortness of breath. Chronic bronchitis and emphysema can occur together.

Risk factors associated with chronic bronchitis are smoking, long-term exposure to smoke, pollution and some jobs such as coal mining and working in textile manufacture. Chronic bronchitis can also be caused by allergies.

If they smoke, sufferers should be advised to stop immediately and they may be prescribed drugs to widen the airways. Antibiotics may also be prescribed if infection is the cause.

If a sufferer is overweight or obese, he or she should be advised to lose weight as carrying extra weight causes the lungs to work harder and increases shortness of breath.

Gentle exercises to increase the muscle power of the diaphragm, chest muscles, arms and legs should be encouraged.

Diabetes mellitus

Blood glucose levels are controlled by the hormone insulin which is secreted by the pancreas. People with diabetes either cannot produce insulin or cannot use it properly, so blood glucose levels become uncontrolled. People with undiagnosed or untreated diabetes suffer from excess thirst, frequent urination, extreme tiredness and weight loss. Long term, there might be more serious complications affecting the kidneys, blood circulation and eyesight.

Type one diabetes

This is known as childhood or juvenile onset diabetes – it first appears during childhood and injections of insulin are needed before each meal because the pancreas is unable to produce any insulin. It is thought to be genetic.

Type two diabetes

This is known as adult or mature onset diabetes, although children as young as nine have been diagnosed. Either a reduced amount of insulin is produced by the pancreas or the body cannot use the insulin that is produced. It is non-insulin dependent and usually treated by diet, exercise and tablets. It occurs more often in overweight or obese people and is more common in people of Asian or Afro-Caribbean origin. It can run in families.

People with diabetes are advised to regulate the amount of fat and sugar in their diet and take regular exercise. Some people with type two are able to control their condition by diet alone.

Did you know?

- Respiratory difficulties can affect anyone at any age and can be acute or chronic.
- Smoking is a major irritant to the lungs and other organs of the respiratory system.
- Environmental factors such as pollution and pollen can also affect the severity of symptoms in respiratory disease.

Key terms

Acute – usually short-term and curable

Chronic – usually long-term and may be progressive or incurable

Just checking

1. Produce a short leaflet outlining the causes, symptoms and ways of treating asthma, emphysema or chronic bronchitis.
2. Visit the Diabetes UK website and find out more about the advice that is given to people with diabetes.

Further effects of malfunctions

Crohn's Disease

Crohn's disease is a chronic disease which can affect the whole of the digestive tract. Most commonly it affects the lowest part of the small intestine and the large intestine. Symptoms include abdominal pain, bleeding from the rectum and abscesses in the anal area. Children can suffer from this disease and may have developmental delay. Certain foods can make Crohn's Disease worse and sufferers are advised to avoid foods that make their symptoms worse.

People who have Crohn's can be symptom-free for quite long periods of time, but at other times the symptoms can be very severe. Drugs can help, but often the affected part of the bowel needs to be removed. Most people are able to lead normal lives but hospitalisation for treatment or surgery can affect young people's lives and education.

Renal failure

The function of the kidneys is to filter waste from the blood to prevent a build-up of toxins in the body. Renal failure can be acute or chronic.

Acute renal failure can occur for several reasons, including reduced blood supply to the kidneys, a drop in blood pressure, severe dehydration or lack of salt. It can generally be treated and cured, although a sufferer may need to have kidney dialysis until full renal function returns. Occasionally a transplant may be required.

Chronic renal failure can occur as a complication of diabetes mellitus, or it may be caused by blockage to kidney drainage or some inherited conditions. It often occurs with high blood pressure. It is not usually curable and sufferers may need to be on long term dialysis until they are able to receive a new kidney.

Osteoarthritis

Osteoarthritis is the most common type of arthritis in the UK, affecting about 8.5 million people. It can affect almost any joint in the body but most commonly affects the hips and knees, which are the main weight-bearing joints in the body. The cartilage can wear away, bony growths can appear round the edge of the joints and the tissues surrounding the joints can become inflamed. This results in pain and loss of movement, although the severity of symptoms varies greatly in different people. Osteoarthritis tends to occur when people get older and is more common in women. There is no cure for osteoarthritis, but it can be treated with painkillers, physiotherapy or surgery to replace the affected joints.

Parkinson's disease

Parkinson's disease is described as a progressive neurological disease and is caused by the loss of nerve cells in a particular part of the brain. It affects movement and symptoms can include rigid muscles, tremors

Key term

Progressive – happening or developing gradually

and slowing of movements. Symptoms can appear in any order and very gradually. In the UK about 120,000 people have Parkinson's and about 10,000 people are diagnosed every year. Usually the disease appears after the age of 50 and men are slightly more likely to develop it than women.

Multiple sclerosis

Multiple sclerosis or MS is also a progressive neurological condition in which the myelin sheath (the protective covering) over the nerves becomes damaged. When this happens, impulses cannot travel up and down the nerves. Symptoms are varied and most people only experience a few of them. They include pins and needles or numbness, fatigue and visual problems. About 100,000 people in the UK have MS. Treatments such as physiotherapy and occupational therapy can help and drugs are also available, but there is not yet a cure. Women tend to be affected more than men, and most people with MS tend to have a near normal life expectancy, although they may lose mobility and have problems with swallowing.

BTEC

Assessment activity 7.4

Using the two body systems investigated in assessment activity 7.2 outline one common malfunction that might occur in each of the systems.

For **P4** you should outline each malfunction by identifying its main signs and symptoms and making a few notes, for example on the changes that occur in the structures and functioning of the body system.

For **M2** and for each of the two malfunctions, you should describe how routine measurements and observations of the body system might be affected in the presence of the malfunction.

Grading tip

There are many websites (such as The British Heart Foundation website) that will explain a lot about a malfunction, including signs and symptoms and how people may be treated. This should help you with your research but remember that everything you write and hand in must be your own work: you cannot copy word for word or cut and paste information from these websites. For **M2**, you should state what observatoins and measures might change, and in what way they may change, e.g. whether they increase or decrease and under what circumstances. For example, what will happen to an individual's pulse rate when they are experiencing a heart attack?

PLTS

Taking responsibility for researching your chosen malfunctions makes you an **independent enquirer**. As a **reflective learner** you will be reflecting on what you have learned and how this may affect sufferers. Working with a partner enables you to develop skills as a **team worker**, and planning your work within a time scale will help you to become a **self-manager**. Planning your work and collaborating with your partner will help you to become an **effective participator**.

Functional skills

Writing a report about the two malfunctions will help you to practise **ICT** and **English** skills. You may wish to import diagrams or pictures to illustrate the points you are making.

Just checking

1. Find out what dietary restrictions there might be for people who have renal failure.
2. Visit the MS Society website and find out more about multiple sclerosis. To obtain a secure link to this website, see the Hotlinks section on p. x.

Potential risk

Key term

Socio-economic – relates to social and economic or financial factors

Sometimes body systems stop working as efficiently as they should and this can result in the onset of illnesses or diseases. In this section, you will learn about potential risk factors that could contribute to malfunctions and how people are cared for.

Factors

There are different risk factors that will contribute to how susceptible a person is to becoming ill. Lifestyle, environmental and inherited factors can all increase the risk of developing a disease or condition that affects the daily activities of individuals. Age is also considered to be a risk factor as certain diseases and conditions become more common as we age.

Table 7.9 Risk factors that contribute to illness

Lifestyle Factors	Environmental Factors	Inherited Factors
Diet	Quality of housing	Chromosome abnormalities such as:
Exercise	Air quality	Down's syndrome
Stress	Water quality	Haemophilia
Use of drugs	Noise pollution	Cystic fibrosis
Use of alcohol	Employment	Achondoplasia
Smoking	**Socio-economic** status	
	Safe neighbourhood	

Lifestyle factors

Lifestyle factors tend to relate to the choices we all make about how we want to live our lives. As you can see in the first column above, an individual can choose whether or not to take exercise and eat a healthy diet, or take drugs, drink alcohol or smoke cigarettes. Many people are aware of the health risks of their lifestyle but believe their health will not be affected, or that they have plenty of time to change their behaviour when they get older. However, there are clear links between some behaviours and disease. Obesity, a poor diet and lack of exercise coupled with smoking can contribute to coronary heart disease and stroke, and a diet high in fat and sugar can contribute to type two diabetes.

Stress can play a large part in determining the onset of some diseases. This may be due to overwork or personal problems and may be short or long term. Sometimes, environmental factors such as those described below can be a cause of stress to people, resulting in anger and raised blood pressure.

Environmental factors

Environmental factors are not necessarily related to choice. People who live on a low income or are unemployed will not have the means to move out of an area that could be harmful to their health and – in the case of air or water quality – may not have the ability to change their environment. Various diseases have been linked to environmental factors; for example asthmatic attacks can be triggered by particles of dust, animal dander and pollen in the atmosphere, as well as by other allergens.

Inherited factors

Inherited factors are a result of genetic abnormalities. Whether or not someone develops an inherited condition or disease is often down to chance, although people are more likely to develop some diseases if both their parents were affected by, or were carriers of, the disease. The age of the mother is a key factor in a baby being born with Down's syndrome, with the children of mothers over 35 being much more at risk. Some people who have Down's syndrome have heart and lung problems.

Age

Some diseases and conditions become more common as we age, but there are some conditions that develop in childhood and may disappear as children reach adolescence or adulthood. As you have seen on earlier pages diseases such as Parkinson's and MS tend to develop after the age of 50. A lot of people develop osteoarthritis as they age and carrying excess weight can make this condition worse.

Activity: Risk factors

In groups, investigate the different types of risk factor in the table above; find out what they are and how they could affect people's health. Make a poster of your findings.

Assessment activity 7.5 **BTEC** **P5**

Refer back to your work for Assessment activity 7.4 and identify the potential risk factors that may cause or worsen each of the malfunctions you described. You could produce a table with brief notes in order to identify the risk factors. This will allow you to achieve **P5**.

Grading tips

Think carefully about the two malfunctions you are using and consider what you have learned in this unit so far. You might want to refer to specialist websites to find out what causes the malfunctions and what the risk factors are.

You could link this assessment activity to assessment activity 7.6 (page 228) and produce a written report to cover **P4**, **P5** and **P6** (**M3**/**D2**).

PLTS

This task will give you the opportunity to develop skills as an **independent enquirer**, as you plan and carry out research into risk factors for the two malfunctions. Planning your work and organising your time and resources in relation to other demands will help you to become a **self-manager**. Planning your work and collaborating with your partner will help you to become an **effective participator**.

Functional skills

Writing a report about risk factors will help you to practise **ICT** research skills and **English** skills. You may wish to import diagrams or pictures to illustrate the points you are making.

Just checking

1. What is a risk factor?
2. Find out who you would contact if you were concerned about noise pollution and air and water quality in your area. How would this be investigated?

5. Routine care given to individuals with body malfunctions

This topic will look at the routine care which needs to be given to individuals with body malfunctions.

Monitoring body systems

The care given to individuals will be based upon measurements and observations, and regular monitoring of a patient's condition will give health care workers an indication of how successful their care and advice is being. For example, the respiration rate of an individual suffering from chronic bronchitis, or the blood pressure results of someone with high blood pressure, will be important indicators of health status.

Lifestyle changes

Often, doctors will advise patients to make some lifestyle changes to help to reduce the risks of becoming ill or to aid recovery if they have become ill already. For example, after a heart attack, a patient may be advised to stop smoking, take exercise and change their diet, to try to reduce fatty deposits in their blood vessels. Similarly, patients with type two diabetes will be advised to reduce the amount of fat and sugar in their diet.

Use of aids

There is a wide variety of aids available for people who need help with daily activities, including special cutlery for people who have had a stroke, or walking sticks, crutches and walking frames for those whose mobility is reduced. In some cases (for example, following a hip or knee replacement) the use of aids will be temporary during the convalescent period. Maintaining mobility is important because it helps to retain a person's independence, which has a positive effect on self esteem and self confidence. Weight bearing activity such as walking can help to prevent osteoporosis and is a good form of exercise.

Activities

Healthcare aids

Visit a website that supplies aids for people who need them (such as NRS or Handy Health Care) and research the different types of aids that are available. To obtain a secure link to these websites, see the Hotlinks secton on p. x.

Monitored dose systems

Find out more about monitored dose and nomad systems. What are they and who can use them?

Service users who have been treated in hospital may need to have their homes assessed before they are discharged – especially if they live alone – to ensure that they will be able to manage. A home visit will allow the Occupational Therapist to see how someone copes, and what aids or adaptations to their home may be needed.

Support for self administered medication

Some service users are determined to maintain their independence for as long as possible and wish to be in charge of their own medication. Many individuals are completely able to do this, but others may need to use a monitored dose system where a week's supply of drugs is provided in labelled daily doses. Items such as inhalers can safely be left with some service users, as they know when and how much they can take, and people with diabetes are usually familiar with calculating and injecting the correct dose of insulin for themselves.

Appropriate environment: temperature

Service users in residential care should be in an appropriate environment where the temperature is comfortable and the accommodation is well-lit and ventilated. People living in their own homes should try to maintain the temperature at a comfortable level. People on a low income may try to save money by not putting their heating on and may be in danger of hypothermia, where the body becomes too cold to function. Every year, older people receive the Winter Fuel Allowance to help with the cost of heating.

Maintenance of mobility

Maintaining mobility helps to retain a person's independence which has a positive effect on self-esteem and self-confidence. Weight bearing activity such as walking can help to prevent osteoporosis, and is a good all round form of exercise. In addition, movement creates heat in the body and keeping active may help to prevent hypothermia. Even sitting in a chair and exercising can help by maintaining muscle time and strength and lung function for someone with breathing difficulties.

Controlling risks: infection

The immune system tends to be less effective as we age, so older people are more at risk from infections. It can take a long time to recover so it is important to do as much as possible to prevent any infection taking hold. A good diet with plenty of fresh fruit and vegetables will provide the body with essential vitamins and minerals and good personal hygiene, including careful hand washing, can also protect against infection. Care workers who deal with food should know the basics of good food hygiene and can gain a food hygiene certificate.

Activity: Winter Fuel Payments

Find out about the Winter Fuel Payment. Who receives it and how much do they get? To obtain a secure link to this website, see the Hotlinks section on p. x.

Controlling risks: falls

Minimising the risk of falls can be as simple as ensuring that carpets and rugs are in good condition, there are no trailing leads on the floor and there are no obstacles in walkways. However, someone who is unsteady on their feet or has balance problems may need aids and other assistance to move around. People living in their own homes may need to have a stair lift fitted and steps into and out of the house could be replaced with a ramp.

If someone is unsteady on their feet or has balance problems, such as a service user who has Parkinson's disease or multiple sclerosis, they may need to use aids and/or be assisted to move around. People who have high blood pressure may have dizzy spells. People with diabetes who do not manage their condition are at greater risk of collapsing due to blood levels of glucose being too high or too low.

PLTS

Working on this task will allow you to conduct some research and explore issues surrounding care giving which will give you practice in becoming an **independent enquirer**. As you prepare your work you will be able to manage your time efficiently, set yourself goals and review your progress as a **self-manager** and **reflective learner**.

Functional skills

You should be able to refine your **ICT** research skills and **English** skills. You may wish to import diagrams or pictures to illustrate the points you are making. Make sure that you have read through your work thoroughly before submitting it, checking grammar, spelling and punctuation carefully.

BTEC **Assessment activity 7.6**  **P6** **M3** **D2**

Refer back to the two malfunctions you have researched for assessment activities 7.4 and 7.5 and find out about the routine care that would be given for each malfunction. You should consider the role of monitoring and observation, discuss possible restrictions to diet or lifestyle, and refer to appropriate first aid or medication where relevant.

To achieve **P6**, you must identify the routine care necessary for each malfunction; to achieve **M3**, you must describe each aspect of this care in more detail; and to achieve **D2**, you will need to explain how this care will affect the body systems.

Grading tips

You should be able to find much of the information you need in text books in your learning centre or via reliable websites and you may find the Student BMJ is useful or using leaflets from relevant charities, e.g. the Stroke Association, the British Heart Foundation, or the Arthritis Research Campaign. If you are doing work experience in an appropriate care setting, the staff you are working with may have relevant and useful information. Public libraries are also useful places to find information on disorders.

Just checking

1. Why is it important for some service users to self administer their medication?
2. How can you help to control the risk of infection and why would this help service users to remain as healthy as possible?

Sunny Bhatti
Operating Department Practitioner Trainee

I am training to be an Operating Department Practitioner (ODP) in a large hospital which provides treatment and care for most of the major specialities. I am based in the Operating Department, where there are 12 operating theatres. I am learning about anaesthetics and recovery, which involves looking after patients before they are anaesthetised and after their surgery, as well as assisting surgeons during operations.

Most patients are under anaesthetic when they are being operated on, so it is vital that I and the rest of the team know what their needs are and make sure that they are being met.

Learning about anatomy and physiology is very important because, when I am preparing theatre before operations, I need to know what is going to be done so that I can prepare the correct instruments. I want to make sure I know and understand as much as possible about the different body systems because, during the operation, I need to know what is going on and what instrument the surgeon might need next. It's much more difficult to do my job well if I don't know what's going on!

Think about it!

1. Being an Operating Department Practitioner is just one job within health and social care where a good knowledge of anatomy and physiology is necessary. How many other jobs can you think of where this would be a requirement?

2. Carry out some research into some other body system malfunctions that have not been covered in this chapter. You could investigate the following:

   A fractured hip   Prostate cancer

   An ovarian cyst   Tuberculosis

3. What health and safety issues would need to be considered when working as an Operating Department Practitioner?

Extension activity

Charlie is 58 years old. He is a pub landlord in a run-down area of a large town. There is a high turnover of staff which means that he rarely gets a day off. His working day usually starts at about 9 am and he doesn't normally stop until midnight. He watches television to relax after he finishes and goes to bed at about 2 am most nights. Occasionally he manages to have about two hours off in the afternoon. Charlie played football semi-professionally in his youth and would like to regain his fitness, but although he has joined a gym he either doesn't have the time or feels too tired to go.

The pub does employ a chef but the food on the menu is limited to pies, fish or chicken and chips with everything. Because he is so busy, Charlie eats the pub food every day and will often snack on chocolate bars, pork scratchings and crisps. He has at least a couple of pints of lager most evenings and often has a double whisky after closing "to help him sleep".

One morning, the cleaning staff arrived to find the front door of the pub still locked. They managed to get in through the back door, which was unlocked, and found Charlie semi-conscious on the floor of the bar. He was cold and could not speak clearly. There seemed to be something wrong with the right side of his body as he hadn't been able to get up off the floor, and it looked like he had been there all night. An ambulance was called and Charlie was admitted to hospital.

1. What do you think might have happened to Charlie, and which body system has been affected?

2. Can you identify any risk factors that might have contributed to Charlie's condition?

3. What care could be given to Charlie to help him to recover? Which health care professionals might be involved in his care?

4. You have identified the risk factors that might have contributed to Charlie's current health problem. Devise an action plan with short-, medium- and long-term targets that Charlie can aim for. Remember to take into account his current lifestyle and try to be as realistic as possible about what he can achieve.

5. What might stop Charlie from sticking to the action plan? Can you think of some alternative strategies for him to try?

edexcel :::

Assignment tips

- This unit is about how the body works and what can happen when things go wrong. If you study the systems carefully and understand the structure and function of each system, you will find it much easier to learn about what happens when there is a malfunction.

- Make sure that you understand the importance of taking accurate measurements and observations, as these can be indicators of a change in a patient or individual's physical condition.

- It is important to ensure that all equipment is properly used and maintained. As an employee you have a responsibility to protect yourself, to use equipment provided for its intended purpose and to report safety hazards. Make sure you are familiar with all possible hazards, and ways in which to prevent these.

- When you are caring for individuals, remember that they are individuals and you cannot treat everyone the same. Take the time to get to know the people you are looking after and support and encourage them to be as independent and self-caring as possible.

8 Human lifespan development

There are many aspects of human growth and development which make this a fascinating subject to study. Much of our thinking about this field today is based on work by Abraham Maslow in the 1950s. He considered that our health and well-being were based on many different influences and needs which include physical, intellectual, emotional and social (PIES) factors. Although you will be looking at these factors separately it is important that you remember how each of them is linked. This holistic approach is the basis of much in your work in health and social care and you will often come across PIES. It is also important to remember that the different ages at which various events occur are only guidelines, and people do grow and develop at different rates.

This unit provides a broad overview of human growth and development and explores some of the different aspects of physical, intellectual, emotional and social development that occur across the main life stages. It also encourages you to consider some of the positive and negative influences on human growth and development and the impact these can have on the development of an individual's self-concept. As someone who may work in health and social care, you should be able to take account of these factors when considering the changing care needs of people at different life stages.

Learning outcomes

After completing this unit you should:

1. know developmental changes that occur at different life stages
2. know positive and negative influences on individuals at different life stages
3. know factors that can influence an individual's self-concept
4. understand the different care needs of individuals at different life stages.

Assessment and grading criteria

This table shows you what you must do in order to achieve a **pass**, **merit** or **distinction** grade, and where you can find activities in this book to help you.

To achieve a **pass** grade the evidence must show that you are able to:	To achieve a **merit** grade the evidence must show that, in addition to the pass criteria, you are able to:	To achieve a **distinction** grade the evidence must show that, in addition to the pass and merit criteria, you are able to:
P1 Identify key aspects of physical, intellectual, emotional and social development at each of the life stages. [IE1, SM2, SM3] **Assessment activity 8.1, page 255**	**M1** Outline key aspects of physical, intellectual, emotional and social development at each of the life stages **Assessment activity 8.1, page 255**	
P2 State the positive and negative influences on growth and development [IE3, IE5, SM2, SM3] **Assessment activity 8.2, page 261**		
P3 State the factors that influence an individual's self-concept [IE3, IE5, CT4, SM2, SM3] **Assessment activity 8.3, page 271**	**M2** Outline how factors can influence the development of an individual's self-concept **Assessment activity 8.3, page 271**	**D1** Describe how factors can influence the development of an individual's self-concept **Assessment activity 8.3, page 271**
P4 Explain potential differences in the care needs of individuals at different life stages [CT1, CT2, SM2, SM3, EP3, EP4] **Assessment activity 8.4, page 274**	**M3** Discuss potential differences in the care needs of individuals at different life stages **Assessment activity 8.4, page 274**	**D2** Justify care provided to individuals at their different stages **Assessment activity 8.4, page 274**

How you will be assessed

This unit will be assessed by internal assessment tasks that will be written and marked by the staff at your centre. All of the assessment tasks are checked before they are given to you and some of your work will be internally moderated by other members of staff to make sure it has been assessed fairly. It may also be subject to sampling by your centre's External Verifier as part of Edexcel's quality monitoring process.

Your assessment tasks could be in the form of

- written assignments
- case studies
- presentations
- reports
- posters
- leaflets.

Marek, 16-year-old carer

I really enjoyed this unit because it made me think about all the different things that have gone on in my life and how they have made me the person I am. I liked the work we did on self-concept as I hadn't properly thought about how so many things affect who we are. And many of those things are things we can't do anything about – so we shouldn't always be comparing ourselves to people who have different experiences.

I have been helping my Mum ever since I can remember and this unit has also helped me to understand why she is the way she is. Sometimes I have felt angry that I have to help look after her but now I know I want to help other people who have disabilities. I hope to go to university to become a nurse or maybe someone who works in a centre for people with disabilities.

One thing I liked about this unit is that we got to produce our work in lots of different ways. I was a bit nervous when I started college because I am quite shy. I really enjoyed doing small group work because I felt that other people in my group listened to me. I think by the end of my course I might even be the one who can stand up in front of the class to present our ideas!

Over to you!

- Every individual's life experience is different. Can you see why it is so important to understand some of the general characteristics of human development across a lifetime?
- Why do you think it is important that care workers should promote choice and independence with service users?

1. Know developmental changes that occur at different life stages

Growth is usually described as an increase in size, weight or shape. This is quite easy to measure and most of us know how tall we are and how much we weigh.

Development is usually meant to describe changes in complexity. This is harder to measure, although most of us are aware that we can do more complex activities now than we used to. This topic and the following ten will help you to explore developmental changes that occur at different life stages.

PIES

When we think about growth and development we usually do this under the headings of physical, intellectual, emotional and social (PIES). These are all interlinked and influence each other but sometimes it is easier if we look at them individually when studying.

Physical

This refers to things to do with your body. It will include the development of each of your body systems and is affected by both inherited or genetic factors and lifestyle factors.

Intellectual

Intellectual development is to do with the growth of the brain and the development of your thought processes. This includes things like memory, problem solving and an understanding of the world around us.

Emotional

Emotional development is about the growth and understanding of feelings. The ability to receive and give love, care and affection and to feel secure is found in Maslow's hierarchy of needs (see page 52). Emotional development is closely linked to the development of self-esteem.

Social

Social development is about making connections with people and becoming a part of society. It includes your immediate family and friends as well as the community in which you live.

The start: conception and birth

Humans have both internal fertilisation and internal development. Internal development means that the embryo develops inside the mother's body, where it absorbs food and oxygen from the blood. This means the mother is free to lead a reasonably normal life until just before the birth of her baby.

Conception occurs when a sperm meets an egg and fertilises it. The fertilised egg is called an embryo which implants into the wall of the uterus or womb. At about 2 months it is usually called a foetus and it continues to grow and develop for about 9 months.

Did you know?

When a girl is born she already has all her eggs inside her and releases them, usually one at a time, from puberty until the menopause.

Activity: Growing inside the mother

Can you think of things that might affect the baby while it is growing and developing inside the mother?

After about 9 months the baby is usually ready to be born and the mother goes into labour. The uterus walls begin rhythmic muscular contractions, the cervix dilates and the baby passes into the vagina, or birth canal, and out of the mother's body. The baby now has to live on its own as an independent person although of course, human babies remain dependent on their carers for many years.

Mothers and babies start to bond straightaway

Just checking

1. What is the difference between growth and development?
2. Who developed the hierarchy of needs that we often refer to when studying growth and development?
3. How does a baby receive its food and oxygen when it is growing inside the mother?

First steps 1: infancy (0–3 years)

Key term

Reflex – an unlearned and quick response to a stimulus which is usually needed for survival and/or protection

Infancy is a time when growth and development are at their most rapid. This section will look at the physical and intellectual development of infants.

Physical development

Humans are quite helpless and dependent when they are born compared with most other animals and in order to survive they need to be looked after. To ensure this happens they are born with several **reflexes**. These include rooting, sucking, swallowing, grasping, stepping and the startle reflex.

Activity: Health checks

Regular health checks are made on babies to measure their height and weight. Who carries these out? Why do you think this is done?

Babies are almost immobile when they are born and have very little muscular co-ordination. Very quickly, however, they are able to focus their eyes and follow a sound from side to side as well as being able to cry and make gurgling sounds.

Soon the muscles begin to strengthen and babies start to control their movements. This allows them to begin exploring their environment and learn how their world operates. Physical control and co-ordination progress downwards, beginning with the head and moving through the neck, trunk, arms and finally the legs.

Table 8.1: The pattern of physical development in babies

Muscle control	Approximate age
Able to raise head when lying on stomach	2 months
Can grasp objects using whole hand	4 months
Can sit up without support	6 months
Can start to crawl	8 months
Can walk without help	12 months
Can climb stairs and run but often falls	18 months
Can control muscles which allow for toilet training	2 years
Can climb on furniture and kick a ball but not yet catch one	2 years
Can jump and ride a tricycle	3 years

Intellectual development

Intellectual development refers to the development of the mind and allows us to recognise, remember, reason, know and understand things around us. We also develop communication skills which allow us to make ourselves understood and to develop relationships.

As children interact with the environment they gradually organise their thoughts and develop an appropriate set of responses for dealing with the world. These become adapted as new experiences occur giving us all a better understanding of our world.

The best known and most influential theory of intellectual development was proposed by Jean Piaget (1896–1980), a Swiss psychologist.

It is important to remember that development is a continuous process. Piaget suggested that intellectual development takes place through four stages and, although we pass through the stages in the same order, the ages are approximate because children move through them at different rates depending on their environment.

Did you know?

Piaget researched and wrote about children's cognitive development from the 1920s until the 1980s. He believed that children think in an entirely different way to adults and his work has had a huge impact on how we educate children.

It is thought there is a critical period for language development. If this is missed young people never really acquire true language, as has occurred in feral children. Noam Chomsky (born 1928) and Eric Lenneberg (1921–75) are two theorists associated with the development of language.

Activity: Piaget's stages of development

Find out about Piaget's different stages of development. You could do this in the form of a table.

Do you agree with the ages and things Piaget proposed we can (and cannot) do at each stage? Some psychologists suggest that when he carried out his research he asked questions in a way which children could not understand.

Some people think we may not all reach the last stage – what do you think?

PLTS

This task will give you the opportunity to develop skills as an **independent enquirer**.

Language development is another aspect of intellectual development. The milestone is that children should know at least six words by 18 months. Most one-year-olds should be able to name simple objects and by the age of two most are able to put two or three words together into a simple sentence. By the age of three years, most speech should be understandable and children should be able to speak in complete sentences. Children at this age love to have stories read to them, often the same ones over and over again!

Just checking

1. What is meant by a reflex?
2. What are the names of Piaget's different stages of development?
3. What do we mean by the acquisition of 'true language'?

First steps 2: infancy (0–3 years)

My life

Babies' social needs

Can you think of different ways in which a baby's social needs are met?
Try to think of formal and informal ways.

Infancy is a time when growth and development are at their most rapid. This section will look at the emotional and social development of infants.

Emotional development

The way in which we are able to form successful relationships depends very much on our early experiences. Many of our ideas are based on the work of the psychiatrist and psychoanalyst John Bowlby (1907–90) who used the term 'attachment' to describe the strong, two-way, emotional bond between a young child and his or her main caregiver. This is necessary for a sense of security and the development of trust and self-worth.

One-year-old babies are able to learn about the effect their behaviour has on their caregivers and can express emotions through tears, laughter and facial expressions.

Two-year-old children are known for their temper tantrums as they struggle to express their emotions. They are able to show a certain degree of empathy which is often expressed through play, for example, punishing or praising a doll.

By the age of three years, children are more sensitive to others' feelings and are willing to share toys and take turns when playing. They are interested in having friends and this is often when children start nursery or playgroup.

Case study: Susie at playgroup

Susie, aged 3 years, has just started playgroup and she misses her mum. She is always quiet for the first ten minutes but when she sees her favourite toy she settles down. However, she gets cross when someone else wants to play with the things she is playing with.

1. What is the term often used to describe the emotional bond between carer and child?
2. Why do you think Susie behaves the way she does?
3. What advice might you give to Susie's mum to make the transition to playgroup easier?
4. Have you got any ideas of how the nursery could make things easier for Susie?

Social development

Our need to be sociable seems to be something we are born with. Even babies of a few days old will react to the sound of human speech and focus on pictures of human faces more than on other pictures. If you watch and listen you will observe that older babies and toddlers make social moves towards each other and are pleased to see each other.

Social development is very closely linked to emotional development as described above. At first the most important relationships are those with primary carers and other family members whereas relationships with peers become more important as children get older.

Young children form friendships and tend to show preferences for particular people. Language skills are important in the development of these relationships and, as children develop, they are more able to express their feelings verbally. Contact between ages is part of normal family life and children benefit from spending time with both older and younger people. Often children start nursery at this age and this provides an opportunity for them to share time with different age groups. If you watch closely you can see that children adjust their communication styles and understand that different types of communication are needed depending on who they are with.

One way in which children develop social relationships outside their families is through play.

Activity: Playtime

Try to arrange a visit to a nursery or playgroup where you can spend a morning observing the children at play. Are there differences between the ways different aged children play? What about boys and girls – do they show differences in their play? Note how the children communicate with each other and the workers.

Play is an essential part of growing up

Just checking

1. What do we mean when we talk about attachment in terms of human development?
2. Name the different stages of play which are a part of our social development.

Childhood (3–11 years): 1

Childhood is such an exciting stage of development with physical skills developing as well as children learning about the society in which they live. They become much more independent and in some cultures already start to take on many responsibilities.

Physical development

Growth continues to be rapid during this phase, although not as fast as in the first three years, and body proportions are beginning to be more adult-like.

The main feature of this stage is that *gross* and *fine motor skills* are becoming more advanced.

Activity: Gross or fine motor skills

Copy out the table and for each of the activities say whether you think a child would be developing gross or fine motor skills, or both. You might want to discuss this with a partner and see if you agree. At which age do you think a child is able to carry out each of the activities?

Activity	Gross motor skills	Fine motor skills	Both
Tying shoes			
Making and decorating a cake			
Playing football			
Building a brick tower			
Playing a musical instrument			
Throwing a ball			
Gymnastics			

What skills can children learn through these activities?

Intellectual development

We can only guess what children are thinking by what they do and later by what they say. During this stage of development many changes take place and in many countries this is the time when children often start formal schooling. Many ideas about what we should be teaching children at this stage are based on Piaget's theories about what children are capable of understanding.

Activity: Conservation

Go back to your work in the previous section on Piaget to remind yourself of the stages of intellectual development. Make sure you understand the terms pre-operational and concrete operational.

If you have access to a child in this age group try this experiment. Get two glasses, one tall and thin and the other short and squat. Get a measuring jug and pour the same amount of water into each glass – you can even let the child watch you do this. Ask the child which glass has the most water.

As a group you may be able to try this out on children of different ages and see if there is a difference.

Piaget called this concept *conservation*. Try to find out what this means.

You can also do a similar experiment with Smarties. Find out how.

PLTS

This task will give you the opportunity to develop skills as an **independent enquirer**.

As children get older they are able to carry out more logical activities. They can begin to understand different concepts but often need to actually see concrete objects in order to understand them. For instance, when learning about fractions children can understand the concept but only if they can use a concrete example such as dividing up a pie so that a number of people can each have some.

As children progress through this stage they become fluent in language and may develop a good vocabulary. They become able to construct sentences and use grammar fairly well, which is what psychologists call *true language* – it involves more than just knowing words. Interest in reading and writing develops.

It is also during this stage that children begin to be able to see things from perspectives other than their own, in other words they begin to become less **egocentric**. They also have a sense of past, present and future.

Moral development is something that also begins during this phase. This is the process by which children adopt the rules and expectations of the society in which they are brought up and develop a sense of right and wrong. This is learned from the people around them.

Key term

Egocentric – centred on the self; thinking chiefly about oneself

Just checking

1. How do your body proportions change as you move through the stages of development?
2. Explain what is meant by the term 'concrete operational'.
3. Who do we learn our moral sense from?

Childhood (3–11 years): 2

Emotional development

Case study: Martha

Anna was half an hour late picking up her daughter, Martha, from nursery and when she got there Martha was anxiously looking out of the window. As soon as Anna opened the door Martha rushed over and jumped into her arms. The next day Martha was upset when Anna dropped her off at nursery.

1. Do you think Martha's response was a 'normal' one?
2. How could Anna help Martha?

As children progress through this stage they begin to loosen the bonds with their main carers although they still need their support. They begin to be more independent and start to develop a sense of 'self'.

Most of our emotional responses are learned from our primary caregivers. Children learn to be in control of their emotional responses and to resolve conflict and carers should praise them when this occurs while trying to understand the temper tantrums of frustration that do occur.

Children begin to show signs of compassion and empathy and again, carers need to encourage this. During this stage children also develop the ability to talk about their feelings. Even at a young age children will say things such as, 'I feel sad' or, 'That makes me happy'.

Case study: Joe

Sunita knew there was something wrong as soon as Joe (aged 11) came in from school. He was trying to act normal because Sunita's friend, Sheena, was there. He tended to bottle up his feelings like his father but later blurted out that one of his friends was very ill and in hospital. Sunita could see how upset he was because his eyes started filling with tears but he went up to his room and started listening to his music.

1. What do you think about the saying 'Big boys don't cry'?
2. Are there cultural differences in the expectations of how boys and girls express emotion?

Social development

As children develop into social beings they go through what is termed *socialisation*. Primary socialisation takes place within the family although there are many different types of family.

Relationships with people outside the family become more important as children move through this stage. As mentioned in the previous section, one way in which these relationships develop is through play.

Table 8.2: Ages and types of play

Type of play	Approximate age	Features
Solitary	0 to 2 years	Young children like to explore and play with a wide range of toys by themselves. They also like games of imagination and make-believe.
Parallel	2 to 3 years	Toddlers will play alongside others and will even watch what they do but do not play together.
Simple co-operative	3 to 5 years	Children join in many different activities with others and learn to share and take turns.
Complex co-operative	5 years onwards	Children make up complex games with others, organising themselves and making up their own rules.

Activity: Types of family

Find out about the different types of family.

How do you think your family has influenced the way you have developed?

You might think about things like the food you eat, whether or not you eat together as a family, the television you watch, and the kinds of things you do at the weekends.

Are these different from the way things happen in your friends' families?

Activity

Look at the table below and decide at which stage of play these children are.

Case study	Stage of play
Jo and Nathan are playing with a cardboard box, pretending it is a car. They take turns to climb inside and be the driver.	
Erin is sitting on her own on the mat, stacking a pile of bricks.	
Joshua, Joel and Lisa are playing monsters. Joel tells Joshua he must hide under the climbing frame. He tells Lisa to go to the corner and count to ten before coming to look for them.	
Janine and Jason are at the play dough table. Jason is copying Janine as she rolls play dough into a long sausage.	

Just checking

1. Name three different types of family.
2. What do you understand by the term socialisation?
3. Can you give some examples of how a parent can provide emotional support to their children?

Teenagers (11–18 years): 1

Key term

Puberty – time of rapid growth during adolescence when a young person becomes physically able to reproduce

Think about it

What does it feel like when a girl gets her period for the first time?

How does a boy feel when his voice cracks when he is talking?

How does it feel to get a spot on your face just before going out to meet up with friends?

How does a short boy feel when his friends seem to grow faster than he does?

Adolescence is the stage during which we move from childhood to adulthood. It is a time of important physical changes which include **puberty**, after which we are biologically able to reproduce. There are also intellectual changes, which develop as we learn to understand more complex concepts, emotional changes, during which we develop our individuality, and social changes which, in some cultures, change our status in society. This is often marked by a *rite of passage*. Can you think of any?

Physical development

At puberty, chemicals in your body called hormones (see Unit 7, page 203) trigger many physical changes, including growth spurts and weight increases, and boys and girls begin to change and look different as they grow into young men and women.

Figure 8.1: Many changes take place in boys and girls during puberty.

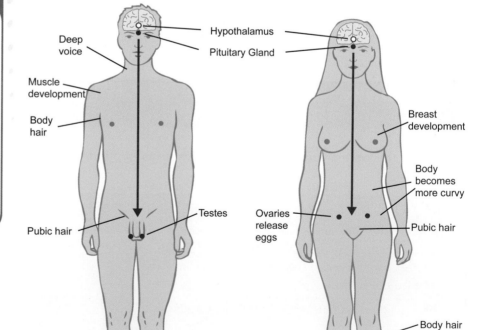

Intellectual development

If you look back at your work on Piaget, this is the stage at which people develop the ability to work with abstract concepts and develop problem-solving skills.

Activity: Questions

Young children would find it hard to answer the question below. How about you?

Anna is taller than Eleanor.

Eleanor is taller than Alison.

Who is tallest?

Think about it

Some people think that genetics is a major influence on intelligence while others think environment is more important.

What do you think?

Ideas about religion and politics may also begin to occupy the minds of teenagers as they realise that the world is more complex than it might have seemed when they were younger and that issues are not 'black and white'. Long-term memory also develops which enables teens to study for and pass exams.

Adolescents are able to start thinking about possibilities for both their immediate and long-term futures and plan ahead. Decisions such as whether or not to continue in education or to go out to work may be options for some, for example.

Moral codes develop during adolescence. Kohlberg (1927–87) was an American psychologist who studied this in the 1960s and 1970s. Kohlberg devised a theory of stages of moral development which described the different ways we decide on what is right and wrong at different stages in our lives. Many people find they have to challenge their ideas about right and wrong during adolescence.

Just checking

1. Give three examples of physical changes that take place during puberty for boys and girls.
2. What is meant by an 'abstract concept'?
3. What is moral development?

Teenagers (11–18 years): 2

My life

Yeah, whatever

Write down all the words you can think of that are used to describe teenagers in today's society. Are these positive or negative?

Key terms

Storm and stress – the English translation of 'Sturm und Drang', a German literary movement that emphasised the volatile emotional life of the individual

Peer group – a group of people who share at least one identifying characteristic, for example, age group, gender, job role or living environment

Think about it

How would you describe your adolescence?

What is, or was, your relationship like with your parents/carers?

What are/were the good things about being an adolescent?

What are/were your biggest sources of unhappiness?

What do/did the adults around you get wrong when dealing with you?

What do/did they get right?

Emotional development

Erik Erikson (1902–94) saw adolescence as the most important period in the development of adult personality. Many other psychologists have described this period as one of **storm and stress** as young people try to develop their own individual identity and *emotional intelligence*.

Often teenagers alternate from behaving like children and then behaving as adults. They also often feel misunderstood and may challenge parental values, deliberately pushing against boundaries which are often perceived as too restrictive or controlling. This, in turn, is perceived as rebelliousness by carers and family tension can result.

Teenagers become less dependent on family for emotional support and turn to their friends for advice. This is called the influence of the **peer group**. Young people want to be accepted by their friends and this can sometimes lead to difficult situations, affecting both self-esteem and self-concept – these topics will be covered later in this chapter.

Case study: Tamara

Tamara was 15 when she met Joe at a local youth club. He was several years older than her and she found him very good looking and mature. He asked her out and before long they were meeting regularly. Tamara felt very grown up now she had a boyfriend like Joe although her friends were worried about her. Tamara's parents were also very unhappy and there started to be frequent rows at home. Tamara's parents were keen for her to concentrate more on her schoolwork and to get good grades.

Joe soon persuaded Tamara to sleep with him and Tamara started lying to her parents about where she was and who she was with. Joe also encouraged Tamara to start drinking and she soon found it difficult to concentrate on her schoolwork.

A few months later Joe suddenly stopped wanting to see Tamara and seemed to be hanging around with another set of friends. Tamara was shocked and upset and felt let down and used. A few weeks later Tamara discovered she was pregnant.

1. What should Tamara do?
2. Do you think adolescents can make good parents?
3. How do you think Tamara's parents might deal with this situation?

Social development

Social and emotional development are intertwined and, as teenagers gain independence, they spend more time with friends. This allows them to practise social skills, sometimes called *social intelligence*.

Albert Bandura (born 1925) is a psychologist who called learning from our social environment *social learning* and its influence depends very much on the culture in which we are born. For some adolescents factors such as living in poverty, living in a dysfunctional family and/or living in an area of high crime make this period of life more difficult.

As teenagers turn more to their peers they often struggle because they want to be liked. Peer recognition is very important and things like the types of clothes worn and interests that are followed become significant.

Peer pressure can also present difficulties as it can challenge many of the ideas learned from families. This is often a period during which issues such as experimenting with alcohol, sexual orientation and attitudes towards education are examined.

Think about it

What do you think is the difference between social intelligence and social learning?

Activity: Statements

Do you agree with the statements below?

I should be a nice person and live up to the expectations of people I know and care about.

I want others to think well of me (social approval).

I should be good so that the social system I live in doesn't fall apart.

Figure 8.2: Teenagers are often stereotyped unfairly

Wayside Road

Just checking

1. What is meant by social learning?
2. What is meant by emotional intelligence?

Grown-up (18–65 years): 1

This is a stage of great change because it covers such a wide age range. For this reason it is often divided into early adulthood, mid-adulthood and late adulthood. This section will only deal with the first two of these as there is a separate section on late adulthood. Before people have reached this stage there is a tendency to think it must be so easy: you can go out and do what you like, go to bed when you want, have money, etc. But ask any adult if they think it is easy and many will say that there are so many big decisions that they have to make.

Physical development

People in their twenties and thirties (early adulthood) are usually at the peak of their physical development. They are fully mature and it is at this stage that many people have children.

Most elite athletes perform at their best in their twenties and even have to think about retiring after this! Good exercise regimes and a healthy lifestyle can help to extend this and many individuals decide to start to develop their fitness after this age.

From about the age of 30 the physical ageing process begins and people begin to notice a number of changes. These can include:

- wrinkling of skin
- greying and thinning hair
- hearing and sight decline
- bones lose calcium
- circulatory system not as efficient
- flexibility reduces
- the menopause for women over 50.

Some people have trouble accepting these changes.

Intellectual development

Intellectual development certainly does not stop after the age of 18. Most people in our society either continue with their education or start work at this stage.

Many young adults continue with their education at a college or university. Here they study a wide variety of programmes which may be purely academic or more vocational. Even after this, intellectual development does not stop. Once at work, many new skills will be developed and individuals may well also follow a number of more formal training courses. Young adults continue to develop problem-solving and decision-making skills.

Many adults return to formal education if circumstances have prevented them from achieving all they wanted when they were younger. They may be juggling work and families as well as studying, which requires considerable organisation and commitment (which are intellectual skills in themselves).

There is some evidence that memory declines with age and, just as your physical self needs exercise to keep flexible, so your mind also needs to be kept active.

Intellectual health is as important as physical health. It includes creativity, general knowledge and common sense and does not just involve knowing a lot of academic facts.

Did you know?

Using your mind strengthens the connections between brain cells and so boosts mental sharpness.

Exercise your mental muscles:

Call phone numbers from memory.

Remember your shopping without taking a list.

Try to do a Sudoku or some other kind of puzzle.

Activity: Intellectual health

Answer the following questions:

1. Are you easily bored?
2. What do you do to 'exercise your mind'?
3. Do you enjoy reading?
4. What TV programmes do you regularly watch?
5. Do you have a job? How long do you work and do you find it challenging?

Asking questions, playing games and reading informally are all ways to stimulate your mind and to keep you intellectually healthy.

Just checking

1. Describe some of the physical changes that take place during the later stages of adulthood.
2. What do we mean by intellectual health?

Grown-up (18–65 years): 2

Activity: Emotional development

1. Look up Erik Erikson and read about his eight stages of development.

   What are the outcomes for adulthood?

   Do you agree with the outcomes he describes for each of the other stages?

2. Draw a timeline with as many of the different emotional changes you can think of that take place during adulthood.

Functional skills

This activity will give you the opportunity to develop your **ICT** skills if you create your timeline on a computer.

Emotional development

Erikson looked at people's emotional development throughout the life stages. This is often known as Erikson's 'Eight Stages of Man'.

Erikson divided adulthood into two, with individuals in their twenties and thirties thinking about life partners and developing close emotional bonds with one person. This is also the time when many people decide to start a family, which means new responsibilities. This is usually a positive experience although there are often conflicting pressures on young families. Most young adults have the emotional maturity to manage these, although there are sometimes too many pressures and they may need to access outside help.

Middle adulthood, from the forties onward, is also a period of change and for some these changes can cause a *mid-life crisis*. People will start to become aware of their physical ageing, women will go through the menopause, there are fewer job options, many children are thinking of leaving home and middle-aged adults may be helping look after their own ageing parents, who are themselves experiencing difficulties.

But for most people it is a positive time. Their experience is valued, they have been productive, there is more freedom as children leave home and individuals are usually established in their communities. Individuals can look at the contribution they have made to society which gives them a sense of belonging and well-being.

What sorts of pressures might this young family face?

Social development

Social changes are significant throughout this life stage. In our twenties we usually do not have too many responsibilities and most people are able to spend quite a lot of their free time socialising. Friendships are important, both same sex and opposite sex, and meeting new people is often an exciting activity.

There are many different types of relationships that develop, both personal and public. The personal ones will be the extended family, long-term friends and, possibly, a life partner.

Public relationships are those that take place in the wider world, including the world of work. Social networks are developed and maintained through a number of different ways.

Activity: Social networking

How many different examples can you think of where you are developing or maintaining your social network?

Can you think of how technology has changed this over the years?

Do you think that maintaining social networks is different for 20-year-olds and 50-year-olds?

In our society there are norms of behaviour – what society expects. For example, it is the norm that people in this society will work for a living. This gives us a role and a sense of identity as well as extending our social world. When people meet for the first time one of the questions that is often asked is 'What do you do?' Work is seen as very important as it gives individuals a social identity, social status and contact outside the family. We will look at the effects of unemployment in a later section.

It can be hard to balance all the demands of family and work and still have time for fun and personal relationships. However, communication makes all of our social interactions possible and there are many different types of communication depending on the situation.

Activity: Communication

Try writing a short holiday postcard to:

1. Your best friend
2. An elderly relative
3. A small child

Is the way you have written this different for each?

Just checking

1. Describe the main features of young adulthood and mid-adulthood.
2. What do we mean by social networking?

Never too old (from 65 years): 1

Different societies have different ideas about what is meant by old age. In this society we usually take it to mean from 65 years as this is the normal time for people to retire from the world of work. Whichever society you are in the end of this stage is death.

Physical development

The ageing process progresses more quickly once most people reach their sixties. At some point almost all older people will have to deal with some sort of disability as they are no longer able to do the same things they did when they were younger. But it is important to remember that being older is not an illness!

Activity: Effects of ageing

Complete the table below on some of the different physical effects of ageing and what can be done to remedy these. The first couple have been done for you. Can you add some more to the list?

Body organ/system	Effects of ageing	Remedy
The brain	Some memory loss	Keep mentally active
The eyes	May find difficulty reading	Get reading glasses and have good light
The ears		
The skeleton and joints		
The skin		
The hair		

Intellectual development

Think of many of our senior politicians or judges – they are older but still contribute to our society in a positive way. Many people do not retire until much later and often act as advisors due to long life experience and wisdom.

Older people can still learn different skills and hobbies, which has been shown to help people age in a positive way. They can learn a foreign

Did you know?

The study of ageing is called gerontology.

What ways can you keep socially active in older age?

language, play scrabble or bridge, learn to play a musical instrument, or join a painting or pottery class. Many of these activities also involve increased interactions with other people, which in itself provides mental stimulation.

But there is also evidence that some older people are less able to solve problems as quickly. Often they are less flexible in their approach and may sometimes be described as 'set in their ways'. The risk of memory loss increases with age and most cases of dementia are recorded in older people.

Some lifestyle factors seem to be important. For example, studies have shown that older people who walk regularly, who eat a lot of leafy green vegetables and who eat fish at least once a week keep more mentally active than those who do not.

Social factors can also be important. Older people who live with family members and who have a lot of human interactions tend to do better both in terms of physical and intellectual health than those who are more isolated in old age.

On a positive note, when we look at the overall perspective, a vast majority of older people are intellectually sharp and creative. The fact that they may be a little slower at some tasks than they were in their youth impacts only minimally on their lives.

Just checking

1. Describe five physical changes that we associate with older age.
2. Why is it important for an older person to keep mentally active?

Never too old (from 65 years): 2

Activity: In control

Studies have shown that having a sense of control over one's life makes you feel happier. One group of older people in a care home were told they didn't have to worry about anything and that everything would be taken care of for them. Another group were told that they would have to organise all their own activities although they would be supported.

Can you guess which group were happier?

Emotional development

As with all aspects of development in older age there are positive and negative aspects to emotional development.

In many societies the wisdom of old age is valued so those individuals feel they are making a contribution to their communities. But if this is not the case it can make people feel that they are just a burden.

Many older people are pleased to have more free time and are able to spend their retirement visiting family and friends or pursuing their hobbies. According to Erikson they have come to terms with their lives and have a sense of satisfaction with what they have achieved.

Case study: Monica

Monica is 78 years old and her husband died eight years ago. She has osteoarthritis which affects her fingers, hands and back. This causes her pain when she tries to carry out regular daily living activities. She also becomes breathless when she walks to the shops. Monica is a little forgetful and worries about making mistakes when she has to do things like pay bills.

Monica has little social contact. Her son lives abroad and although he contacts her regularly he rarely visits. Monica's daughter, son-in-law and their three children live nearby. Monica does get visits from them but finds the children tiring after a while.

Monica has been feeling a little depressed lately.

1. Have you got any suggestions for Monica which might make her happier?

2. What could Monica's family do to help?

Social development

Not working usually means less social contact but more time to spend with friends and family. Many people prepare for retirement by developing interests that can be followed later and others may do voluntary work. These kinds of social interactions have been shown to be important for a healthy older age.

Social isolation can, however, still happen. If families do not live nearby, when partners and friends die or health problems make it difficult to get out, it is easy to become isolated and depressed. But there are now many services designed to help avoid this situation.

Activity: Social encounters

Talk to an older person and ask them how often they go out, who they go out with and what they do. For example, they may have coffee with a friend, go shopping or start on a DIY project.

You could also compare this with adults and teenagers.

Based on this information which group would you say were the most social?

Which group had the most variety of activities?

What kind of organised activities for older people are there in your neighbourhood?

There are many ageist assumptions made about older people which are not true. For example, most older people do not suffer from dementia or have a physical disability and many do not have to use the health service particularly often.

Think about it

Think of words which are used to describe older people. Are they stereotypically negative or positive? Why do you think we have these views?

Assessment activity 8.1

 BTEC

PLTS

This activity will give you the opportunity to develop skills as an **independent enquirer** and **self-manager**.

You are going to produce a magazine article for each aspect of development for each age group you have covered.

For **P1**, identify in your article key aspects of physical, intellectual, emotional and social development at each of the life stages. For **M1** you should also outline the key aspects of development by adding further detail for each aspect across each life stage.

As you finish each section in the book, it would be a good idea to jot down the main points for each aspect so that you can use them for your assignment.

It would also be a good idea to start collecting pictures you might use to make your article more interesting.

Think about the types of magazines you like to look at and what it is about them that makes you want to read the articles.

Functional skills

When you write your magazine article you are developing functional skills in **English**, and also **ICT** if you use a computer.

Grading tips

There is a great deal of information available about the development of individuals at different life stages so you will have to select the main features of the PIES development for each age group to present in your assignment for **P1**. For **M1**, you should include a few more notes about each aspect of development at each stage.

Just checking

1. What is meant by the term 'ageism'?
2. Describe three different activities older people might do in order to keep socially engaged.

2. Positive and negative influences on individuals at different life stages

You have looked at the physical, intellectual, emotional and social development of individuals over the lifespan in a general way. Obviously where and how we live our lives will affect this development. These factors are known as *socio-economic* factors and they can sometimes be a positive or a negative influence. This section will introduce you to some of these influences at different life stages – it will be up to you to decide if the influences are positive or negative.

Figure 8.3: There are many factors which influence how we grow and develop

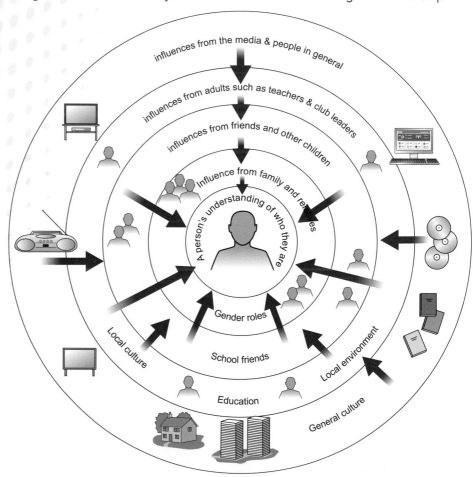

Income

Income is the money a person has to pay for what they need to live their life. This usually comes from paid employment or benefits a person may receive from the government.

According to the Annual Survey of Hours and Earnings (Office for National Statistics) the average weekly earnings in the UK (in 2009) are:

- £531 per week (£27,612 per year) for men

- £426 per week (£22,152 per year) for women.

Low income is considered to be 60% of average income or below. Many people find themselves in debt because they cannot afford to live on the money they have.

Activity: Adequate financial resources

Look at the diagram below which highlights some of the benefits of having adequate financial resources. How might each of these affect your PIES development?

Do you think money makes people happy?

Think about it

Do you know what the National Minimum Wage is? Do you think it is enough to live on?

What kinds of things do you think would be considered good housing and poor housing?

Do you think it is important to have a garden or access to an outdoor play area?

Do you think it is important for each child to have their own room?

Figure 8.4: Having enough money can make a lot of things easier

Housing

Where you live affects many aspects of growth and development. Some people live in cities and towns, some live in the suburbs and some live in rural areas. Where you live may be because of where you grew up, due to your job or down to your choice. There are many benefits to both urban and rural living which can also depend on your stage in life. For example, many young people like living in towns as there are often more social activities and facilities that are accessible to them. Rural life is often quieter, which might suit families with young children.

There are many different types of home and accommodation and this can also affect your health and well-being. Housing standards have improved a great deal in the UK although there are still people who live in inadequate housing.

Just checking

1. List five benefits of having adequate financial resources.
2. What is the National Minimum Wage?
3. List five things you would consider to be found in poor accommodation.

More influences on my life!

Environment

As well as the type of home in which you live, the local environment and your community also affect your growth and development. People often make assumptions about you based on your address, for example. Other environmental factors can include living in overcrowded areas with no recreation spaces, living close to busy roads which are noisy, living near a source of pollution or living a long way away from health and welfare services. Some areas have high crime rates which can be stressful and possibly dangerous. It may also make people afraid to go out and this can impact on their social contacts.

There are several types of pollution that can affect growth and development. These include air, water and noise pollution. Some of these effects can lead to illness or stress.

Education

Education affects development mainly because it affects job opportunities. Higher educational achievement usually gives individuals more choice of the type of career or employment they can follow. In the UK, education is compulsory between the ages of 5 and 16 although many people study beyond that age. Once in work many people continue to develop their skills through training courses which may provide opportunities for promotion.

If a young person chooses to study away from home, for example at university, it helps to develop their independence and allows that person to meet a range of people from a variety of backgrounds.

Culture

We are all influenced by the family and friendship groups we grow up in and every family and friendship group is different. Families and small groups are also influenced by the culture that surrounds them. Culture involves the pattern of behaviour and thinking shared by people living in a group. This includes their beliefs, language, style of dress, religion and the rules they live by.

People are categorised by themselves and others in different ways; for example, race, social class, ethnicity or religion. Sometimes this can lead to stereotyping and people may make generalisations about others based on, for example, the types of clothes they wear.

Key components of culture are *values* and *norms*.

Values are ideas about what in life seems important to a particular group of people.

Norms are the expectations of how people will behave. If people do not conform to those norms there are sanctions. Sometimes these may

What assumptions might you make about each of these people?

Think about it

How many different ways can you think of to categorise yourself?

be things like being snubbed by your peer group and this can affect your self-esteem. Other sanctions imposed by society include fines or even being sent to prison.

Rituals are carried out by all societies. Some of these are simple things which you might class as good manners. Sometimes there are rituals which mark the passage of a young person into adulthood. Other rituals involve how a wedding ceremony or funeral is carried out, for example.

The UK is classed as a multicultural society. Sometimes this can cause problems as people do not always understand the ways of other societies. This is called a culture clash. It can also cause problems between generations within the same culture as parents may have different expectations from their children as to how to conduct their lives.

Gender

Gender and sex are two different things. A person's sex is genetically determined whereas their gender is about the expectations of behaviour of that sex. If, for example, you look at a toy catalogue you will find many gender-stereotyped examples: girls' toys are often pink and involve nurturing types of behaviour whereas boys' toys are often rough and tumble action toys.

Gender stereotypes are also reinforced by the types of jobs people are directed to. For example, the health and social care sector is mainly staffed by women although today many more men are choosing jobs in this area. Once in work there are employment laws against discrimination.

Sometimes people feel they are a different gender from their biological sex. In the past, and still in some cultures, this was treated as something to be ashamed of. Today in many societies it is beginning to be more accepted.

Activity: Be ladylike. Act like a man

Get two large pieces of paper. Write 'Be ladylike' on one and 'Act like a man' on the other. On each piece of paper write some of the words that are often used to describe men and women. You might include words like 'strong' and 'don't cry' for men and 'giggling' and 'sensitive' for girls.

It might be fun to do this as a group – you could use post-its and all contribute.

Just checking

1. What do we mean by values and norms?
2. Give some examples of gender stereotypes.
3. List some of the factors to do with the environment which can affect your growth and development.

People influence my life

My life

Relationships

Think of all the different people you are involved with and the type of relationship you have with them.

Relationships

People need relationships to feel happy and thrive and we have a wonderful skill which allows us to be sociable, friendly and co-operative with each other. Of course there are many different types of relationship, some formal and some informal. Also, different types of relationship form at different life stages and each of these will affect our growth and development in different ways, sometimes positively, sometimes negatively.

Friendships

First relationships are with your parents or carers and are important as they set the tone for future relationships. You may remember from your work on attachment that infants learn how to express emotions and interact with others based on these first relationships.

Throughout our lifetime we make friends. Friends provide stimulation and they certainly influence you. Friends can be reassuring but can sometimes make you feel bad. People usually choose their friends from those they meet regularly and with whom they share interests and values.

During childhood, friends are often within same-sex groups. During adolescence relationships change as puberty results in feelings of physical attraction to others. During this stage peer pressure can have a huge influence.

Adult relationships often develop through work, hobbies or through activities carried out with children.

Older people also need friends and when they retire can sometimes feel lonely if they are no longer meeting people on a daily basis. However, many older people do have more time and may meet new friends through leisure activities as long as they are able to keep active. As we get older some friends will be lost through illness or death and this can also lead to loneliness, especially after the death of a life partner.

Case study: George

George is 15 and seems to be having a difficult adolescence. He feels his family don't like his friends and he is always having rows with them about how he dresses and what time he should come home after an evening out.

He really prefers to go out with his friends or stay in his room when at home these days rather than join in with the family because of the constant nagging. He feels his parents are always on at him about his school work – most of his friends do not like school and are often bunking off. He has started to join

them and is now often in trouble at school as well as at home.

Some of the time George feels pleased that he has got a gang of friends, but lately they have started doing things he feels uncomfortable with, such as drinking and shoplifting. He knows these things are wrong but feels strong when he is part of a group.

1. What do you think George could do to make himself feel better?

2. Who could he talk to?

Sexual relationships

Intimate relationships develop as you grow up and begin to be able to put someone other than yourself first. You become more comfortable with your sexuality and, as you become more emotionally mature, long-lasting relationships develop. Sexual intercourse is an expression of physical attraction but is also a powerful expression of this intimacy. Many young people often confuse sex with love and distinguishing between these can be difficult.

Sexual orientation depends on whether you are attracted to someone of the same or the opposite sex. Because of society's expectations, if your sexual orientation is different from the norm it can have an effect on your self-concept.

Family relationships

Becoming a parent is a natural and fulfilling role. However, having a child is a huge commitment – another person is totally dependent on you – and this responsibility requires many skills and qualities, such as patience and unselfishness. Some parents experience difficulties with their children and there is no one right way to bring up a child.

Sibling relationships are relationships between brothers and sisters. Having siblings can teach you how to co-operate, which is a useful skill for later relationships. Sometimes sibling rivalry happens if brothers and sisters compete with each other, but this also helps children learn how to deal with disputes, and usually having brothers and sisters is a positive experience.

Working relationships

Most adults spend a lot of their time working and so form relationships with the people with whom they work.

There will be formal relationships with managers and the influence these have on your development will depend on how that manager makes you feel. Good managers will make you feel valued and part of a team and a good atmosphere at work is important.

Activity: Families

Think about the different types of family groups listed below:

- Nuclear families
- Single parent families
- Stepfamilies
- Extended families
- Foster families

How might belonging to each of these affect someone's development?

PLTS

This activity will give you the opportunity to develop skills as an **independent enquirer** and **self-manager**.

BTEC Assessment activity 8.2   P2

Use a case study to produce a report on factors that might influence the development of individuals (P1). You should base your report on an elderly individual who may be someone you know and can interview or a case study similar to the one about George on the previous page. Alternatively, your report could be based on a case study of a family made up of different generations.

Grading tip

Before starting your report, review the previous section of this chapter and read the following section about life events to remind you of the factors that might influence the development of the individual or individuals in your case study. Remember to always relate what you say in the report to the case study you have chosen.

Just checking

1. List the different types of relationships that influence people.
2. Describe the different family types that are found in societies today.

Things happen

Life pushes us through changes at particular points. These periods of change are all **transition** points which can be a little unsettling. They are usually counterbalanced by periods of calm and stability. These changes may make us feel awkward or even be painful but they are necessary because life does not stand still.

Some change is inevitable. For example, your body changes as you grow and develop; you learn many new things and you become more independent and develop different types of relationships as you grow up. These changes are predictable life events and our society generally prepares us for them. Other life events are unpredictable such as developing a serious illness, family break up or moving to a new country. These events are usually more stressful because they are unexpected and you may have had little control over them.

This section looks at a range of such life events and helps you to consider the effects they may have on human growth and development.

Activity: Timeline

Get a large sheet of paper and draw a line across it with a mark for each year of your life. For each year, think of something that happened to you and write it either above your timeline if you felt it was a positive experience or below it if you felt it had a negative impact. You might include things like starting school, birth of a sibling, parents separating or best friend moving away.

Compare what you have included with a classmate. Did you have similar things written down?

Predictable life events

Expected life events tend to happen at particular points in your life. You have already considered some of the physical changes that occur through the lifespan. This section looks at expected events at different stages rather than developmental changes.

Of course not all of these events are necessarily expected in all families and the positive and negative effects will be different for everyone. You can probably think of many more positive and negative effects of each event in your own life.

There are also many other expected life events that take place and there may be some different ones in different cultures. Can you think of any more?

Table 8.3: Predictable life events and their possible effects

Life stage	Predictable life events	Possible effects	
		Positive	Negative
Infancy and Childhood (birth to 10 years)	Birth of a sibling	Proud, important as older child, responsible	Jealous, threatened due to less attention
	Starting school	Stimulating, grown-up	Uncertain, sad at leaving carers
Adolescence (11–18 years)	Development of close relationships	Someone to share concerns with	Loss of innocence of childhood
Adulthood (18–65 years)	Leaving home	Feeling of independence	Financial concerns
	Marriage	Sharing life with someone who cares for you	Have to make compromises
	Parenthood	Intense emotional relationship with child	Scared of responsibility, loss of sleep, impact on social life
	Starting work	Regular income	Less free time
Older age (65+ years)	Retirement	More free time	Less structure to day, less money, loneliness, may become ill

Case study: Nathan

Nathan was 3 years old when his baby brother was born. He could not understand why everybody was making such a fuss over this new baby and no one seemed to take much notice of him anymore. Not long after the baby was born Granny came to stay and she definitely seemed to like the baby more than she liked him. One day Granny told him she was going to take him to nursery school but Nathan did not want to go. He wanted to stay with Mum and cried all morning. Then people started to tell him not to be silly and that made him feel even worse.

1. What emotional effects do you think the birth of the baby had on Nathan?

2. Do you think it was a good idea to send Nathan to nursery just after the birth of his brother?

Just checking

1. List three expected life events that occur in your culture at your age.
2. How does starting school affect your PIES development?

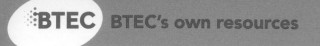

Unpredictable life events

Sometimes events happen that take us by surprise and we will not have had any preparation for them. We may well see them taking place in other people's lives but never think it will happen to us. If these events do occur they can change your life forever. Most of these events seem to be ones which involve some sort of loss and require a great deal of adjustment.

Dealing with these unplanned events can often be very difficult and people often ask the question, 'Why me?' Reactions such as anger and frustration are common and research has shown that it is better to allow the grief that is usually associated with these events to be expressed and form part of the healing process. If those feelings are repressed there are often long-term psychological problems. In some cultures it is more accepted to demonstrate grief and there are often rituals associated with this. Do you know of any?

Serious illness or injury

Most of us have had some sort of illness in our lives and, usually, this is not serious. Sometimes, however, people can develop a condition or become ill where the consequences are permanent. Such conditions may be genetic, developmental, environmental, because of accidents or they may have developed as a result of an infection. There are many types of disability which can result from any of these conditions.

People with disabilities have to make adjustments to their lives. They may lose their independence and the loss of a job as well as having to deal with the reactions of others. Many wheelchair users, for example, feel that people talk to their carers rather than to them which makes them feel as if they do not really exist. People with mental disabilities are often ignored as people do not understand their situation. There are many support groups available which many people find helpful in these circumstances.

Divorce

When a couple decides to marry they usually promise to look after each other, be faithful and share responsibility for any children they may have. Unfortunately, for a variety of reasons marriages sometimes fail and, although there are many more divorces today than in previous years, it is a difficult time for the couple and their families. Usually the individuals will be financially worse off as two homes need to be maintained. Arrangements for children are made so that they are able to spend time with both parents and although many children find this difficult, if handled sensitively, it need not have a serious negative impact. Many parents will go on to develop new relationships and this also requires many readjustments.

Case study: Ryan, age 15

Ryan was 7 when his father left his mother. He does not remember him very well now because, although he used to speak to him on the phone occasionally at first, he has not heard from him for several years. His mother thinks he has moved abroad for work. Money was tight because Ryan's father did not help them financially. Ryan's mother had a job which provided them with the basics but there was never any left over for extras. This made Ryan feel left out with his school friends.

Ryan's mother started seeing a new man and although that helped things financially, Ryan was not really sure he was the right person for his mum. He often had rows with this man and the atmosphere at home was not very relaxed.

1. What aspects of PIES were affected when Ryan's father left home?
2. What changes is Ryan going through now?

Redundancy and unemployment

Starting work is an expected life event for most people in the UK. Sometimes, however, people are unable to get a job and find they are unemployed. Others may have worked for many years and are made redundant because either the job is no longer needed or the company has gone bankrupt. There are many adjustments that need to be made in such situations and it is a difficult time for most people. Financial pressures, lack of a daily routine and a loss of a sense of identity can result in considerable stress for the individual and their families.

Bereavement

Bereavement can be an expected or an unexpected event depending on when and which family member or friend has passed away. As we get older we expect to lose our parents or our partners but we do not expect to lose a child, sibling, parent or close friend when they are young. In any of these situations a grieving process takes place and people experience a range of emotions. There may be disbelief that the person has died; there may be sadness, anger or guilt depending on the circumstances. It is hard to change but adjustments have to take place as you learn to cope without that significant person in your life.

Abuse

Unfortunately sometimes individuals are the victims of abuse. This can be physical or emotional and usually happens when someone wants to exert some sort of power over someone else. The abuser has often been the victim of abuse themselves and doesn't know any other way to behave. Abuse can take place with children or older people, at home or at work. Sometimes at school children suffer from bullying, which is also a form of abuse and needs to be dealt with appropriately.

Just checking

1. List three different types of disability and describe how people make adjustments to accommodate these.
2. Make a list of some of the effects of redundancy on a person and their family.
3. Think of two examples of physical abuse and two examples of emotional abuse.

3. Factors that can influence an individual's self-concept

Self-concept

Self-concept is the knowledge you have about who you are; it is sometimes described as self-awareness. Self-concept is usually thought of as being based on three things:

- **self-image** which is your idea of who you are
- **ideal self** which is who you would like to be
- **self-esteem** which is how you like and value yourself.

You have seen in the previous section that as you go through the different life stages there are many factors which will influence who you are. The way in which you perceive yourself and how you feel about it will also develop and change.

It is important to have a sense of yourself because it affects what you say and do in relation to others. It can make you feel self-confident or anxious, it can help you to lead an enjoyable life or lead you into difficulties; it can motivate you to do better at things or stop you from getting into trouble.

Self-image

When you are describing yourself to someone you usually use four types of description. These might describe:

- your social role, for example, I am a student
- your personality, for example, I am outgoing
- your physical self, for example, I am sporty
- your intellectual abilities, for example, I am good at maths.

Information about your self-image comes from many places but there are three main ones. These include:

- reactions of others. Your idea of who you are depends a lot on how you think other people see you. As you interact with people you build up an idea of the kind of person you think you are based on people's gestures, words, actions and facial expressions.
- social comparison. We often compare ourselves to others in order to build up a picture of who we are. For example, when school work is returned you usually want to know how you have done in comparison with everyone else. Or, if you are running a race, your sense of your sporting abilities depends on how well you have done.
- observing your own behaviour. The ability to do this is something that develops as you become more mature. You may not always like how you act in certain situations and try to do something differently. A lot of work in health and social care depends on this ability to be self-reflective.

Figure 8.5: What you see and what others see may not be the same

Ideal self

Your ideal self is the kind of person you would like to be. This may well be influenced by a variety of role models. There will be people you admire and you may wish you could be like them. Of course, unless you know them well, you are only seeing a very small aspect of their lives but they can still have a very large influence on your ideal self. If your self-image and ideal self are close then you are likely to feel good about yourself but, if they are not, then you may have low self-esteem.

Self-esteem

Self-esteem is really about how you value yourself. It is certainly not fixed and can be different in different areas of your life. For example, you may feel that you are clever because you have always done well at school and this would raise your self-esteem. But you may not be very popular with your classmates and this might lower your self-esteem.

Activity: Self-concept

How do you rate yourself on the questions below? Rate yourself from 1 to 5 with 1 for the lowest opinion and 5 for the highest opinion.

Physical self: How good are you generally at sport and physical activity?

Intellectual self: How good are you at general academic work?

Emotional self: How good are you at understanding other people's feelings?

Social self: How good are you at relationships with your peers?

Obviously there are many more questions you could ask but these sorts of questionnaires can help you to build up a picture of who you are in relation to others. Many similar questionnaires are used by interviewers to help decide if a person is right for a particular job or career.

PLTS

This activity will give you the opportunity to develop skills as a **reflective learner** as you think about the questions.

Just checking

1. What do we mean by self-image?
2. How is self-image different from self-esteem?

Why am I me?

Factors affecting self–concept

There are many factors that affect your self-concept, just as there are many factors that affect your growth and development.

Age

Our self-concept changes as we age. We learn what other people think about us from a young age and from that develop a sense of self. Your parents or carers will have had a huge impact on the development of your self-concept. Parenting classes try to help parents who may be struggling so that their children will feel valued and develop into self-confident people.

Each different age presents different challenges to our self-concept and feelings of self-worth. When you are a teenager, what your peer group think about you probably matters more than what your parents think. When you are an adult you may well define yourself in terms of your job and your ability to provide for your family. As you get older the visible signs of ageing can be difficult and the phrase 'growing old gracefully' becomes more relevant.

Appearance

What we look like is very important to most of us. Faces are usually the most important feature by which we recognise each other and babies respond to pictures of human faces after only a few days. We make assumptions about people from their faces, the way they dress and their general body shape.

Figure 8.6: What do you think their self-concept is?

Table 8.4: Self-concept at different life stages

Life stage	Self-concept
Infants (0–3 years)	Self-concept mainly limited to descriptions of visible characteristics like boy or girl or age.
Children (4–10 years)	Children describe themselves in terms of various categories such as hair colour, their family, which school they go to. They are also able to start describing how they feel.
Adolescents (11–18 years)	Self-concept is often described in terms of how they compare to others and their relationships with peers. They can also describe their beliefs and what they think is right or wrong.
Adults (18–65 years)	Self-concept develops as individuals become more confident in their personal relationships and establish themselves in a particular career.
Older adults (65+)	Most older adults are self-aware and have a lot of 'wisdom'. Once they have lost their work role they may not feel valued.

If someone has a birthmark on their face or if they have had an accident which has affected their face, it can have a huge impact on their self-concept depending on how people respond.

Many adolescent girls think they need to be thin, probably because of some of the role models they see in magazines or television. This can lead to the development of eating disorders in some cases.

Activity: Role models

We learn our roles through socialisation and we learn attitudes, behaviours and skills from role models. From about the age of eight we start to choose who we will imitate rather than just copying those in our immediate surroundings. It is important, therefore that we have good role models.

Each of the different types of role models below can be positive or negative. Complete the table to describe behaviours for a positive role model and a negative one for each.

Role model	Positive	Negative
Parents		
Gender role models		
Peers		
Celebrities		

Media

We are much more exposed to many different forms of the media today than previous generations. This has probably affected our ideas of who we are and how we should behave.

Activity: The media

The media has a large influence on our ideas of the ideal self. We see adverts with 'the ideal family', 'the ideal shape' or 'the ideal holiday'. Most of us do not have lives like that and sometimes people can feel bad if they are unable to live that kind of life.

What do we mean by the media? Can you give some examples?

Discuss media representations of female weight. Have these changed in the last few years?

Think about media representations of disability and list disabled characters in popular TV programmes. What effect do these have on disabled and non-disabled viewers?

Discuss media representations of mental health problems.

Just checking

1. What do we mean by role models?
2. Name as many different forms of media as you can.
3. Identify five aspects of your appearance and say how these can affect your self-esteem.

269

Why else am I me?

Culture

As we have seen in the previous section, culture has an effect on your development. It is what binds groups together and provides a sense of belonging and shared identity. It sets norms of behaviour about many features of life including diet, morality, dress and gender roles. Your culture forms a part of your socialisation process.

If a group of people feel discriminated against due to their culture it will affect their self-concept. The attitudes of others are important in how we feel about ourselves and it is important to be aware of cultural differences when interacting with a variety of people. People who work in health and social care need to be aware of these differences so that they deal with service users in a sensitive manner.

Gender

There are expectations of behaviour for men and women. These may have changed over time, for example it is more acceptable today for women to work outside the home than it was in previous generations; but there are still ideas about gender roles that exist in society.

The value we as a society place on these roles can have an effect on a person's self-concept.

Education

Experiences at school can certainly affect how we feel about ourselves. Educational achievement can increase our self-esteem but not everyone is successful in the school environment. Education can also challenge our values and it gives us an opportunity to explore new ideas.

Income

The self-esteem of people who grow up in low income families may well be affected, especially when we are surrounded by images of people who have a lot more material wealth. It is important to remember that possessions are not the only important things in life, as long as a basic standard of living is maintained. In the UK we have a social service provision for this.

Relationships

The quality of our emotional relationships influences how we feel about ourselves throughout our whole lives. If the relationships are positive we will probably be happy and successful and feel good about ourselves.

Abuse

We all respond differently to the range of life events that occur. Some of this will be to do with our personalities; some will be to do with the age at which different events take place and some with how long the events last.

Unfortunately there are some people who suffer abuse. This can take several different forms, including physical, sexual or emotional abuse. Abuse can happen to people at any age: children may be abused by their carers; young people may be bullied by their peers; couples may abuse each other and yet still stay together and older people can be abused if they are being cared for by others. Whatever form of abuse has occurred, the effects are harmful. Sometimes the abuse is short term and most people recover from this but abusers often frighten the abused person into not saying anything and the abuse can continue for many years.

There are laws to protect vulnerable people but much abuse takes place behind closed doors and is not always detected. If abuse is detected there are many organisations which can provide support.

Just checking

1. Which sorts of people are vulnerable to abuse?
2. How can knowledge of different cultures be useful when dealing with people who use services?
3. Explain how gender stereotypes can affect your self-esteem.

Case Study: Zac

Zac is 43. He has spent 17 years of his life in custody for various crimes including theft and grievous bodily harm. His childhood was made difficult by abuse and violence. He grew up with feelings of anger, injustice and bitterness. He often found it difficult to control these feelings and it led to him committing offences. Sometimes his responses were out of proportion to the event such as beating someone up for looking at his girlfriend. He is now out of prison and is trying to keep straight.

1. What sort of self-image do you think Zac has?
2. What sort of things would help Zac to remain out of trouble?
3. What kind of things might tempt him to return to his old ways?

Assessment activity 8.3

Use a case study of an individual provided by your tutor for this task. State the factors that have influenced the individual's self-concept (P3). For M2 you will need to add some notes about how the factors have influenced the individual's self-concept and for D1, describe these in more detail.

Grading tips

You could present your case study for P3 using a visual format such as a wall chart, leaflet or presentation. To achieve M3 and D3 you will need to allow room in your evidence to include the notes and extra detail required for these criteria. For D1 you will need to consider how the factors that influence self-concept are not straightforward and are often interrelated.

PLTS

As you complete this activity you will develop skills as an **independent enquirer, self-manager** and **creative thinker**.

Functional skills

As you complete this activity you will develop functional skills in **English** and **ICT** if you type up your factors.

4. Understand different care needs of individuals at different life stages

People may need support or help at different times in their lives. This may be short-term support or full-time complete care and different people and services can help to provide this. There are many aspects of care and a lot of different factors to consider. Multi-disciplinary teams are best able to meet the differing care needs of people on an individual basis, giving people choice and trying to maintain their independence for as long as possible. This involves careful assessment of a person's needs and a plan as to how these needs can best be met.

Providing for care

Abraham Maslow (see page 52) identified different needs which he considered important to each individual. Health and social care workers in particular must be familiar with these needs when providing support to service users. Obviously these needs will vary for each individual but you should be able to identify broadly what some of these needs are. The next stage is to determine how these needs can be met and who is the best person or service to provide them.

Informal care

Informal care is provided by family, friends, neighbours or others. It is usually unpaid and not overseen by any organisation. There are several million informal carers in the UK although it is hard to know the exact number. Sometimes children may care for a parent who has a disability, a neighbour may well do some of the heavy shopping for an older person or someone may just pop in for a coffee to give that person some company.

Formal care

Providers of formal care can be separated into three sectors: public, private and voluntary (or not-for-profit).

Historically the provision was split into health care and social care but today there is a holistic approach to care and there is a huge overlap between these. Multi-disciplinary teams also ensure that the appropriate service is used to best support the differing needs of the particular service user.

Social care providers include: residential homes; day-care centres; domestic help; home care; support group; refuges; family support; Youth Offending Team; palliative care; housing; fostering; young carers; child protection; adoption; telephone helplines; learning disabilities team; occupational therapy; counselling; Citizens Advice Bureau; physical disabilities team.

Health service providers include: chiropodists; pharmacists; health care assistants; hygienists; doctors; opticians; dentists; midwives; physiotherapists; health visitors and nurses such as community, hospital and practice nurses.

Care needs at different life stages

Look back at your work on individual needs and remind yourself of Maslow's hierarchy of needs. These needs should be met at all ages and there will be many similarities. There will also be differences as to how these needs are met at each life stage and who is best able to meet that need. Carers for people at each of these stages need to be aware of developmental stages so that they can treat all individuals with respect.

Infancy

Infants are completely dependent on carers to meet all their needs. The most important of these are physical, such as food, warmth, shelter and safety. They also have emotional needs and initial relationships are important.

Childhood

Children are still dependent on their carers to meet their physical needs as well as providing an emotionally secure environment. Intellectual needs are generally met by school attendance. Relationships begin to develop and social needs should also be met.

Adolescence

Adolescents become more and more able to function independently although it is still important that they have an emotionally secure environment. Social acceptance is generally crucial, as is a group of peers with whom they can interact. Carers who work with adolescents need to appreciate their growing independence.

Adulthood

Adults in need of care services may well need help with the activities of daily life but should be enabled to lead as independent a life as possible. Adults will also need to feel part of a group and social activities are important.

Older adulthood

As people face the end of their lives they will probably require some sort of support. As well as helping with their physical needs it should not be forgotten that older adults also have intellectual, emotional and social needs which must be met.

Activity: Health and social care providers

1. Find out what each of these health and social care services, such as health visitor, occupational therapist and social worker, actually does.

   This is the kind of information a health and social care worker would need to know before they are able to refer a person to the most appropriate service. Remember that much support is provided by several providers working together as a multi-disciplinary team.

2. Make a list of all the different services you think a family with an adolescent with a learning difficulty might need.

Think about it

Can you think of any barriers there might be for each group in accessing health and social care services?

Case study: Margaret

Margaret is 76 years of age and until recently lived an independent life. She had worked as a housekeeper and was able to manage both her daily and financial arrangements. Four months ago Margaret suffered a stroke which affected her speech and mobility. Initially she was very frustrated and found daily living arrangements such as washing, dressing and feeding a struggle. After discussion with a social worker Margaret now has the support of her neighbour, a

home help and a physiotherapist. The support has helped Margaret enormously and she now feels much happier and more confident.

1. Think about how Maslow's hierarchy of needs has been addressed in Margaret's situation.

2. How do you think Margaret's self-concept might have been affected by her situation?

Just checking

1. What is the difference between formal and informal care?
2. How does a family support worker help families?
3. Name three services that an adult might use but young people are unlikely to access.
4. What kind of services can support children with health issues?

Functional skills

As you complete this activity you will develop functional skills in **English** and **ICT**.

PLTS

As you complete this activity you will be a **creative thinker** a **self-manager** and an **effective participator**.

Care for the carers

It is important to remember that carers also need support. Informal carers especially will not have a professional organisation for support. There are many voluntary support groups and these are extremely valuable as many carers can feel isolated.

Professional carers usually work in teams and are supervised which gives them an opportunity to discuss individual cases and any concerns they may have.

 **BTEC** Assessment activity 8.4   P4 M3 D2

Explain how the care needs of individuals differ in each of the life stages you described in assessment activity 8.1. You should consider what the likely day-to-day needs of individuals in each life stage would be, explain why they have these needs and then compare them to identify differences between potential needs at each life stage (P4). You could present their needs as might be done in a care plan. For M3 you should discuss the differences by including more detail and considering similarities as well as differences in care needs of individuals at each life stage. For D2 you should develop the care plans to identify how the care needs of individuals at each life stage could be met and to justify the plan add a short piece of writing to explain how the plan will meet needs at each stage.

Grading tips

Potential needs (P4) are those which are likely to arise in most individuals at that life stage but do not necessarily arise for every individual at that life stage. For example all newborn infants need to be fed, bathed and toileted but older adults may or may not need help with some or all of these activities. For M3 examples of the detail you could discuss how the needs of individuals can be met so that the individual remains as independent as possible for example, special aids and adaptations at home. For D2, your justification should consider the benefits of the care plan to the individual's choice, dignity, independence etc.

Julie Carson

Early years worker

I am an early years worker in an inner city nursery. I really like that I work with people from a range of backgrounds although this can sometimes present challenges! One of the things we learn in our training is the importance of treating each child as a unique person. We help the children to be strong and independent from a secure and loving base and to help this we are each assigned children for whom we are key workers. As well as developing personal relationships with the children we help them to develop their social skills. We need to appreciate that children learn and develop in different ways and that they are all important. As

workers we need to learn this as well as helping the children appreciate diversity and difference. This helps them to get the best possible start in life.

People think that working in a nursery is just about playing all day. Play is a valuable way of learning many skills, and we use this as a way of supporting all aspects of children's development, but it is not the only way. We also need to understand which aspects of development are helped by various activities. The training to become an early years' practitioner introduces us to all aspects of children's development and we keep up to date with new ideas through CPD activities.

This job is very rewarding although it can be very tiring! The part of the job which I like least is the paperwork although I know it is important. We keep records which help us keep the parents informed about their child's progress.

Think about it!

1. What have you learned in this unit which would help Julie carry out her job effectively?
2. What are all the different roles within a nursery setting?
3. Can you think of other places where you might find an early years worker other than in a nursery?
4. Which skills do you think would be useful if you were applying for a job as a nursery assistant? You might consider things you have learned in other units as well.

Extension activity: Nature or nurture?

You are a social worker visiting a single-parent family where the son, Matthew, aged 13, is getting in increasing trouble with the law as well as missing a lot of school and staying out late at night. Matthew's father left the family home when Matthew was just one and now has no contact with him. Matthew's mother says his father was violent towards her and was constantly in trouble with the police. She says, 'Matthew takes after his father. There's nothing I can do about it.'

1. Which parts of this case study might make you think nature was responsible for Matthew's problems?
2. Which parts of the case study might make you think it is to do with nurture – Matthew's life experiences?
3. Which do you think is the most likely?
4. How do you think Matthew feels about himself?
5. What might be a suitable service to work with this family?
6. What sorts of things might be suggested to support Matthew and his mother?

Assignment tips

*   When you are writing your assignments, it is important to think about all the different age groups. Use your family and friends to get lots of ideas to use as examples to support the things you have learned about. Don't forget to use your own experience as well!

*   Always keep your eyes open for articles in magazines and newspapers – there are a lot of items about the things you have learned because this unit teaches you about things that affect every one of us.

*   Television, especially soaps, can provide you with examples of family relationships and social interactions. Some of them address important issues such as the effect of peer pressure, teenage pregnancy or dealing with disability.

*   You are all pretty knowledgeable about lifespan development, possibly without being aware of it, because you live in communities with a variety of people from different backgrounds and age groups. So, you should be aiming for more than the pass criteria!

*   If you have done a placement, or if you are able to visit different care settings, it would be good to ask the service users about their care needs and who provides them. (Don't forget to ask permission to do this first.)

9 Creative and therapeutic activities in health and social care

What creative or therapeutic activities do you know about?

Have you ever considered how creative and therapeutic activities might be used within health and social care settings?

Have you ever been involved in either a creative or therapeutic activity yourself?

There is a wide range of very different creative and therapeutic activities available that health or care settings can use to benefit the health and well-being of their service users.

This unit will help you to understand more about the various creative and therapeutic activities available and the different settings which use these activities. You will look at the legislation that regulates the practice of these activities and protects the service providers and service users from harm or injury. You will also consider the benefits of these activities for the health and well-being of the service users.

This unit gives you the opportunity to plan and carry out a creative or therapeutic activity for a service user and then from this evaluate the effectiveness of the activity for the service user.

Learning outcomes

After completing this unit you should:

1. know different creative and therapeutic activities and their benefits

2. know legislation and regulations relevant to the implementation of creative and therapeutic activities

3. understand the role of the professional in supporting individuals who undertake creative and therapeutic activities

4. be able to implement appropriate creative and therapeutic activities.

Assessment and grading criteria

This table shows you what you must do in order to achieve a **pass**, **merit** or **distinction** grade, and where you can find activities in this book to help you.

To achieve a **pass** grade the evidence must show that you are able to:	To achieve a **merit** grade the evidence must show that, in addition to the pass criteria, you are able to:	To achieve a **distinction** grade the evidence must show that, in addition to the pass and merit criteria, you are able to:
P1 Identify creative and therapeutic activities for people using health and social care services [IE3, TW1, SM3] **Assessment activity 9.1, page 303**		
P2 Identify the benefits of creative and therapeutic activities for individuals using health and social care services [IE3, TW1, SM3] **Assessment activity 9.1, page 303**	**M1** Outline the benefits of creative and therapeutic activities for individuals using health and social care services **Assessment activity 9.1, page 303**	
P3 Identify legislation, guidelines and policies relevant to the implementation of creative and therapeutic activities [SM3] **Assessment activity 9.2, page 305**	**M2** Outline legislation, guidelines and policies relevant to the implementation of creative and therapeutic activities **Assessment activity 9.2, page 305**	**D1** Describe the importance of relevant legislation, guidelines and policies relevant to the implementation of creative and therapeutic activities **Assessment activity 9.2, page 305**
P4 Explain the role of the professional when planning creative and therapeutic activities in a health and social care environment [IE3, SM3] **Assessment activity 9.3, page 311**		
P5 Plan a creative or therapeutic activity for an individual using health or social care services. [IE2, CT1, CT5, RL4, SM3, EP3,] **Assessment activity 9.4, page 320**	**M3** Carry out a planned creative or therapeutic activity in a health or social care environment **Assessment activity 9.4, page 320**	**D2** Present an evaluation of the effectiveness of your planned activity to meet the holistic needs of an individual **Assessment activity 9.4, page 320**

How you will be assessed

This unit will be assessed by an internal assignment that will be written and marked by the staff at your centre. The External Verifier for your centre may ask to sample coursework as part of Edexcel's ongoing quality assurance procedures. The assignment is designed to allow you to show your knowledge and understanding of activities that would be suitable for service users, either as an enjoyable pastime or for therapy.

These relate to what you should be able to do after completing this unit.

Your assessment could be in the form of:

- presentations
- case studies
- written assignments.

Charlotte, Level 2 college student

I always knew I wanted to work with people. Before I started this health and social care course I thought that I wanted to be a nurse and work in an intensive care unit, but my ideas have changed since I did my second work experience placement. I went to a Day Centre for Adults with Learning Disabilities and I absolutely loved it. I was dreading it at first because my friend Natalie who did the same placement last year told me that it was awful and very frightening because some of the service users find it difficult to communicate. She got very upset because she didn't understand what they were trying to say to her. In the end she asked to be moved.

On my first day I was quite worried because I was thinking about what Natalie had said. But I needn't have been because everyone was really friendly as soon as I walked in the door. Sheila, the manager, explained everything to me and asked Bob, the Senior Carer, to look after me for the day. I had a brilliant time and got involved in all sorts of activities from singing to making cakes for tea. The staff and service users all got on really well together. I have been here one day a week for half of the term and don't want to leave. I hope there will be a job for me here when I finish the course, as I have decided that I really want to work in a setting like this.

Over to you!

- In this unit you will be learning about the different types of activities that you could organise and carry out with service users. Make a list of as many activities as you can and which service user groups they might be suitable for.
- What do you think you could do to prepare yourself for working in a setting where providing different activities is a major part of the work carried out by the carers?

1. Different creative and therapeutic activities and their benefits

Activity: Being creative

You have already read that art and craft activities may require lots of materials to be available for service users to use. Find out where the nearest scrapstore is in your area and find out what it does. As a group arrange a visit, and buy some materials. When you return to school or college, create something useful or decorative with the materials you obtained. This could be done individually or as a large group project.

Did you know?

The word 'photograph' was coined in 1839 by Sir John Herschel and is based on the Greek word *phos* meaning light and *graphe* which means representation by means of lines or drawing, together meaning 'drawing with light'.

Creating a piece of art work, or making something that is decorative and useful, can give people an opportunity to express themselves in a way that doesn't need words and can give a great sense of satisfaction. This can be particularly important in helping people to come to terms with emotional or physical difficulties that they might be experiencing. This topic and the following eleven will help you to explore different creative and therapeutic activities their benefits and the settings in which they may take place.

Expressive art

Expressive art is described as a way of expressing your feelings through different forms of art. People who use it as therapy do not need to have special training or even be particularly talented in any art form. It is quite often spontaneous and those taking part can use many different art forms to create personal art work. These could include painting, drawing, sculpture and collage. People who use expressive art can work alone or with others.

Art and craft

Art and craft activities can include those mentioned above and also pottery, jewellery making, making cards and calendars or even more complicated things such as modelling, making boxes or photograph albums or flower arranging. They often require lots of materials and may also need a model or theme to focus on, for example a bowl of fruit or a vase of flowers. Normally people who do art and craft work alone, but they often enjoy working alongside others for company or to discuss and get ideas.

Photography

Photography includes capturing both still and motion pictures, either with film or, increasingly, digital cameras. People who still use film may also choose to develop their pictures themselves using a dark room, or they may have them developed and framed. They can combine this with digital technology and capture pictures on compact discs which can then be printed. Depending on how interested an individual might be in ICT, various techniques can be used to create different types of art work.

Motion pictures of films are recorded nowadays on digital camcorders which can be transferred to hard disk drives or onto DVD. Again, people who have an interest in filming can create their own storyboards with the appropriate software.

Photo therapy can be used by counsellors as a technique in psychoanalysis and has been described as using therapy as a healing process. People who use this technique see it as a way to effect active change in their lives.

Therapeutic photography does not need to be practised by a counsellor as it can be a way of using photography to work on personal issues or to make sense of life events.

ICT

Information and Communication Technology is becoming more and more popular with many people of all ages, and knowledge of computing is necessary in most workplaces. Computers stimulate the mind and can be a very useful source of information as well as being used for recreational purposes, such as gaming or finding flights and holidays quickly and easily on the Internet. Service users with communication difficulties may find that using different programs on a computer can help them to develop skills, and children can also use ICT to learn. However, using computers for hours on end might lead to isolation as it can be very solitary, and this may not be a good activity for some service users. Although people use computers a lot for learning, they should also be reminded that other sources of information such as books are equally useful as learning tools, and some websites may not contain accurate or reliable information. However, ICT can be an excellent way for people who have limited mobility to stay in touch with friends and relatives.

There is a lot of concern about how the Internet is used, especially on social networking sites. There have been recent stories in the media about adults using these sites inappropriately to try to make contact with children and young people by pretending to be the same age as the users. This has led to the government providing guidance that is intended to protect the vulnerable from possible danger.

Remember

If you are working with service users whose hobby is photography, you need to bear in mind that they will need to obtain consent from anyone who is to be photographed.

Did you know?

You may have heard the term 'silver surfers' which refers to older people who have developed an interest in ICT, particularly after retiring. The Queen is understood to text and email her grandchildren from time to time.

Activity: Networking guidance

Social Networking Guidance provides advice for industry, parents and children about how to stay safe online. You could visit the Information Commissioner's Office website and find out what information is provided. To obtain a secure link to this website, see the Hotlinks section on page x. Then create a leaflet or poster for children and young people, giving advice about how to avoid putting themselves at risk when using the Internet.

Just checking

1. What types of art and craft activities could you carry out with service users?
2. How can computers be used as an activity?

Benefits of expressive art, craft, photography and ICT

Key term

Hand–eye co-ordination – the co-ordinated control of eye movement with hand movement. It allows the brain to process what the eye sees, so that the hand can reach for and touch or grasp an object. Many actions could not be done without it

Activity: Creative activities for children

You are working in a nursery and the room leader has asked you to prepare two creative activities to help the children develop fine motor skills. As a group, discuss the options and decide the most appropriate activities. What equipment would you need for each activity? Identify all of the different benefits that the children might gain from doing the activities.

Caring for people used to focus on what was wrong and how it could be cured or treated. However, nowadays people are looked after *holistically* which means that health and social care professionals care for the whole person – that is, making every effort to meet their PIES needs.

Physical benefits

You may not immediately think that there are very many physical benefits to doing art and craft activities, but there are some that can provide physical benefits. For example, some people might enjoy making furniture which could involve carrying heavy items and some physical work; and someone who enjoys photography, particularly if it involves wildlife or nature, could do a lot of walking. Activities that involve using fine motor skills, such as knitting, sewing or using a computer keyboard, can help to keep fingers nimble, although some people with osteoarthritis may find this difficult. A Nintendo Wii uses interactive technology and there are many Wii games and activities, including golf and tennis, that can be played which will provide physical benefits such as improving **hand–eye co-ordination** for anyone who uses them. The Nintendo DS can help with fine motor skills, as well as providing mental activity with some of the games available.

Cognitive benefits

Any activity that means that you have to think about what you are doing, such as looking at perspective or colour when painting or working out a complicated knitting pattern, helps to keep the brain active. The brain is a bit like a muscle – it needs to be stimulated to prevent boredom and keep it active. If people don't have anything to do they may become bored and this might cause them to suffer some memory loss. Taking part in activities that require concentration will have positive benefits for service users. There are many educational activities that can be accessed on a computer, and 'brain training' with the Nintendo DS may also help to keep the brain active.

Emotional benefits

Raised self-concept and self-esteem are emotional benefits that help service users to remain positive. Being able to create or produce something gives people a sense of achievement and satisfaction, and can provide the motivation to develop new interests. Photography can allow the world to be seen through the eyes of the service user, which can be used by health care workers to develop an understanding of how someone feels, especially if they have communication difficulties.

Figure 9.1: What benefits do computer games offer?

As well as providing a sense of satisfaction and achievement, this can also help a service user to feel valued.

Social benefits

Although many people prefer to work alone when they are being creative, for some people it is an opportunity to work with other people and make new friendships. Sometimes people are quite happy just to take up an artistic hobby for their own amusement, but there are many who prefer to join an art class or club, especially if they are a bit isolated and want to make new friends. Sometimes a hobby such as art can be so successful that it leads to a new career for some people. Using computers can allow people who live alone and are isolated to keep in contact with friends and family.

Just checking

1. Find out what activities are available for the Nintendo Wii that will help people to gain physical benefits from using it.

2. Get together in small groups and identify as many artistic and creative activities as you can. Then come together as a large group and compare your lists. How many activities have you come up with?

Activity: Discussion

Discuss the following view points. Do you agree or disagree?

View 1: 'Only young people should use computers. Old people don't know how to use them and are too old to learn.'

View 2: 'Learning to use a computer helps the mind to work and learning a new skill provides a sense of achievement. Age is not a barrier to learning.'

PLTS

This activity will help you to develop skills as a **reflective learner**.

Dancing, drama and music

Key term

Therapeutic – the treatment of disease or other disorder, something that may benefit health

Activity: The Lebed method

Using the Internet for research, visit the Breast Cancer Haven website to investigate a therapeutic exercise and dance movement programme called the Lebed Method. This was originally started to help those with breast cancer regain their movement. To obtain a secure link to this website, see the Hotlinks section on page x.

You can access this by going into 'How we can we help' and then 'Our therapies' where you select the Lebed Method.

You will also see on this site many other recommended creative and therapeutic activities used with cancer patients and their families.

Discuss your findings and thoughts with your peers.

Living every day with a long-term illness or disability, or recovering from a short-term illness, is not just about treating the part of the body that is affected. Holistic care means looking after the whole person, not just treating the illness or part of the body affected. Activities like dance, drama and music can provide a variety of benefits to service users and can be so enjoyable that they inspire people to take up one or more of them as a lifelong interest.

Dancing

Dancing comes in many forms and is lots of fun at all levels. People of all ages and from all backgrounds can do it. It is an inclusive activity as even people with reduced physical mobility and reduced mental ability can get involved in dance. Some health or social care settings may use dance for the health and well-being of service users or individuals can just access dance in their community as and when they wish to.

Dancing is **therapeutic** because it uses movement to improve the physical and mental well-being of a service user. It is a holistic activity as it focuses on the connection between the mind and body to promote a sense of well-being and, where appropriate, healing.

Dance is available to healthy people and as a complementary method of reducing stress for people with an illness and also for care givers.

As a therapy dance is used in a variety of settings with people who have emotional, social, physical or cognitive conditions and concerns, e.g. children's settings, elderly day care centres, community clubs, residential homes and hospitals to name just a few.

Drama

Drama is classified as an active approach that can help the service user to tell their story, sometimes to solve a problem and to understand the meaning of images. Drama can also be used to strengthen and build relationships. It can involve service users being able to express themselves through different roles and not necessarily acting out specific roles. Similar to drama is role play, however this is more to do with taking on the role of someone else.

Drama can help to set up a supportive and safe environment for service users to express themselves and explore areas that they may have otherwise avoided. This activity is particularly useful when working with children whose speech and vocabulary are not developed enough to enable them to interact with the professionals working with them.

Belonging to a drama group or society is a very popular hobby. It is a very creative activity and people who do not necessarily have a condition or illness can use drama as a way of expressing themselves and purely for enjoyment.

Music

We all respond to music and it can often provide a sense of release or therapy for an individual. A group of people could sing and/or listen to music or songs together or an individual may wish to do this as an activity on their own.

Creating music can be fun as an individual or as a member of a group. Using music as a therapy may be expensive considering the cost of instruments, but these can also be made quite inexpensively out of many household items, e.g. yoghurt pots with lids filled with rice as a shaker.

Music therapy is often used with children and young people with challenging behaviour or with people who have mental health problems. There is some evidence to suggest that music can be helpful in caring for people with Alzheimer's disease.

Did you know?

A master's degree is required to be a dance therapist.

The use of dance to complement traditional and conventional medical therapy started in the 1940s.

Activity: Who?

In pairs, identify the types of client group that you would use drama and role play with.

Who do you think would benefit the most? Why?

Which client groups would be least likely to enjoy drama or role play?

Discuss this with your peers.

Activity: You shall have music wherever you go...

1. In groups or pairs you are to investigate how you can make a musical instrument out of household items. When you have sourced your materials to make your musical instrument, make it and then play it.

   Share your inventions with the rest of your peer group and all play your musical instruments together. Think about how these instruments could be used with service users as a musical activity in a health or social care setting.

2. Chicken Shed is an inclusive theatre in North London. Find out more about what it does and who is involved.

3. Carry out further research into dance, drama and music opportunities in your local area. Put together a booklet that includes information about these opportunities and who can access them. How many are inclusive (available to everyone in the community)?

Did you know?

The Music Therapy Charity was founded in 1969. It promotes and supports research, training and projects using the therapeutic intervention of Music Therapy.

Just checking

1. What benefits does dancing have for young children and older people?
2. What is role play?
3. Identify three household objects that could be used to make musical instruments.

Benefits of dancing, drama and music

People who take part in activities like dance, music and drama often feel a huge sense of satisfaction and achievement because they have been involved in a creative process. Performing in public can seem very daunting to people who have never done it before, but setting a challenge and getting over nerves can provide a real boost to confidence, self-esteem and self-concept.

Physical benefits

Dance is a form of exercise which improves mobility and muscle coordination and reduces muscle tension. People who are overweight can lose weight and tone up at the same time and they can enjoy it so much that it doesn't feel like taking exercise. There have been claims that exercise of the muscles during dancing strengthens the immune system and can actually prevent disease. Television shows such as 'Strictly Come Dancing' have contributed to the growth in popularity of dance, and there are dance classes all over the country offering classes including salsa, tap, hip hop and even belly dancing. Service users who have a physical disability, or who have suffered loss of mobility following a stroke or accident, may be able to regain movement that they have lost.

Children may benefit greatly from being involved in drama as it may help to develop their gross and fine motor skills. People of any age will benefit from the movement and flexibility that drama can provide.

Anyone playing any kind of musical instrument has to have good hand-eye coordination and dexterity. Energy expenditure will depend on the instrument being played, and musicians playing brass or woodwind instruments will have to learn how to use their diaphragms and respiratory system to play effectively.

Cognitive benefits

Drama can stimulate the brain to remember how to play as well as practising a person's language skills. A service user who is recovering from a stroke may find that this activity helps them to regain their speech and provides an opportunity to improve their social interaction and communication skills. Adults and children can benefit a great deal by being involved with drama. Drama can help to stimulate the brain by providing opportunities to think, to remember lines of text and to reason. A person's imagination can be developed through drama as it allows the individual to express their feelings. Communication skills are also helped by the use of drama and role play for any age of service user.

Listening to or playing music can be very stimulating for the brain, and a stimulated brain is a healthy one; i.e. we can see music as exercise for the brain. When a person does not keep their brain active and stimulated it starts to deteriorate, just as any other organ and muscle in the human body does. The deterioration may be seen as a loss of memory. Remembering how to read music, play an instrument or sing a song 'word perfect' ensures the brain keeps working and benefits the service users' overall health and well-being. Learning something new, such as a new song or a piece of music, helps to support cognitive development of service users. Research indicates that the benefits of music for people with Alzheimer's disease can include improved sleeping patterns and behaviour as well as helping to trigger memory and reality awareness.

Emotional benefits

Dance and drama can improve a person's self-awareness, self-confidence and interaction with others. They can be outlets for people to communicate a message or express their feelings, which can be done verbally or non-verbally. In drama people can use mime successfully to convey different feelings. Body language and facial expressions can be used in drama and dance to convey a message.

Music can be helpful for relaxing and it can also be useful to help people to change their moods and feelings when they listen to music or create different types of music. Music can also be used with other types of creative or therapeutic activities, such as yoga, art and crafts, exercise, drama and dancing. Taking part in music – creating it, playing it or singing – positively develops an individual's self-esteem and self-concept.

Social benefits

Dance can be a solitary activity, but is more often a social activity. Even if it is just you and the dance instructor or therapist, you are socialising with another person, but often people will attend classes and develop new friendships. An elderly service user who has recently moved into a residential home might find that dancing could be an activity which helps them to get to know other people and to feel more at ease. Drama may help a service user to form and develop friendships. By taking part in a drama-based activity people will work together as part of a team and they will have the chance to interact with each other. Music brings people together. Going to concerts or festivals to listen to music and see bands and artists playing and singing is a very social activity. Music therapy is often carried out in groups. Creating music, playing music or singing can bring people together and make them feel united and it can also be fun. It can be worrying and lonely for an individual to move away from their familiar surroundings, such as their own home and their family, if they have to move into residential care, for example. Music is an excellent way of including people and making them feel welcome in their new home and environment, and it may also help them to make new friends.

Figure 9.2: How can dancing and playing music help people?

Did you know?

Music therapists work to promote well-being, manage stress, reduce or eliminate pain, enhance the memory and expression of feelings, improve communication and promote physical rehabilitation.

Just checking

1. Who do you think would benefit the most from drama and role play? Why?
2. Which client groups would be least likely to enjoy drama or role play?
3. Create a list of benefits that drama, dancing and music can offer.

Exercise and sport

Key terms

Fibromyalgia – a condition which causes widespread pain and severe fatigue

Depression – a mental illness. It can be a chronic condition or a short-term one related to a life circumstance

Many people enjoy taking exercise and some do this by playing a sport. Sometimes it is just for enjoyment, although many people will play competitively on a regular basis. It is well known that taking exercise releases hormones in the brain called endorphins which give us a feeling of well-being.

Exercise

There are lots of different ways in which people can take exercise, from simply going for a brisk walk to playing soccer at a top class level like Wayne Rooney. If you go for a walk or a jog you can do exercise that costs nothing or, alternatively, you can join an exercise class or gym for which you might pay a subscription or pay at each session. People of all ages and abilities can do some form of exercise that will contribute to health and fitness, even those with very limited mobility. Exercises done in a chair can help to lower blood pressure and can help people with osteoporosis and arthritis, who may not be able to place extra strain on legs, hips and arms. People with Down's syndrome can benefit greatly from exercise. They often have poor muscle development and a tendency to obesity. Taking exercise can help to maintain a healthy heart and control weight.

Sport

You can probably think of many different sports that you and your friends and family take part in, from very popular ones like soccer, rugby and tennis to those that are enjoyed less commonly like ice hockey and lacrosse. Some people who do sport like to play in a team and get great satisfaction from playing together and winning. Others prefer individual sports, like running or cycling, where they are completely reliant on their own ability, strength and stamina. It is important to bear in mind that many people who have disabilities are very keen to play sport and some do this to a very high level, even taking part in the Paralympics.

Swimming

Swimming is good all-round aerobic exercise. It can be a lifetime activity that benefits the whole person and it is classified as being a holistic activity. When an individual is in water, the buoyancy of the water reduces the weight and strain on the body's joints and so it is a great activity for those who have arthritis as it keeps them moving with reduced pain.

Service users with **fibromyalgia** can get benefit from a variety of different water therapies and not just swimming. Warm water exercise can help service users with fibromyalgia by reducing pain, raising the pain threshold, and helping to lessen anxiety and **depression**. Warm water is used because cold water can make the body's muscles tense up.

Not every swimming pool centre has a warm water pool, but there will be a list available from your GP as to your nearest warm water pool where water therapy activities take place. Many hospitals have hydrotherapy pools which are used to treat patients with certain physical and mental conditions, and some special schools have pools so that pupils with disabilities can swim as part of their school routine.

Did you know?

In 2008 in Beijing, China, Ellie Simmonds – who was 13 years old at the time – became Great Britain's youngest-ever individual gold medallist in either the Paralympic or Olympic Games. She won two gold medals in the 100 metre and 400 metre Women's Freestyle races.

Ellie Simmonds was awarded an MBE in 2009.

Activity: EMDP Paralympics

EMDP is the Exercise, Movement and Dance Partnership. It is the lead national governing body for exercise, movement and dance. Carry out some research and find out the physical, cognitive, emotional and social benefits of taking part in movement.

Find out what keep fit and movement classes are available in your area. You can do this through the EMDP website. (To obtain a secure link to this website, see the Hotlinks section on page x.)

Stoke Mandeville Stadium in Aylesbury, Buckinghamshire was the birthplace of the Paralympics, and Stoke Mandeville Hospital is world renowned for its spinal injuries centre. Find out about British Wheelchair Sport and produce a poster which identifies the sports that can be done in a wheelchair.

Just checking

1. What type of exercise and sport can be beneficial?
2. Ellie Simmonds became very well known following her double gold medal performance in the Beijing Paralympics. Find out who else won medals and in which sports.
3. Is swimming best for a particular age group or is it good for anyone?

Benefits of exercise, sport and swimming

It can sometimes seem like a lot of effort to do some exercise when you are tired after a hard day at school or college and you have homework and a paid job as well. However, if you do find the time to fit it into your life then you will get many benefits from it.

Physical benefits

Any kind of physical activity is known to reduce the risk of developing many major illnesses and premature death. Some of the specific physical benefits from exercise are that it can reduce the risk of developing type 2 diabetes, coronary heart disease and some cancers, reduce high blood pressure, protect against osteoporosis by building bone density, help to maintain a healthy weight, treat depression and help to improve sleep and reduce stress. Many types of sport and exercise can help to improve hand–eye co-ordination and build muscles.

Swimming provides an all-over body workout, as nearly all of the body's muscles are used during swimming. It increases flexibility, tones muscles and builds strength; it also builds endurance and cardiovascular health. Swimming provides a low impact therapy for some injuries and conditions, and it can be of particular benefit to people who are obese. There is no strain on the joints of the body when swimming, which makes it an excellent way for someone who needs to lose weight to access an exercise programme.

Cognitive benefits

Researchers are beginning to establish a link between exercise and brain function in humans. It is believed that exercise improves learning and intelligence scores. It helps to improve memory, and can promote recovery after a brain injury. Exercise in childhood is also thought to make the brain more **resilient**. Some sports can help participants to develop problem-solving skills.

Swimming lessons for children help them to develop co-ordination as they learn to move their arms and legs together while staying afloat and breathing.

Emotional benefits

Many people report that they have a real sense of well-being after taking exercise. This is thought to be due to the release of endorphins by the pituitary gland in the brain. These have the effect of providing a feeling of well-being and also suppressing pain. However, scientists now are questioning whether or not this is the case, and believe that perhaps the feeling of well-being comes just from achieving something positive. However, taking part in a sport where there is a competitive

Figure 9.3: Can you think of any memorable sports celebrations?

element can make people feel good when they win, whether it is a solo effort or as part of a team.

Swimming alleviates stress and can be a very relaxing and peaceful activity. It can give a person the space to think over things that might be troubling them without interruptions from everyday life such as ringing phones and constant texts or emails.

Social benefits

Being friends with a group of people can lead to taking up a sport or activity together; alternatively, taking part in team activities provides an opportunity to develop social friendships. This is not only based on the shared aims and team effort required to win a football match, for example, but the after-match activities that take place where genuine friendships can develop through having a shared interest. Some sports teams go on tour which provides opportunities to combine sport with a holiday. This can also have cognitive benefits if different countries are being visited, where groups have the chance to sightsee and learn about different cultures.

Swimming can be a solo activity but it can also be a great way of meeting new friends and it can be a very social activity. There are swimming clubs at most swimming pools where people can meet on a regular basis. Many swimming pools and leisure centres offer free swimming for the elderly. This can be a real benefit for people who live alone as it is an activity they can afford and they get to meet other people rather than being on their own. Many public pools also offer women-only sessions for women who feel uncomfortable about exposing themselves in a swimming costume in front of men, or because there are cultural or religious reasons why they cannot swim at the same time as men. Muslim women who like to swim use these sessions.

Just checking

1. Explain how improving bone density can help to prevent osteoporosis.
2. Suggest some suitable sports that would help to prevent osteoporosis.
3. Identify other exercise or sport that can be done in water and what the benefits might be. Put together a table showing the benefits of each activity.

Gardening, cookery, games and quizzes

My life

Can you dig it, or cook it or play it?

Can you think of times when you have had to do things that you are not particularly interested in and have not enjoyed them very much? Just as you are different from your friends and siblings, service users are all different and have different interests. As a health and social care worker, it is important that you can offer a wide variety of activities to your service users. Brainstorm with a couple of your classmates some activities that have not yet been covered. How easy do you think it would be to organise some of them?

Some service users may want to take part in activities but are not necessarily keen on or able to do something that is very strenuous. It is important as a health and social care worker that you are able to think about and identify alternative activities.

Gardening

Some people develop a lifelong love of gardens and gardening and it can be the thing that many service users miss most if they eventually have to be admitted to residential care. Elderly people who grew up during the war, especially in the countryside, may have been involved in growing vegetables to feed the family. Other people may have developed an interest in a particular species of flower or type of garden, and may just enjoy looking at or being in gardens rather than working in them.

Gardening can be a therapeutic activity for many people with learning disabilities, mental health problems, dementia, physical disabilities and sensory impairment. Specially trained horticultural therapists work with people either in small groups or on a one-to-one basis. The programmes are very supportive and provide a variety of benefits to service users. Thrive is a charity that was set up in 1978 to provide gardening opportunities for people with disabilities. You can find out more about it at the Thrive website. To obtain a secure link to this website, see the Hotlinks section on page x.

How do you think gardening could be beneficial for people?

Cooking

Cooking is an activity that can be done with any age group and with people with different abilities. It is likely that carers will have to supervise cooking sessions for health and safety reasons. If food is being prepared for consumption by members of the public, then at least one member of staff should have a food hygiene certificate.

Cooking and baking can become much more than just producing a cake or a meal. Preparation and planning is important and this can help service users to develop organisational skills. If buying ingredients is required, this can provide opportunities to go out to shops and learn to deal with money. Service users get the chance to see and eat the results of their efforts, and they can progress from making cakes and biscuits to producing a whole meal.

Games

Games can include board games, bingo and various card games. Most board games require at least two people to play and many can involve up to six individuals joining in, or even teams playing against each other. Some board games can be very expensive, but you can make your own for a fraction of the price and can develop your own theme. A pack of playing cards is not very expensive and can be used to play a variety of games – either alone or with a group of people. Many games are suitable for a wide age range, which means that they can be played by families. However, if you are planning to play a game it is important that you consider the ages and abilities of the client group you are working with. Some games are often played mainly in pubs or clubs such as billiards, pool or darts, and there are some traditional games that are unique to different parts of the country, such as Northamptonshire Skittles, or Aunt Sally, which is a popular pub game in Oxfordshire.

Quizzes

There are lots of quiz shows on the television which are very popular, ranging from shows where the public can win large sums of money like 'Who Wants to be a Millionaire?' to a game where celebrities play for fun like 'Never Mind the Buzzcocks' or 'A Question of Sport'. Normally the quiz shows require contestants to have a level of knowledge, sometimes about specific subjects like music or sport, although to appear on 'Mastermind' you need to have extensive knowledge of a specialist subject as well as a wide general knowledge. Many people enjoy being part of a team playing in pub quizzes or for a local community, but for people who have difficulty getting out, there are many quiz magazines that are available.

Activities:

1. Cooking

What types of food could be prepared or cooked by different client groups? How much supervision do you think would be required for each group? Do you think it is possible to carry out cooking activities in every care setting? Why?

2. Quiz

Design or make a game or quiz for a particular client group in a health and social care setting. Make sure that you think carefully about the client group and don't make it too difficult or easy. Make sure that everyone in the setting can take part if they wish to.

Just checking

1. Identify three cooking activities that would be suitable to do with children in Years 1 and 2 at a primary school.
2. In groups, choose three board games that you are familiar with and decide which client groups they would be most suitable for. Then get together as one big group and create a table identifying which client groups each game would be suitable for.
3. Which games are best for the most groups and which would be less suitable?

Benefits of gardening, cookery, games and quizzes

Activity: Organisations

Find out if there are any other organisations in the UK that provide gardening opportunities for people with disabilities or mental health problems.

Find out whether there are clubs and societies in your local area for the following activities:

Chess	Bridge
Snooker	Scrabble
Backgammon	Dominoes

When do they meet and where?

Key terms

Spatial awareness – understanding where things are in relation to other things

Manual dexterity – an ability to perform tasks skilfully with the hands so that it looks easy

Some people find that taking part in activities can be very therapeutic as doing something quiet can be relaxing and allow the brain to rest. Winston Churchill, Prime Minister during the Second World War, used to build brick walls in the garden to help him to relax and switch off from affairs of state.

Physical benefits

Gardening can range from gentle weeding or deadheading plants to an activity that can be surprisingly physical, such as vigorous digging or chopping down trees. A person can burn up about 300 calories doing one hour of moderately active gardening. If gardening includes producing fruit and vegetables then these can also provide the basis for a healthy diet.

Cookery can be a learning opportunity for service users to explore the value of healthy eating. Information about the components of a balanced diet, and how to cook healthily, can help service users to maintain their weight within acceptable limits and help to prevent ill health.

Some games can be useful to help in the development of hand–eye co-ordination, for example darts, snooker, pool and billiards.

Cognitive benefits

A study in Australia that lasted for 16 years, and followed nearly 3,000 people over 60 years of age, found that the risk of their developing dementia reduced by 36 per cent when they gardened every day. The opportunity to learn new practical skills or information about plants and flowers can help to keep the brain active and provide a sense of achievement for those taking part.

Cookery is often used as a learning experience, especially in primary schools. Children can learn about weighing and measuring and the nutritional value of food. In the new Secondary School Curriculum, due to be introduced in 2011, cooking in the form of food technology will become compulsory for all 11–14 year olds, partly as a result of Jamie Oliver's campaign to make school meals more healthy and to educate people about healthy eating.

Playing games and quizzes can be an important part of keeping the brain active. Taking part in quizzes or working on puzzles like sudoku can help to develop analytical skills and logic. Doing crosswords also helps to develop the vocabulary and spelling. Other games can help young children learn colour, number and word recognition, **spatial awareness** and **manual dexterity** among other things.

Emotional benefits

Any creative activity that produces an end result can provide a huge sense of satisfaction and achievement for a service user. Gardening can help to relieve stress and tension and have a very calming influence.

Cooking is a very good way to encourage service users to create something which then allows them to enjoy eating what they have made at the end. Many people get great satisfaction from cooking for others and seeing them enjoy what has been produced. Research suggests that children who eat with their families regularly tend to do better at school, are less depressed and are less likely to smoke, drink alcohol and smoke cannabis than children who eat with their families less than twice a week.

Playing games where there is a chance to win can be very good for an individual's self-esteem and confidence, but it is important to be aware that children sometimes struggle with the concept of losing or seeing their counter drop down a snake in Snakes and Ladders. It is unlikely that children under the age of six will be able to understand the concept of fair play, so it is important that a balance is found between winning and losing. Making sure that the game is pitched to the right age or ability is important. There is no point in playing a game that is too difficult for an individual or a group. They will soon lose interest and feel that there is no point in continuing. Many mainstream games now have junior versions such as Junior Scrabble and Monopoly that can be more enjoyable for children or adults with learning disabilities.

Taking part in quizzes, in whatever form, can provide a sense of satisfaction for lots of people. Many individuals enjoy the challenge of working things out, and usually the harder something is, the more enjoyment can be had when it has been successfully completed. Puzzles such as sudoku can be attempted at different levels of difficulty so they can be suitable for people of differing abilities.

Social benefits

Gardening can be a very social activity when people work together to achieve a goal such as designing a garden from scratch. Friendships are formed based on a common interest and a sense of belonging to a group can make a huge difference in the life of someone who might previously have lived a very isolated existence. The charity Thrive supports about 900 gardening projects throughout the UK so there are many service users who benefit from the social opportunities on offer from this charity.

Cookery can be a very social activity. Working together to produce food, whether it is one item or a whole meal, can help to create friendships, and an interest in a particular style of cookery, such as Italian or Indian food, can strengthen the friendship further. Eating together has always been seen as a very social activity and families who eat together and discuss the day's events around the dinner table tend to be closer. The Women's Institute runs residential themed cookery courses on a regular basis. Some of them are available to non-members, and they are very popular among people who have retired.

Cooking allows service users to enjoy their creations

Just checking

1. What are the benefits of cookery?
2. Who might be helped by gardening activities?
3. What are the benefits of games and quizzes?

Yoga, massage, multi–sensory stimulation and animals as therapy

Alternative and complementary therapies are becoming more popular in the United Kingdom, particularly for helping people to cope with some long-term illnesses or conditions. Alternative therapies tend to be used instead of traditional medical treatments, while complementary therapies can be used alongside conventional medical treatment.

Yoga

Yoga is a Hindu discipline or philosophy that originated in India. It is said to bring the mind and body into harmony or balance using a series of postures, breathing and meditation. It can be done as a group activity or on an individual basis and many people practise yoga every day to help them to feel calm and balanced. There are several different types of yoga. Some focus on spirituality and others can be very physical.

Chair yoga is a type of yoga that has been developed for people who are over the age of 60 or who have disabilities which mean that taking part in normal yoga progammes is impossible. Chair yoga is done in sitting and standing positions and is seen as a programme for achieving physical and mental fitness. Many of the poses have been adapted from traditional yoga poses and it is one of the gentlest forms of yoga available.

Figure 9.4: Yoga is a great way to de-stress

Massage

Massage is a therapy that involves stroking, kneading, rubbing and pressing on different parts of the body with the hands. It is used to help people relax and feel calm. There are many different types of massage, but all are designed to help with the circulation of blood and can reduce pain and stiffness. Sports massage is a specialised form of massage that can be used to treat sports injuries. You do not have to be a sports person to have a sports massage, but they are particularly useful in aiding recovery. Massage is not seen as a cure for any ailment, more as a way of relieving pain and discomfort.

It is very important that service users who want a massage ensure that their therapist is a qualified practitioner to ensure that no damage is done during the treatment. Remember too that some people do not like to be touched so massage may not be an activity that they would choose, even if it might help them.

Multi-sensory stimulation

Multi-sensory stimulation or snoezelen is a method of providing soothing stimulation in rooms specially equipped with equipment that is designed to stimulate all the senses. This includes the use of different fabrics and the use of light, sound, colour, music and scent. Snoezelen can be used for many different service users, with children and adults with profound and multiple learning disabilities, autism, dementia and brain injury. The rooms are not used in any formal way; the equipment in the room tends to be adjusted according to the mood of the service user at any given time.

Animals as therapy

There are a variety of ways in which animals can help people with disabilities or illnesses. Lots of different animals can become involved in therapy, including dogs, cats, dolphins, rabbits and birds. The animals have very specific characteristics and become a fundamental part of the therapy.

Pets as Therapy is a charity that has volunteers who own dogs and cats and take them to different care settings for service users to stroke and cuddle. All the animals have been temperament tested and they are usually very friendly.

Equine assisted psychotherapy is a therapeutic activity that is mainly used with people who have mental health problems. Most of the work is ground based and does not tend to involve horse riding. Equine assisted psychotherapy helps people to explore their feelings and behaviour.

Riding for the Disabled provides opportunities for people with disabilities to ride horses and to take up carriage driving.

Think about it

Find out how many different types of massage there are and what they might be used for.

Activity: Taster event

With a friend, or on your own, enroll in a class or take part in a taster event for an alternative therapy (Yoga, reflexology, aromatherapy, massage). Did you enjoy it?

Evaluate it as an activity that could benefit service users and identify groups of users and how they would benefit.

Just checking

1. Find out how many different types of yoga there are and what each is used for.
2. Which do you think you would be most interested in trying?
3. Find out more about the Riding for the Disabled Association. Which client groups would be most likely to use this charity?

Benefits of yoga, massage, multi-sensory stimulation and animals as therapy

Obviously not every creative and therapeutic activity will provide the same benefits to service users; some will provide many more physical than social or emotional benefits, and some will concentrate much more on developing cognitive skills. A service user might have to be persuaded to take part in activities and it may take some time for them to find something that they are interested in, but it is worth persevering if the final outcome is going to provide benefits.

Physical benefits

There are many physical benefits that people can get from doing yoga. It improves flexibility, muscle tone, posture, respiration and cardiovascular function. It can also help with other disorders particularly relating to the musculo-skeletal system. It also stimulates the endocrine system and boosts the immune system, which will help to fight off infections.

Research has shown that massage can be successful in reducing blood pressure, increasing blood circulation and relieving pain for migraine sufferers. There is also some evidence to suggest that massage can increase the number of white blood cells produced, which helps to boost the immune system. It also aids recovery after an illness or operation. Research has established a link between stroking animals and lowering blood pressure. Stroking animals is also thought to release endorphins in the brain and aid recovery from illness. Horse riding can help to develop gross and fine motor skills and improve muscle tone and posture.

Activity: The Cinnamon Trust

Visit the website of the Cinnamon Trust and find out about the services offered. Look to see how many care establishments in your area allow animals to stay with their owners. Find out how you could become a volunteer for the Trust. To obtain a secure link to this website, see the Hotlinks section on page x.

Cognitive benefits

Any of these activities can help people to learn new skills. Yoga and massage can help people to develop greater concentration skills and increase awareness. Studies have shown that massage improves alertness and performance in office workers. Occupational therapists can work with animals to help children with disabilities so they learn new skills and become more self sufficient. Children are so keen to work with animals that they are highly motivated to learn and achieve.

Emotional benefits

Practising yoga on a regular basis helps to relieve stress and enables people to deal with stressful situations more calmly. Research showed that office workers were less stressed and children with autism were much calmer after massage. Massage also helps to relieve anxiety and depression. People who work in establishments where animals visit have seen some very depressed residents, who didn't interact with anyone, starting to respond when the animals came in. Many people who are no longer able to look after themselves have had to part with their pets to go into residential care, as many care homes do not allow animals to stay with their owners. This can be a great wrench for some elderly people, who find it very difficult to leave a pet which might have been their constant companion for years. The Cinnamon Trust keeps information on care homes and sheltered housing associations which allow pets to live with their owners.

Being able to achieve a new skill such as horse riding can be very positive emotionally, and people who take part in Riding for the Disabled can develop huge self confidence as they achieve different goals.

Social benefits

A lot of people like to practise yoga alone on a daily basis, but there are many yoga classes where people can do yoga together and make new friends. Although massage is generally an activity that is done on a one-to-one basis with a therapist, it is possible that the relaxation it provides can help people to develop social relationships.

Being involved with animals can help service users to become more confident and it is often a way to help people to develop or improve communication skills. Once confidence levels have increased, service users can find it much easier to build relationships with other people. Riding for the Disabled helps people to take part in riding events and competitions and this can have emotional benefits too, especially if they win. It can also help people to become team players and work together.

What benefits can horse riding have?

Just checking

1. In small groups, organise a discussion about which client groups you think would benefit most from yoga and massage. Explain why you think this.

2. In the last few pages you have been introduced to Pets as Therapy, Riding for the Disabled Association and the Cinnamon Trust, all charities that are involved in using animals as therapy. Carry out some research and find out what other organisations use animals as therapy or to help people with disabilities or sensory impairment.

Health and social care settings: 1

There are many different health and social care settings that provide a variety of services for many service users. These services may be related to age, physical or learning disabilities or mental health, and may be community-based, day centres or residential care. You may have to take any or all of these factors into account when you are planning creative or therapeutic activities for service users.

Pre-school care

Pre-school care includes any care that is provided for children before they can go to school at the age of five. It can be held in local community or church halls, or in nurseries that are linked to local primary schools – which can make the transition to school easier. In England every 3 and 4 year old is entitled to 15 hours free early learning per week taken over at least three days for 38 weeks per year, but if the parents want or need more child care they have to pay for it. The child care settings that can provide this free pre-school education include nurseries, preschools and playgroups, primary schools that admit 4 year olds, accredited childminders and Sure Start Children's Centres. All of these settings have to be inspected by OFSTED, be in the local authority Directory of Providers and must help children to work towards the Early Learning Goals in the Early Years Foundation Stage. This is because all these settings receive government funding so that the provision is free.

Childminders

A childminder is a carer who works at home looking after pre-school aged children during the day. They provide food, drink and play and learning opportunities for the children in their care. They will also look after older children before and after school. Childminders have to be registered and inspected regularly by OFSTED to make sure that they are providing good quality care in England.

Before and after-school clubs

Breakfast and after-school clubs are useful for parents who work longer hours than the school day, and who want to be sure that their children are being looked after while they are at work. Breakfast and snacks are usually provided and there is a range of activities available to keep the children occupied. Any club that looks after under-eights for more than two hours a day has to be registered and inspected, and if it is registered, at least half the play workers employed must be trained.

Nannies

Nannies are usually employed by families and a nanny will normally work for just one family, although there are 'nanny shares'. They can work days only or be live-in, and their main duties are to care for the children although some will do light housework. Nannies do not have to have any childcare qualifications and there is currently no registration body for nannies, so it is very important that parents wanting to employ a nanny interview carefully and take up references. This is one of the most expensive forms of childcare with nannies in London currently able to earn about £500 per week. However, the hours can sometimes be long.

Day care

Day care can be for children, as shown above, or may be provided for older people or for people with disabilities who live in their own homes independently but need some support. Hospital day care provides services for people who need medical care or other treatment, such as physiotherapy, as well as providing a meal and social contact. Social services provide day care for people who may be socially isolated and lonely. Some day centres provide many sorts of services and activities from hairdressing and podiatry to lunches, games and outings.

Did you know?

Residential homes are for people who do not usually require nursing or medical care and are staffed mainly by care workers. Nursing homes are for people who require nursing and/or medical care and there must be qualified nursing staff on duty at all times.

Activity: Day centre activities

Find out where your local day centres are for older people and adults with learning disabilities. If possible, arrange to visit one or both of them to see what activities they provide for their service users. Can you think of any other activities that would be suitable in either setting – taking into account the needs of the service users and the resources that are available?

Residential care

Residential care can vary from very large buildings that cater for many residents to a house where three or four service users can live together with support. Residents have their meals provided and are helped with personal care and management of any medication. Most residents have their own rooms and some have en-suite bathrooms. Residential care is staffed 24 hours a day, although in some places where residents are quite independent there will be an alarm system to call a member of staff in an emergency at night. Some residential homes allow service users to bring their own furniture and some even allow pets by arrangement.

Although we tend to think of residential care as being something that people use at the end of their lives, there are also homes for children whose parents have died or cannot look after them. Sometimes people will go into residential care for a short time to convalesce after an illness or operation because they are not yet well enough to cope independently. They may also be admitted for short term respite care to give their regular carers or family members a break. Residential and nursing homes can be quite expensive.

Just checking

1. Find out how many primary and secondary schools in your area provide breakfast and after-school clubs.
2. Which groups of service users might live in residential care?

Health and social care settings: 2

Activity: Community groups

Community groups often advertise in local newspapers. Have a look to see what groups there are in your area.

Key term

Warden – an official person in charge of a home or building who makes sure that the residents are well and happy and that everything is maintained properly

How can a community group benefit people?

You have already found out about child care settings and residential care on the previous page. But did you know that there are lots of other types of settings which plan and provide activities for service users?

Domiciliary care

This is provided in the client's own home and helps people to remain independent for as long as possible. The support is provided by carers and does not include nursing care. The help provided can range from helping clients to get out of bed and get washed and dressed to doing shopping for them or going on outings with them. This type of care can be done on a temporary or permanent basis, and some service users may choose to have live-in carers.

Community groups

Community groups are different groups and clubs that cater for various ages, genders, abilities and interests. A day centre can be classed as a community group. Community groups tend to meet together on a regular basis to share interests and include Rainbows, Brownies, Beavers, Cubs, Guides and Scouts for children and young people, Gingerbread for lone parents, the Women's Institute, drama, music or singing groups, different support groups and groups based on different sports. All of these can provide useful support and social contact for many people. There may also be church and religious groups providing support and help.

Independent living

This is also known as sheltered accommodation and it enables service users to maintain their independence. Residents have their own flat or bungalow, but also have the security and reassurance of a **warden** who lives on site or who can be contacted by an emergency alarm system of pull cords in each room. The accommodation can be specially adapted to suit the residents who are normally over the age of 50 or have disabilities. Although people in independent living have their own space, most buildings have communal areas where those who wish to can meet up with other residents for company. Some will provide extra services, such as laundry or meals, if required.

Hospitals

Hospitals provide different types of care to all types of service users. Some hospitals will be local and the services will be limited, e.g. wards for older people, a day centre and maybe a minor injuries unit. Others will be much bigger and will cater for all or nearly all of the medical specialities. Some will be regional specialist units for specific problems. For example, Stoke Mandeville hospital in Aylesbury is a regional spinal injuries unit and Pinderfields General Hospital in Wakefield is a regional burns unit, while the Churchill Hospital in Oxford has a regional endocrine and diabetes centre.

Hospitals are open 24 hours a day to provide care for people who are ill. However, not all departments will be open all the time – some have staff on call out of hours who will come in to the hospital if needed. Over the last few years keyhole surgery and day surgery have become more common and as a result patients do not need to stay in hospital as long as they used to and recover more quickly from surgery.

Some people choose to pay for treatment and operations in private hospitals. This is paid for by an individual or by a health insurance scheme. A monthly sum of money is paid into a health insurance scheme which can then be used to pay for care when needed.

PLTS

This task will give you the opportunity to develop skills as an **independent enquirer**. You will be exploring the issues involved from different perspectives. You will have to be able to be a **team worker** and collaborate with placement managers and possibly service users to get the information you need for the poster. As a **self-manager** you will organise your time and resources well, prioritising tasks.

Assessment Activity 9.1 P1 P2 M1

The tasks in this activity will help you to achieve **P1**, **P2** and **M1**.

You are applying for a job as Activities Development Officer at your local council. You will be expected to advise on and help to develop the provision of creative and therapeutic activities for service users in all the different health and social care settings in your area.

As part of the selection procedure you have been asked to do a presentation on different activities that could be provided for client groups in different settings. You should create a large table for a poster that will include the following:

1. A column identifying different creative and therapeutic activities that could be used in different settings. **P1**

2. A second column that identifies the benefits of the activities that you have selected to the client groups. **P2**

You will then have to present your poster to the interviewing panel. You must make sure that you have produced notes outlining in much greater detail the benefits of the activities which you will also present to the panel as a PowerPoint® presentation **M1**. Remember that your chances of getting the job depend on how detailed your information is and how well you perform.

Grading tips

Make sure that you take enough time to read through this part of the chapter carefully so that you know about the different activities and settings you will be writing about. Try to find out what is available in your own work placement setting that you could make use of or, if you are not in a placement, arrange a visit to a local setting to find out.

Functional skills

In this activity you will have the chance to develop **ICT** skills by researching the information you need and creating the poster and the PowerPoint® presentation. You should be able to create some eye-catching artwork by including pictures or photos. To make sure that you are developing **English** skills you should make sure that you proof read your work carefully as well as using the spell and grammar checks.

Just checking

1. Draw up a table listing all the care settings mentioned in this section. For each care setting identify all the creative and therapeutic activities that you think would be suitable. Remember to think about the different service users and what their needs and abilities might be.

2. Can you think of any other activities that have not been mentioned in this chapter? If so which settings do you think they would be most suited to? Add them to your table.

2. Legislation and regulations relevant to the implementation of creative and therapeutic activities

Figure 9.5: Do you know how to lift safely?

You might be wondering why you need to learn about legislation in a chapter about creative and therapeutic activities in health and social care settings. This is because everything that you do that involves service users is governed by the laws that are made by Parliament. You need to have an understanding of the most relevant ones so that you know how to protect yourself and others. Additional information about legislation can be found in the table at the end of the book.

The Health and Safety at Work etc. Act 1974 is the main piece of legislation that covers health and safety in workplaces, and both employers and employees have to make sure that all work is carried out as safely as possible. Employers have to protect employees and other people, and employees have every right to expect that their employer is doing all they can to protect them at work. But employees are also responsible for protecting themselves and others.

The Food Standards Act 1999 was passed by the government so that the Food Standards Agency could be established. It sets out the functions and powers for the Food Standards Agency so it can make food safe and protect public health. It has powers to intervene at any stage in the process of producing and supplying food to ensure that consumers are protected and food is safe.

The European Parliament introduced new powers and penalties relating to food businesses and the British government introduced **The General Food Regulations** in 2004. The main regulations are that food cannot be sold if it is harmful or unfit for human consumption and it has to be recalled if it does not comply with food safety requirements. There are also regulations relating to the labelling, advertising, presentation and supply of food.

The Manual Handling Operations Regulations (1992) are in place to ensure that the lifting and carrying of heavy objects is done safely. As with the Health and Safety at Work Act, both employers and employees have a duty to ensure that they are complying with the regulations.

The Control of Substances Hazardous to Health Regulations (2002) (COSHH) ensure that employers have to control hazardous substances that employees and others may be exposed to at work. Hazardous substances are any products that could pose a risk to health if they are not controlled. They can include glues, paints, cleaning agents, fumes, dust or bacteria. Warning labels on packaging will show whether the product is subject to COSHH Regulations. In a health or social care setting they will apply to certain substances that might be used for cleaning, such as bleach.

The Reporting of Injuries, Diseases and Dangerous Occurrences Regulations (RIDDOR) (1995) allow the Health and Safety Executive and local authorities to identify where and how risks arise. The HSE can then give employers advice on how to reduce injury, illness and accidents at work. Some work-related accidents, diseases and dangerous occurrences must be reported by an employer or self-employed person, and a record must be kept for at least three years.

Organisational policies and codes of practice

An organisational policies manual is a crucial tool for any organisation and it sets out the regulations of the business and how they should be implemented. It should also inform employees about what is expected of them. Codes of practice set out the standards of conduct and practice expected of employees within which they should work.

Activity: Main points

Find out the main points of the General Social Care Council Code of Practice.

PLTS

This task will give you the opportunity to develop skills as a **self-manager**.

Functional skills

In this activity you will have the chance to develop **ICT** skills by researching the information you need and creating the leaflet. To make sure that you are developing **English** skills you should make sure that you proof read your work carefully as well as using the spell and grammar checks before you hand it in.

Assessment activity 9.2   **P3** **M2** **D1**

Produce a poster that identifies the legislation, guidelines and policies that should be considered when carrying out creative and therapeutic activities in health and social environments (**P3**) and add brief notes to highlight how they could affect the implementation of these activities (**M2**). Add to the notes on the poster to describe why the legislation, guidelines and policies are important when carrying out such activities (**D1**).

Grading tips

P3 Use a placement or visits to the health and social care environment where you are planning to do assessment activity 9.4 to research the legislation, guidelines and policies (**P3**) and how they apply when carrying out creative and therapeutic activities (**M2**). You could pay particular attention to the relevant polices of the environment where you will carry out the activity. Make sure you explain the reasons why the legislation, guidelines and policies are important when doing these activities with individuals in health and social care (**D1**).

Just checking

1. Find out the steps to COSHH set out by the HSE that employers must carry out. To obtain a secure link to the HSE website, see the Hotlinks section on page x.
2. Find out what information must be kept in the records regarding an injury, disease or dangerous occurrence under RIDDOR.
3. Find out what the health and safety policy is for your school or college and make sure that you read it.

3. Understand the role of the professional in supporting individuals

Key term

Diversity – the ways in which people are different from each other

Dignity – the state of being worthy of respect

This topic and the following three will help you to understand the role of the professional in supporting individuals who undertake creative and therapeutic activities.

Principles and values

Unit 2 is concerned with individual rights in health and social care. It considers the principles and values that underpin health and social care and the responsibilities of professionals to ensure that service users' needs are respected and valued. This section will look at how professionals support individuals who take part in creative and therapeutic activities.

Anti–discriminatory practice and equality of opportunity

When working with service users, carers need to ensure that they do not discriminate against them in any way and they must respect the **diversity** of the groups of people that they look after. It is very important that you do not prevent service users from receiving the best possible care because of their race, gender, ability, religion, sexuality or age. This means that when you are planning an activity for a group of people everything should be done to ensure that they can all take part and enjoy it. This provides equality of opportunity, because you may have to provide extra resources for some people to take part. An example of this is going to a pool where there is a hoist to lower people with physical disabilities into the water so that they can enjoy a swim.

Empowering

Empowerment is the process of increasing an individual's capacity to develop their skills, knowledge and understanding so that they gain more self-confidence and control over their lives. Supporting a client to learn how to do things enables them to become more independent and helps to increase self-esteem. Learning a new skill or how to do a task provides a sense of achievement.

Ensuring dignity

Ensuring the **dignity** of a service user means that you respect a client's cultural needs and privacy. Showing sensitivity to service users and being compassionate is all part of providing holistic care and failure to take account of these factors can have devastating effects. Small acts of kindness and courtesy can have a huge impact on how clients feel. For example, you should make sure you know what a client likes to eat, whether they take sugar in their tea and what they prefer to be called (Mrs Jones or Florence?) because it maintains their dignity at a time when they might otherwise feel very vulnerable.

Promoting independence

Promoting independence helps people to develop a positive self image and good self-esteem. Supporting clients to do things for themselves rather than having things done for them prevents them from developing something called 'learned helplessness'. This is when clients can become totally dependent on carers even though they are capable of doing things for themselves. Taking part in different activities can be a way of encouraging service users to remain as independent as possible for as long as possible.

Confidentiality

Confidentiality is one of the most important components of caring for others. Disclosing information to other people about a service user can destroy trust and the relationship between client and carer. Safety may be put at risk if sensitive information is disclosed to people who should not have access to it. Of course if you are organising a therapeutic activity, you will need to discuss information with the therapist but this is a professional relationship so disclosure is accepted. However, if you are working with a group of clients and chatting, you need to ensure that you do not discuss sensitive issues that might embarrass or hurt any of them.

Respecting diversity, culture and beliefs

During the second half of the twentieth century, Britain started to become **multicultural** and now people of many different cultures, religions and beliefs make up a hugely diverse society.

Having an opportunity to learn about other cultures and customs helps us to learn about how other people live, and using this as an educational tool in activities can help to develop understanding and respect. Carers should ensure that they ask clients or check on the care plan for any religious beliefs so that these can be taken into account when planning activities. Jewish or Muslim service users would not want to take part in any cooking activities that involved pork, and Muslim women would only swim in a women-only session at a public swimming pool. Failure to be observant about diversity, culture and beliefs can be offensive and will affect self-esteem in a negative way. You can read more about this in Unit 6.

Supporting service users to do things for themselves and not taking over helps them to retain their independence

Key term

Multicultural – Multi means many so multicultural means many different cultures

Case study: Day out

You and a colleague are taking two service users with mild to moderate learning disabilities out for the day to a new shopping centre that has just opened. You will use public transport and have lunch out.

1. What would you both do to ensure that you don't breach confidentiality while you are out?

Just checking

1. What is empowerment?
2. Why is promoting independence so important for service users?
3. What effect could failing to respect diversity, culture and beliefs have on service users?

Supporting inclusion

Figure 9.6: Friendships and a feeling of belonging can boost self-esteem for service users

Inclusion means ensuring that people with different abilities can feel that they belong in our society, are engaged in what is going on around them and have goals and objectives that relate to every other person in the society in which they live. Increasing opportunity and provision means that inclusion becomes more a part of everyday life, so that everyone in an organisation can celebrate and value the abilities of everybody else.

Development of friendships

We can probably all remember the first day we started school or college and how we felt about it. The place was different and unfamiliar and if you remember your first day at primary school you probably remember feeling lost when you were left there. You probably soon made friends and settled in quite quickly, but people do not always find this easy. Some service users have difficulty in communicating so others may be unsure about how to make friends with them. Carers can contribute hugely to this. They can help service users feel comfortable in their new surroundings and organise activities to help introduce people to each other – this can help people to develop friendships and a feeling of belonging to a group.

Methods of communication

In Unit 1 you will have learned about different methods of communication and how valuable they can be for people who have difficulty communicating verbally. There are other ways of communicating that can be as effective as speaking and, with patience, carers can make a big difference to a service user's communication skills. Using signs and symbols such as Makaton or British Sign Language can help to open a new world to some service users and learning one of these methods can help carers to improve their own communication skills as well as those of their clients.

Encouraging new experiences

Sometimes service users can be fearful of new experiences and will resist any attempt to get them to try something they have not experienced before. Carers who have developed a trusting relationship with service users over time might be able to use that trust to encourage them to try to take up a new hobby. Sometimes it might be necessary to build up confidence slowly, so if a carer wants to encourage a service user to swim, for example, it might be necessary to start with a visit to a swimming pool. It may be some time before an individual will even get into the water because the steps need to be taken very gradually.

If you are working as a carer and an activity is a new experience for you, doing this with one of your service users can help them to gain the confidence to have a go themselves.

Activity: Social networking

You may use Facebook, My Space or Bebo to keep in touch with friends or to make new friends. Obviously communication in the evenings and at weekends with friends you see most days is different to that with people you only have contact with through the Internet. Do you think that your cyber friendships are developing into real friendships? How can you be sure who you are talking to? Take another look at the Social Network Guidance on the Information Commissioner's Office website (to obtain a secure link to this website, see the Hotlinks section on page x). Make sure that you are not giving away too much personal information to someone you don't know. How can you make sure that you keep yourself and your friends as safe as possible?

Figure 9.7: Signing can be a very useful tool for people who find verbal communication difficult.

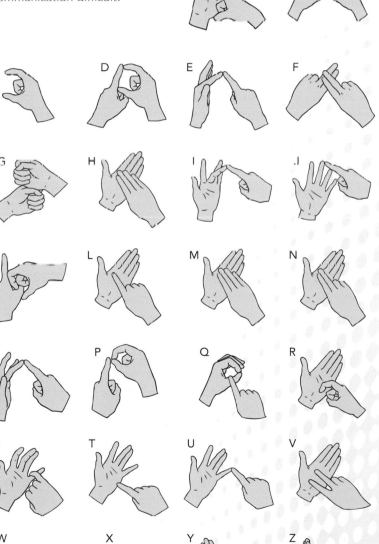

Just checking

1. Why is it important to develop friendships for all members of society and at all ages?
2. What benefits could a service user gain from trying out new activities or experiences?

Role of the professional in supporting activities

Earlier in this chapter you had the chance to explore different activities and the benefits to service users of taking part in them. While some service users will be very enthusiastic and keen to try out any or all the activities offered to them, others will not want to take part. Sometimes the support of health and social care workers will make the difference.

Motivation

An individual who has experienced something in their lives that has caused them to feel depressed may well lack the motivation to fully engage with activities of daily living, let alone creative or therapeutic activities. People who have suffered an injury that requires painful treatment such as physiotherapy may not be motivated to do the exercises because they hurt. Health and social care professionals can sometimes make the difference to service users by helping to motivate them to improve their state of mind or physical ability. It is useful to spend time talking to service users to find out what their interests are, or if there are any new things they would like to try. It will often be easier to get someone motivated if you are offering them something that they know about and which is familiar. People can often lose motivation if they cannot see progress being made and may prefer to give up rather than keep going. If this happens with a therapy as important as physiotherapy, it could lead to reduction or loss of movement in a limb or other part of the body which could well be permanent.

Support enjoyment

People who really love taking part in a sport or pastime will gain huge enjoyment from doing it on a regular basis, especially if they can see improvement or they gain satisfaction from working as part of a team. Even people who work alone can get great enjoyment from what they do. However, it is always an extra reward when there is someone supporting you who can see what you have achieved. This can provide positive reinforcement and spur people on to achieve even more. Taking photographs and making a pictorial record in the form of a photograph album or a collage can help to retain the memory of what a service user has achieved and the enjoyment from this can be very supportive.

Offering practical help

We have already discussed barriers that might prevent service users from taking part in some activities. Offering practical help can take many forms, from making sure that a service user has money or transport to attend an activity to helping to provide equipment or clothing. Support workers who work with families who have children with profound and multiple disabilities may be able to provide help such as weekly respite care to allow parents to spend time with their other children or just to have a chance to have some time off from 24-hour care.

Providing resources and being available

Carers who work in organisations sometimes have access to resources that can be used to provide activities for service users. In some cases this might be a small charity that has been left money by someone who has died, or it could be a Lottery grant to provide some kind of facilities for a charity or community group. Arguably the two most important and useful resources are money and time. Very often, service users might indicate that time is the resource that they most want. Older people who are lonely will often feel much better for having had a cup of tea and a chat with a carer or volunteer on a regular basis.

Health, safety and security

Earlier in this chapter you found out about the legislation that should be considered when planning and implementing creative and therapeutic activities for service users. Make sure that you are aware of the basics of the legislation that relates to health, safety and security when planning activities. Carrying out a risk assessment is compulsory in many settings before an activity can take place, and carers should ensure that this is carried out and action is taken to minimise the risks as much as possible.

PLTS

This task will give you the opportunity to develop skills as an **independent enquirer**. You will need to make sure that you explore issues, events and problems from different perspectives. You also need to develop skills as an effective **self-manager**. You will work towards the overall goal of achieving the unit and you will organise your time and resources well.

Functional skills

In this activity you will have the chance to develop **ICT** skills by researching the information you need and creating the booklet. You may develop skills in using Publisher for this. You should be able to create some eye-catching artwork by including pictures or photos. To make sure that you are developing **English** skills you should make sure that you proofread your work carefully as well as using the spell and grammar checks before you hand it in.

BTEC

Assessment activity 9.3

Completion of this task will help you to meet **P4**

You are a care assistant in a residential home for older people and you have been working there for five years. Two years ago the manager asked you to take responsibility for co-ordinating activities for the residents with their individual key workers. She would now like the key workers to take on this role for their own clients, and has asked you to produce a booklet for the staff on the role of the professional when planning creative and therapeutic activities that could be used in any care setting.

You need to make sure that you produce a user-friendly booklet with information about underpinning principles and values when caring for service users, how to ensure inclusion and how to support the various activities that might be planned. She would like a colourful word-processed booklet for every member of the care staff.

Grading tips

Remember that you have been asked to produce a booklet that would be suitable for any care setting so you need to keep it general, although you could give examples of different types of setting. Remember also that you only have to meet one pass criterion for this learning outcome, so make sure that the time you spend on it is proportionate to the requirements.

Just checking

1. What might you notice in a service user's behaviour that would indicate to you that they were very motivated to maintain an interest in a particular activity?
2. Choose two activities that have been covered in this chapter and make notes on how you could provide practical help and resources to help an individual or a group to complete a creative activity.
3. What health and safety factors would you have to take into account for each activity?

4. Be able to implement appropriate creative and therapeutic activities

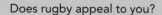

Does rugby appeal to you?

This topic and the following three will help you to implement appropriate creative and therapeutic activities and plan them effectively.

Factors affecting choice of activities

The choice of activity that you make is very important and depends on several factors. You need to think about and understand what activities benefit client groups in different ways and which activity you should choose, based on the needs and abilities of the client groups.

Potential benefit

When you start to think about planning an activity for an individual or client group, you have to think about what benefits they would gain from taking part. This means that you have to think about how appropriate it is. Swimming, for example, would provide physical benefits to almost anyone who takes part, but it would be pointless to arrange this for someone who is afraid of water. Similarly, horse riding would be no good for someone who is allergic to horses.

Interests and preferences

Just as you would get bored and fed up if you felt forced into doing something you had no interest in, so will service users. This is why it is important to get to know your client group or individual and find out what their interests are. Providing the wrong type of activity for someone could be as bad as providing nothing at all, and you need to make sure you provide what service users actually want, not what you think they want!

Physical ability

Care workers should not assume that a lack of physical ability will stop service users from enjoying activities that are physical. Taking part in these activities can provide a boost in self confidence and self-esteem for people who have physical disabilities. Many activities and sports can be adapted to provide for the needs of people with different physical disabilities. Tennis for people with visual impairment uses larger balls with bells inside so that players can detect their position. There are organisations that provide adventure holidays for people with disabilities, and many local clubs provide activities such as sailing. Someone who has poor hand–eye co-ordination (a skill learned in early childhood) will find playing ball games difficult, so playing tennis or badminton may not be enjoyable for them.

Intellectual ability

People with learning disabilities are able to take part in many activities although, as for people with physical disabilities, adaptations may need to be made. Taking part in some activities will help to develop cognitive skills, and children learn through play as they grow and develop. Health and social care workers need to assess the level of intellectual ability and pitch activities at the right level. If an activity is too easy interest is lost quickly and if it is too difficult a service user may lose self confidence and self-esteem if they can't achieve goals.

Communication skills

Some people who have reduced intellectual ability may have problems with communicating. Staff should ensure that there are other methods of communication available such as communication books which contain pictures that service users can point to. A lack of communication can mean that a client is unable to take part in an activity and their needs are not being met. Although it can be difficult, carers need to persevere to ensure that service users are being given choices and are getting enjoyment and satisfaction in their lives.

Age

Much of children's play involves using lots of energy and running around, which helps them to develop gross motor skills. Children enjoy doing physical activities so planning some that include opportunities to develop cognitive or social skills would provide many benefits.

Older teenagers and young adults will not want to be seen doing something that might be considered 'uncool' by their peer group. It can help to organise a group activity so no individual stands out, or activities combining physical and intellectual elements could be used to develop new skills or improve existing ones.

Some older people might be limited in what they can do because they are no longer as physically able as they were or because they have some memory loss. Games and activities that are less physically demanding or help to retain memory could be suitable.

Culture

When you plan activities you will need to consider all aspects of a person's culture such as beliefs, religion and way of life. If someone is a strict vegetarian it would be unprofessional and insensitive to ask them to join in a cookery activity using meat.

Gender

In the past it was thought that there should be a difference in activities and games enjoyed by males and females, with boys and men being encouraged to take up tough physical activities, such as rugby or soccer, and girls taking up sewing and knitting or netball and tennis. Women today are more involved in activities that were previously considered for men only, such as rugby, and some of the top football clubs in the United Kingdom have women's teams. Arsenal Ladies Team won the FA Women's Cup in 2009 and they also have a Women's Centre of Excellence and Academy.

Activity: PHAB

PHAB is a charity that brings together able-bodied people with people with disabilities to take part in activities together. You can find out more about it at the PHAB website. To obtain a secure link to this website, see the Hotlinks section on page x.

Did you know?

In October 2007, 28-year-old Bern Goosen from South Africa broke his own record for the fastest ascent of Mount Kilimanjaro in a wheelchair. He has cerebral palsy and is classified as quadriplegic. He took 6 days, 3 hours and 20 minutes to reach the summit and is the only man in a wheelchair ever to have achieved this. One of the other successful members of the team was Neil Stephenson, another South African who had lost his leg in a shark attack a few years previously.

Just checking

1. Why is it important to make sure that the activities you provide for service users are things they are interested in?
2. How could age affect the activities that service users might be interested in?
3. Why should you take account of people's culture and beliefs when planning activities?

Needs of the individual

Case study: Kwame and Stephanie

Kwame and Stephanie are both physically disabled and live in domiciliary care. Kwame had a stroke a couple of years ago. The left side of his body is still very weak and he finds it difficult to move round because it takes so long.

Stephanie is 19 and lost her right leg in an accident on her motor scooter three months ago. She is currently using crutches and a wheelchair to help her get around while she adjusts to her disability.

1. Identify Kwame and Stephanie's physical needs.

2. Plan an activity that you would do with Kwame and one that you would do with Stephanie. You need to include the materials that you will require.

3. Are they the same activities? Would they suit other client groups? Explain why.

You will have already explored the needs of the individual and how they can be met in Unit 3. In this section you will explore how activities can meet the needs of individuals.

Physical needs

Physical needs are the needs we have that keep our bodies working efficiently. In health and care settings you will meet people who have had an accident, an illness or have been born with a disability that affects their physical health. Some physical needs will change across the lifespan.

Sensory needs

The five senses are sight, hearing, taste, touch and smell, and being able to use all of these helps us to make sense of the world around us. People who are sight and hearing impaired can find it very difficult to live in an environment where they cannot see and hear everything that is going on around them, although many adapt very well and have aids to help them. Guide Dogs for the Blind Association and Hearing Dogs for Deaf People train dogs for sight and hearing impaired people and you can find out more about them through their websites. To obtain secure links to these websites, see the Hotlinks section on page x.

Social isolation and depression

We all have a social need to make friends and build relationships. If people have to move into residential accommodation because they are no longer able to cope in their own homes, it can be very upsetting as often they will not know anyone. They might have to move some distance from their home and leave their friends. This can be very socially isolating for service users and they will need plenty of activities that will help them to settle in and get to know other people.

There can be many causes for depression, such as the loss of a partner, child or job, and this can lead people to experience negative feelings and develop low self-esteem and lose interest in the world around them. It can become a vicious circle as depression leads to withdrawal and social isolation and this can make depressed people feel even worse. Encouraging them to take part in a creative and therapeutic activity and develop new interests can help them to overcome feelings of grief or depression.

Learning disability

When considering the needs of people with learning disabilities you need to assess the level of disability and plan activities accordingly. Some people may have associated physical disabilities, or have short concentration spans, so you will need to take into account what they can do and how long they might be able to do it for. It is very important that carers understand that service users who have a learning disability are still able to make decisions and choices in their lives, and although they may need advice and guidance their wishes must be taken into consideration.

Developmental needs

While we tend to think of growth as physical growth that usually ends as we reach adulthood, we continue to develop throughout our lives, and our needs will change accordingly. Intellectual, language, emotional and social development in children is rapid and the activities they do should aim to support and assist that development. Adolescents, adults and older people also need to be supported but some may be more able to do this independently and will gain a great boost to their self-esteem if they can. It is important to plan activities so that they will meet developmental needs and are designed at the right level for people's understanding and enjoyment.

Communication needs

We all need and want to be able to communicate with other people. Being unable to communicate makes people feel isolated and lonely. There are several reasons why people may have difficulty communicating. It might be because they have a physical or intellectual disability or because they do not speak the same language as you. It does not mean that you cannot communicate with them, just that you might have to find alternatives to speaking.

Activity: Speaking without words

We communicate with each other verbally but in fact much of communication is non-verbal. Working with a partner, try to communicate a message without speaking, writing or drawing. How hard is it? Did your partner understand your message?

Just checking

1. How can social isolation or depression affect an individual's health and well-being?
2. Why is it important to assess a client's level of ability when planning activities?

Case study: David

David is 49 years old and has Down's syndrome. He lived at home with his parents until 10 years ago when he moved into residential accommodation, and since then both his parents have died. David lives a very full life and has a part-time job at the local supermarket helping with stacking shelves. He is very well known in the small town where he lives. David loves steam trains and knows a lot about them even though he has never been on one. His colleagues know that his fiftieth birthday is coming up soon and have asked the home's managers if they can arrange a day trip on a steam train for him as a birthday present.

Divide your group into two, with one group being the management team of the home and the other being the group of David's colleagues, and complete the tasks below:

Management Team

You must draw up a list of factors that the colleagues will have to take into consideration when planning the day trip, including health and safety. You will then hold a meeting with the Colleagues Team to brief them.

Colleagues Team

Respond to the list, detailing how you will deal with each factor on the list and feed this back to the Management Team.

When you have done this, have a whole group meeting to write an itinerary and risk assessment for the day trip. Make sure that you are all in agreement.

When you have done this, you will be able to tell David about his surprise.

Plan creative and therapeutic activities

Activity: Planning

Identify two activities that you would like to plan – one that can be done inside and the other that involves being outside or going on an outing or visit. Think about the resources you might need, such as equipment and materials, and whether or not you will need money. Make a list of all the resources you can think of for each activity.

Create a grid to help your planning. Use the headings:

- Needs
- Timing
- Resources
- Space and setting
- Barriers
- Health and safety

Although it is possible to organise some activities quite spontaneously and without very much planning, they are usually more successful when you have taken all factors into consideration and have planned what you are going to do.

Needs of the individual

The first thing you need to consider when you are planning an activity is who you will be doing it with. You might be working with an individual or a group and you will have to establish their level of ability to do things. You have already considered on previous pages the factors that might affect the choice of activities, and you should keep them in mind when you are planning an activity to meet the needs of the individual or group. It can be very easy when you are inexperienced to stereotype people, for example to assume that an older person won't like pop music, but 50 years ago today's 80 year olds may well have been dancing to rock and roll!

Timing

There are timing issues you need to take into account when you are planning to organise activities, such as how long it will take to complete an activity. A trip to a theme park would probably take a whole day, but a painting activity in a residential home might only take an hour or two. You will have to make sure that you know when meal times are, or if a service user has a treatment session, so that the activity doesn't end up being rushed and unsatisfactory. Careful planning and organisation will mean that time isn't wasted and you and the service users can concentrate and enjoy what you are doing.

Resources

The materials and equipment that you have available to you may be restricted so you may have to be quite inventive in thinking about what you can use. Going for a walk in a local park does not require any resources and can be just as enjoyable as planning something that costs a lot of money. Obviously if you don't have access to a kitchen it may be difficult to do much cookery, but if you have a couple of mixing bowls and access to a microwave oven, you could make chocolate rice crispie cakes for example. Earlier in the chapter you found out about scrap stores. Remember that this can be a very good way of obtaining materials quite cheaply, and don't forget all the junk modelling that you did at primary school; what objects did you use to make things? Some art projects can revolve around a theme such as nature – collecting fallen leaves costs nothing but you may need paper, glue and paint to create a piece of art work from them.

Space and setting

Depending on the type of activity you want to plan, you will have to assess the physical environment that you are working in. Trying to organise a dancing session in a residential home might not be very successful if there is not a big enough room with an appropriate floor surface; and if you plan to do a cookery session you will need to take into account how big the kitchen is and how many service users can work safely in it. The setting where you are working might determine the activities that you can do. Some activities may not be suitable for a certain service user group, or activities that you plan for young children in a nursery might not be appropriate for a residential home that caters for adults with learning disabilities. However, you might consider how you could adapt the activity so that it can be used for people with a variety of needs and abilities.

Barriers

You have discussed barriers to services in other units that you are studying, and it is very important that you consider any barriers that might prevent someone from taking part in an activity. Some of these are identified below.

Physical barriers can include physical access to a building where an activity is taking place, especially for service users who have poor mobility or use wheelchairs, or the health of the service user who might be too ill to take part.

Psychological barriers could be when people may not want to take part in an activity because of fear. This can be fear of being hurt, of looking silly in front of other people, or being too afraid to leave their home. Individuals who are anxious or depressed might not want to participate, possibly because they are unable to understand that taking part in some kind of activity may help them to feel better.

There would be **financial barriers** to taking part in activities if you have a very low income and there just isn't the money to spend on what some might see as luxuries or the transport to get somewhere. People who are on low incomes might need some advice on facilities that are available to them for free or a very low fee. The government's Swim for Life initiative is designed to allow the under-16s and over-60s to swim for free in many public swimming pools.

Health and safety

Sometimes there are situations where there are barriers that cannot be overcome. One way of establishing whether or not an activity is safe to do is to complete a risk assessment. This will enable you to identify any hazards associated with a particular event or activity and how severe the risks might be. Remember that your actions are governed by legislation and this has been covered earlier in the chapter. Risk assessments are covered in Unit 4.

Activity: Barriers

What other barriers can you identify that might prevent people from taking part in activities. Can you think of ways that the barrier can be overcome? Why is it important to try to remove barriers?

Just checking

1. Identify three indoor activities that four people with learning disabilities living together in a house could take part in together.
2. What activities might be suitable for a group of people who do not all speak the same language?
3. In small groups, identify five different activities and list the risks associated with them. When you have done this, rank them in order of safety. Which would carry the most risk and which the least?

Resources and specialist resources

Activity: Materials

You have been asked to lay out a table with lots of different materials for arts and crafts. What materials would you put on the table? Would you put out the same materials in different care settings? Identify and describe what materials you would use for different care settings and explain why.

For some activities that you plan you do not need many resources, but if you are planning to do something that is a little bit more specialised, you will need relevant equipment to be able to provide an enjoyable experience for service users.

Resources

Art and craft materials

You have already researched scrap stores so should know how useful they are in providing materials for art and craft. Depending on the interests of the service users and what you plan to do, you might need a variety of art and craft materials such as paper, glue, pens, pencils, scissors and paints, clay, play dough and even different pasta shapes.

Games

Some games are played purely for enjoyment, but there are others that can provide opportunities for people to develop physical, intellectual or social skills. Games like Twister or Connect 4 can help with gross and fine motor skills, whereas Nintendo DS games such as brain training will help to develop thinking skills. Active participation in karaoke can help people to develop self confidence. Remember, however, that you will need to take into account the age and ability of the target group when planning.

Music

Music can be used in many different ways, from getting people up to dance to quiet enjoyment of a favourite piece of music. Singing can be a way of bringing people together and can help to prevent memory loss. Music therapists can be invited to different care settings to help people to enjoy music by playing, listening and singing. Service users are encouraged to use instruments and voices to create sounds. Ready-made instruments can be used or individuals can make their own.

Equipment

Depending on the interests of the individual service user, other equipment may need to be provided or health and social care workers may have to find out where they can go to access equipment for service users. It is quite likely that some people will have their own digital camera or camcorder for example, but often care settings will also have them. Some service users will be interested in recording music and might have access to appropriate equipment to do this. Many people today are computer literate and there is wide access to computers at local libraries or in internet cafés if people do not have their own or cannot access them at care settings.

People who enjoy cooking, or would like to learn a new culinary skill, will not only need a kitchen and equipment but will require ingredients.

Although this is not a problem, responsibility for meeting the costs of providing them would have to be agreed between the service provider and the service users. Gardening is an interest that can be encouraged, and gardening equipment can be quite expensive. If you plan to introduce service users to gardening, you could start small by using basic tools such as trowels and pots to grow plants for sale and use the proceeds to buy a range of bigger, more expensive equipment as skills and interest develop.

Specialist resources

It is now possible to find quite a lot of specialist resources for people who have a physical or sensory impairment which can make it much easier to take part in activities. Companies are beginning to produce large versions of games which may not be designed specifically for people with disabilities and impairments, but which can make playing easier. The Disabled Living Foundation provides advice on daily living aids and Nottingham Rehab Supplies sells a wide range of games and equipment to aid daily living, such as easy grip scissors, grips and non-slip mats. (To obtain secure links to the websites for these organisations, see the Hotlinks section on page x.) Computers with touch screens are very useful for people who have limited movement in their hands and there are specialist IT companies which provide adaptations to computers for people with different types of disability.

The RNIB provides a talking book service that currently costs subscribers £79 a year. This includes the loan of an unlimited number of books on CD during the year and a special player to play them on. Large and giant print books, games, cards and texts are also available for people who are visually impaired.

Activity: Home caring

You are a home carer who has a number of service users with very different abilities and interests. All of them over the past month have mentioned to you that they are having difficulty with retaining as much independence as possible, working or socialising. Visit the websites mentioned in this section and see if you can find any aids that could be useful for the following people:

- Margaret, 67, has multiple sclerosis and very limited movement. She loves reading books, but has difficulty turning the pages on her own and hates disturbing her husband to do it for her.

- Sunil, 48, had a motorbike accident and now has limited mobility in his right hand. His work involves doing a lot of word processing at the computer but he has difficulty pressing the keys.

- Adam, 55, has gradually become totally blind over the last five years and manages to do most daily activities very well with the help of his guide dog Bessie. He really enjoys meeting up with his friends at the pub every week, but would like to carry on playing some of the games that they play when they are together.

Compile a fact sheet for each client with the information they will need. Try to include at least two on each sheet.

PLTS

This task will give you the opportunity to develop skills as an **independent enquirer** by researching a suitable activity for your client. As a **creative thinker** you will be able to generate ideas and explore different possibilities. You may also be able to try out alternative activities. Getting feedback on your plan will help you to develop skills as a **reflective learner** as you get feedback from your supervisor. Organising your time and resources and breaking down tasks into manageable steps will demonstrate the development of skills as a **self-manager** and **effective participator**. You will work towards the overall goal of achieving the unit and you will organise your time and resources well.

Functional skills

In this activity you may have the chance to develop **ICT** skills by researching the information you need producing your evaluation. To make sure that you are developing **English** skills you should make sure that you proof read your work carefully as well as using the spell and grammar checks before you hand it in. The development of other functional skills will depend on the activity you decide to plan and implement.

BTEC Assessment activity 9.4

In this activity you will complete tasks that will help you to meet **P5**, **M3** and **D2**.

You may use your work placement setting or another appropriate setting to complete this activity. Make sure that you have the permission of the service user and his or her key worker to do the activity, and make sure that you take all health and safety factors into consideration.

Plan one creative or therapeutic activity for one individual who uses health or social care services. You must produce a detailed plan indicating what you intend to do, where you intend to do it, what resources you will need and how you will carry it out. You will also have to consider whether or not a risk assessment will need to be done. **P5**

When you have completed your plan, discuss it with your placement supervisor to ensure that it is suitable and then carry it out with a service user. **M3**

When you have completed the activity, write an evaluation of what you did. How well did you plan the activity? Did you achieve the result you intended? Did the service user enjoy the activity? Do you think you remembered to do everything you needed to do? What would you change if you decided to do this activity again? **D2**

Grading tips

Good planning is the key to a successful activity. Make sure you research your chosen activity thoroughly and make sure that you have everything prepared before you start. If you are not sure, keep it simple as things are less likely to go wrong. Remember to reflect on every stage of your activity in your evaluation so that you can achieve the distinction criterion.

Just checking

1. Identify two games that could help children to develop gross motor skills.
2. What activities might help older people to maintain fine motor skills?

Jed Moreton

Art Therapist

I wasn't really much good at the academic stuff at school and spent nearly all of my time in the art room. I decided that whatever I did in the future would have to involve art in some way. When I told my parents, my Dad was really worried. He thought I'd always be struggling to make money. I did A Levels at school and then did a Foundation Art Degree for a year. It was really hard work with very long hours but it was great. Then I did a fine arts degree. At the end of the second year a friend on my course persuaded me to go and work at a summer camp for children with learning disabilities.

I helped with the art activities. I wasn't sure that I wanted to do this for the whole of the summer but I had a brilliant time. Seeing the kids having a go at all sorts of art and really enjoying achieving something was very rewarding. I got talking to one of the Leaders and he told me about Art Therapy, which I had never heard of, so I did some research to find out about it.

When I finished my degree I did a Post Graduate Diploma in Art Therapy which took another two years. It took a bit of time to get a job when I finished and I had to do quite a lot of pub work, but I now work in a special hospital with people with learning disabilities. I love the job and working with the same people for a period of time gives me the chance to see them really developing and producing great art work. It may have taken a long time to get here, but I reckon I've got one of the best jobs. My Dad doesn't worry any more about my career prospects!

Think about it!

1. What benefits do you think Jed's clients get from the art therapy they do with him?
2. What special qualities does an art therapist need to have?
3. Art therapy is one of many therapies that can be used to help service users. Find out what other types of therapy are available and what qualifications are needed.

Extension activity: Helping Dan

Dan is 82 years old and a widower; his wife died 18 months ago. He used to work as a gardener on a very large estate owned by the National Trust and spent his spare time following football, especially supporting Everton, his favourite club. He was also a keen photographer, and particularly enjoyed taking photos of the gardens he worked in. Although Dan had been managing quite well living alone in the family home, his balance is now not very good and he has had two falls in the past three months. His two children live quite far away and do not often get the chance to visit him, but they are worried about how he is coping. Dan has reluctantly agreed to move into independent living and is now in a ground floor warden-assisted flat.

Many of Dan's friends have died and he feels quite lonely. Although he has seen some of the other residents around the block of flats, he is quite shy and doesn't really feel confident about getting to know other people.

Ann, the warden, has noticed that Dan keeps very much to himself and is starting to worry that he might be getting depressed. She is thinking of organising a fun day for everyone who lives in the flats but doesn't know where to start. Her daughter works at the local college and has told her that your group has to organise some activities as part of your course. She has phoned your tutor to ask if you can help.

1. In groups, identify what Dan's physical, emotional and social needs are.
2. Decide which three different creative and therapeutic activities would help to meet Dan's needs.
3. Give detailed reasons for your choice and identify the materials you would need for each of the activities.

edexcel :::

Assignment tips

- This unit is about how to plan and carry out creative and therapeutic activities for service users with different needs and abilities. Although many of the activities can be fun to do, you must remember that you are working with service users and must adhere to the legislation to maintain the health, safety and security of clients. A very clear plan is essential.

- A knowledge and understanding of the different types of activities that are available and how they will benefit service users is vital in ensuring that you meet their needs.

- You need to understand the role of the professional in supporting clients to undertake creative and therapeutic activities, and you need to be able to plan and implement activities effectively.

10 Health and social care services

If you are on a health and social care course you already have an interest in health and social care but you may not have thought about the different services and how they work together. For example, who decides whether a patient is cared for at home or in hospital, or how do social workers work with doctors? You may also wonder, if you have had some experience of health and social care services, how some people have priority over others for the treatment they receive. This unit will give you a real insight into how the services work and how people within the services communicate and work together. You will find that being an effective team member is one of the most important skills that health care professionals need and there will be opportunities in this unit for you to look at the implications of good team working and what happens if people do not work together.

This unit will also help you to understand exactly what health and social care workers do and the skills they need. You may be thinking about a career as a social worker, an occupational therapy assistant, a nurse or an early years worker and want to explore these professions and the skills and qualities you need to work in this sector.

This unit links well with the other units in the book, particularly the units relating to communication and work experience. It is also an important unit for you if you are intending to move on to the BTEC National Qualification in Health and Social Care.

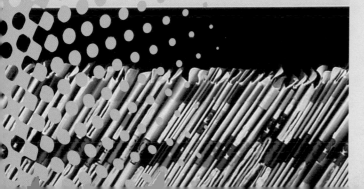

Learning outcomes

After completing this unit you should:

1. know key elements of health and social care services
2. know barriers to accessing health and social care services
3. understand the principles of partnership in health and social care
4. understand the requirements for job roles in health and social care.

Assessment and grading criteria

This table shows you what you must do in order to achieve a pass, merit or distinction grade, and where you can find activities in this book to help you.

To achieve a **pass** grade the evidence must show that you are able to:	To achieve a **merit** grade the evidence must show that, in addition to the pass criteria, you are able to:	To achieve a **distinction** grade the evidence must show that, in addition to the pass and merit criteria, you are able to:
P1 Identify the key elements of health and social care services (IE2, RL5, TW1, SM2, EP2) **Assessment activity 10.1, page 333**		
P2 Identify the main barriers to accessing health and social care [IE1, CT1, RL5, SM2, EP2] **Assessment activity 10.2, page 339**	**M1** Describe how the barriers to accessing health and social care may be overcome **Assessment activity 10.2, page 339**	
P3 Explain the benefits of inter-agency partnerships [CT1, CT3, CT4, CT5, RL5, SM2, EP2] **Assessment activity 10.3, page 345**	**M2** Discuss the ways in which the agencies work together to benefit individuals **Assessment activity 10.3, page 345**	**D1** Assess factors that could prevent these organisations working together **Assessment activity 10.3, page 345**
P4 Explain the skills required for two different job roles in health and social care [CT3, CT4, CT5, RL5, SM2, EP2] **Assessment activity 10.4, page 362**	**M3** Compare the skill requirements of the two different job roles in health and social care **Assessment activity 10.4, page 362**	**D2** Assess potential workforce development activities for the two job roles **Assessment activity 10.4, page 362**

How you will be assessed

You will be assessed by means of an internal assessment which will be designed and marked by the staff at your centre. It may be sampled by your centre's External Verifier as part of Edexcel's ongoing quality assurance procedures. The assignment is designed to show your understanding of the unit outcomes. These relate to what you should be able to do after completing this unit. Your assessment could be in the form of:

- presentations
- case studies
- practical tasks
- written assignments.

Sam, 16-year-old BTEC First Diploma in Health and Social Care student

I found this unit really interesting; I learned about the ways in which health and care services are organised and how different organisations work together to provide support for people. I really didn't know about any of that but now it makes much more sense when I think of going to the doctor and how, if I needed to go to hospital for anything, people would work together. I also learned about why some people find accessing services difficult and what can be done to help them get over the barriers and receive the support they need. I want to work in social care and so I really need to know about how best to meet the needs of individuals who will use the service.

I think that the best part of this unit was looking at what everyone does in more depth. I liked my work placement in a day centre for people with learning disabilities, but I think that I would like to work with older people in my next placement. It's amazing what careers are out there. My aunt is a social worker and now I think of everything that she has to do and all of the different people she has to work with, I think that she does a great job! I hope that I can go on to the BTEC National after this and then who knows what I might be able to do?

Over to you!

- How will you use the information contained in the unit?
- Which area of health and social care would you like to work in?
- Can you think of any barriers to receiving health and social care?

1. Know key elements of health and social care services

You have probably come across lots of different health and social care services without really thinking about them. This topic will start to help you to understand what they are and who provides them.

Statutory care

There are different ways of providing health and social care in the UK. Quite a lot of it is provided by the government and we call this **statutory** – it is provided by law. This means that the government has decided that everyone who has a particular need must be able to access the service. Governments provide money to support these services and to pay the wages of people who work in them:

- Social services
- the National Health Service and National Health Service Trusts
- Strategic Health Authorities
- Primary Care Trusts
- Mental Health Trusts
- Children's Trusts.

All of these organisations are funded (paid for) by the government but there are other sources of funding. Some funding comes from charges made to users of health services, for example prescription charges, dental and opticians' fees for adults over 19 and under 65 who are not entitled to some form of benefits. In the same way, some support provided by social services is means tested, which means that people have to pay a fee if they have an income over a certain level. For example, fees for residential care, community home support and the mobile meals service. In addition, some statutory care facilities such as hospitals and hospices are supported by groups of volunteers often composed of people who have benefited from the service, who raise funds to pay for particular projects such as incubators in a special care baby unit.

Private care

Some health and social care services are privately funded, which means that people either pay directly for the services or have **private** healthcare insurance; examples of private care services include:

- private medical and nursing care
- private residential care.

Voluntary care

Other support is provided by **voluntary** groups which support people who have a particular need. These organisations may have paid staff working for them who are professionally qualified, but they rely mainly on donations from individuals and many of the staff are volunteers. You might do voluntary work yourself. Volunteering is a very good way of getting more experience in health and social care.

Organisations which provide voluntary care include:

- the Autistic Society
- the Alzheimer's Society
- Age Concern.

Informal care

Much social care support is provided by **informal** carers; these are relatives, neighbours and friends who often give up their paid employment to support people who cannot take care of themselves. Although they may be eligible to claim a 'Carer's Allowance', informal carers work mainly out of concern for their relatives and are a valuable community resource.

Many informal carers appreciate the support they receive from the voluntary services. For example carers of individuals with long-term conditions may receive support from organisations such as the Dementia Society, whilst relatives of individuals with terminal illnesses may appreciate contact with Macmillan Nurses. Some informal carers have formed self-help groups to provide a forum for discussion and mutual support. An example of this is S.P.Y.C.A.T. (support for parents of young children with autism); groups of parents meet in each other's homes and also community centres to discuss strategies for coping and to share friendship with people who share the same issues. All of these groups are a valuable source of support for families who can feel isolated as they deal with the challenges on a daily basis.

Activity: Who pays?

Make a list of the different health and social care services you know; try and find out how many are statutory, private and voluntary and how many statutory services also provide a private service.

Key terms

Voluntary – support which is provided by organisations funded through public donation

Informal – support which is provided by relatives and friends

Did you know?

Some people who have used health and social care services are so impressed by the quality of the support they have received, they go on to train as professionals themselves.

Think about it

When you were unwell, what types of support provision did you receive?

Just checking

1. Name two voluntary groups which provide support for individuals.
2. Name two ways in which private support could be funded.
3. What is informal support?

Health and social care settings

Key terms

Ophthalmic – care and treatment of eyes; usually provided in an out-patient clinic, but serious issues are treated in hospital

Maternity – support for women before, during and after the birth of a baby

Paediatric – nursing and medical care of children

Terminal illness – an illness where the individual does not recover

Respite care – short-term support in a residential setting for individuals who are supported by family

Holistic support – supporting all of the needs of an individual

Community nurses – nurses who visit people in their homes and provide nursing support

Community care assistants – people who have usually completed an NVQ level 2 in social care or a BTEC First Diploma in Health and Social Care who provide personal care for individuals in their own homes

Everyone is an individual and when they need to use the health and social care services it is important that they have access to the setting which precisely meets their needs. Different settings are designed to do just that and the trained staff within those settings have the skills and knowledge to meet those particular needs. For example, an older person recovering from a fall may have different needs from a much younger person – even if they also have an injury resulting from a fall. It is important that settings meet the needs of the individual if they are to provide effective support.

Key elements

If everyone who needed support all turned up at the same place, things would become rather crowded; more importantly, not everyone would receive the support that they really needed. Health and social care services are designed to meet particular needs and are staffed by professionals who know how to do this. Here are some examples of the different settings.

Hospitals

Hospitals provide support for people who have an illness or who are recovering from one. Many hospitals provide support for a variety of conditions and illnesses and are staffed by people who are trained to do this. Some hospitals provide support for particular conditions such as **ophthalmic** (eye care), **maternity** (care of the mother and baby during pregnancy and birth) and **paediatric** (children).

Hospices

Hospices are usually smaller than many hospitals and provide support for individuals who have a **terminal illness**. Some hospices provide **respite care** which means that an individual may come for a few days in order to provide their relatives with a break from caring. The staff receive special training in order to give the **holistic support** required.

Domiciliary support

Domiciliary support is provided in an individual's own home and can be either health or social care. (Domicile is a word meaning 'home'.) For example, **community nurses** will visit a person at home and provide nursing care; sometimes this could be removing stitches after surgery or changing a dressing. **Community care assistants** may help an older person with their personal care if they can no longer manage this. Domiciliary care enables people to either return to or remain in their own homes and provides a choice.

Residential homes

Residential homes are designed to meet the needs of individuals who cannot take care of themselves. Many older people who can no longer meet their own personal care needs, or who are lonely following the death of a partner, may prefer to live in a residential home rather than remain in their own home. Residential homes provide the companionship which people are missing, and staff will deliver the personal support if this is needed, in a way which preserves the dignity of the older person whilst providing necessary safeguards. Other residential settings provide a home for younger people who have physical needs which prevent them from living independently. The staff in both types of settings usually include an activity coordinator who arranges events and activities designed to encourage the use of skills such as memory and physical mobility.

Day centres

Day centres are designed to provide a social space for individuals who would otherwise spend much of their time alone. Many day centres provide companionship and a midday meal for older people, enabling them to meet with people of a similar age and receive support from trained staff. Many day centres have regular visits from health and social care professionals such as counsellors, chiropodists and even opticians. They may also provide other services such as hairdressing and nail care.

Other day centres provide similar facilities for younger people who have multiple physical disabilities, enabling them to enjoy friendship in a pleasant atmosphere. Day centres also provide many relatives with a respite from the demands of caring for family members, enabling them to spend time on their own needs.

Fostering arrangements

For a variety of reasons some children cannot be cared for in their own homes. When this happens social services may arrange for a child to be looked after by foster carers who will have received training in order to provide a suitable, temporary home for a child. This can either be a short-term arrangement, for example if both parents were ill and there were no other relatives available to provide a home for the child, or long term if that was thought necessary. Foster carers do receive some financial support, but their main reward is in seeing the children thrive.

Activity: Funding

Visit your local library or community information centre and see how many different health and social care settings you can find out about in your local area. Choose two to research, finding out the answers to the following questions:

- Where does the funding come from?

- What support does the setting offer?

- For each of your two chosen settings, find out the average age of the users of the service.

- Produce a booklet with your information.

PLTS

When you are researching your two chosen settings, you will be an **independent enquirer.**

Just checking

1. Give one reason why some people would prefer to receive domiciliary support rather than residential support?
2. Name one task which a community nurse might perform.
3. What type of hospital unit would deliver babies?
4. What is respite support?
5. What would an ophthalmic clinic treat?
6. What are foster carers?

Hospitals are just one type of health and social care setting. Where else could you work?

Providing support in the right setting

Primary and secondary health care

Health care delivery is divided into three general categories which are **primary, secondary** and **tertiary.** Health care settings fit into these three categories and are arranged so that people have their needs met in the most appropriate way. Many people experience health care from all three categories during their lifetime, whilst others only receive primary healthcare for the majority if not all, of their lives.

Primary care

This refers to the health services which are the first point of contact for people with a health need. The organisations responsible for this service are the Primary Care Trusts (PCTs) which are large local organisations at the heart of the NHS. Primary Care includes GPs, dentists, pharmacists, opticians, NHS Direct and the Walk-in Centres. PCTs manage 80 per cent of the NHS budget. This type of health care is known as primary because it usually comes first; for example if we are ill we visit the GP, who may refer us to a hospital department if this is necessary. However, the need may be something that the GP can deal with, such as a sore throat or a simple ear infection, in which case we will only require primary health care. NHS Direct and the Walk-in Centres tend to be used when GP surgeries are closed, for example at the weekend or later in the evening and on bank holidays. They are staffed by professionals, usually registered nurses, who are able to prescribe antibiotics and give health care advice. Patients are always advised to follow-up the contact with a visit to the GP as soon as possible, particularly if the problem continues. Other primary health care services, such as opticians and dentists, provide support through an appointment service but will meet emergency needs when required.

Secondary care

Some patients need health care which cannot be provided by primary care services, either because they require more specialist or in-patient treatment, or because they have developed a condition which requires emergency care. People would then require secondary care services such as those provided by NHS Hospital Trusts, usually in an NHS hospital. They may need to be taken to hospital in an ambulance which is provided by an Ambulance Trust. Some patients also need support from a Mental Health Trust if they have emotional needs and also support from social care services. For example, if a child's sore throat developed into a more serious infection then her mother might contact the emergency ambulance service by dialling 999 and the child would be taken to the nearest hospital with the appropriate facilities. If there is no one to take care of any other children in the family while the parent was at the hospital, then the social care services would have provided temporary foster care, perhaps overnight, and day care during the day.

Social Services

Social care services look after the health and welfare of the population. Some of the main client groups that may require social services include children or families under stress, people with disabilities, elderly people needing care in their own home or people with housing or financial difficulties.

Social Services are run by local authorities sometimes working in partnership with the NHS or private or voluntary organisations.

Services available include:

- fostering and adoption
- home help for elderly people
- day care services for elderly people or people with disabilities
- occupational therapy
- personal care at home
- blue badge parking schemes

Activity: Social Services

In groups, choose one of the social services listed and find out as much as you can about them from your local social services department. You may be able to get information from your GP surgery or local library. Make a display which shows what services are available and who they help.

Case study: Secondary care

Beryl Grey was 82 years old and lived alone in her bungalow in a small village. Beryl woke up very early one morning and felt most confused. She could not remember who she was or where she was. Beryl wandered out of her house and into the street, still wearing her nightgown and without putting on her slippers; at one point she slipped and fell over in the street. A neighbour saw Beryl and took her home. The neighbour rang the GP who decided that Beryl may have broken her arm and telephoned for an ambulance to take her to the Accident and Emergency Unit at the local hospital. The doctor in the unit arranged for Beryl's arm to be x-rayed and treated but decided that the confusion was due to **dementia** and arranged for a specialist from the **NHS Mental Health Trust** to examine Beryl to decide on the support she may need. Beryl remained in the hospital for a few days and then was transferred to a nursing home for people who had dementia. The unit was staffed by trained staff who understood Beryl's needs and took good care of her.

1. Why did Beryl's neighbour contact the GP first rather than telephoning for an ambulance?
2. Why did the GP telephone for an ambulance?
3. Can you find any evidence of partnership in the case study?

Activity: Accessing services

Find out about the health care services in your area; how many primary and secondary services are there? How accessible are they for people who live in your community?

Why should people only attend the accident and emergency unit in the case of an emergency?

Key terms

Dementia – condition which may occur in older people which includes memory loss and confusion

NHS Mental Health Trust – a secondary care organisation which meets the health care needs of people with emotional disorders

Just checking

1. What is primary care?
2. What is secondary care?
3. Name three examples of primary care.
4. Name three examples of secondary care.
5. What is an optician?
6. Give three reasons why someone might need to visit the dentist.

More providers of care

Key terms

Dialysis unit – a hospital unit which contains specialist equipment for treating long term kidney disease

Neonatal – newborn

Tertiary care

This type of health care is provided by more specialised departments or hospitals. Often these hospitals are linked to medical schools and are known as teaching hospitals. People who have conditions which need more specialised help are treated in tertiary health care units. For example, people who have long-term kidney disease may visit a renal (kidney) **dialysis unit** for regular, specialised treatment by doctors, nurses and technicians who have had extra training in order to provide the care needed. **Neonatal** units for babies who have been born prematurely or with particular needs also come under the title of tertiary care.

Activity: Tertiary health care units

1. Using the internet or resources in your local library, research the tertiary health care units which are local to you. Find out about volunteers who support one of the units either by working in the setting or by raising funds to buy additional equipment or other resources. Could you become involved?

2. Can you link the settings (i) a nursing home (ii) an antenatal clinic (iii) a dental surgery (iv) a hospital ward for patient with acute medical conditions, to the correct health care area – primary, secondary or tertiary? Check your answers with your tutor.

Children's Trusts

The requirement for all Local Authorities to have a Children's Trust came as a result of Lord Laming's review of the death of Victoria Climbie. Lord Laming said that it is vital for all agencies who work with children, young people and their families to work more closely with each other and to communicate better with each other. Children's Trusts work hard to ensure that children and young people feel safe, valued and supported, so that they can make a full contribution to society. Children's Trusts work in partnership with the agencies that provide services for children, young people and families.

Mental Health Trusts

Mental health services are provided through primary health care providers such as GPs or secondary health providers such as specialist units. Services might include counselling, psychiatric therapies, community and family support. People with mental health problems such as depression, severe anxiety or psychiatric conditions such as bi-polar disorder would receive care from these services.

How do services work in partnership to ensure that people receive the best care?

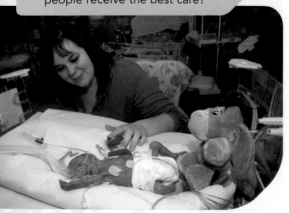

Case study: An emergency delivery

Mrs Jones is a community midwife who works for her local Primary Care Trust. One of her patients, Gemma Davies, is due to have her baby in two months time. Gemma has been receiving primary health care; she visits the community midwife regularly and the GP if she feels unwell. However, on her last visit to see the midwife, Gemma was found to have high blood pressure and was transferred by her GP to the **antenatal services** at the local hospital to be under the care of an **obstetrician**. Gemma began to have her baby the day after her visit to the hospital and was taken into the labour suite where her baby was born, two months prematurely. The baby had breathing difficulties and was transferred, by ambulance, to the **special care baby unit** at another hospital where they had the required equipment and staff with additional training.

1. Name the primary, secondary and tertiary health care services which all cared for Gemma and her baby.
2. Why is it necessary for these services to work in partnership with each other?
3. Why do you think Gemma's GP referred her to the hospital?

Key terms

Antenatal services – midwives and specially trained doctors who care for pregnant women

Obstetrician – a doctor who is trained to care for mothers-to-be

Special care baby unit – a hospital unit which cares for newborn babies with health issues

BTEC Assessment activity 10.1 P1

Identify key elements of health and social care services.

Produce a booklet for learners who are planning their work experience which identifies:

- four types of health and social care settings
- the main source of funding for each of the four settings
- how each of the four settings meets the needs of the individuals who use them.

Grading tip

P1 To improve your presentation, try to cover all of the bullet points for each of the settings you have chosen, in turn; for example, a residential home for older people, source of funding, how the setting meets the needs of the older people and so on. Remember to read the unit content carefully to ensure that you include all of the necessary details.

PLTS

When you are researching the information for your booklet you are becoming an **independent enquirer**; discovering information for yourself. You will also be reflecting upon your research and learning from this which makes you a **reflective learner**. As you organise your priorities in order to complete the activity in addition to your other assignments, you will be a **self-manager**.

Functional skills

When you are producing your booklet you will be extending your **English** by using your reading and writing skills. If you word process the booklet you will also be demonstrating your **ICT** skills.

Just checking

1. Name four examples of tertiary health care.
2. Give one example of where an individual may need all three types of health care – primary, secondary and tertiary.
3. Why might the staff ratio be higher in a tertiary unit?

2. Know barriers to health and social care

Key terms

Welfare State – the provision of health and social care services by the State

Barriers – reasons why some people cannot access health and social care provision

Financial burden – costs which make life difficult for people

Rural locations – places in the countryside where houses may be in small groups or quite isolated

Britain is a **welfare state**: health and social care services are provided for all citizens. Even so, many people experience difficulty in accessing the services they need because of **barriers** which are just as real as the barriers which prevent us from crossing the road in some areas.

Financial

For some people the cost of travelling to the service is a large barrier. Many people in modern Britain work long hours for low wages and use much of their pay to provide food and a home for themselves and their families. This means that there is very little left to pay the transport costs for a visit to a clinic or social services centre. Individuals in this situation who have young children will have particular difficulties; providing for a family may mean that the adults neglect their own needs and use all available funds to provide for what they see as the necessities of life. Other charges may also be a burden, for example individuals who are not eligible for exemption from prescription, dental or optician's fees may still have difficulty paying these and providing for their family. People may face hard choices, for example, between buying new spectacles and shoes for the children; paying for a school trip or dental treatment for themselves. These choices may form a barrier which prevents some individuals from accessing the services which would improve their well-being.

The **financial burden** can be increased when people live long distances from their nearest health or social care settings.

Geographical location

Not everyone lives in a big city where services may be within walking distance; some people live in villages and more **rural locations**. This can mean far less access to health and social care services; for example some family doctors provide services for more than one village and the nearest social service centre is in a town several miles away. For older people, there may be a problem with lack of transport if they do not have a car – some villages just have one bus a day – which may

Figure 10.1: Lack of transport can be a serious barrier to services

Activity: Counting the cost

1. Work out a monthly budget for a family of four, considering the cost of staple foods, energy costs, essentials such as soap and toilet paper.

2. Find out how wide an area your local medical centre serves; do some people have to travel a distance? Calculate the cost in bus fares. Visit a local supermarket and calculate the cost of feeding a family of four for one week and add that to the bus fares; how much does this all add up to?

mean that they leave problems until they become emergencies; for example medical conditions, or the need for help in the home due to reduced mobility. Some people who live a distance from health and social care services find that the long journey aggravates their condition or increases their discomfort so much that they prefer to stay at home. Others are concerned that admission to hospital will mean further expense and travel for relatives. It could be suggested that the transition from smaller local facilities, to large multi-service units, for example some of the larger hospitals which have replaced more specialist units, has increased the barriers for some individuals who now have to travel further for treatment and support.

Social class

Politicians now speak about a 'classless society', but for many people class is linked with wealth or income. Lack of money can make people feel that they belong to an **underclass** which exists at the edge of society. They are unable to enjoy many of the things which money can provide, for example leisure activities, comfortable homes and holidays. All of these things, which some people take for granted, contribute to our sense of well-being and without them we can feel excluded. Although we live in a Welfare State, some people still live disadvantaged lives; without jobs people can lose hope and their health is affected.

Case study: The Greens

The Greens are an average family in modern Britain. Dad is employed by a construction firm; he works long hours and comes home very tired. Mum works at the local supermarket, but cannot work in the school holidays because there are two younger Greens, Lucy who is 6 years old and Sam who is 9. The Greens cannot afford to pay for a childminder in the school holidays, so the manager of the supermarket allows Mum to take unpaid leave in school holidays.

Dad has been feeling unwell recently but his manager will not allow him to take time off to visit the GP in work time and Dad is too tired to go after work. In addition, the Greens live on a housing estate at the edge of a village and the GP is in the next village. Getting an appointment is difficult, and the bus fares are expensive. Mum is concerned about Dad's health but hopes that he will recover without having to take time off work. Sam needs new shoes and Lucy is growing out of her clothes so quickly – she seems to need something new every week. Mum is becoming stressed and has begun to use alcohol to relieve this. The **health visitor** is concerned at the bruises on Mum's face, but she has claimed that she fell over and bumped her face on the stairs when she was tired.

1. Which health and social care professionals could support the Green family?
2. What could be the risks to the family if Dad does not receive medical attention?

Did you know?

Some people earn wages above the level of entitlement to benefits but may still find the travel costs involved in accessing health and social care services difficult to meet.

Community health and social care services are the only social contact for many older people in rural areas.

Think about it

Can you think of one other reason why people may not choose to access health and social care services?

Just checking

1. Why might the cost of travel discourage someone from using health and social care services?
2. What is a welfare state?
3. Name one role which a Health Visitor would perform.

Barriers to health and social care: disability

Disability

People with disabilities would say that they have an impairment; it could affect **mobility**, vision, hearing or understanding. The disability comes from the environment – preventing them from accessing the services they need. Many centres now have wheelchair access, **induction loops**, access to information in **Braille** and large print. Staff are trained to use equipment and support users of services in appropriate ways. Why then do the barriers still remain for some? Some possible reasons include the following.

- Older centres are not always suitably adapted to meet all needs; financial costs may prevent this.

- Financial costs may also reduce the number of appropriately trained staff and the amount of available transport; some individuals have a medical condition which affects their ability to travel or to wait for the attention of professionals.

- Some individuals feel that they would prefer not to access support, rather than encounter the difficulties which it involves.

- Sometimes lack of understanding about the nature of some disabilities can produce barriers, as can be seen in the case study on page 337.

How can we stop disabilities from being a barrier?

Activity: How accessible is your health centre?

1. Conduct a survey of your local health centre. (i) Note how accessible it is for users of wheelchairs and visually impaired individuals. (ii) Could it be improved? (iii) Find out what is meant by a 'disabling environment'.

2. Speak to your centre youth worker; find out about access to provision for young people who have a disability. Do they have equal access or are there barriers?

Case study: Yasmina's visit

Yasmina is a young woman who has a visual impairment, which occurred following an attack of **meningitis**. Yasmina does have some vision, but finds it difficult to distinguish between different surfaces if they are not brightly coloured. Yasmina also has severe asthma and visits her local medical centre regularly for check ups. The centre has clear access and the edge of the steps up to the door are painted a bright yellow which enables Yasmina to enter without tripping over. The waiting room has a rail all the way round which enables Yasmina to reach her seat independently. Unfortunately, due to a bad cold, her asthma became worse and she was referred to her local hospital to be seen by a consultant. The out-patient clinic at the hospital had recently received a large donation from a branch of a national bank and had used the money to re-decorate the area. The manager of the bank suggested that the clinic should be re-decorated in the bank's colours, which were pale blue and cream. In addition to this, the bank provided new chairs in the waiting room – also pale blue and cream.

Yasmina is an independent person and insisted that her parents allow her to visit the clinic by herself. She arrived at the clinic and went through the doors, tripping over the pale blue mat and walking into an equally pale blue and cream chair. A nurse saw her fall and ran to assist her. 'You should look where you are going,' she said. 'I would if I could see where everything was,' replied Yasmina. The nurse helped Yasmina into the clinic and helped her out again, which made Yasmina feel helpless, an emotion she did not like.

When her next appointment was due, Yasmina decided that she would not attend, because the environment reduced her independence. This meant that her asthma did not improve as quickly as it could have.

1. What did both the bank and the clinic staff forget when they re-decorated the clinic?

2. What information could Yasmina's GP have given to the clinic when he referred her?

3. Why would Yasmina be reluctant to re-visit the clinic?

Key term

Meningitis – a serious infectious illness which can leave a person with a disability

Just checking

1. Name two ways of removing barriers to health and social care for a person with a disability.
2. What does the word mobility mean?
3. Who would use Braille to communicate?
4. Why is it important to enable a person who has a disability to be independent?

337

Barriers to health and social care: ethnicity, culture and faith

Where do I fit in?

Ethnicity

This means our ethnic origins; i.e. where our ancestors were born. Britain is a multi-ethnic society; if you look around any big town or city you will see that this is true. Ethnicity can affect the colour of our skin, eyes and hair, but these are all about appearance, ethnicity may go much deeper than that. For many people, belonging to a particular ethnic group means having a shared history, customs and a distinct culture where particular customs and practices are important to daily living. For example, in some ethnic groups, it is important that a woman is only examined by a female doctor; this can mean that a woman might refuse to receive medical treatment rather than go against this.

Culture

Culture involves all of the acceptable practices for good manners and ways of doing things which are important to a particular group. For example, in some cultures an individual would not make eye contact with a professional, such as a social worker or a teacher, as a sign of respect, whereas for other groups, lack of eye contact would be regarded as bad mannered.

Culture can also mean the customs which are particular to families and individuals. For example the use of first names may be restricted to close family members and individuals would be offended if you used their first name rather than addressing them as Mr, Mrs or Miss. It is important that we recognise the customs and values which are part of a culture and show respect even if we disagree or cannot understand the reasons. The observance of culture and customs is part of what makes us an individual but also enables us to feel part of a group and provides us with a sense of identity. If we do not respect the culture and customs of the users of the service, we are not meeting all of their needs.

Faith

Although many people follow faiths which are not connected with either their ethnic group or their culture, faith is still an important part of everyday life for some ethnic groups; it is intertwined within their culture. It is important for health and social care professionals to be aware of this when organising events for people from groups other than their own. For example, someone from the **Rastafarian** faith may not wish to receive Christmas presents, and a group of **Muslim** women would not attend a group counselling session where refreshments were served during the holy month of **Ramadan** when they were observing the **fast**.

For some people, their personal preferences and choices are not an option; they are connected with a set of beliefs or strongly held views and opinions. But not every set of beliefs is connected with a religious faith. For example, vegetarians may avoid eating meat because they believe that it is wrong to kill animals for food; vegetarian beliefs can be connected with a religion, for example Buddhism, where all life is believed to be sacred, but people have many reasons for being vegetarian. Other people do not believe in taking western medication but would prefer to use 'natural' cures obtained from **alternative healers**. There are also **humanists** who believe that life is precious and to be celebrated, and do not practise any religion.

These beliefs are all-important to those who hold them and should be respected when delivering health and social care. If the support offered does not include this respect, people may refuse to attend for support or treatment.

Key terms

Ramadan – a holy time when Muslims do not eat or drink between sunrise and sunset in order to draw nearer to God

Fast – going without food and sometimes drink to purify the soul and draw nearer to God

Alternative healers – individuals who use non-medical ways of supporting people with medical and social issues

Humanists – believe in the importance of respect for all and celebration of life; they do not follow a religion

---

 Assessment activity 10.2

Produce a set of information leaflets identifying barriers to health and social care. In these leaflets you should provide information on:

- what the barriers are
- the problems these barriers cause
- how these barriers can be overcome.

Grading tip

Carry out research relating to your own neighbourhood and how accessible the services are for different groups of individuals and consider several different factors that cause barriers (**P2**). Your local research could help you outline how barriers could be overcome (**M1**).

 PLTS

When you are finding out about cultures, customs and beliefs you will be developing your skills as an **independent enquirer**.

Functional skills

When you are researching information about different beliefs you will be developing your **English** reading skills.

Just checking

1. What is one of the main differences between a vegetarian diet and a non-vegetarian diet?
2. Name one belief which humanists may hold.
3. How can ignoring personal beliefs and preferences prevent some individuals accessing health and social care?

3. Understand principles of partnership

Figure 10.2: Why is it important to work together to solve problems?

There are several ways in which health and social care professionals can work as partners, supporting individuals and providing a 'package of care' which meets all of the needs rather than just a few or even none. These are some examples of professional partnerships which can be successful if used in the right way:

Multi–disciplinary working

People who are employed by the same service, for example social services, will work together as a team to provide support for an individual. This could include a social worker, a family support worker, a probation officer and a youth counsellor all working together to support a family where there are a variety of social issues. It is important for each individual to regard themselves as a member of a team, even though they do not usually work with each other, sharing information and discussing progress on a regular basis, otherwise the partnership will fail and the individual service users will not be supported. You will also find multi-disciplinary teams working within the health service; for example, a person who has had a hip replacement will need the services of a nurse to change the dressing and check the progress of the wound, a physiotherapist to support the development of mobility and the surgeon who performed the operation to check on overall progress. All of these professionals work together to plan and carry out the support needed so that the patient can recover fully.

Inter–agency working

People who are employed by different agencies may also work together to provide support for an individual or a family. For example, a social worker, an occupational therapist and a community nurse could work in partnership to support an individual who has physical disabilities. It is essential that all of these professionals recognise themselves as a team, share information and co-operate to prevent mistakes occurring and also to prevent support being duplicated. There have been terrible mistakes made when professionals working across agencies have not communicated essential information; effective team work can be critical. It is also important to include the user of the services in all planning and decision making; they should be considered the most important team member and all planning should be fitted around them in order that all needs are fully met.

Users of services forums

Services forums are composed of individuals who use a particular service and some of the professionals who provide this. For example, some of the people who use a particular health centre, the practice manager and doctors who are partners in the practice may meet once a month to discuss how the service could be improved for the people who use it. Other forums may include individuals who have a particular, long-term medical problem and act as a source of support in addition to discussing any issues or changes which may be necessary to the service. The overall aim of these forums is to enable people who use this service to become involved so that they can put forward their points of view and contribute to the way the service is run. It is important that a service meets the needs of those people who use it and a forum can help this process as the users explain how, in their opinion, delivery could be adapted, or how they would prefer their needs to be met.

Voluntary and statutory sector liaison

Voluntary groups such as the NSPCC may work with statutory organisations such as Children's Services to protect a child who is at risk from harm. It is essential that such groups lay aside any professional bias and recognise each other as professionals who are all working towards the same goal. Other voluntary groups, such as Age Concern, work with statutory agencies such as social services and health visitors, to support older people and their families.

Integrated Workforce Agenda

This is a government initiative which is intended to cross professional boundaries and support organisations in working together as one workforce. Workers will see themselves as being health *and* social care workers rather than health *or* social care workers. There will be **core competencies** or skills which both health and social care professionals are expected to have. Examples of these could be communication skills and report writing; both of which are necessary for either profession. Professionals are being encouraged to recognise the benefits of working in partnership in order to provide a more consistent service for individuals. While this is important for everyone, it is seen as being particularly crucial for children. We now speak of 'joined-up services' for children and young people, which means that health, social care and educational services should be working together, to plan support for individuals. This will help to ensure that every child and young person has an equal chance of succeeding in achieving their goals and are not disadvantaged because they have needed support in some areas of their lives.

Remember

The user of the service is also a member of the team; support should always be discussed with them.

Activity: Who works in teams?

In pairs, make a list of all of the different examples you can think of, where health and social care professionals work in teams. Compare your lists with each other and then show them to your tutor.

What do you think are the benefits of working in teams?

Key term

Core competencies – skills which are essential to performing a role accurately

Just checking

1. What is meant by multi-disciplinary working?
2. What is meant by inter-agency working?
3. What is a user of services forum?

Purposes of partnerships: Why work together?

Key terms

Occupational therapist – a health care professional who works with individuals to increase mobility and independence

Housing officer – a social care professional who usually works for a local authority, ensuring that individuals in need have appropriate housing

Holistic approach – an approach to delivery of support which takes account of all the needs of an individual

Activity: Sharing resources

What kind of resources could be shared between professionals? Look again at the example of the lady who can no longer climb her stairs; what resources could the professionals share when working with her?

Much of health and social care work is delivered in teams; even if someone is being supported by a community nurse or a social worker, these professionals will be part of a team which includes other professionals, administrative support and often technical support. Teamwork is essential if the individual is going to receive all of the support they need. This section will provide you with some reasons for working in partnership with other professionals, across agencies and within agencies with people from different disciplines, all contributing their expertise for the good of the individuals in need.

Working in a team means that you are always supported and someone will help you if you are having difficulties with completing a task. In many teams, everyone has different tasks to complete but they are all just as important. Some people work best as team leaders, while others are more efficient and comfortable working as a member of the team. It can be a positive experience when everyone works together, completing their own tasks and being willing to help others within the team. The experience becomes negative when one or more members do not complete their tasks fully or are unwilling to help anyone else. This can cause resentment and prevent the team functioning at its best.

Purposes of teamwork

Teams are always composed of several people, who must all work together otherwise the service will not be delivered effectively. Here are some examples of teamwork which will help you to understand the topic more easily.

Instead of viewing the individual's needs from the point of view of your own profession only, the need is viewed from several angles – in other words from all sides of the issue. For example; a person may come for help with housing because she can no longer use her stairs. She may need re-housing and you as a **housing officer** could organise that; if you were working in partnership with the health service, an **occupational therapist** could assess the house and suggest that a stair lift be fitted, enabling the lady to remain in her own neighbourhood amongst her friends.

A holistic approach

Professionals will discuss the individual's needs following assessment, and find that their aims are the same, even though the approach may be different. A **holistic approach** means that both the housing officer and the occupational therapist would identify the common aim of increasing the lady's quality of life.

Promotion of integration

Health and social care services are encouraged to work together and see themselves as being part of one team rather than several. For example, you as the housing officer and the occupational therapist would regard yourselves as one team for the purposes of finding a solution to the lady's mobility problem.

Prevention of duplication

When different professionals work together, seeing themselves as partners, they can reduce the times when the same support is delivered. Previously an individual may have been assessed by several professionals separately, with no communication between any of them. This could mean that valuable resources were wasted and the service user would also feel that time was also wasted.

Pooling of resources

When professionals work together, they can share resources; this can mean that services can reduce costs, leaving more to be used by others.

Maximisation of expertise

All professionals are experts in their own field; working in partnership with professionals from other services will mean that everyone can use their own skills and not have to perform functions where they are less skilled. In other words, everyone does what they are good at!

When everyone is working in partnership, they can agree on the most effective and consistent approach for delivering the services. Recording this can mean that all professionals and the user of the services are fully aware of how support will be delivered.

Think about it

Why do you think that it is important to record all meetings between partners in health and social care?

Just checking

1. What does a dietitian do?
2. What does reduction of duplication of services mean?
3. What is a holistic approach?

Key term

Dietitian – a health professional who works with individuals who need to adapt their diet for health reasons

Case study: Tremayne

Tremayne was a 42-year-old man who lived independently in his own home. He was unmarried and worked as an accountant for a local firm. Tremayne had been diagnosed as having high blood pressure by his GP and had been advised to give up smoking. The GP referred Tremayne to a government-sponsored organisation which would support him in this. Tremayne did manage to give up smoking; however, his appetite increased as food tasted better and he began to gain weight, which was also bad for his blood pressure.

The GP now referred Tremayne to a **dietitian** who worked with him to design a more healthy approach to eating. Tremayne also decided to visit a gym to help to reduce both his weight and his blood pressure. The gym was a private one, owned by a national sports organisation. The trainer worked with the doctor's advice to support Tremayne in improving his health.

1. How many partnerships can you find in this case study?
2. What points will they all need to remember?
3. How will Tremayne benefit from the services working in partnership?

Planning support

Figure 10.3: The planning cycle

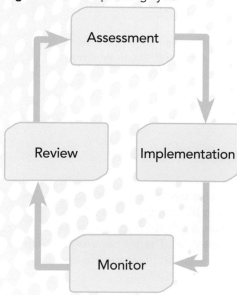

Individual people need individual plans

When individuals have health and social care needs, they may require the services of several professionals working together. Sometimes the professionals all come from the same service; for example a physiotherapist, a doctor, and several nurses may work together to support a patient who is recovering from a stroke. The doctor will prescribe medication, arrange for tests to be made and examine the patient. The nurses will administer the medication, take care of the patient's skin to prevent pressure sores, interact with the patient and ensure that they are clean and comfortable. The physiotherapist will examine the patient and then work with them to encourage mobility and restore movement. This type of partnership is known as **multidisciplinary,** which means that several people from different disciplines or professions but the same service are working together. When the professionals come from different services; for example, a social worker, a community psychiatric nurse and a representative of a mental health charity such as **MIND** work together to support a patient who is suffering from depression, then this is known as an **inter-agency** partnership because people from different services are working together.

Planning cycle: whether people are receiving health support or social support, or even a combination of both, the professionals will have worked through a process of planning to ensure that the support matches the need. This is a good example of professionals working together.

Stage 1 The team will come together to discuss all of the needs of the patient and record their meeting. Usually the patient will have a file and all information will be stored in this.

Stage 2 The team will then decide how best to meet these needs and arrange for treatment to be carried out. For example the doctor might order some tests and prescribe medication, the nurses will organise any practical care and administer the medication and the physiotherapist will decide on the regime for recovery.

Stage 3 The plan will be monitored to ensure full implementation. All of these decisions will be discussed with the patient and also the nearest relative if this is appropriate.

Stage 4 The treatments will be delivered, but will be reviewed at regular intervals to ensure that the plan is working and that nothing else should be added.

Recognising needs

When we are planning support for someone it is important to recognise all of their needs which are at the centre of the support they receive. It is easy to forget that a problem belongs to a real person; they are not the problem, they are a person who has a problem.

When planning you will need to:

- provide continuity and consistency

- provide support and advice

- allow the person to be included in the planning discussions, so that they are involved in decisions rather than being presented with them

- ask someone about their choices and preferences and invite them to present their own solutions to the issues.

A full recognition of someone's needs will involve taking a holistic approach to the planning of support. External factors may affect the planning process, for example, current availability of resources; availability of a member of staff, funds to pay for work.

BTEC Assessment activity 10.3

Elizabeth is an older lady who is in the early stages of Alzheimer's disease. Elizabeth becomes quite flustered and upset, because she is aware of her needs but finds them difficult to express. She says that her family do not understand her and are no longer interested in her well-being. Her family are actually very concerned but are not sure how to deal with Elizabeth.

In groups of two or three, discuss how a Health Visitor and a representative of the Alzheimer's Society could work together to support Elizabeth and her family, using the following bullet points to guide you.

- Using the Internet, research the role of a Health Visitor in supporting older people.
- Using the Internet, research the different ways in which the Alzheimer's Society work with families.
- Write down what you see as the main issues which the family are dealing with.
- Discuss how each of the professionals could support Elizabeth and her family.
- Decide where they could work in partnership and combine their services

Record your discussion and individually, write a short report based on this, which explains and discusses how the partnership would benefit Elizabeth and her family (P3, M2). To achieve a distinction grade, you should include in your report an assessment of factors which might prevent the partnership from being successful.

Grading tips

Remember that to achieve P3 and M2, you must be sure to explain and discuss how the inter-agency partnership would benefit Elizabeth and her family. To achieve D1, you will need to add an assessment of those factors which could prevent the partnership being successful.

PLTS

When you are considering the support for the case study you will be a **creative thinker** by generating ideas and considering possibilities.

Functional skills

When you are writing your report based on the case study, you will be developing your **English** skills in writing.

Just checking

1. What is the planning process?
2. Name one way of recognising an individual's needs.

4. Understand the requirements for job roles in health and social care

What makes a good nurse or a good care assistant? Personality, skills, something else? What do you think? This topic will explore some of the general characteristics and approaches you will need to develop if you are thinking of working in a health or social care environment.

Appearance/attitude

Appearance does matter; would you really like to be cared for by someone whose appearance was untidy, perhaps unclean? Of course not, a professional appearance inspires confidence. If someone cannot look after themselves, will they be capable of looking after you properly? Combined with appearance is attitude, which can be revealed in body language and tone of voice. Someone who is interested in their work and interested in the individuals they are supporting will convey this in their approach to work.

A positive attitude will also demonstrate itself in your approach to punctuality. If you are late you are showing a lack of respect to colleagues, who are having to complete your work until you arrive, and a lack of respect to individuals who are waiting for your support.

By appearing confident you will give the impression to the users of the service that you are committed and able to support them.

Empathy

Empathy means the ability to see the world from another person's viewpoint and experience. Some of the people you will be supporting may have had difficult experiences and this may be reflected in their appearance or behaviour. It is part of your role to see the world from their point of view; you have to accept service users as people rather than making judgments.

Ability to work with others

The ability to work as an effective team member is essential in health and social care. Staff have to work under a lot of pressure and must be able to rely on each member to complete their tasks and to support each other.

Although each member of staff will have particular tasks to complete, all members of staff are expected to ensure that the needs of patients and users of services are fully met. This may mean that you would complete a task for someone else, if they could not. A well functioning team recognises the need to deal with disagreements or differences of opinion which would reduce the quality of relationships and reduce communication.

It is essential that team members do not gossip about each other as this would reduce team effectiveness. Ill feeling between team members can be conveyed in body language and tone of voice, which in turn may cause lack of confidence in patients and service users.

Competence, qualifications and registration

Health and social care staff at all levels are required to prove that they are competent to perform their role. Anyone who has caused harm to an individual or group of service users through incompetence is not allowed to work in the services. Staff are monitored and reviewed in order to ensure that all delivery of support is of a high standard, underpinned by principles of good practice. Staff are now required to complete relevant qualifications, for example National Vocational Qualifications in **Pro-active Support**, and also in particular techniques such as safe lifting and handling of users of services, **basic food hygiene** and first aid. Nurses, social workers and members of similar professions are required to register with the appropriate body and renew that registration annually. Evidence of poor practice can mean that the person's name is removed from the register, preventing them working as a professional.

All health and social care workers have to follow codes of practice; for example Social Care Workers have to follow the General Social Care Codes of Practice. There are six codes for employees and six for employers. These codes are designed to ensure that all support is delivered in a way which promotes the rights of an individual and meets their holistic needs. Health care workers have to follow similar codes of practice. Some of the legislation which provides a framework for professional practice in health and social care also includes codes of practice which are designed to safeguard the rights of service users. For example, the Mental Health Act 2007 has a code of practice which ensures that patients are safeguarded from abuse and have the right to have their case reviewed when detained in hospital.

Remember

Not everyone can work in health and social care – it is hard work and requires particular types of people.

Key terms

Pro-active support – support which encourages people to make choices and retain independence

Basic food hygiene – a course which instructs people in the correct storage and preparation of food

Did you know?

The work may be hard but it is very rewarding, challenging and full of variety.

Activity: Do you match the requirements?

Make a list of all of the personal requirements described in this section and put a tick against the ones you meet. Discuss this with your tutor. Find out about the personal requirements for a work role outside the area of health and social care, for example working in a shop, and compare them with your list. Are they quite similar?

Just checking

1. What is empathy?
2. Give an example of incompetence in health or social care.

Care skills in a caring environment

Figure 10.4: Principles of good practice in health and social care

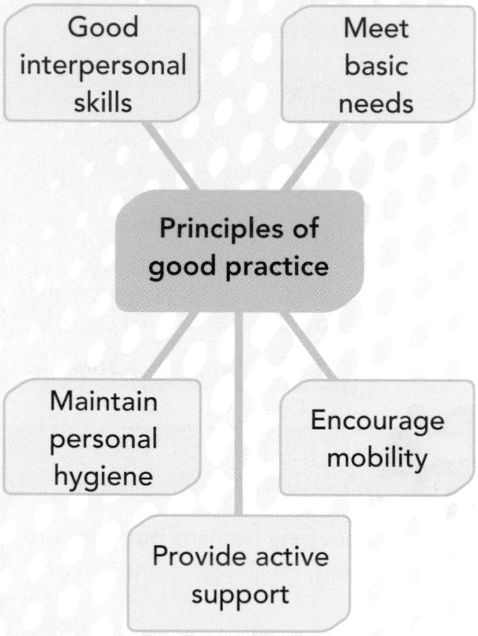

- Good interpersonal skills
- Meet basic needs
- **Principles of good practice**
- Maintain personal hygiene
- Encourage mobility
- Provide active support

Think about it

The principles of good practice apply to all areas of health and social care. Why do you think that these principles are so important?

Key term

Empower – give people the right to decide for themselves

When we are supporting individuals, we need to do so competently, following the procedures, policies and guidelines provided. Not everyone who works in health or social care follows these carefully – which is one reason why mistakes sometimes happen. We need to ensure that our professional practice is of the highest standard at all times – taking pride in our work and developing confidence in our abilities. Imagine yourself as a user of a service – how would you feel if the support you received was not of a good standard? You would feel neglected, uncared for and perhaps afraid. Part of the role of the professional is to safeguard the well-being of individuals through the competent use of appropriate skills in a safe manner.

Principles of good practice in health and social care

Principles are the important ideas which underpin the way we deliver health and social care. They ensure that we perform even simple, everyday tasks to the best of our ability and in a way which meets standards set by government legislation and the codes of practice set by health and social care professional bodies. These are some of the basic ones; you may find more.

- Follow all set procedures when completing tasks; these may be written in a procedure book, so do check when you are on work experience.

- If you are unsure of how to complete a task, check with your supervisor; mistakes can be dangerous.

- Treat every user of the service with respect; allow them dignity and privacy.

- Always address users of services by their preferred name; you do not have the right to use their first name unless they give you specific permission.

- Challenge any discrimination and challenge yourself if you feel that you may hold prejudices.

- Always take a person-centred approach; the user of the service is the most important person – support should always be matched to their needs.

- Always follow health and safety rules; never take unacceptable risks for others or yourself.

Active support

Take an active approach to support; encourage, enable and **empower** individuals to make choices, make decisions and take control. Never force choices onto individuals.

- Your role is to enable users of service to become as independent as they can, while providing support for those who need this.

Interpersonal skills

Effective interpersonal skills are essential in health and social care – not only to prevent mistakes happening, but also to build and maintain relationships with users of services, their relatives and also other members of the staff team. The following skills are ones which you should develop:

- clear speech, without jargon, slang or regional expressions

- appropriate paralanguage; polite tone which is not sharp or too loud to cause offence

- non-aggressive body posture; remember, folded arms may look as though you wish to argue

- good eye contact, a professional smile and a cheerful facial expression

- excellent listening skills

- good awareness of personal space.

Meeting basic needs

Basic needs must be met every day; if an individual requires support for these, they must receive respect, dignity and privacy where appropriate. Staff must be aware of those individuals who cannot support themselves and complete their own personal care. For example, toilet doors must be closed to preserve privacy and screens should be drawn around a patient in a hospital bed when personal care is being delivered. Bed bathing should be conducted sensitively, not uncovering the individual any more than is necessary. Always try to imagine yourself in that situation: what would you want and how would you like to be cared for?

Maintaining personal hygiene

The maintenance of personal hygiene is essential to an individual's well-being – emotional and physical. For example if the skin is not kept clean for an individual who is immobile, it can result in serious infections and extreme discomfort. A person-centred approach to care includes meeting all of the basic needs, including the maintenance of personal hygiene.

Encouraging mobility

Part of the role of a health or social care worker is to encourage mobility in the users of the service. It is essential that people retain as much mobility as possible, whatever their underlying condition. It will increase and improve a person's quality of life if they are allowed their independence rather than if it is removed (however well meaning the 'help' is).

Figure 10.5: Why is it important to stay calm and be patient?

Activity: What are our rights?

Many people would say that all of the points described in this section are their basic human rights, but are there other human rights? Conduct an internet search to find out what other people consider to be basic human rights. You might begin by looking at the Human Rights Act; a piece of legislation which states what our rights as citizens are. When you have found your information, produce a poster and ask your tutor if you can place this in your classroom.

Just checking

1. Name three basic rights of all individuals.
2. List three principles of good practice.
3. Describe what you think is a positive attitude towards work.

Working in health and social care: 1

My life

Florence Nightingale again?

Think of nursing roles which you have seen either in person or on television or at the cinema. Are there any other qualities you would add to this list?

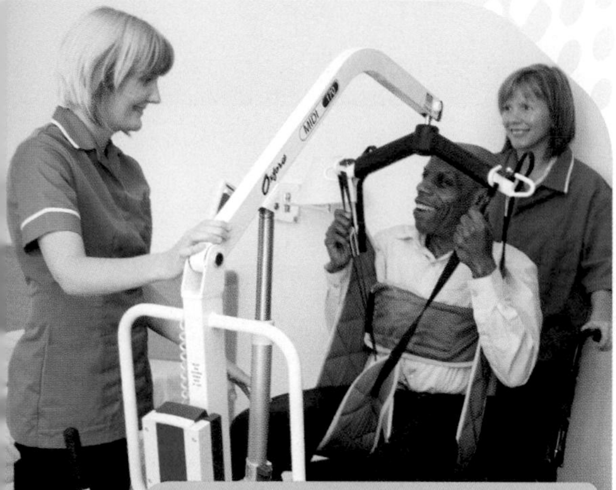

Nurses work with a range of people in a range of settings.

The following pages will explore a range of professional roles of people who work in the health and care sectors. We have chosen the following professions for you to learn about but of course there are many more. You will be investigating the personal qualities you need, the work they do and the skills you need to carry out this work. There will also be an overview of the qualifications you need. You will explore the role of the adult nurse, nursing assistants, hospital porters, physiotherapists and social workers. The roles of other health and social care professionals are considered throughout this book.

Nurses

Nurses are well-qualified professionals who deliver support to individuals in hospital and also in the community. Nurses undergo three or four years training during which they experience a wide variety of health care situations working with people who are sick or in need of health care support in the community or in a hospital setting.

Personal qualities

Nurses need many personal qualities and here are some examples:

Figure 10.6: Are there any qualities you would add to this list?

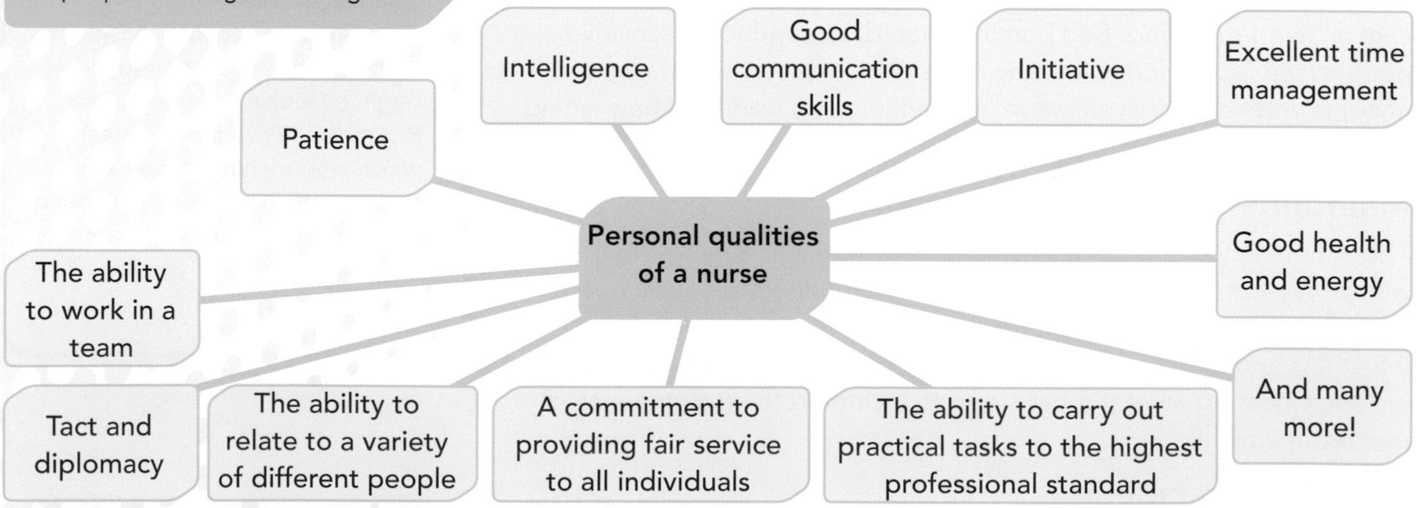
Personal qualities of a nurse
Patience
Intelligence
Good communication skills
Initiative
Excellent time management
Good health and energy
And many more!
The ability to carry out practical tasks to the highest professional standard
A commitment to providing fair service to all individuals
The ability to relate to a variety of different people
Tact and diplomacy
The ability to work in a team

Did you know?

People who have completed a period of work experience in health and social care are more likely to be granted a place as a student nurse.

Role

Nurses work in shifts usually seven and a half or eight hours split between morning, afternoon or night. A nurse receives the report (handover) from the staff they are taking over from, will liaise with doctors and other professionals, and deliver personal care such as assisting with a bath, shower or shave. A nurse will administer medication at the appropriate time of the day. They may dress wounds using correct techniques. They may liaise with relatives or community staff if the patient needs any more care at home. The nurse may remove **surgical stitches**, and will take physiological measurements, (see Unit 7) and communicate with doctors and other professionals. They may also consider the dietary needs of their patients.

Skills

As well as the personal qualities and skills described above, nurses need to learn a range of practical skills to carry out tasks such as dressing wounds, removing stitches or providing personal hygiene in a caring and **person centred** way. They learn to work safely with the correct techniques to enable healing while preventing the spread of infection. Hand washing and cleanliness are very important. Nurses also learn about the medications which need to be administered and how these work so that they can give them to patients safely.

Qualifications

To become an adult nurse you will usually need to complete your BTEC First Diploma in Health and Social Care to at least merit standard and then move on to study on the BTEC National Diploma in Health and Social Care. You will also need to have GCSEs at C or above in English and mathematics. Learners who have these qualifications can then apply to a university to study for the Diploma in Nursing (Adult Branch) or a degree in nursing. The Diploma takes three years to complete and brings with it registration to practise. From 2013 all new nurses will have to complete degree courses in England (this happened in Wales in 2004).

Case study: Rachel

Rachel is a district nurse based in a busy GP practice. She visits patients in their own homes so that they do not have to go to hospital but can be cared for in a familiar home environment. It is Tuesday today and after a meeting, with the doctors and the other nurses at the practice, she makes her first visit – to Mr Ralph who has diabetes and leg ulcers. Rachel changes Mr Ralph's dressings and discusses his insulin. Is he coping with injecting himself? Is he eating well and still managing the stairs to go to the bathroom? Mr Ralph enjoys Rachel's visits as she gives him confidence that he can still manage most things by himself. She then visits Mrs Bandara, who needs an injection and a blood test, following which Rachel checks up on Michael who has had heart surgery and is recovering at home with the help of his wife. They discuss his medication and also his next visit to hospital as an outpatient. After this it is time to return to the GP practice to write up her notes, have a sandwich and prepare for her afternoon visits.

1. What personal qualities did Rachel use today?

2. Do you have the personal qualities to be an adult nurse?

Key terms

Surgical stitches – stitches inserted by a surgeon to close a wound created by surgery

Person centred – treating each person individually according to their needs

Activity: Nurse training

Use the internet to research the requirements for a Registered Adult Nurse at three different universities and write down your findings.

Did all of the universities ask for the same qualifications, or did they ask for different ones?

Remember

While universities are required to request GCSEs in English and mathematics at C or above for a Diploma in Nursing, they are also entitled to ask for other qualifications in addition if they choose to.

Just checking

1. List three personal qualities needed by an adult nurse.
2. Name two tasks which an adult nurse might perform.

Working in health and social care: 2

Social workers

Social workers are busy and well-qualified professionals who perform a variety of tasks in the community. They also work with healthcare staff in hospitals, dealing with issues and improving the lives of many people. Social workers are concerned with the safeguarding of children but they also support families who need help, for example if a family member has a disability, and work with individuals who have mental ill health. Social workers often work under stressful and difficult conditions and many people do not realise how important the role is.

Personal qualities

Social workers need many personal qualities to perform their roles effectively. Look at the spider diagram below; could you add any more qualities?

Figure 10.7: Can you think of any more qualities needed by a social worker?

Role

Social workers generally arrive at the local office at 8 am to see if they had any calls from users of the service. In a typical day they may be due in court, for example to speak for a mother who wishes to regain custody of her child. They may then go on to visit a family. They will have to write up case notes and move on to the next visit. Social workers may also attend case conferences regarding individuals they are involved in supporting. Case conferences can last long after office hours but the social worker must remain until they finish. Sometimes they do not arrive home until after 9 pm, having started at 8 am. The role is not for you if you want to work 'office hours', but it is an essential one.

Skills

Social workers need a thorough understanding of social work law and an ability to apply this to their cases. They need to be able to relate to a variety of different people, manage a case load and be **assertive** when necessary. They will need to take a non-judgemental approach when dealing with individuals who have difficulties. They must also know when to refer a case to a senior colleague or to another professional, such as a doctor or the police. They also need to work with professionals from other services, including voluntary organisations such as the **NSPCC** .

Qualifications

You would need to go onto the BTEC National Diploma in Health and Social Care and also gain GCSEs at C or above in English and maths. You would then need to gain at least merits to move on to the university course. Social workers complete a three to four year degree course at a university. They complete work placements with practising social workers and also gain experience of attending court as part of their degree. A full driving licence is very important if you plan to follow this route.

Key terms

Assertive – confident and able to state his/her own views

NSPCC – National Society for the Prevention of Cruelty to Children – a voluntary organisation

Activity: Social work training

Use the internet to research the entry requirements for two degrees in social work and compare them. Do they both ask for the same or are they different?

Case study: Kendra

Kendra is a social worker who has a busy case load. Today she is visiting an older lady who wishes to move from her flat into sheltered accommodation. Kendra is doing her best to arrange this, but there are not many spaces and a lot of people want them. The older lady feels that Kendra is not trying hard enough but does not realise that Kendra has a full case load and not just one person to support. Kendra has just had a telephone call to say that there is a space in a sheltered housing complex which would suit the lady and is looking forward to telling her. When she arrives, Kendra finds that the lady no longer wishes to move because her son has invited her to live with him and his wife. Kendra is concerned because the lady does not really like her daughter-in-law and feels that it would not be a good idea. Kendra manages to persuade the lady to visit the accommodation before she makes a final decision.

1. What personal qualities does Kendra need to use in this situation?
2. Do you think you have the qualities needed to be a social worker?

Just checking

1. List three personal qualities needed by a social worker.
2. Why would you need good writing skills to be a social worker?

Working in health and social care: 3

Care assistants

Many care assistants work in residential and day care settings, supporting more qualified staff in delivering the routines necessary for the comfort and safeguarding of residents and daily attendees of the centres. Care assistants must have all of the personal qualities that a nurse needs; the role is demanding and work with people will always be challenging, but also enjoyable.

Personal qualities

Care assistants need many personal qualities.

Figure 10.8: Are there any more personal qualities you would add?

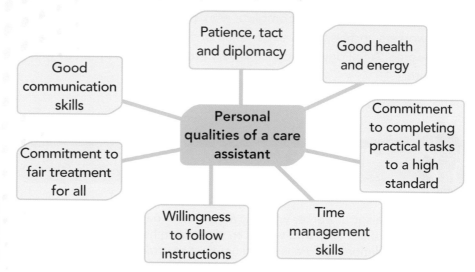

Role

The care assistant will take a major role in a day centre and take responsibility for many tasks. Care assistants usually greet the users of the service, offer them a drink and help them to find a place to sit. The care assistants may work with the activities co-ordinator or, in smaller centres, run the activities. These can be anything from a game of bingo to quizzes or gentle exercises to increase mobility. Care assistants will organise the meals and need to be aware of any dietary requirements. While they are at the day centre, care assistants are always working; they may even eat their lunch with the members to ensure that everyone is coping with the meal.

Skills

Care assistants must be competent in carrying out practical tasks such as delivering personal care, for example, dressing and bathing. All tasks must be completed in such a way that the person is not placed at risk of harm. Care assistants must be able to manage their time well and prioritise tasks. They need to understand the needs of each individual and how to meet those needs, for example allowing independence but giving support if required. Care assistants must be able to learn the routines of the setting and follow these in a way which meets the requirements of policies and procedures within the setting. They must also be aware of any guidelines and legislation, for example laws concerning health and safety.

Qualifications

You will need to have fully completed your BTEC First Diploma in Health and Social Care and have a clear **Criminal Records Bureau check**. Once you are employed at a centre, you may be encouraged to complete a higher qualification such as an **NVQ** level 3 in Pro-active Support. This will enable you to take up a more senior position as you become more experienced.

Key terms

Criminal Records Bureau check – a method of ensuring that people who work in health and social care do not have criminal records

NVQ – a qualification achieved while working in a setting-National Vocational Qualification

Case study: Lucy

Lucy has recently been appointed to her first job as a Care Assistant at the Acorn Day Centre for older people. Lucy had spent her work experience at the centre and was looking forward to working there.

On her first day Lucy was greeted by the manager, who was pleased to see her. Lucy had worked hard as a learner, and the manager felt that she would make a good member of staff. 'Hello Lucy,' she said, 'I'm glad to see you, can you just take Mrs Ali to the toilet please? She has had an accident; you will need to help her change.' Lucy was surprised – as a learner she had not been asked to perform personal care. The manager explained that the delivery of personal care was part of Lucy's role now that she was a care assistant. Lucy thought for a moment and then realised that Mrs Ali would feel much better once she had been supported. She also remembered all that she had learned about treating people with respect and allowing them dignity; helping Mrs Ali was a way of doing this. Lucy realised how important her role was in supporting the well-being of the people who came to the day centre.

1. Why was Lucy surprised to be asked to deliver personal care?
2. Should she have been surprised?
3. What does it mean to allow people to have dignity?
4. What does well-being mean?

Care assistants play an important role in the life and routines of any setting. Would you like to be a care assistant?

Did you know?

If you complete higher training whilst employed as a care assistant, you could progress to being a care manager, with experience.

Just checking

1. What are two differences between the role of a learner and the role of a care assistant in a residential setting?
2. Why are Criminal Record Bureau checks performed before staff are employed as care assistants?
3. List three personal qualities required by care assistants.

Remember

Your First Diploma is the first step to a career in care; have confidence and move on.

Working in health and social care: 4

Key term

Outpatient clinic – patients may visit a clinic for a follow-up appointment after being in hospital

Activity: Nursing assistant

Using the internet, find the website of your nearest National Health Service Trust and find the job vacancy section. Write down the personal qualities and skills required for a nursing assistant. Match them against the list on these pages. What are the differences? What qualifications do you need to apply for a job as a nursing assistant?

Do you have the qualities needed to be a nursing assistant?

Nursing assistants (Clinical Support Workers)

Nursing assistants and hospital porters perform an essential role within a hospital setting. Other staff would find it very difficult to function without the support of these people. They work shift patterns similar to other staff, including night duties. Hospitals must be staffed for 24 hours a day and patients may need taking for an X-ray at 2am for example, if they are involved in a car accident.

Personal qualities

Nursing assistants (also known as clinical support workers) need to have many of the same personal qualities as qualified nurses. They work on hospital wards and in outpatient clinics, supporting people who have a variety of health and social care needs. These qualities include:

* patience, tact and diplomacy
* good listening skills
* team work
* willingness to follow instructions
* ability to treat people fairly
* ability to complete practical tasks to a high standard.
* ability to follow routines
* time management skills.

Skills

In addition to the personal qualities listed above, nursing assistants have to develop a variety of skills to carry out such tasks as testing urine (for example to measure glucose) or blood, checking patients' temperature, pulse and respirations. In a busy **outpatient clinic** a nursing assistant will need to show initiative, tact and diplomacy to deal with the many patients who will visit in one day.

Role

Nursing assistants perform many tasks during their working day; when they work on a hospital ward they will work the same shifts as the nurses. They check all of the clinic rooms to ensure that everything is ready: that the examining couches all have clean paper sheets spread across them and the doctor's desk has all of the necessary paperwork, for example cards to refer the patient for an X-ray, scan or blood test.

Nursing assistants will check that the scales for weighing patients are accurate and dust free, the treatment room has a clean couch, the **sharps bin** has been emptied and that the drawers are full of syringes and disposable needles. The nursing assistant may collect the patient's notes from the medical reception and place them in the consulting rooms and call patients one by one from the waiting area and bring them to the clinic.

Hospital porter

Personal qualities

Hospital porters need many of the personal qualities which are required by other staff in a caring role. These include:

- good health and energy
- willingness to work hard
- patience, tact and diplomacy
- good communication skills
- ability to complete practical tasks to a high standard
- excellent time management skills.

Role

Hospital porters are expected to collect equipment and transport it to different parts of the hospital, to give directions to visitors and patients new to the hospital and will help to transport patients to and from operating theatres. They know who most of the staff are and are usually the people everyone relies upon to know where **central stores** are kept and what time deliveries to the hospital are made. In very big hospitals, there are large groups of porters who will work shift patterns so that there will always be someone available. Porters need good health, physical strength and lots of energy as the role is busy and demanding; you may have to stand still but the work does not. Hospital porters have the respect of staff from all levels; they need good communication skills and have to be organised in order to fulfil their important role.

Skills

A hospital porter needs to be able to move heavy equipment safely; he needs to be able to operate lifting and handling equipment safely and will usually have completed a training course as part of his introduction to the job. Hospital porters will also need a good sense of direction as many hospitals are large organisations and they cannot waste valuable time trying to find their way around. A porter will need to work well with others; he is a member of a team which relies on good relations and co-operation in order to function. Porters will also have to learn the correct way to push wheelchairs and trolleys safely and be able to communicate clearly as many people will ask for directions during the working day.

Key terms

Sharps bin   a special yellow bin for depositing sharp objects such as needles

Central stores – large stores where much of the equipment is kept

Activity: Hospital porter

Go onto the website for your nearest NHS Trust hospital and look for a job vacancy for a hospital porter. Read the qualities and skills required in the person specification. Do you have those qualities and skills? How will your present course help you to gain these?

Would you like to be a hospital porter?

Just checking

1. List three qualities which a nursing assistant needs.
2. Name two places where a nursing assistant might work.
3. Why would a hospital porter need to know about safe lifting techniques?

Working in health and social care: 5

Would you like to be a physiotherapist?

Key term

Arthritis – a condition affecting joints which is more common in older age

Physiotherapist

Physiotherapists work in hospitals and also in the community. Their main aim is to enable people to become more mobile. People may lose their mobility for a variety of reasons, for example, through accidents, stroke, illness or following major surgery.

Personal qualities

Physiotherapists require many of the same personal qualities as other health professionals. Look at the list below and see if you would add any:

- good health and energy
- intelligence and knowledge of the anatomy and physiology
- excellent time management skills
- a commitment to treat everyone fairly
- good communication skills
- patience, tact and diplomacy.

Skills

A physiotherapist must have a thorough understanding of the human body and how it works, particularly the muscles and joints. They must be competent in performing the practical tasks such as demonstrating the exercises and manipulating muscles. Physiotherapists must be able to recognise when to refer a patient to another professional, for example following surgery if a patient is still in more pain than would be expected. In addition, a physiotherapist must be assertive and firm when necessary, encouraging independence and mobility in their patients.

Role

Physiotherapists often work in the community although they are employed by the NHS Trust. The working day may begin at 8.30 but they may have to leave home earlier to arrive at their first appointment on time. They will attend a number of house calls, for example the first call may be to a patient who has had a hip replacement because of **arthritis**. He now needs to move around and regain mobility. The physiotherapist will spend some time ensuring that the patient is doing his exercises correctly and checking that he can use the aids he has been given to put on his shoes and sit on the toilet comfortably. Patients in such situations need encouragement and support; they may have lost confidence and be afraid to try. Physiotherapists may also have appointments in hospitals and will have to complete patient notes.

Mobile meals staff

Mobile meals staff are employed by local authorities to deliver meals to people who are restricted by reduced mobility. The meals are hot and include a cooked lunch and a pudding. The users of the service pay a small fee unless they are on benefits and cannot afford to pay.

Personal qualities

Mobile meals staff need many personal qualities in order to fulfil their role. These include:

- good health and energy
- sense of humour
- good communication skills
- excellent time management skills
- patience
- respect for individuals and commitment to treating everyone fairly.

Skills

Mobile meals staff will need to be good at managing their time so that people are not kept waiting unnecessarily. They will also need a clean driving licence and must be careful drivers, as speeding with a van full of hot meals is not to be recommended. They will need to have an excellent sense of direction and an ability to read a map in rural areas. The ability to remain cheerful is also important; they are providing a service and should remain professional. Like all staff in a caring role, they will need to be CRB checked as well.

Role

Mobile meals staff will have to be up early to collect the meals from a central point and a list of the individuals who are expecting a meal, checking to see if there are any special diets. They also need to be able to deal with unexpected situations, such as arriving at a person's home to find that they have had a fall, or have become ill and need immediate medical help. The role is suitable for people who love to interact with others as people will often want to chat, particularly those who live alone. The drivers are obviously out delivering meals whatever the weather, and so a strong constitution and good health is also essential. The job is busy and demanding but rewarding; most people really appreciate the service, particularly when they are unable to prepare a hot meal for themselves.

Just checking

1. Why would a clean driving licence be useful for both these roles?
2. Why would a physiotherapist need tact and diplomacy?
3. List three requirements for the role of a mobile meals worker.
4. Why would you need a clear CRB check?

Did you know?

Like many services, mobile meals are **means-tested benefits**. This means that a person's ability to pay is assessed. Some private firms also deliver hot meals on order, but these are generally more expensive and many older people and those receiving disability benefits cannot afford them. For some older or disabled people, the mobile meals worker is one of their few social contacts.

Key term

Means-tested benefits – benefits paid by the State to individuals, on the basis that their income is below a certain level

Think about it

Delivering the meal is only half of the job; the social contact is just as important. Mobile meals staff will need excellent communication skills and a genuine interest in people. How pleased would you be to have a meal delivered if your mobility was reduced?

Activity: Fit for purpose?

Make a list of the skills and qualities needed to be a mobile meals worker. Then make a list of the personal qualities and skills that you think you have. Are they the same, or are there some which you still need to develop? Work with your tutor to develop an action plan for the areas which require some work.

Developing the workforce

Key term

Inset – short for 'in-service training' when teaching staff are given training in teaching techniques or learn about new methods of teaching

Remember

The reason for improvement is so that we can continue to support individuals to the best of our ability.

Many people in employment are regularly required to undertake training programmes to update their skills and knowledge and to improve the service they deliver. For example, teachers and teaching assistants attend **inset** days, supermarket employees attend customer service training and office workers receive training on a variety of matters including improved telephone skills and the use of the latest computer software package relevant to their organisation. In health and social care it is particularly important to keep up-to-date with our knowledge and skills in order to provide the very best support for the individuals who need this. It is also important that employees everywhere have a working knowledge of any government legislation and guidelines which affect the way they work, as it could mean serious trouble if these are not followed.

Developing the workforce

Once you enter the health and social care workforce you will never stand still! Your initial qualifications get you through the door; after that you will just keep moving. There is a need for improved standards, which must be raised in order to make services better for the individuals who need help. Here are some of the ways in which we can all become more professional.

Sector Skills Councils

The Care and Development and Health Sector Skills Councils have a responsibility to ensure that all care and support is delivered to particular standards. They provide the health and care services with regulations which are designed to ensure that all users of the services receive a high standard of support delivered by competent professionals.

Codes of Practice

All of the health and social care professions have their own Codes of Practice which are designed to ensure that individuals all adhere to standards of behaviour and competence when working in a professional capacity. For example, the Nursing and Midwifery Council Code of Practice (2009) covers standards of conduct, performance and ethics for nurses and midwives. The Code includes the following instructions:

- make sure that the care of people is the first concern of nurses and midwives
- treat people as individuals and respect their dignity
- work with others to protect and promote the health and well-being of those in your care
- treat people kindly and considerately.

The General Social Care Council Codes of Practice apply to all people who work in social care, from social workers to care assistants. All are expected to deliver care to the highest possible standards. The codes are intended to promote good practice and their requirements include:

- treating people with respect and dignity
- doing people good and not harm
- maintaining confidentiality.

You can see from both of these codes that health and social care workers are expected to follow standards and promote the reputation of their professions.

National Occupational Standards

These are set by members of professional bodies and are, again, designed to ensure competence in health and social care. The competencies are those skills which are considered to be essential for the health and safeguarding of individual users of services. Workers who do not achieve these competencies will be required to re-train in areas of poor practice. These include the carrying out of practical tasks such as administering medication, taking blood pressure and delivering personal care.

Induction

All new members of a workforce are required to take part in an induction process. This process may last from two days to two weeks, depending on the organisation and the amount of information involved. Induction is designed to introduce new employees to the mission aims, the important policies and ways of working within an organisation.

Transitions

Induction also helps new staff with the **transition** or movement from their former occupation to becoming part of the new team. You will have enjoyed your time as a student, and are looking forward to your career, but you will find that induction helps you to become a team member far more easily.

Continuing Professional Development (CPD)

Where would health and social care be if the practices were still the same as they were many years ago? Can you imagine being cared for without all of the benefits of modern medical and nursing treatments? Can you imagine how difficult it would be without up-to-date residential care and day centres, for people whose lives are enriched by this type of support? There is a need to raise our standards; to increase our skills and knowledge, in order to provide the best support possible for people who use the services. Continuing professional development – or **CPD** – is a way of doing this. Health and social care staff are encouraged to attend training days to:

- upgrade their practical support skills
- learn more about relevant legislation.
- upgrade their knowledge about relevant policies and procedures
- upgrade their knowledge about medical conditions.

Staff are also encouraged to read relevant journals and articles to increase their knowledge in appropriate ways.

Key terms

Transition – movement, for example from one work role to another or one department to another

CPD – Continuing Professional Development

Did you know?

Continuing professional development is an expectation for many professional services who are not involved with health and social care.

Appraisal

The appraisal system is a way of encouraging staff to participate in continuing professional development. The individual meets with their immediate manager, usually once or twice a year, to discuss their progress in the work role, together with any plans for training and development. A record of the appraisal with notes for development and the action plan will usually be stored in a portfolio.

Monitoring performance

There are several ways of monitoring the performance of staff in health and social care:

- observations of practice
- completion of progress surveys
- service users' surveys.

All of these methods help to ensure that standards of support are maintained at an excellent level. If staff are not achieving the required standards, additional training may be suggested or the individual could be provided with a mentor who would demonstrate excellent practice.

BTEC **Assessment activity 10.4** P4 M3 D2

Choose two work roles in health and social care: you could use two of the roles described in this chapter or investigate two others, and investigate the skills required for each. When you have completed your investigation you could produce an information booklet for people who are interested in working in the health or social care sector. Your booklet should contain all of the following information:

- an explanation of the skills which are required for each of the work roles with a full explanation of what each skill involves and why it is necessary for the work role
- a comparison of the skills requirements for each of the two work roles – which are the same and where the differences are
- you should then propose one workforce development activity for each of the work roles, stating how they would help an individual in each of the roles to progress as a professional.

Grading tips

To achieve P4 you must remember to **explain** the skills saying exactly what each consists of and why they are necessary for the work role.

To achieve M3 you must remember to **compare** the required skills of the two work roles, noting any that are the same and the ones which are different. You may find that your chosen work roles have several skills which are the same.

To achieve D2 you must **assess** (suggest) one workforce development activity for each of your chosen work roles; explaining how each activity will enable someone in the work role to develop their professional skills or knowledge.

Katy Clarke
Dental Nurse

I am a dental nurse and part of the dental care professional team working in a community dental practice. I completed my two years of training at a large dental hospital and moved to work in the community afterwards. Before this I had completed my BTEC First Diploma in Health and Social Care and then moved onto the BTEC National Diploma in Health and Social Care, which I finished with an overall merit. I begin work at 8.30 am and finish at 5.30 pm. I work with people of all ages, including older people and children. During my working day I might have to complete all of the following tasks:

- Care and maintenance of equipment; usually this will take place at the beginning of the day before patients arrive, or at the end of the day when all of the patients' appointments are over.
- Preparation of the surgery and setting out of the instruments; I will usually do this first when I get in so that everything is ready for the dentist to use when the first patient arrives.

- Decontamination and sterilisation of instruments and equipment: this will usually happen in between patients because leaving everything until the end of the day will mean that dirty instruments will be left in the surgery to build up infection when patients are being treated. I always wash my hands thoroughly when I have completed this task.
- Recording and charting: when the dentist is examining a patient's teeth he or she will be describing the condition of each tooth to me so that I can record this on the patient's chart. This will enable the dentist to have a complete picture of the patient's dental condition.
- Passing instruments and treatments such as fillings to the dentist as they work.
- Holding the hands of nervous patients.
- Providing the patients with mouth wash and tissues.
- Supporting patients after treatment if they are not feeling well.

I need to perform all of these tasks efficiently and quickly as the dentist will not want to wait because this may make the patient nervous. I also have to reassure patients and deal with those who become ill or feel faint. It is a busy and demanding role, supporting the dentist and ensuring the smooth running of the surgery. My training prepared me to work as a professional and I might go on to complete further courses, for example in dental hygiene, where I can support patients in improved dental care.

Think about it!

1. Why is it important that dental instruments are sterilised once they have been used?
2. Why is it necessary for Katy to record what the dentist says as he is examining a patient's teeth?
3. What would Katy have to remember when she is preparing filling mixtures for the dentist?
4. Why would it be important for Katy to remain calm when working with patients?
5. Why does Katy wash her hands after sterilising dirty instruments?
6. Why do you think some people are nervous when visiting the dentist?
7. How can Katy help nervous patients?
8. Why is it important to receive training before working as a dental nurse?

Extension activity: Skin deep?

Fatima is a senior clinical support assistant in an NHS Trust, based in the Dermatology clinic. Many of the individuals who come to the clinic are very distressed. They have skin conditions which disturb their sleep through extreme irritation and often pain. Some of the conditions cause red and scaly skin, and patients may be embarrassed because other people stare at them on public transport. Part of her job is to reassure people and prepare them for the doctor to examine them.

Fatima says: 'I love my job, it is so rewarding and, as many people have been coming to the clinic for several years, I feel that I have become a professional friend to them. Just recently I began to feel that I would like to gain more knowledge and skills in order to provide a better service to the individuals who use the clinic.'

1. List three ways in which Fatima could gain further knowledge and skills.
2. How could Fatima's annual appraisal help her to progress?
3. Why is it important that Fatima should remember that she is a professional even though she takes a friendly approach with the users of the clinic?
4. Design a short professional development plan for Fatima.

Assignment tips

- Make sure that you understand exactly what the grading criteria mean.
- Always check with your tutor if you are unsure what something means.
- Find out about how continuing professional development (CPD) is conducted on your work experience.
- For one of your chosen work roles in the grading activity, consider finding out about a professional who works in the voluntary sector, for example Age Concern, Mencap or the NSPCC.
- Find out about the National Occupational Standards for one of your chosen work roles and include the skills requirements in your activity for **D2** .
- Gain functional skills by using ICT to produce your work.
- Include direct references from the student book and internet sources to enhance your work.
- Always include a bibliography at the end of your assignment.
- Research local private healthcare provision to include as information for **P1** .
- Find out about one local partnership in health and social care to use as an example in **P3** .

11 The impact of diet on health

This unit will help you to gain a knowledge and understanding of diet and the effect it has on people's health. It is important that health and social care workers have a good understanding of the principles of nutrition so that they can maintain or improve their own health as well as that of service users or patients. You will learn about the components of a balanced diet, how the diet changes over the lifespan, the effects of diet on health and the dietary needs of individuals. You will also learn about the importance of food safety and hygiene.

Learning outcomes

After completing this unit you should:

1. know dietary needs of individuals at different life stages
2. understand effects of unbalanced diets on the health of individuals
3. know specific dietary needs of service users
4. understand the principles of food safety and hygiene.

Assessment and grading criteria

This table shows you what you must do in order to achieve a **pass**, **merit** or **distinction** grade, and where you can find activities in this book to help you.

To achieve a **pass** grade the evidence must show that you are able to:	To achieve a **merit** grade the evidence must show that, in addition to the pass criteria, you are able to:	To achieve a **distinction** grade the evidence must show that, in addition to the pass and merit criteria, you are able to:
P1 Identify the components of a balanced diet (IE4, IE5, CT1, CT2, RL1, TW1, SM2, SM3) **Assessment activity 11.1 page 387**	**M1** Discuss how the components of a balanced diet contribute to an individual's health at different life stages **Assessment activity 11.1 page 387**	
P2 Identify different dietary needs at each life stage (IE3, CT2) **Assessment activity 11.1 page 387**		
P3 Explain two medical conditions related to unbalanced diets (RL1, TW1, SM2, SM3, EP2) **Assessment activity 11.2 page 391**		
P4 Identify two service users with specific dietary needs (RL1, TW1, SM2, SM3, EP4) **Assessment activity 11.3 page 397**	**M2** Outline a two-day diet plan for two service users with specific dietary needs **Assessment activity 11.3 page 397**	**D1** Justify how the two-day diet plan meets the dietary needs of the two service users **Assessment activity 11.3 page 397**
P5 Outline relevant legislation in relation to preparing, cooking and serving food (IE4) **Assessment activity 11.4 page 404**	**M3** Discuss the effects of unsafe practices when preparing, cooking and serving food in a health or social care setting **Assessment activity 11.4 page 404**	**D2** Assess the effectiveness of safe practices when preparing, cooking and serving food in a health or social care setting **Assessment activity 11.4 page 404**
P6 Explain safe practices necessary in preparing, cooking and serving food in a health or social care setting (RL1, RL2, TW1, SM2, SM3, EP2, EP3) **Assessment activity 11.4 page 404**		

How you will be assessed

This unit will be assessed by an internal assignment that will be written and marked by the staff at your centre. The External Verifier for your centre may ask to sample coursework as part of Edexcel's ongoing quality assurance procedures. The assignment is designed to allow you to show your knowledge and understanding diet and nutrition. These relate to what you should be able to do after completing this unit.

Your assessment could be in the form of:

- presentations
- case studies
- written assignments
- Food Hygiene Certificate.

Laila, 16–year–old health and social care learner

When I started doing this course I was pretty sure that I wanted to work as a Health Care Assistant and perhaps even go on to do my nurse training. I never would have thought that I'd enjoy learning so much about nutrition and diet, and it's not just because I am doing a course and have to pass the unit. I have found that I am really interested in diet and nutrition and improving my own diet and health, as well as finding out more about how diet affects people who have different health issues.

I've become much more aware of making sure that food is stored safely and I often tell my Mum and Dad and brothers off for putting food in the wrong place in the fridge! I'm always asking them if they've washed their hands every time I see them making food in the kitchen.

Now that I have had a chance to find out a bit about food and nutrition I think I might do some research to find out about careers in diet and nutrition. I don't know yet what qualifications I might need, but it's definitely a career option that I want to know more about.

Over to you!

- In this unit you will be finding out about different food groups, nutrients, diet-related disorders and food hygiene. There are three macro- and two micronutrients that you will be studying. Try and find out what they all are.

- How many diet-related disorders or illnesses can you think of? Do you know how diet affects the disorders you have identified?

1. Know the dietary needs of individuals at different life stages

Key term

Weaning – introducing solid foods to a baby from the age of about 6 months

Dietary needs change throughout our lives. There may be many reasons for these changes, such as growth and development, ageing, an illness or disorder or a change in levels of activity. A suitable balanced diet for a small child will not be suitable for an adult or older person, so individual needs must be considered when planning or providing meals.

Infancy (0–3 years)

From birth, breast milk contains all the baby needs in the right amounts. Although it is low in iron and copper, the baby has enough of these stored until **weaning**, when the baby starts eating solid foods. Breast milk is free, clean, provides immunity against disease and does not have to be prepared. Some mothers cannot or choose not to breastfeed and use formula, which is modified cow's milk. However, if they are able to breastfeed even for two weeks, this will provide some immunity for the baby. Formula must be made up according to the instructions on the packaging to prevent damage to the immature kidneys, and equipment must be sterilised to prevent infection. Parents are usually advised not to wean their babies until six months of age, as early weaning may lead to obesity or allergies later.

Table 11.1 Daily energy needs of babies and children

Age Range	Males		Females	
	MJ	Kcal	MJ	Kcal
0–3 months (formula fed)	2.28	545	2.16	515
4–6 months	2.89	690	2.69	645
7–9 months	3.44	825	3.20	765
10–12 months	3.85	920	3.61	865
1–3 years	5.15	1230	4.86	1165
4–6 years	7.16	1715	6.46	1545
7–10 years	8.24	1970	7.28	1740

(Source: DEFRA, *Manual of Nutrition*, 10th Edition, 1995)

Childhood (4–10 years)

Children aged between four and ten years of age tend to be very active and are growing fast. Although their energy requirements are not as high as those of adults, they need almost the same amount of some vitamins and minerals. Some children seem to have big appetites; this is not due to greed but to the fact that they have high nutritional needs. During childhood children should be encouraged to eat healthy meals consisting of a mix of meat, fish or eggs and potatoes, pasta or rice with vegetables. They should not eat too many sweets, crisps, biscuits and fizzy drinks, as these can lead to obesity and tooth decay.

Adolescence (11–18 years)

The nutritional needs of adolescents are greater than for any other age group. This is because they have large appetites and are still growing. Boys aged 11–14 years need 2220 Kilocalories a day, rising to 2755 from 15–18 years. Girls need 1845 and 2110 Kilocalories respectively. It is important that people in this age group are encouraged to eat sensibly at regular intervals and not to go through phases of overeating or starving themselves in order to lose weight. In addition to encouraging healthy eating, they should be advised to maintain a regular amount of physical activity. Again they should not eat too many sweets, crisps, biscuits and fizzy drinks.

Adulthood (19–65 years)

An adult's nutritional needs reduce with age. Men need approximately 2550 Kilocalories daily and women 1940. In general adults need to eat a healthy diet consisting of complex carbohydrates, such as bread, potatoes, rice or pasta, protein such as meat, eggs, cheese or fish and fruit and vegetables. Fatty and sugary foods should be kept to a minimum and adults should be advised to take physical activity on a regular basis. Alcohol intake should be limited as it contributes extra kilocalories to the diet.

Pregnancy and breastfeeding

During pregnancy and breastfeeding a woman's nutritional needs are increased to provide nutrition for the growing baby and for making breast milk after the baby is born. Although there is a belief that being pregnant means that a woman can 'eat for two', only about an extra 200 kilocalories are required in the last three months of the pregnancy, and about 450–570 kilocalories extra during breastfeeding. This is to give the mother the energy she needs to carry the extra weight of the baby and to make breast milk. Women planning to become pregnant should be advised to eat a diet rich in folic acid (and take a folic acid supplement) to prevent damage to the foetus, particularly spina bifida.

Old age (65 years +)

Although there is not much difference in the dietary needs of adults and older adults, as we age we become less mobile and we need less energy for our daily needs. Men and women between 65 and 74 need 2330 and 1900 Kilocalories daily and over the age of 75 need 2100 and 1810 Kilocalories. Older people have smaller appetites so the diet should provide concentrated sources of protein, vitamins and minerals in smaller portions. Gentle exercise should be encouraged. Older people should be encouraged to eat foods that do not require much preparation but are high in nutrients.

Activity: Food and drink

- Visit the Change4life website and find out what advice there is for children encouraging them to eat healthy meals. To obtain a secure link to this website see the Hotlinks section on page x. Make a leaflet for 7–10 year olds that will give them advice on making healthy food choices.

- Use the Internet to research weaning. Find out at what stage different foods should be introduced to a baby and make a chart showing which types of food should be introduced when.

Just checking

1. What is weaning and when should it start?
2. What problems might be associated with eating in:
   - adolescence
   - older age.

369

Concept of a balanced diet

There is not one single food or type of food that provides all the nutrients that your body needs to function efficiently. A balanced diet will depend on the different types of food you eat over a period of time and your nutritional needs. The wider the variety of foods eaten, the more nutrients you will get from them. It is now known that some health problems are caused by dietary intake, such as too much fat causing heart disease and too much salt contributing to strokes.

Intake and needs

Dietary needs will vary for each individual. As you have seen from the previous pages, dietary needs will differ according to age, but other factors should be considered. Such factors will include:

- the level of exercise taken
- the type of job a person does
- religious or cultural decisions
- likes and dislikes
- a person's health
- availability of food.

Energy balance

It is important that there is energy balance in the diet. The diet should contain a wide variety of foods so that energy comes from different sources. As you will see later in the unit, different food groups provide different amounts of energy per gram of the food, and balancing these will help to provide an overall healthy diet. Current advice is that about 50–60% of energy in the diet should be provided by starchy carbohydrates such as potatoes and pasta, 15–25% by proteins and 25–35% by fats – although the lower end of the range for fats is advised.

Dietary Reference Values

In 1991 the Committee on Medical Aspects of Food Policy (COMA) published Dietary Reference Values (DRVs), which were designed to

Activity: Vitamin C

Use the DRV definitions in Table 11.3 to help you answer the questions below:

What is the average requirement for vitamin C for people aged 11–14?

A pregnant woman asks you how much vitamin C she should consume daily. What would you advise her?

You are planning a school lunch. How much vitamin C should you include to make sure that most people's needs are met?

A survey shows that a group of 12-year-olds have an average intake of 16mg of vitamin C a day. Do you think they need to increase the amount of vitamin C in their diet?

Table 11.2 Dietary reference values

	Definition
Estimated Average Requirement (EAR)	An estimate of the average need for food energy or a nutrient. Most people will need more than this average and many will need less.
Reference Nutrient Intake (RNI)	The amount of a nutrient that is enough for almost every individual, even those with high needs. The RNI is generally much higher than most people need. The RNI supplies enough of a nutrient for at least 97.5% of the population.
Lower Reference Nutrient Intake (LRNI)	The amount of a nutrient considered to be sufficient only for the small number of individuals with low nutrient needs (only about 2.5% of the population).

Table 11.3 Dietary Reference Values for vitamin C (mg per day)

Age	LRNI	EAR	RNI
0–12 months	6	15	25
1–10 years	8	20	30
11–14 years	9	22	35
15+ years	10	25	40
Pregnant women	20	35	50
Breastfeeding women	40	55	70

(Source: Adapted from *Dietary Reference Values – A guide* HMSO 1991)

provide guidelines by which doctors and nutritionists would be able to assess the adequacy of the diets of different groups of people. These are shown above.

Nutrient deficiencies

If a person's diet is deficient in a particular nutrient, then the diet will not be balanced. If the deficiency is long term, it is possible that an individual will develop what is known as a *deficiency disease*. In some cases these can be very serious and some may even cause death. You will learn more about specific nutrient deficiencies later in this chapter.

Malnutrition

Maintaining good health depends on the consumption of sufficient amounts of nutrients and energy. **Malnutrition** can describe under-nutrition or over-nutrition. Under-nutrition is the result of not taking in enough energy or nutrients and, if this continues over a length of time, starvation and other deficiency disorders will occur. In particular, children who suffer from under-nutrition can suffer from physical stunting or mental retardation.

Over-nutrition results from an excessive intake of energy or one or more nutrients and can result in medical problems such as obesity, heart disease or diabetes. Further information on these and other nutrition disorders will be covered in more detail later in the chapter.

Think about it

Malnutrition in older people is often caused by poor fitting dentures or bad teeth. Why do you think that is?

Key term

Malnutrition – not having sufficient food or nourishment for your energy needs

Just checking

1. Give definitions for EAR, RNI and LRNI.
2. Explain what is meant by under-nutrition and over-nutrition.
3. Why might a person's health have an effect on their intake and needs?

The balance of good health

1. Base your meals on starchy foods
2. Eat lots of fruit and vegetables
3. Eat more fish
4. Cut down on saturated fat and sugar
5. Try to eat less salt – no more than 6g a day
6. Get active and try to be a healthy weight
7. Drink plenty of water
8. Don't skip breakfast

Relative proportions of five food groups

The Balance of Good Health is based on the Government's Eight Guidelines for a Healthy Diet. It forms the basis of the Food Standards Agency Nutrition Strategy. They are listed in the margin. Read through them and decide how many of them you follow. Could you follow more of them?

The Balance of Good Health was set out in pictorial form to show the recommended balance of foods in the diet. If people follow the recommended amounts as shown on the plate and make sure that they choose different foods, they should ensure that they have a balanced diet.

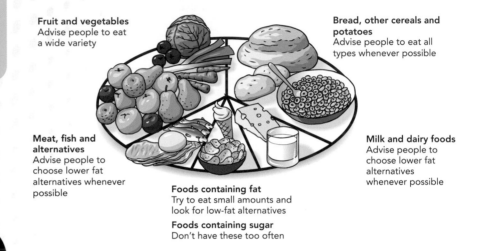

Fruit and vegetables
Advise people to eat a wide variety

Bread, other cereals and potatoes
Advise people to eat all types whenever possible

Meat, fish and alternatives
Advise people to choose lower fat alternatives whenever possible

Milk and dairy foods
Advise people to choose lower fat alternatives whenever possible

Foods containing fat
Try to eat small amounts and look for low-fat alternatives

Foods containing sugar
Don't have these too often

Figure 11.1: The Balance of Good Health

Just checking

1. What foods are in the bread, other cereals and potatoes group?
2. What recommendations are made concerning eating milk and dairy foods?
3. Why are beans and pulses good alternatives to meat?

Although the main components of the diet should be healthy, people can still eat less healthy foods, but less of them. This is sometimes known as the 80/20 rule – 80% of the time people should eat healthily and they can then eat less healthily 20% of the time. It does not necessarily mean that people have to vary their diet daily – as long as they can achieve a good balance over a week or two week period. It is sometimes shown as a pyramid.

Food	What's included	Main nutrients	Message	Recommendations
Bread, other cereals and potatoes	Other cereals means foods such as breakfast cereals, pasta, rice, oats, noodles, maize, millet and cornmeal. This group also includes yams and plantains. Beans and pulses can be eaten as part of this group.	Carbohydrate (starch), Fibre, Some calcium and iron, B vitamins	Eat lots	Try to eat wholemeal, wholegrain, brown or high fibre versions where possible. Try to avoid: • Having them fried too often • Adding too much fat (e.g. thickly spread butter, margarine or low fat spread on bread) • Adding rich sauces and dressings (e.g. cream or cheese sauce on pasta)

Fruit and vegetables	Fresh, frozen and canned fruit and vegetables and dried fruit. A glass of fruit juice also counts. Beans and pulses can be eaten as part of this group.	Vitamin C, Carotenes. Folates, Fibre and some carbohydrate	Eat lots – at least 5 portions a day. Fruit juice counts as only one portion however much you drink in a day. Beans and pulses count as only one portion however much you eat in a day.	Eat a wide variety of fruit and vegetables. Try to avoid: • Adding fat or rich sauces to vegetables (e.g. carrots glazed with butter or parsnips roasted in a lot of fat) • Adding sugar or syrupy dressings to fruit (e.g. stewed apple with sugar or chocolate sauce on banana)
Milk and dairy foods	Milk, cheese, yoghurt and fromage frais. This group does not include butter, eggs and cream.	Calcium, protein, Vitamins A, B_{12} and D	Eat or drink moderate amounts and choose lower fat versions whenever you can.	Lower fat versions means semi-skimmed or skimmed milk, low fat (0.1% fat) yoghurts or fromage frais, and lower fat cheeses (e.g. Edam, half-fat cheese and Camembert). Check the amount of fat by looking at the nutrient information on the labels. Compare similar products and choose the lowest – for example 8% fromage frais may be labelled 'low fat', but it is not actually the lowest available.
Meat, fish and alternatives	Meat, poultry, fish, eggs, nuts, beans and pulses. Meat includes bacon and salami and meat products such as sausages, beefburgers and pâté. These are all relatively high-fat choices. Beans, such as canned baked beans and pulses, are in this group and they are a good source of protein for vegetarians. Fish includes frozen and canned fish such as sardines and tuna, fish fingers and fishcakes. Aim to eat at least one portion of oily fish such as sardines and salmon each week.	Iron, protein, B Vitamins, especially B_{12}, zinc, magnesium	Eat moderate amounts and choose lower fat versions whenever you can.	Lower fat versions means things like meat with the fat cut off, poultry without the skin and fish without batter. Cook these foods without added fat. Beans and pulses are good alternatives to meat as they are naturally very low in fat.
Foods containing fat; foods and drinks containing sugar	**Food containing fat:** Margarine, butter, other spreading fats and low fat spreads, cooking oils, oil-based salad dressings, mayonnaise, cream, chocolate, crisps, biscuits, pastries, cakes, puddings, ice cream, rich sauces and gravies. **Foods containing sugar:** Soft drinks, sweets, jam and sugar, as well as foods such as cakes, puddings, biscuits, pastries and ice cream.	Fat, including some essential fatty acids, but also some vitamins. Some products also contain salt or sugar. Sugar, with minerals in some products and fat in others.	Eat foods containing fat sparingly and look out for the low fat alternatives. Foods and drinks containing sugar should not be eaten too often as they can contribute to tooth decay.	Some foods containing fat will be eaten every day, but should be kept to small amounts, for example margarine and butter, other spreading fats (including low fat spreads), cooking oils, oil-based salad dressings and mayonnaise. Foods containing fat such as cakes, biscuits, pastries and ice cream should be limited and low fat alternatives chosen where available. All foods and drinks containing sugar should be eaten mainly at mealtimes to reduce the risk of tooth decay.

Source: Food Standards Agency, 2001, The Balance of Good Health

Components of a balanced diet: 1

Key terms

Macro – large or large scale

Micro – very small

Poly – Many or much

Mono – One

A balanced diet is made up of proteins, carbohydrates, fats, vitamins, minerals, fibre and water. Carbohydrates, proteins and fats are known as **macro**nutrients because they are required in the body in large amounts. Vitamins and minerals are known as **micro**nutrients because they are needed in quite small amounts. This topic and the next four topics look more closely at macro and micronutrients.

Macronutrients

Carbohydrates

Carbohydrates are made up of carbon, hydrogen and oxygen. There are three main groups of carbohydrates in foods. These are starches, sugars, and cellulose and related products (fibre or NSP – see below). They provide the main source of energy in the diet. Foods high in carbohydrates include grains, pulses, fruit and vegetables, and should make up about 50–60% of the diet.

Starches

Complex carbohydrates are known as starches and are **poly**saccharides – many sugars linked together. They are found in widely eaten foods such as wholemeal cereals such as oats, wheat, barley, rye and rice. Many of these can be used to make foods like bread and pasta, but this group also includes potatoes, root vegetables, some fruits and pulses and beans such as lentils, baked beans and chickpeas. One gram of starch provides approximately four kilocalories of energy.

Some complex carbohydrates are refined starches and these foods include pizza, and some sugary foods such as cakes, biscuits and sugary breakfast cereals. However, these are often high in fat so should be limited in the diet.

When carbohydrates are eaten and digested they break down into glucose, which is needed to provide energy for all the cells in the body. The glucose is absorbed into the bloodstream and a hormone called insulin is released by the pancreas to control the absorption of glucose into the cells.

The energy from complex carbohydrates is released slowly, so your energy levels remain steady over periods of time.

Sugars

Sugars are referred to as simple carbohydrates and are found in natural and refined forms. There are many different types of sugars, such as glucose and fructose, which are known as **mono**saccharides or simple sugars. (The 'ose' part of the word tells you it is a type of sugar.)

Glucose is found naturally in fruit and plants and in the blood. Glucose syrups are refined and used in the manufacture of cakes, sweets and

Figure 11.2: These foods are rich in carbohydrates

jams. Fructose is found in some fruit and vegetables and honey. It is the sweetest sugar known.

Sucrose is commonly known as table sugar. It occurs naturally in sugar cane and sugar beet and in some fruits and root vegetables such as carrots. Lactose occurs in milk and is less sweet than glucose or sucrose. Sucrose and lactose are two sugars linked together and are known as **di**saccharides.

The refined sugars found in sweets, cakes, biscuits and pastries are digested more quickly than the starches. This means that they can be absorbed and used more easily, but it also means that they cause peaks and troughs in blood glucose levels. Because of this, energy levels are much less stable. Refined sugars should only make up about 11% of your total daily carbohydrate intake and the remainder should come from complex carbohydrates.

When you are hungry and in a hurry, you might just decide to grab a chocolate bar 'to keep you going'. But because chocolate bars contain refined simple sugars, the energy will be quickly used up. You may then find that you are even hungrier than you were before you ate it! A sandwich made with wholemeal bread would provide a more sustained release of energy and provide you with fibre to keep your bowel healthy.

Activity: The F-plan

There are two types of fibre, soluble and insoluble. Carry out some research into both and find out how they act in the body to contribute to good health.

Non-starch polysaccharides (NSP) are also known as cellulose or fibre. It is found in the fibrous structure of plant material such as cereals, fruit and vegetables. It is classed as a carbohydrate, but it cannot be digested and absorbed by humans. It is a very important part of the diet as it has a role in the maintenance of good health and helps to prevent hunger. Fibre has the following functions:

- it encourages chewing
- it adds bulk to the diet and helps with digestion
- it helps to prevent constipation
- it helps to prevent bowel disorders.

Key term

Di – two

Did you know?

The report of a survey published by **Consensus Action on Salt and Health** (CASH) in January 2008 stated that many parents have no idea how high the levels of salt are in some sweet foods.

A blueberry muffin contains 1.1g salt – more than two packets of crisps, which contain 0.5g each. A serving of rice crispie-style cereal with milk contains more salt than one packet of crisps.

Just checking

1. Explain the action of insulin in controlling blood glucose levels in the body.
2. Why do you need fibre in your body?
3. What is a complex carbohydrate?

Components of a balanced diet: 2

My life

Animal or vegetable?

You are probably aware that protein is one of the macronutrients that we all need to help us stay fit and healthy. Protein is found in both animal and plant foods. List as many protein foods as you can under the headings of Animal protein and Plant protein. Get together with your group and discuss what you have all written. Together how many different animal and protein foods can you identify?

Did you know?

When they are cooked, proteins denature. This means that they change their appearance. For example, clear runny egg white solidifies and turns white, meat changes colour and texture and cheese melts. This tends to happen more with animal proteins.

Figure 11.3: These foods are rich in proteins

Proteins

Proteins are made up of carbon, hydrogen, nitrogen and oxygen. Most also contain sulphur and some contain phosphorus. Proteins are essential components of all cells. They have two main functions – to regulate body processes or to provide structure in the body. They also help to make antibodies and enzymes. Protein is needed in the body for growth and repair, but any excess taken in will be used to provide energy.

Proteins are made up of chains of amino acids. About 20 amino acids are needed in the body and, of these, nine are said to be essential. This does not mean that they are more necessary than the others, but you have to get them from the food you eat because they cannot be made in the body. About 15% of your daily dietary requirement should come from protein foods.

Animal and vegetable proteins

Proteins are classed as animal and vegetable. Animal proteins are called high biological value (HBV) proteins because they contain all the essential amino acids. These include meat, fish, cheese and eggs. Cooking animal proteins at high temperatures creates chemicals that are thought to increase the risk of cancer. This does not seem to happen if they are cooked at low temperatures. Many animal proteins, especially meat, are high in saturated fat, and studies have shown that eating large amounts of red and processed meat can contribute to stomach and bowel cancer.

Plant proteins are called low biological value (LBV) proteins because they are usually deficient in one or more of the essential amino acids. Low biological value foods include pulses such as nuts, beans, peas and soya or tofu, although tofu is the most complete vegetable protein. Generally LBV proteins are high in fibre, vitamins and minerals and low in fat. They also contribute to disease prevention and good health.

Because LBV proteins tend to be deficient in one or more of the essential amino acids, if foods are mixed in the same meal they will complement each other and become a complete protein. An example of this is baked beans on toast. Bread is deficient in one essential amino acid and beans are deficient in another so by eating them together you can have a complete protein meal. Food combining is a way that vegetarians and vegans can obtain complete proteins in food. Figure 11.4 shows how this can be done.

Figure 11.4: Combining foods for more complete protein

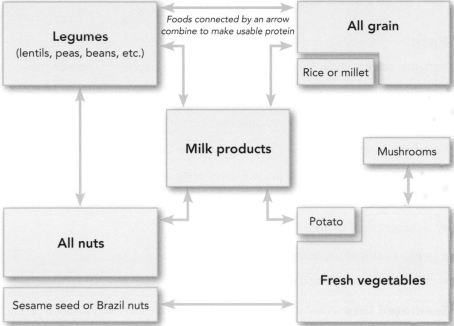

Source: Patrick Holford (1997) *The Optimum Nutrition Bible*, Piatkus

Manufactured protein foods

In addition to proteins found naturally in animal or plant food, there are alternatives to meat that have been developed by the food industry. Texturised vegetable proteins (TVP) have been developed from the plant proteins in soya beans and are considered suitable for use by vegetarians. They are produced as soya mince or chunks and are fortified with vitamins and minerals.

Mycoprotein is another alternative to meat. One well-known product produced from a fungus is Quorn. The fungal microorganism is grown, harvested and processed and is produced as slices, chunks, mince, burgers and sausages. Both TVP and mycoprotein will take up the flavour of other foods they are being cooked with. Many non-meat eaters find this a suitable alternative to animal protein.

Activity: Combining food

1. Food combining is important for vegetarians and vegans because they have to make sure that they mix vegetable-based foods to get high biological value protein in their diets. Devise three dishes using the food combining chart that will provide HBV protein for them.

2. Find out more about texturised vegetable proteins and mycoprotein. How are they manufactured and how valuable are they in vegetarian and vegan diets? Do they have any particular health benefits?

Just checking

1. Explain the difference between HBV and LBV proteins.
2. Why do we need protein?
3. How much protein should you have in your diet?

Components of a balanced diet: 3

My life

Cholesterol levels

Cholesterol is a type of fat that is found in the body. It is mainly made in the liver from the fat in the diet. Many people believe that cholesterol is very bad for you, but it does have some useful functions in the body. Carry out some research into cholesterol and find out the benefits and risks of cholesterol.

Fats

Fats are compounds of carbon, hydrogen and oxygen. Some of the fats consumed by humans are visible – that is they can be easily seen – such as the fat on meat. Others are invisible and these are generally a component of a food such as milk and nuts.

Fats have several important functions in the body. For example, they:

* provide a concentrated source of energy in the diet
* help to provide insulation against the cold by preventing heat loss
* protect body organs such as the kidneys
* help to transport and store vitamins A, D, E and K
* provide taste to food and make it easier to eat.

Saturated fats

The main sources of fat in the Western diet are animal fats, which come from animal and dairy products. These are called saturated fats and are solid at room temperature. Examples of saturated fats are butter and margarine, hard cheese and suet and the fat on meat. They are less healthy than fats that come from plants as they can contribute to heart disease because they contain cholesterol. Fats should make up no more than 35% of the diet and no more than 10% should be saturated fats.

Unsaturated fats

There are two types of unsaturated fats. Monounsaturated fats are found in olive and rapeseed oils and polyunsaturated fats are found in sunflower and soya oil. These are all vegetable oils as they come from plants. They are usually liquid at room temperature. They are less likely to contribute to heart disease because they do not have the same effect of blocking the blood vessels as animal fats have. Olive oil is particularly identified as an oil that helps to protect against heart disease.

Fish, nut and seed oils

Polyunsaturated fats also include essential fatty acids which are known to be very important in the prevention of heart disease. They are the omega-3 and omega-6 fatty acids. Omega-3 include fish oils and are found in oily fish such as mackerel, sardines, fresh tuna (not tinned) and salmon, as well as pumpkin seeds, linseed, soya beans, walnuts and leafy green vegetables. Omega-6 fatty acids are found in sunflower, grape seed and corn oil as well as cereals, eggs, poultry and evening primrose and borage oils.

Did you know?

Nutritionists are now finding that omega-6s and omega-3s will only maintain their status as 'good' fats when there are relatively balanced amounts of both. Unfortunately, most Western diets today are heavy on omega-6s, often at the expense of omega-3s. This means that omega-6 supplements are probably not necessary except for a few conditions.

Fat content of a range of foods:

25g serving sour cream and onion potato crisps 8.5g

25g serving reduced fat crisps 5.2g

25g Cheddar cheese 8.3g

25g Low fat Cheddar cheese 1.8g

100g cooked pork sausage 28.4g

100g roasted chicken leg meat (no skin) 8.4g

100g dry baked cod 0.9g

100g chocolate 29.9g

300g chicken korma curry 31g

Figure 11.5: These foods are rich in fats

Hydrogenation and trans fats

The Food Standards Agency website describes hydrogenation as 'a process that turns liquid oil into solid fat. During the process, a type of trans fat may be formed.' Hydrogenated vegetable oil has to be declared on the ingredients list of foods, but trans fats do not. If a label on a margarine tub says that the product contains hydrogenated vegetable oil, there may also be trans fats in the product. Trans fats and saturated fats have a similar effect on blood cholesterol to saturated fats. They raise cholesterol in the blood which increases the risk of coronary heart disease and that is why it is important to replace these in the diet with unsaturated fats.

Activity: What type of fat?

Go to your local supermarket and look at the labels of the different margarines and spreads that are on sale. Check the labels to find out which have hydrogenated or trans fats and which do not.

PLTS

This activity will help you to develop skills as an **independent enquirer**.

Just checking

1. Explain the difference between saturated and polyunsaturated fat.
2. Suggest three ways that fat intake in the diet can be reduced.

Components of a balanced diet: 4

Vitamins and minerals

Until the beginning of the twentieth century, it was believed that the only necessary components of the diet were proteins, carbohydrates and fats. However it was then established that there were also other essential elements. Vitamins are essential because they help enzymes to work properly. Most vitamins cannot be made by the body. There are two types of vitamins: water soluble and fat soluble.

Water soluble vitamins

The water soluble vitamins are the B vitamins and vitamin C. They cannot be stored in the body so we need to have a daily intake of foods that contain them.

Fat soluble vitamins

The fat soluble vitamins are A, D, E and K. They dissolve in fat in the body, which is why we need to consume fat in our diet. They are stored in the body in the liver.

Figure 11.6: These foods are rich in vitamins and minerals

Table 11.4 Functions and sources of vitamins B and C

Vitamin	Sources in diet	Function	Effect of shortage
B_1 Thiamin	Bread, nuts, cereals, flour, meat, eggs, potatoes, poultry, milk	Converts carbohydrate to glucose, aids digestion and nerve function, building of blood, growth	Beri beri, apathy, poor appetite, pins and needles in legs, depression
B_2 Riboflavin	Milk, liver, kidney, cereal, yeast, meat extracts, eggs, cheese	Converts glucose to energy	Cracking at corner of mouth, soreness of tongue, light sensitivity
B_3 Niacin	Meat extract, yeast extract, wholemeal bread, eggs, liver, cereals	Also converts glucose to energy, healthy skin and nervous system, cell metabolism	Pellagra, redness of skin, exfoliation of hands and face, diarrhoea, memory loss, irritability, insomnia
B_5 Pantothenic Acid	Animal products, cereals, legumes	Converts glucose and fat to energy, maintains healthy immune system	Weakness, depression, lowered resistance to infection
B_6 Pyridoxine	Meat, green vegetables, bran, wholemeal flour, eggs, bananas	Protein metabolism, converts tryptophan to niacin, formation of Haemoglobin	Fatigue, nerve dysfunction
B_9 Folic Acid	Yeast, leafy green vegetables, meat, avocado, bananas	Produce red blood cells and tissue cells, normal growth, healthy digestive tract	Megaloblastic anaemia, neural tube defects in foetus
B_{12} Cyanocobalamin	Widely distributed in animal foods	Involved in manufacture of red blood cells in bone marrow, nervous system	Pernicious anaemia, red sore tongues, degeneration of nerve cells
C Ascorbic Acid	Blackcurrants, citrus fruits, green vegetables, peppers, tomatoes	Formation of bones and teeth, essential in blood, wound healing, immune system, skin and gums	Scurvy, incomplete cell repair, bruise easily, physical and mental stress

Table 11.5 Functions and sources of fat soluble vitamins

Vitamin	Sources in diet	Function	Effect of shortage
A	Fish oil, liver, butter, cheese, eggs, milk, fruit and vegetables	Night vision, keeps skin and epithelial linings healthy	Night blindness, itching, thickening of horny layer of skin, dry skin, loss of taste
D	Fish liver, oily fish, eggs, milk, margarine, sunlight	Absorption of calcium in intestine, regulates calcium and magnesium in bone tissue	Rickets, osteomalacia, spontaneous fractures
E	Eggs, cereal oils, vegetables, nuts, seeds	Maintains healthy muscular system, anti-oxidant, protects cell membrane	Poor muscle, circulatory and nerve performance
K	Green vegetables, fish liver oils, alfalfa tablets, molasses, yoghurt	Blood clotting	Rare – babies may need supplement at birth, diarrhoea

Minerals

Minerals are also known as micronutrients because, like vitamins, they are only needed in very small amounts in the body. They are found in the earth and in the sea. They are necessary for many different processes in the body and these are shown in the table below.

Activity: Minerals

Research the functions, sources and deficiency effects of zinc, iodine and fluoride.

Table 11.6 Functions and sources of minerals

Mineral	Sources in diet	Function	Effect of shortage
Calcium	Milk, cheese, bread, flour and green vegetables. For some the bones in canned fish are important.	Builds strong bones and hard teeth. Essential for blood clotting. Helps muscles and nerves to work. Activates certain enzymes. Requires vitamin D for absorption.	Rickets in children, osteomalacia in adults, muscle cramps
Sodium	Naturally in eggs, meat, vegetables, milk. Added to many processed foods such as meat and canned food.	Maintains balance of body fluids. Maintains blood pressure although excess is linked to high blood pressure. Aids muscle contraction and nerve transmission. Intake must be restricted in renal disease.	Muscle cramps but shortage is unlikely
Iron	Meat (offal), bread, flour, cereal products, potatoes and vegetables	Needed by all cells. Needed to form haemoglobin in red blood cells and myoglobin in muscles. Vitamin C increases absorption of iron.	Anaemia, fatigue, brittle finger nails
Potassium	Potatoes, fruit (especially bananas), vegetables and juices	Balance of fluids in body (with sodium). Needed for muscle and nerve function. Controls pH of blood. Excess can cause heart failure.	Irregular heart beat, muscle weakness, confusion

Activity: Vitamins and minerals

Find the recommended daily allowances of the vitamins and minerals in the tables above. Make sure that you use UK sources, as recommended daily allowances differ in other countries.

Just checking

1. Find out what the symptoms of beriberi, and pellagra are.
2. What are the best dietary sources of iron for vegetarians?

Our need for vitamins and minerals

The previous pages referred to the need for vitamins and minerals generally in the body, but needs will vary according to different factors. This is an important point, as although it is difficult to develop an excess or a deficiency of most vitamins and minerals, you should still be aware that in some cases these do occur.

Temperature control

Vitamin E is thought to maintain the heat regulation of the body, particularly for women during the menopause, and magnesium is a trace element that is also thought to regulate body temperature. Fat is known to insulate vital organs like the kidneys, and iodine regulates fat metabolism which may have a role in temperature control. Water also has a role in maintaining body temperature. It is known that alcohol, coffee and tea can produce heat in the body.

Activity

As you learned on the previous pages, vitamins and minerals play vital roles in the metabolism of proteins, carbohydrates and fats. This means that if they are not present it will not be so easy to use the macronutrients in the body. Exercise will increase the need for some vitamins and minerals, especially the water soluble vitamins that can be lost in sweat. However, in general in the UK, provided that a very active person is eating a well balanced diet they will not become deficient in them and the body processes will be efficient.

Age

Folic acid or Vitamin B_9 is very important in the diet of women who want to become pregnant or are in the early stages of pregnancy. This is because it helps to protect the foetus against spina bifida, which is a condition where the spinal cord does not develop normally.

Babies who are breastfed will normally get all the vitamins and minerals they need in the breast milk. Some are not present in breast milk but a baby usually has stores of those in the body which will last until weaning begins. Formula milk is fortified with the necessary vitamins and minerals.

Young children need a balanced diet to make sure that they get all the nutrients they need, but arguably the most important micronutrients are calcium and Vitamin D. These two micronutrients work together to ensure strong bones and teeth. Calcium cannot be absorbed without Vitamin D.

As far as the micronutrients are concerned, teenagers tend to need increased amounts of calcium and iron. Some nutritionists recommend that a good intake of calcium is necessary in the teenage years to ensure that osteoporosis does not occur in old age.

Teenage girls usually need extra iron to compensate for the iron lost in blood when their periods start in order to prevent anaemia.

Although there is not a need for extra micronutrients during adulthood, older adults are advised to make sure that they eat a diet rich in iron, calcium and vitamin D. These will help to prevent anaemia and osteoporosis, a condition that makes bones less dense and brittle. Vitamin D can be obtained from sunlight as well as from some foods.

Diet and lifestyle

Some people may follow a particular diet or lifestyle which means that they need to pay particular attention to what nutrients they are getting. Vegetarians will usually have a balanced diet provided they eat a varied diet and know how to combine vegetable proteins. Vegans eat no animal products at all and so they must know which vegetable foods are rich in the vitamins and minerals that are usually found in animal products, most particularly Vitamin B_{12}.

Athletes and sports people will have a higher energy requirement and will have a high carbohydrate intake. Water soluble vitamins may be lost through excessive sweating and will need to be replaced.

Alcoholics can be deficient in many nutrients, mainly because they tend to replace meals with alcohol. This means that their diet will probably not contain the daily requirements. B vitamins tend to be destroyed by alcohol, and extra vitamin A and C are needed to help to protect the liver.

Smokers have a higher vitamin C requirement than non-smokers because smoke tends to destroy vitamin C.

Water

Water plays a vital role in the body's processes. People can live for some time without food but they cannot live for more than a few days without water. It makes up about 55–60% of the body's weight, and is an essential part of all body cells and helps in many chemical reactions in the body. Water carries nutrients to and waste away from the cells, helps to regulate body temperature, digest food and lubricate joints. Excess water leaves the body via urine, faeces, sweat and breathing. The kidneys regulate water levels in the body and hormones control the amount of water excreted by monitoring the concentration of the blood. You should aim to drink about eight glasses of water a day, but in warmer climates you would need more.

Activity: B12

You have read above that vegetarians and vegans need to know how to combine foods to ensure that they have a healthy diet. Find out which foods are rich in Vitamin B_{12} that vegans could eat instead of meat.

Did you know?

Nearly all foods contain water, especially apples, pears, melons, cucumbers, cabbage and tomatoes. It is also present in cottage cheese, white fish and boiled rice.

Water contains no calories.

Activity: What's in water?

Go to your local supermarket and have a look at the range of bottled still and sparkling mineral waters. Make a list of the mineral content of each and then compare your findings. How does the mineral content differ? Why might you be concerned about someone who drinks a lot of mineral water?

Just checking

1. How can vegetarians and vegans access all the vitamins and minerals they need?
2. Why do teenage girls need extra iron? Where can they find this?

Diet variation during life stage development

From our birth to the end of life we all need food which we use as fuel to keep us going. Just as you would not expect a small baby to eat a roast dinner, you would not expect to see an adult drinking formula milk from a bottle. This is because our diets vary through life. Although we all need the same macro- and micronutrients, we need them in different quantities and different formats at different stages in our lives.

Babies

At about six months, babies start to need more nutrients than can be supplied by milk alone. Weaning is the term used to describe the introduction of solid food to babies. A baby's kidneys are not mature enough to cope with solid food before this.

Table 11.7 The stages of weaning

4–6 months	Start with spoonfuls of baby rice, mashed potato or puréed fruit or vegetables such as apple, carrot, peas or parsnips. When they are used to the spoon lots of tastes can be introduced, such as puréed meat, pulses and other fruit. By six months all infants should have started on some solid food but advice is not to rush babies who are not ready.
6 months	Introduce food with soft lumps. Do not give nuts as infants may choke or be allergic to them.
9 months	Minced or finely chopped food can be given. Infants at this age should be given different textures so that they can get used to different foods and textures.
12 months	A good mixed diet should be given by this stage, including 3 meals and 2–3 healthy snacks each day.

Babies should start drinking from a cup at about six months of age and ideally not given bottles after the age of 12 months. Prepared baby foods are available in shops or they can be homemade. It is important not to add salt to food that is homemade and it is also advisable not to add sugar unless there is a need for it in small amounts, such as in puréed fruit which may be too sharp for babies.

Children and adolescents

Schoolchildren grow very fast and are very active so they have large appetites. Children should eat concentrated sources of vitamins and minerals and protein to help with growth and development. Obesity can be a problem for children, which will remain a problem in adulthood, if they are given the wrong types of food. Children should eat plenty of fruit and vegetables along with protein and carbohydrate, and not too much fatty and sweet food. Sugar only provides calories and has no nutritional benefit. If children get used to eating healthy foods they are more likely to develop a habit of healthy eating for life.

Adolescents probably have the highest nutritional needs of any other group of people and often have big appetites. They should be advised to eat as healthily as possible. They may snack on high fat and sugar food and drinks because parents have less influence on what they eat. Adolescent obesity is often caused as a result of a poor diet and lack of exercise. It is important to encourage regular healthy eating rather than periods of dieting as this can be dangerous and lead to nutritional deficiency. It may also lead to eating disorders.

Adults

In developed countries, adults are more likely to suffer from over-nutrition. There is a lot of hidden fat, sugar and salt in processed foods and ready-made meals and they contribute to heart disease, Type two diabetes and high blood pressure. Heart disease is the commonest cause of death in Britain, diabetes is increasing in the UK and high salt intake can cause strokes.

Adults should follow the government's guidelines for healthy eating and eat plenty of complex carbohydrates such as bread, potatoes, pasta and rice, moderate amounts of meat or alternatives (oily fish about three times a week will help to prevent heart disease), and plenty of fruit and vegetables.

Pregnancy

During pregnancy and breastfeeding a woman's diet should contain plenty of energy-rich foods, protein, iron, calcium, folic acid and vitamins C and D so that the foetus develops normally; otherwise the baby will use up its mother's stores and she may become undernourished. Eating foods high in vitamin A such as liver, can cause birth defects and should be avoided. Soft cheeses and pâtés can be contaminated with listeria, a bacterium that can be harmful.

Older people

Older people should be encouraged to eat little and often and to make sure that the food they choose contains concentrated amounts of the necessary nutrients. This is because activity and appetite decrease with age. Older people should not eat too many foods that contain saturated fat in order to help prevent heart disease. Gentle exercise should also be encouraged.

Lifestyle, occupation, activity level and weight management

People who live a busy lifestyle and are constantly rushing about may eat a lot of fast foods which may be high in salt, sugar and fat, or they may eat out at restaurants which means their diet could be unhealthy. It is very easy to put on weight through eating like this and not taking much exercise, perhaps because of a **sedentary** job.

People who are very active at work or take a lot of exercise are more likely to burn off any excess energy that they take in and their blood pressure is likely to be lower than those who do not take exercise. Keeping weight within normal limits by eating a well balanced diet will help to prevent nutrition related conditions.

Did you know?

Current guidelines on alcohol recommend that women shouldn't regularly drink more than 2 to 3 units a day and men no more than 3 to 4 units a day. Pregnant women should drink no more than 1 to 2 units once or twice a week if they do not want to give up alcohol altogether.

A unit of alcohol is half a pint of beer, a small glass of wine or a single measure of spirits.

Activity: Foetal Alcohol Syndrome

Carry out some research into Foetal Alcohol Syndrome. Find out what characteristics and behaviours children with this syndrome have. A useful source of information is the website of Foetal Alcohol Syndrome Aware UK. To obtain a secure link to this website, see the Hotlinks section on page x.

Key term

Sedentary – tending to sit down a lot, taking little exercise

Just checking

1. What is the alcohol content of different alcoholic drinks such as different types of beer and alco-pops? Create a poster showing the differences.
2. What sort of diet is suitable for an older person, living alone and with limited mobility? Suggest some daily meal plans.

Factors influencing the diet of individuals

What we eat is influenced by more than the physical needs of our bodies. Different factors such as our religion or culture, or what we like and dislike, also make a difference.

Religion/culture

Religion and culture play a large part in the food that people eat. Various foods are forbidden in certain religions. In general, Jews and Muslims do not eat pork products, Hindus do not eat beef and Buddhists are vegetarian.

Social class and financial resources

People from higher socio-economic classes with more money tend to eat healthier and better quality food, whereas poorer people eat fewer fruit and vegetables and more processed foods that are high in fat, salt and sugar. Women in the lower social classes are more likely to be obese than women in the upper social classes. People in lower social classes are more likely to substitute cheap processed food for more expensive fresh food.

Personal preference

Personal preference plays a part in the choices someone makes about food. This may not just be linked to likes and dislikes but other factors, such as people who choose not to eat meat because they do not agree with killing animals for food. Personal preference is also influenced by taste, texture, culture and social habits.

Peer pressure

Peer pressure can have an effect on the food choices that are made, especially by children and teenagers. Many young people develop a stereotyped view of people who eat healthy and unhealthy food and some may choose less healthy options, such as fast food, to fit in with what their friends eat because they do not want to seem different.

The media

Information publicised in the media can influence food choice. Food scares can often be caused by what is reported in the news. In 1996, beef exports to Europe were banned when scientists found a link between eating beef and variant CJD (Creutzfeldt–Jakob Disease), a fatal brain disease linked to BSE – also known as 'mad cow disease'. This had a huge impact on consumption of beef, which was banned from school menus. More recently there has been a lot of publicity about rising levels of obesity in the UK.

Position in family

If food is in short supply, it is known that mothers will often give more protein or fruit and vegetables or larger quantities to their husband/partner or children. They will then fill up on lower quality food and their own nutritional status may suffer as a result; this may be especially significant if they are pregnant.

Location and food availability

Where you live will have an effect on your diet. There is enough food in the world but it is not evenly distributed. More wealthy countries can afford to buy food and so have a greater variety than countries that are poor. Food that is grown in poor soil will have fewer minerals in it and so the quality of the diet will be poorer.

In addition, many developing countries suffer from flooding and drought which means harvests fail and food becomes scarce. Diets that are high in carbohydrates and not so rich in protein and fats can lead to under-nutrition. However in developed countries people have access to a good variety of foods from all over the world which are available all year round. This can lead to over-nutrition.

Activity: In season

See if you can find out which months each of the following fruit and vegetables is in season in the UK: parsnips; spinach; rhubarb; strawberries; apples; carrots; pears; Brussels sprouts.

PLTS

This task will give you the opportunity to develop skills as an **independent enquirer** by carrying out research into the different nutrients. You will need to analyse and evaluate information and decide what is relevant and valuable to your work. As a **creative thinker** you can decide how you want to present your findings and the M1 task will enable you to extend your thinking. As a **reflective learner** you will be reflecting on what you did and the work you produced. As a **self-manager** you will work towards the overall goal of achieving the unit and you will organise your time and resources well.

BTEC — Assessment activity 11.1 — P1 P2 M1

You have just started working as a care assistant with the District Nurses at a health centre. The doctors and nurses are concerned at the number of people they see who don't seem to know much about healthy eating and think that more information should be available for the patients who use the health centre.

Produce a series of fact sheets for patients that cover the nutritional needs of each life stage. Make sure that you include:

- the dietary needs of each life stage
- different types of food needed for a well balanced diet
- how each food group contributes to an individual's health at each life stage.

The fact sheets must be user friendly and contain enough information so that patients can make informed choices about their nutritional choices.

Grading tips

To discuss (for M1) you need to examine the topic through arguments for and against – write as if you are going to take part in a debate. You might find it helpful to complete your evidence for M1 after you have completed assessment activity 11.2 (see page 391).

Functional skills

In this activity you will have the chance to develop **ICT** skills by researching the information you need and creating the fact sheets. You should be able to create some eye-catching artwork by including pictures or photos. To make sure that you are developing **English** skills you should make sure that you proofread your work carefully as well as using the spell and grammar checks before you hand it in.

Just checking

1. What would you cook for lunch for an elderly Buddhist and a Hindu who both follow strict dietary laws?
2. What are the causes of over-nutrition in the UK?
3. Why might someone living in an isolated village have problems including lots of fresh fruit and vegetables and fresh fish in their diet?

2. Understand effects of unbalanced diets on health

Many medical conditions and diseases can be related to the unbalanced diets that people may eat. There may be many reasons why a medical condition occurs, but many links have been made between what we eat and how this affects our health. An example of this is the known link between high intake of salt and high blood pressure leading to strokes.

Medical conditions

Malnutrition

A balanced diet is based on the consumption of appropriate amounts of nutrients and energy. Malnutrition can result from people eating too much or too little of some nutrients over a period of time. Insufficient intake can result in under-nutrition or starvation and excessive intake can result in over-nutrition and obesity.

Over–nutrition

Coronary heart disease

Coronary heart disease (CHD) occurs through eating too many foods, such as animal proteins, that are high in saturated fats. To maintain a healthy heart people are advised to eat two to three meals per week containing oily fish such as salmon, mackerel, sardines or fresh tuna (not tinned) and plenty of fresh fruit and vegetables. See Unit 7 page 194 for more information about how a heart attack happens.

Obesity

Obesity results from eating too much food. Any food that is eaten in excess will be converted to fat and stored in the body, which leads to overweight and obesity. A healthy balanced diet together with exercise will help people to lose weight. Maintaining a healthy weight might require a lifestyle change. Nutritionists confirm that changing what you eat and taking regular exercise is a better way of staying fit, healthy and at the correct weight for your height than trying out different diets.

Type two diabetes

Type two diabetes is also known as late or adult onset diabetes but it is today seen in children as young as nine years old. It is caused by eating too much fat and sugar in the diet. The pancreas is either unable to produce enough insulin for the cells to absorb glucose from the blood or the body becomes resistant to the insulin that is produced. Symptoms of type two diabetes include thirst, excessive urination and extreme tiredness. It can be controlled by diet alone or by diet and medication. Type two diabetics do not normally need insulin.

Under-nutrition

Under-nutrition can result from a general lack of nutrients, particularly protein and energy, or from a lack of a particular nutrient. Two conditions that are seen in underdeveloped countries and which particularly affect children are kwashiorkor and marasmus.

Marasmus

This usually occurs in babies less than a year old and starts as early as five months of age because a baby is weaned onto formula milk early and too suddenly. Often the formula given is too diluted and made up with dirty water. This leads to repeated infections, especially of the digestive system. Children with marasmus have very retarded growth, and very low weight. Their muscles and fat are wasted and this tends to give them an 'old man' look. They are also very deficient in vitamins and minerals.

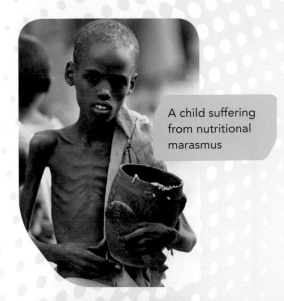

A child suffering from nutritional marasmus

Kwashiorkor

This usually occurs in children aged between one and three years. It happens in poor rural areas when weaning is late and breast feeding stops because another baby is born and needs the breast milk. The child moves onto a starch-based family diet which does not contain enough protein. Children often have acute infections, growth failure, low weight and fluid retention in the feet, legs, face and hands. They have wasted muscles but still have body fat. They are usually miserable and lacking in energy. Hair turns an orange colour, straightens and can pull out easily. The skin on the face often becomes lighter in colour. Stools are loose and the child suffers from anaemia. The skin on the legs and buttocks becomes flaky and may become painful and ulcerated. This may lead to gangrene. The liver is large and fatty which can give the impression that the child is healthy. They are deficient in Vitamins A and B, zinc, potassium and magnesium.

A child suffering from kwashiorkor. How do aid agencies and medical professionals try to treat and prevent marasmus and kwashiorkor?

Tooth decay

Tooth decay or dental caries cannot strictly be described as under-nutrition, as it is caused by an excess of sugar in the diet. Sticky deposits called plaque form on the teeth. Plaque is acid and over time it will dissolve the enamel on teeth, causing cavities. If the cavities remain untreated they can kill the tooth's nerve and blood supply and eventually the whole tooth will die. It is important that sugary foods and drinks are kept to a minimum and good dental hygiene is observed.

Activity: Sweet stuff

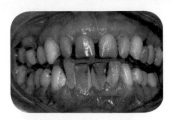

Find out the sugar content of different fizzy drinks and sweet snacks. Make a table of them with the one with the highest content at the top. Apart from tooth decay, how else can a high sugar diet affect the body?

Just checking

1. How can people maintain a healthy heart?
2. How can tooth decay be prevented?
3. How can kwashiorkor and marasmus be prevented?

Medical conditions related to unbalanced diets

Activity: Anaemia

Investigate the causes of anaemia and how it can be prevented.

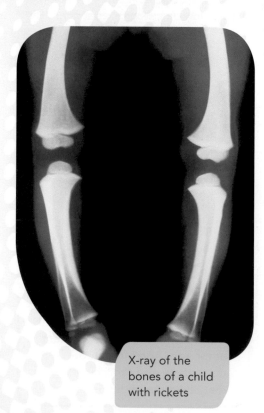

X-ray of the bones of a child with rickets

Nutrient deficiencies

Anaemia

Anaemia is caused by iron deficiency. Iron is used for making red blood cells and in the body's use of oxygen. Symptoms include fatigue and lack of energy, weakness and brittle fingernails. People of Asian origin may be more at risk of becoming anaemic as a traditional Asian diet may not provide enough iron.

Rickets

Rickets is caused by calcium and vitamin D deficiency. Vitamin D has to be present in the body for calcium to be taken up by the bones. Elderly people, adolescents and women who have repeated pregnancies may suffer from osteomalacia (the adult form of rickets) because they absorb too little calcium from a low calcium diet. There is also some evidence that vitamin D metabolises differently in the body in different ethnic groups.

When babies are born, most of their bones are made of cartilage. *Ossification* occurs during growth. This is the development of hard bone which uses calcium and vitamin D. Children with rickets do not receive enough calcium and/or vitamin D and their bones are soft. They also tend to have very tiny chests. The four main bones of the skull are not ossified; this is known as the 'hot cross bun' sign in newborn babies.

Rickets is not often seen in the UK but people of Asian origin, particularly teenage girls, may be deficient in vitamin D, which is known as the sunshine vitamin. Because their religion requires them to cover most of their body, they do not get the opportunity to expose their skin to the sunlight. This can result in conditions known as rickets and osteomalacia. Since the Second World War, margarines have been fortified with vitamin D to ensure that the whole population has enough in the diet.

Night blindness

Night blindness is caused by a lack of vitamin A. It is also known as *xeropthalmia* or dry eye. In its early stages it can be cured by providing sufferers with vitamin A supplements, such as palm oil or other foods high in vitamin A. However, in its later stages it is incurable and leads to complete blindness and, in some cases, death.

Beriberi

Beriberi is vitamin B_1 or thiamin deficiency. Thiamin is found in the husks of grains such as rice. This vitamin is needed to metabolise carbohydrates. Symptoms of beriberi include some or all of the following: neuritis, headache, fatigue, poor memory, diarrhoea, anxiety, insomnia, depression, irritability, eczema, dermatitis, acne, enlarged heart, muscle weakness, wrist and ankle drop (no strength to keep them up) and tenderness in calf muscles.

Scurvy

Scurvy is known as vitamin C deficiency and only occurs when fresh food, especially citrus fruit, berries and green vegetables, are not available. Symptoms include swelling of gums, teeth falling out, bleeding and slow wound healing. It is very easily cured by eating citrus fruits such as oranges, grapefruit and tangerines.

How can scurvy be prevented?

Case study: Dan's diet

Dan is 16 and has been having trouble with his teeth. He is a bit embarrassed because when he cleans them his gums bleed. He thinks that might mean bad breath, but he wouldn't know who to ask! He is also annoyed that he's had a cold for about a month and it won't go away. His nose is red and runny all the time.

Dan lives with his parents, but he hardly ever eats at home. He's always out and only seems to grab a can of cola and some chocolate when he's hungry. Sometimes he has fish and chips or a burger from the burger van in the town square when he can be bothered. Dan's skin is a bit spotty too. In fact, he's decided he looks a bit grey: he'll have to do something about his appearance because he wants to ask Jodie out this weekend.

1. Why do you think that Dan is having the kind of health problems that he describes?
2. What would you suggest he does?
3. What might be the long-term effects on his health if he does not follow your advice?

PLTS

As a **self-manager** you will work towards the overall goal of achieving the unit and you will organise your time and resources well. As an **effective participator** you could identify improvements to diets that will benefit sufferers of the two conditions that you identified.

Functional skills

In this activity you will have the chance to develop **ICT** skills by researching the information you need and creating the case studies. You should be able to create some eye-catching artwork by including pictures or photos. To make sure that you are developing **English** skills you should make sure that you proofread the leaflets carefully as well as using the spell and grammar checks before you hand it in.

Assessment activity 11.2

The District Nurses have been quite impressed by the work you did producing the fact sheets and they have asked you to carry on with the work. They want you to prepare case studies for two people suffering from different nutrition-related conditions. These could then be used to help support and advise other people suffering from the conditions.

Prepare two leaflets, one for each person that describes their condition including signs and symptoms, and give a clear explanation of how an unbalanced diet can contribute to both conditions.

Grading tip

To achieve **P3** you need to explain two medical conditions that are related to unbalanced diets. You could carry out this activity as part of assessment activity 11.1, before you complete your evidence for **M1**. Choosing two health conditions that are common in the UK would be helpful preparation for assessment activity 11.3.

Just checking

1. How do iron and haemoglobin work in the body?
2. Which groups of people might be more likely to become anaemic?
3. What should people do to prevent anaemia from developing?

3. Know specific dietary needs of service users

Many health conditions that are related to nutritional disorders can become very serious and require expensive and lengthy medical treatment. Health care professionals who work in the field of public health work to try to educate the public so that the general health of the population improves and people are less at risk of becoming ill.

Coronary heart disease

People who suffer from coronary heart disease should modify their diet in order to prevent further damage to the heart. Sufferers should be advised to make the following changes to their diet:

- eat at least five portions of fruit and vegetables a day
- reduce the total amount of fat in the diet and substitute saturated fats for poly- and mono-unsaturated fats such as vegetable and olive oils
- eat oily fish such as mackerel, sardines, herring, fresh tuna and salmon two to three times a week
- introduce nuts and seeds into the diet
- maintain a healthy weight
- reduce the amount of salt in the diet to a maximum of 6g per day
- drink alcohol in moderation – 1–2 units per day maximum
- take exercise – a minimum of 30 minutes three times a week.

Obesity

The best way to combat obesity is to maintain a diet low in fat and sugar and high in complex carbohydrates and fruit and vegetables. Regular exercise will also help to burn up any excess energy intake.

Case study: Katya and Natasha

Katya is 16 years old and has always worried about her weight, because that's all her friends seem to talk about. She is 160cm tall and weighs 55 kilos. Her friend Natasha is taller than her. She is 170cm tall and weighs about the same. They both do lots of sport; in fact they are training for the schools athletics championship at the moment.

1. In pairs look at the height/weight chart and see if you think either girl is overweight or underweight.

2. What advice would you give them?

Figure 11.7: A height and weight chart

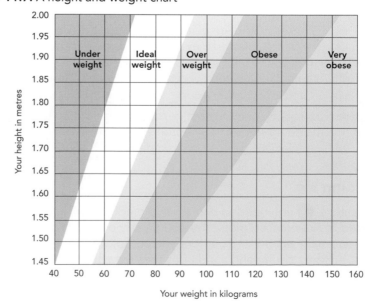

Type two diabetes

People who suffer from type two diabetes can do a lot to help the levels of blood glucose by maintaining a diet low in fat and sugar. Complex carbohydrates should form a part of the diet, as low carbohydrate diets can be high in fat. There is a relatively high incidence of coronary heart disease in diabetics in the United Kingdom.

Lactose intolerance

Lactose intolerance is an inability to digest lactose, the sugar found in milk and milk products. It is particularly common in people of African, Asian and Indian origin and can lead to digestive disturbance, such as cramps, diarrhoea and wind. Milk should be avoided in the diet, but often sufferers can tolerate yoghurt and cheese because the lactose is converted to lactic acid during manufacture.

Food allergies

You might know someone who has a food allergy to peanuts, or milk. These are quite common.

Allergic reactions to food vary in intensity and similar symptoms and illnesses can be triggered by different allergens as well as the same allergens causing very different reactions in different people. Symptoms can include eczema, asthma, urticaria (hives) and other health problems. **Anaphylaxis** is an extreme reaction which must be treated by adrenaline injections. Failure to treat this promptly can result in death. Avoidance of the food that causes allergies is the only way to prevent the onset of symptoms, although some people do have desensitisation treatment which is said to be very effective.

Genetic disorders

Certain genetic disorders can cause problems that can be relieved by diet. Cystic fibrosis is a disorder that causes thick sticky mucus to coat the digestive and respiratory systems. Enzymes produced in the pancreas that are needed to digest food cannot pass into the small intestine and sufferers are given these enzymes in powdered form sprinkled onto their food.

Phenylketonuria (PKU) is a rare inherited condition in which there is a build-up of phenylalanine in the body. Babies are usually tested for this when they are a few days old. Phenylalanine is an amino acid – a building block of protein. A low protein diet is essential for sufferers and has to be supplemented with artificial protein that does not contain phenylalanine. If this diet is not followed learning difficulties can result.

Activity: Coeliac disease

Many people suffer from coeliac disease and this can cause quite severe health problems for those who have it. Find out the following:

What is coeliac disease? Include signs and symptoms.

What foods do coeliac sufferers need to avoid, and what foods are available that have been specially manufactured?

Key term

Anaphylaxis – extreme allergic reaction occurring when the body is extremely sensitive to a substance

Just checking

1. Which foods are particularly common causes of allergies?
2. What is the treatment for anaphylactic shock?
3. How does desensitisation therapy for allergy sufferers work?

Specific dietary needs of service users

Some people would argue that we live in an increasingly secular (non-religious) society where religion and beliefs may not seem to be very important. However, UK society is becoming more diverse, so the knowledge and understanding that health care professionals have of other cultures and religions helps them to develop respect and provide individualised care for service users

Religion/culture

The table below shows the main dietary rules for some common religions.

Table 11.8 Dietary requirements for some of the main world religions

	Judaism	Sikhism	Islam	Hinduism	Buddhism
Eggs	Not if blood spots in the egg	✓	✓	Some	✓
Milk/yoghurt	Meat and dairy are never mixed in the same meal	✓	Not containing rennet	Not containing rennet	✓
Cheese		Some	Some	Some	
Chicken	Kosher only	Some	Halal only	Some Hindus are vegetarian, some avoid pork and none eat beef	Different sects of Buddhists have different rules. Some are strictly vegetarian, others will eat meat, fish and dairy products
Lamb		✓			
Beef		No			
Pork	No	Rarely	No		
Fish	With scales, fins and backbones	Some	Halal only		
Shellfish	No	Some	Halal only		
Animal fats	Kosher only	Some	Halal only		
Alcohol	✓	✓	No	Some will restrict amount of alcohol consumed, some will avoid	Strict Buddhists do not drink alcohol
Cocoa/tea/coffee	✓	Some may choose not to drink these	Some may not drink caffeinated drinks		✓
Nuts	✓	✓	✓	✓	✓
Pulses	✓	✓	✓	✓	✓
Fruit	✓	✓	✓	✓	✓
Vegetables	✓	✓	✓	✓	✓
Fasting	Yom Kippur	No	Ramadan	Some fasting for special festivals	Yes but varies

Vegetarianism

Some people do not like the taste or texture of meat or choose not to eat it because they do not agree with killing animals or fish for food, or object to the way that animals are kept and reared for food. Vegetarian diets are usually high in fibre and low in fat and this makes it a healthy diet to follow. As long as vegetarians are aware of the need to combine vegetable based foods to make HBV proteins they can get all the nutrients they need. There are different types of vegetarian:

- semi or demi vegetarians – no red meat but will eat fish and/or poultry

- lacto vegetarians – will eat dairy foods such as yoghurt, milk and cheese, but not eggs, meat, fish or poultry

- ovo vegetarians – will eat eggs but not dairy, meat, fish or poultry

- lacto-ovo vegetarians – will eat dairy products and eggs, but not meat, fish or poultry.

Choices on restaurant menus are sometimes marked with a green V to indicate vegetarian dishes and labels on packaged foods will be sometimes marked with a green V to indicate that the product is suitable for vegetarians.

Veganism

Vegans eat no animal foods at all, including no eggs or honey. They have to be careful about the plant proteins they eat to ensure that they have a balanced diet. Some vegans will also choose not to wear clothing or use items made from leather, silk or wool.

There is a possibility that vegans may suffer from vitamin B_{12} deficiency as this is mainly found in animal products, although yeast extract is a good source; if vegans know about healthy eating choices they can obtain everything they need from this diet. Nutritionists tend to advise that a vegan diet is not suitable for young children because it contains so much bulk that is filling that they may not eat enough to get the energy they need. However, it is recognised that a vegan diet containing a wide variety of foods will allow children to grow and develop normally although they are likely to be lighter and leaner than meat-eating children.

Just checking

1. Explain what is meant by Kosher and Halal foods and who eats them and why.
2. Identify the main differences between a vegetarian and vegan diet.

Planning a balanced diet

My life

Breakfast

Many people say that breakfast is the most important meal of the day. What do you eat for breakfast? Do you think that this is a balanced meal? How could you improve your breakfast?

This topic will help you to plan a balanced diet, thinking about what you need to include in a diet for different meals, including breakfast, midday meals, evening meal, snacks and beverages.

Two-day plan

Sometimes it is necessary for people who have been newly diagnosed with a nutrition-related disorder to be given advice about how they should change their diet to suit their needs. Creating a two-day plan that will give them ideas about the foods they should be eating, with suggestions for possible suitable alternatives, will help them to adjust to a new way of eating. Plans should include breakfast, midday and evening meals and healthy snacks as well as drinks.

Why do you need to eat lots of fruit and vegetables as part of a balanced diet?

Activity: Food diary

This will help you to prepare for P4 of your assessment.

Keep a food diary for two days of all the food and drink that you have consumed, making sure that you do not cheat! Swap your diary with a partner and make a table of all the foods consumed according to the five food group headings. Analyse what has been eaten and drunk over the 48-hour period.

Make recommendations to your partner about what changes they could make to their diet. Do they eat five portions of fruit and vegetables a day? Do they eat a lot of high fat/sugar/salt snacks? Do they drink enough water?

Devise a two-day healthy eating plan for your partner to follow. After the two days find out:

- How easy was it to follow the plan?
- What did they enjoy and not enjoy?
- Could you make any changes to the plan to include any of your partner's preferences?

BTEC

Assessment activity 11.3

 **P4 M2 D1**

In Assessment activity 11.2 you have already created two leaflets about different dietary conditions and their signs and symptoms, together with some advice about how unbalanced diets affect both conditions (**P4**).

You should now add some supplementary pages to both leaflets which identify the specific dietary needs for each condition. You then need to outline a two-day diet plan for each service user which includes breakfast, lunch, an evening meal, some healthy snacks and drinks for both days. This will help you to achieve **M2**.

To meet **D1** of this assignment, justify the choices you have made and make sure that you can clearly explain the reasons for the suggestions you have made. Include in this section how the food choices will help the service users to manage their condition.

Grading tips

To achieve **P4** in this unit, you need to identify two service users with specific dietary needs. You could use two people that you know who have specific dietary needs or use two service users from a work placement. You need to be able to describe the key points of their dietary needs. If you use people that you know, either personally or from a placement, you must maintain confidentiality and refer to them only as Person A and Person B or by their initials.

For **M2**, if the people you are using are real, then it makes sense to get to know them and to find out if they have any likes and dislikes. Sticking to a diet plan is much more successful if you try to include foods that someone enjoys. To meet **D1** you will need to make sure that you can fully explain and justify the how the diet plan will meet the needs of the service users.

 PLTS

As a **reflective learner**, you will be able to assess your service users and identify opportunities and achievements if you complete the P, M and D criteria. As a **team worker** you will be collaborating with the service users to work towards common goals. As a **self-manager** you will work towards the overall goal of achieving the unit and you will organise your time and resources well.

Functional skills

In this activity you will have the chance to develop more **ICT** skills by creating the two-day plans. You could do this in the form of tables. Again, make sure that you proofread the leaflets carefully as well as using the spell and grammar checks before you hand them in.

Just checking

1. Why is creating a two day plan important?
2. Write a list of some of the foods which are important for a balanced diet.
3. How could you improve your own diet?

4. Principles of food safety and hygiene

Anyone who works in a job that involves providing food for other people must know about the importance of food safety and hygiene. When we go out to eat we want to feel confident that the food we are served has been stored properly, cooked sufficiently and has not been exposed to anything that could cause harm. This section introduces you to the importance of maintaining food safety and hygiene.

Safe practices of food preparation, cooking and service

Hygiene control

When you work with food, it is vital that hygiene is well controlled because food must be kept safe. This is done by:

- protecting food from contamination by harmful bacteria
- preventing bacteria from multiplying to dangerous levels
- destroying harmful bacteria in or on food by thorough cooking
- disposing of harmful food safely.

The basic rules of food hygiene are outlined below.

- Always wash your hands before touching food, particularly after visiting the toilet, after touching animals, your own skin and hair and after touching raw food.
- Always cover any break in the skin of your hands, or sores or spots, with a waterproof adhesive dressing (preferably a highly coloured one so you notice if it comes off).
- No smoking during the preparation of food or in areas where food is prepared or consumed.
- Avoid preparing food if you have any illness (particularly skin, nose or throat infections and sickness and/or diarrhoea).
- Do not allow animals into the food preparation area.
- Cover food to protect it from flies and other insects.
- Wrap all food waste and dispose of it in a covered waste bin.
- Clean as you go. Wash surfaces with hot water and detergent.
- Wipe spills up immediately with kitchen tissue and place this in a covered bin.
- Serve food as soon as possible after preparing it.
- Never allow raw food to come in contact with cooked food; common ways in which cooked food is contaminated from raw food are through the hands, knives and working surfaces.
- Wear clean clothing and be clean yourself.
- Do not cough or sneeze over food.

Temperature control

Bacteria can be found on many foods a lot of the time, but food handlers take precautions to ensure that the bacteria cannot multiply to dangerous levels in the food.

Control of temperature is very important in preventing bacteria from multiplying during cooking and storage of food. The Food Safety (Temperature Control) Regulations 1995 set out the safe temperatures for the storage, heating and chilling of food. Body temperature (37°C) is the temperature at which bacteria like to multiply so they will multiply efficiently inside the human body.

The table below shows the temperatures that must be used for food storage.

Table 11.9 Temperatures required for safe food storage

Method	Temperature
Freezer	–18°C to –22°C
Refrigerator	Legal requirement 8°C, good practice 5–6°C
Hot holding food	Hot food must be maintained at a temperature of 63°C
Reheating commercially manufactured food that has been cooked once during manufacture	Temperature of reheated food must reach a minimum of 82°C

Pest control

A food pest is any animal that can live on or in food, causing damage or contamination. The main types of pests are:

- insects such as flies, cockroaches and weevils
- birds
- rodents such as rats and mice.

Flies land on food and carry bacteria on their bodies. In addition, they defecate and vomit half-digested food onto the food. They also lay eggs and their dead bodies can be found in food. Cockroaches can deposit faeces on food and spread bacteria, and small insects such as weevils live in stored foods and food products such as flour and cereals.

Mice and rats carry bacteria and pass these on by either walking on the food or on work surfaces. Mice have weak bladders and urinate on food. Some birds can carry bacteria. Food can be contaminated by droppings and feathers and by insects that they carry on their bodies.

Evidence of a pest infestation might include droppings, damage, rat runs, egg shells, dead bodies and damage to the building. Protecting premises where food is stored or prepared is the most important way of preventing infection of or damage to food. The owner of the premises must ensure that the building is kept in good repair with no obvious points of entry for pests, and all food handlers have a responsibility to report anything they think is abnormal. Food pests tend to like warm, dark, damp undisturbed places so it is important for food storage and preparation areas to be cool, well lit, dry and clean.

Did you know?

The danger zone for foods that are likely to be affected by bacteria is between 5 and 63°C, so food should be kept and stored outside this zone. Cold temperatures stop bacteria from multiplying, and hot temperatures kill them.

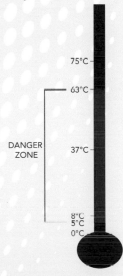

Figure 11.8: Important temperatures for food safety

Activity: Pests!

Find out what the penalties might be under the Food Safety Act 1990 if the owner of a food premises is found to have a pest infestation.

Just checking

1. What checks would you make to ensure that food is being kept at the correct temperature?
2. How long can you leave hot food on a display for before you have to discard it?

Effects of unsafe practices

You probably don't pay much attention to the health and safety aspects of your meal when you go to a restaurant, because you assume that the food you are being served has been stored, prepared and served according to food safety laws. But there are many potential hazards that can affect the food you eat.

Food can be contaminated in a variety of ways – physical, chemical and biological.

Physical contamination

Physical contaminants include bones, shells or pips and stalks from food, food packaging, nuts or bolts from equipment, jewellery, hair, fingernails, plasters, dust, dirt, insects and their droppings and eggs. Some contamination can be prevented very easily by ensuring that food handlers have their hair covered, have short, clean unvarnished fingernails and do not wear jewellery. Proper maintenance and cleaning of buildings and equipment will help to prevent contamination by pests or parts falling off equipment, and proper preparation of food should ensure that bones and shells are fully removed before serving.

Chemical contamination

Chemical contamination can be caused by cleaning chemicals if they are not kept separate from food and food preparation areas, and agricultural chemicals, e.g. on fruit and vegetables if they have been sprayed. They must be cleaned thoroughly or peeled before eating. Leftover food or drink from metal containers should always be transferred to a non-metallic container and stored covered in a refrigerator. Acidic and salty food can attack the metal once a can is opened. All cleaning chemicals should be stored in a locked cupboard away from food preparation areas, and there should be a thorough rinsing stage during the washing up process to ensure that all detergents and sanitisers are removed.

Biological contamination

Biological contamination is contamination by bacteria or viruses that multiply on the food to dangerous levels, or by moulds which cause toxins on food. When they are eaten, they cause illness. Safe preparation, cooking storing and handling of food, together with regular and thorough hand washing, will help to prevent biological contamination. Some of the more common types of bacteria that cause food poisoning are outlined on the next page.

Just checking

1. Identify the main sources of food poisoning bacteria.
2. What simple actions could you take as a food handler to ensure that you are not contaminating food that could put people at risk?

Bacterial food poisoning

Clostridium perfringens is a bacteria found on raw meat, animal and human faeces, soil, dust and insects. It occurs when food (usually meat) is cooked and kept warm for several hours before eating. Symptoms of poisoning by this bacteria are abdominal pains and diarrhoea, and they usually appear between 12 and 18 hours after eating the contaminated food. Most people get better within 24 hours, although older people may be ill for longer.

Staphylococcus aureus

Staphylococcus aureus lives naturally on the skin and in the nose and mouth of most people where usually it doesn't do any harm. But once it is in the wrong place, for example in food that has been handled without wearing gloves, it can cause illness. It is also found in unpasteurised milk. Symptoms appear quite quickly, usually between one and six hours after eating contaminated food, and include abdominal pain or cramp, vomiting and low temperature but people normally recover very quickly.

Campylobacter causes the highest reported intestinal infection in England and Wales. It is found on raw poultry and meat, milk and animals, including pets. The symptoms are diarrhoea, which is often bloody, abdominal pain, nausea and fever and they can take from 48 to 60 hours to develop. The illness lasts about a week but some people have no symptoms at all. The illness is caused by a very small number of organisms – one small drop of raw chicken blood might be all that it takes to infect someone.

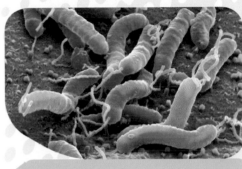

Campylobacter

Bacillus cereus is found in cereals, soil and dust. Symptoms can appear after between one and five hours or 8 to 16 hours depending on the form of the food poisoning. It often occurs in people who eat a lot of take-away food as it is common in re-heated cooked rice which is served extensively in take-away outlets. Symptoms include abdominal pain, diarrhoea and vomiting but subside within about 24 hours.

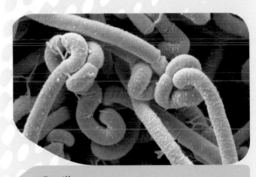

Bacillus cereus

Salmonella is found on raw poultry, eggs, raw meat, milk, animals, insects and sewage and causes abdominal pain, vomiting, diarrhoea and fever. It usually appears about 12 to 36 hours after eating contaminated food – often undercooked poultry. It usually lasts between four and seven days, but the very young and very old can become very ill with it and may require hospitalisation and antibiotics. There are more than 2,500 different strains of salmonella.

E. coli is a bacterium that occurs naturally in the bowel and helps to keep the digestive system healthy. The problems arise when it contaminates food that is then eaten. It occurs in human and animal digestive tracts, sewage, water and raw meat. Symptoms appear within 12 to 24 hours and include abdominal pain, fever, diarrhoea, vomiting, kidney damage or failure. Most recent outbreaks of E. coli have occurred among children who visited petting farms and stroked the animals. Good personal hygiene and thorough hand washing after visiting the toilet and when handling food helps to prevent E. coli contamination.

Salmonella

Legislation, regulations and codes of practice

My life

It's the law

Many people today think that there are far too many laws that we have to follow. However, sometimes it is important that there are laws in place for our protection. Give three reasons why you think it is important to have laws and regulations for the sale and consumption of food.

Case study: NHS fined £15,000 under Food Safety Act

An NHS Healthcare Trust was fined almost £15,000 for having in possession food past its 'Use by' date.

On 17 June 2008, a routine inspection was carried out at the canteen facilities where eleven food products were found to be past their 'Use by' date, the oldest by just over twelve months.

In January 2009, solicitors representing the Trust pleaded guilty to the offences which included selling out-of-date turkey, gammon and fish.

1. What are 'Best before', 'Display until' and 'Use by' dates and which foods do they relate to?

2. Find out why the government is thinking of removing this information from food packaging.

3. How much money might be saved each year if this proposal is introduced?

Food safety legislation requires that any establishment preparing and serving food must ensure that food is safe to eat. Three of the main laws and regulations that have to be adhered to are:

- The Food Safety Act 1990
- The Food Safety (General Food Hygiene) Regulations 1995
- The Food Safety (Temperature Control) Regulations 1995.

The Food Safety Act 1990

The Food Safety Act is the main piece of legislation that governs the safety of food. The Act states that it is illegal to sell or keep for sale food that is unfit for people to eat or causes food to be dangerous to health, or is not of acceptable content or quality, or is labelled or advertised in any way that misleads the consumer. If prosecuted, people who work with food must show that they have taken all reasonable steps to avoid causing any of the above.

The Food Safety (General Food Hygiene) Regulations 1995

These regulations cover the basic hygiene principles that businesses must follow and relate to staff, premises and food handling. They affect anyone who owns manages or works in a food business, whether it is a caravan in a lay-by selling tea, coffee and snacks or a five star hotel. The regulations cover the following:

- the supply and selling of food in a hygienic way
- identification of possible food hazards
- control of identified hazards to prevent harm to customers
- the establishment of effective control and monitoring procedures to ensure that harm does not come to customers.

The Food Safety (Temperature Control) Regulations 1995

These regulations cover the following aspects of food hygiene:

- the stages of the food chain that are subject to temperature controls
- the temperatures at which certain foods must be kept
- which foods are exempt from specific temperature controls
- when the temperature controls allow flexibility.

Hazard Analysis Critical Control Point (HACCP)

HACCP is a universal food safety system. It aims to protect food from contamination by:

- identifying critical points in the food handling process that might cause contamination
- putting controls in place to prevent microbiological, chemical and physical contamination of food
- monitoring the critical points to ensure that contamination does not occur.

This means that all potential hazards at each stage of food handling, from delivery of raw products to the serving of fully prepared food, must be identified. The whole process is designed to ensure that any problems can be dealt with before they cause any problems or illness.

The hazard control chart for pre-cooked meat is shown below:

Figure 11.9: Hazard flow chart for pre-cooked meat

Hazard Flow Chart for				
Stage	**Hazards** *What can go wrong?*	**Controls** *How can I prevent it going wrong?*	**Monitoring** *How can I check my control?*	**Corrective action** *What do I do if things are not right?*
Delivery				
Storage				
Preparation				
Cooking				
Serving				

PLTS

For P5 as an **independent enquirer** you will be researching the legislation relating to food safety. P6 will allow you to be a **reflective learner**, identifying opportunities and setting goals for your work. As a **self-manager** you will work towards the overall goal of achieving the unit and you will organise your time and resources well.

Functional skills

Preparing and delivering the PowerPoint® presentation will help you to practise both your **ICT** and **English** skills, and if you take part in the activities in the kitchen you will be practising **Maths** skills by helping to measure ingredients.

BTEC ## Assessment activity 11.4   P5 M3 D2

You are on a placement at a Day Centre where the service users cook food that they take home. They would like to raise money for an outing by holding a coffee morning selling cakes and biscuits. Your placement supervisor has told you that everyone has to know about food safety before they can sell food products to the public.

You should prepare a PowerPoint® presentation that outlines the relevant legislation relating to preparing, cooking and serving food, and the safe practices necessary in doing so to present to the service users. To get a merit grade you need to include information about the effects of unsafe practices when preparing cooking and serving food.

To achieve distinction level, the service users must make the food that they are going to sell. You must be present to observe them preparing and selling the food. Write a report for the Day Centre Manager assessing how effective you all were in following safe practices.

Grading tips

P5, M3 and D2 all relate to food safety, including safe practices and legislation.

For the presentation you need to make sure that the information is at a suitable level for your service users to understand. For M3 you could include a quiz or question and answer session so that unsafe practices can be discussed in the group. For D2 you may need to ask other people to be present to observe what is happening during the practical activity to ensure that safe practices are being followed. You may wish to invite your tutor and placement supervisor to be present.

Just checking

1. Why is it important to follow legislation when you are handling food for other people?
2. What legislation has to be adhered to?
3. What is the purpose of HACCP?

WorkSpace

Lai Ling Chu
State Registered Dietitian

I am a State Registered Dietitian and I have a degree in Dietetics. I became interested in food and nutrition when I did some work experience in a hospital and shadowed a dietitian. I was really interested in how he worked with patients to help them to understand their condition and what diet to follow to keep them as healthy as possible.

Now that I am qualified I work in a large NHS hospital and I provide people with advice about nutrition, healthy diets and I also work with doctors to help to diagnose nutrition-related diseases.

My work is quite varied as I calculate my patients' nutritional requirements and I also analyse the nutritional content of food. I have also been working with the Catering Manager advising on providing healthy options on the menus for both patients and staff.

I have started to specialise in working with adults and children with diabetes, and I really enjoy helping people to understand their condition and how to manage it.

I love my job because every day is different. I am lucky enough to work with patients and help them to get better and I also get to do some scientific research. It's a good balance.

Think about it!

1. Carry out some research into the work of a Dietitian. What other tasks might they carry out as part of their job?
2. Find out about the following diseases, how they relate to diet and nutrition and what dietary advice could be given:
   - Osteoporosis
   - Irritable Bowel Syndrome
   - Arthritis
   - Diverticulitis
   - Gall stones

Extension activity: Dietary advice

Alf is an 84-year-old widower who lives in a small rural village with only one shop. He worked on a farm from the age of 16 until he retired four years ago, apart from two years when he was away fighting in the Second World War. His wife Ida died in 2003 and he has lived alone since then. His family all live more than three hours away and he does not see them very often. Alf has got a computer, which his daughter set up for him, and he enjoys keeping in touch with his family by email, but he hasn't really done much else with it. He has good neighbours who pop in most evenings to make sure that he is all right, but most of them work full time and the village is very quiet on weekdays. Alf doesn't drive any more because he cannot afford to run a car on his pension, but he does have a bus pass, and the local bus service comes through the village every two hours. The bus journey to the nearest town with a large supermarket takes an hour.

Alf has arthritis and a heart condition and finds it difficult to carry heavy things and walk long distances. He gets most of his shopping from the local village shop but it is expensive and there is not a lot of choice. The fruit and vegetables always look tired and there is no fresh meat or fish on sale.

Alf goes to the local pub on Sundays for a roast dinner. The rest of the time he tends to eat tinned food or anything he can make a sandwich out of.

Alf had a cold last week which has left him with a nasty cough. He had a home visit from the GP who diagnosed a chest infection. She is worried that Alf is not eating properly and that this is having an effect on his health.

1. Identify the different factors that have an effect on Alf's diet.
2. What dietary advice could you give Alf to help him to stay as healthy as possible?
3. Using the information above, identify ways in which Alf's diet and lifestyle could be improved quite simply.

edexcel

Assignment tips

- This unit is about people's nutritional needs and the medical conditions that can occur as a result of eating an unbalanced diet. It is important that you make sure you know what macro- and micronutrients are because unless you know what makes up a balanced diet you will find it difficult to identify problems that arise.

- It is particularly important to know about the nutritional needs of babies and young children. They are more likely to be affected by factors like added salt in foods than other groups.

- Remember that there are other factors besides unbalanced diets that will have an effect on health. These include social class, where you live and how easy it is to have access to healthy foods.

- You must remember that if you are storing, preparing, and serving food to other people you have a legal responsibility to ensure that you are doing this in a way that does not put their health at risk. Failure to do so can result in a fine or imprisonment.

- A general rule to follow is the 80:20 rule: provided that you eat healthily for 80% of the time, you can eat less healthy foods 20% of the time.

Relevant legislation and organisational policy and procedures

This grid provides a list of some of the legislation and organisational policy and procedures relevant to health and social care. The content which is particularly relevant has been listed.

Legislation policy procedure	Website	Relevant content	EU directive implemented by the Act
Care Standards Act (2000) (England and Wales)	www.opsi.gov.uk	Set up an organisation called the National Care Standards Commission. Inspection is now the responsibility of the Care Quality Commission. • Sets standards that all social care workers must meet. These can be found in the booklet *General Social Care Council Codes of Practice*. • Ensures all care provision meets with the National Minimum Standards. • Sets standards for the level of care given to individuals requiring social care. • Requires that all staff have a thorough police check before they begin working with children and adults and that a list is kept of individuals who are unsuitable to work with children or vulnerable adults. The vetting and barring scheme was introduced in October 2009 with the aim of preventing unsuitable people from working with children and vulnerable adults. From July 2010, and phased in over a five year period, anyone working of volunteering with children or vulnerable adults will be required to register with the Independent Safeguarding Authority (ISA). The ISA will make decisions to prevent unsuitable people from working with children and vulnerable adults, using a range of sources including the Criminal Records Bureau (CRB). The CRB will process applications for ISA-registration and continuously monitor individuals against any new information, whilst continuing to provide employers with access to an individual's full criminal record and other information to help them make informed recruitment decisions.	
Children Act (2004)	www.ecm.gov.uk	Introduces Children's Commissioner, Local Safeguarding Children Boards and provides legal basis for Every Child Matters	
Children (Leaving Care) Act (2000)	www.ecm.gov.uk	Requires local authorities to plan for children leaving care. • Children must be provided with support for housing and preparation for independence. • Children must have a personal adviser. • Young people can remain cared for in full-time education until 21 years.	
Children Act (1989)	www.dcsf.gov.uk www.scotland.gov.uk	Made major changes to childcare practice. • Introduced concept of 'significant harm'. • Introduced concept of 'parental responsibilities' rather than 'rights'. • Made wishes and interests of the child paramount.	
Control of Substances Hazardous to Health (2002) (COSHH)	www.hse.gov.uk	Covers the handling of hazardous substances. Gives directions on how to: • Store cleansing materials correctly • Label hazardous substances correctly • Handle bodily fluids such as blood and urine appropriately • Handle flammable liquids and gases appropriately • Handle toxic or corrosive substances/liquids appropriately	67/548/EEC

Community Care and Health Act (2002) (Scotland)	www.opsi.gov.uk	Introduced free nursing and personal care for the elderly in Scotland. • Elderly people who qualify receive payments of between £145 and £210 per week, depending on their needs.	
Data Protection Act (1998) Data Protection Amendment Act (2003) Access to Medical Records (1988)	www.dh.gov.uk www.opsi.gov.uk	Provide for the protection of individuals' personal data with regard to processing and safe storage. The Acts cover: • Storage of confidential information • Protection of paper-based information • Protection of information stored on computer • Accurate and appropriate record keeping.	95/46/EC
Disability Discrimination Act (2005)	www.direct.gov.uk	First came into force in 1995 and was amended in 2005. • Requires the providers of public transport to reduce the amount of discrimination towards people with disabilities on their buses and trains. • Requires public facilities and buildings to be made accessible to those who have disabilities. • Requires employers to make reasonable adjustments to allow an individual with a disability to gain employment.	
Environmental Protection Act, Section 34 (1990) and the Environmental Protection (Duty of Care) Regulations (1991)	www.dh.gov.uk	Impose a duty of care on persons concerned with control of waste. • Anyone who has a responsibility for control of waste must ensure that it is managed properly and recovered or disposed of safely.	2006/12/EC
Food Safety (General Food Hygiene) Regulations (1995)	www.opsi.gov.uk	Provide for the safe handling and preparation of food. Topics include: • Basic hygiene principles for handling and preparing food • Food safety risks. All staff who prepare food for users of services in day centres, residential settings and hospitals must follow the guidelines.	93/43/EEC
Freedom of Information Act (2000)	www.dh.gov.uk	Produced to promote a culture of openness within public bodies. • Everyone has the right of access to a wide range of information held by a public authority. • Individuals can access their health records and can request the information to be provided in Braille, audio format; large type or another language if necessary. Access to information is subject to certain limitations, such as information about an individual.	95/46/EC
Freedom of Information Act (2002) (Scotland)		In Scotland, this Act established the office of Scottish Information Commissioner, which is responsible for ensuring public authorities maximise access to information.	
Health and Safety at Work Act (1974)	www.hse.gov.uk	Aims to ensure the working environment is safe and free from hazards. Employers and employees should share responsibilities for: • Assessing risks before carrying out tasks • Checking equipment for faults before use • Using appropriate personal protective clothing • Handling hazardous/contaminated waste correctly • Disposing of sharp implements appropriately.	89/391/EEC

Human Rights Act (1998)	www.opsi.gov.uk	Came into effect in October 2000. States the basic human rights and that people can take their complaints about how they have been treated to a UK court. • There are 16 basic human rights. They cover everyday things, such as what a person can say and do, their beliefs and issues of life and death. • Human rights are rights and freedoms that all people living in the UK have, regardless of their nationality or citizenship. • Although everyone has these rights they can be taken away from a person if that person does not respect other people's rights.	
Lifting Operations and Lifting Equipment Regulations (1998)	www.hse.gov.uk	Aim to reduce risks to people's health and safety from lifting equipment provided at work. • Equipment must be strong and stable enough for the particular use and marked to indicate safe working loads • Equipment must be positioned and installed to minimise any risks. • Lifting must be planned, organised and performed by competent people. • Lifting equipment must have ongoing thorough examination and, where appropriate, inspection by competent people.	95/63/EC
Management of Health and Safety at Work Regulations (1999)	www.opsi.gov.uk	Explain to managers and employers what measures they must take to keep staff safe. The main focus of the regulations is risk assessment. The regulations explain how to conduct a risk assessment and what the assessment should contain.	
Manual Handling Regulations (1992)	www.hse.gov.uk	Aim to keep staff safe when handling anything. Covers the safe moving and handling of equipment, loads and patients • The environment must be prepared before anything is moved or handled. • Equipment must be checked for safety before use.	90/269/EEC
Mental Capacity Act (2005)	www.opsi.gov.uk	Empowers and protects vulnerable people who are not able to make their own decisions. Deals with the assessment of a person's mental capacity and protects those who lack capacity. The Act created two new public bodies: a new Court of Protection and a new Public Guardian.	
Mental Health Act (2007)	www.opsi.gov.uk	Updates the Mental Health Act 1983. The main changes are: • 16 and 17 year olds can accept or refuse admission to hospital and this decision cannot be overridden by a parent • Patients who are detained in hospital under a section of the Act are entitled to an independent advocate who will speak for them at a review to decide on their future • Under Supervised Community Treatment Orders, patients who are discharged will be visited at home by a mental health professional to ensure that they take their medication.	
Race Relations Amendment Act (2000)	www.standards.dfes.gov.uk	Requires all public bodies, for example Health Authorities and Primary Care Trusts to: • Review their policies and procedures • Remove discrimination from these policies and procedures • Remove the possibility of discrimination from their policies and procedures • Actively promote equality In Health and Social Care, this means that all support must be designed and delivered in such a way that no individual will be treated less fairly because of their race or ethnicity.	
Reporting of Injuries, Diseases and Dangerous Occurrences Regulations (1995) (RIDDOR)	www.hse.gov.uk	Ensures injuries, diseases and dangerous incidents are reported appropriately. • Accidents and injuries must be reported objectively and accurately. • Diseases and dangerous incidents must be reported to the appropriate bodies. • Relevant paperwork must be completed.	89/391/EEC

Temperature and blood pressure chart

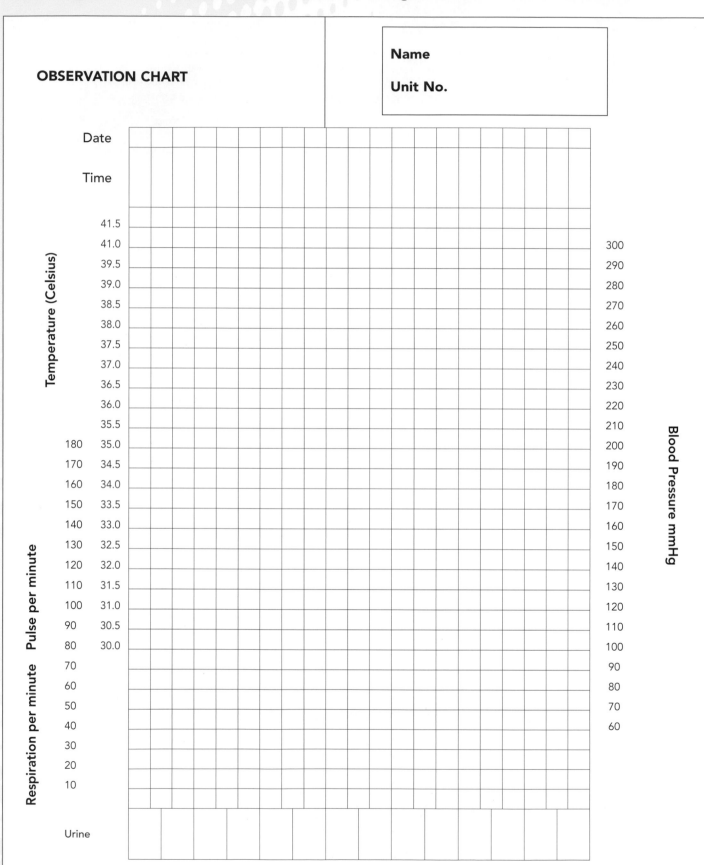

Peak flow chart

Peak flow diary

To take a peak flow reading put the marker to zero, take a deep breath, seal your lips around the mouthpiece, then blow as hard and as fast as you can into the device. Note the reading. Repeat three times. The 'best of the three' is the reading to record. Mark this with a cross on the chart.

Name ....

Date ....

Peak Flow Rate		
600		
550		
500		
450		
400		
350		
300		
250		
200		
150		
100		
Time	am / pm	

Day: 1, 2, 3, 4, 5, 6, 7, 8, 9, 10, 11, 12, 13, 14

Plan to improve health and well being

Below is an example of a partially completed care plan for a young man who needs to spend less time talking to his friends on his computer and more time seeing them face to face within the local community. Sanjay's long term targets are for him to sustain his social networking out in the community rather than to slip back into too much social networking on his computer. Your teacher or tutor may have a copy of this for you or you can copy it and can fill in the blanks as part of an activity with a partner or in a group.

You can also use the headings to draw up your own plan for health as part of your assessment.

Name: Sanjay K   Age 16
Focus: Social and community networking
Date: Assessment carried out on 22nd March 2010

Short term target: To spend less time in my room with my computer and go out more with my friends
Long term target: To join our local youth group and be more sociable

Action plan: Short term targets

When	Task	Alternative strategy	Benefits to Sanjay	Monitor: Parent to complete this	By when	Review: Parent and Sanjay to discuss this	By when	Evaluate: How did doing this make you feel?
Mon.	Meet Bhavin to do some coursework together				Same night			
Tues.	Find out when and where the youth group meets				Same night			
Wed.	Suggest to friends that we all join the youth group				Same night			
Thurs.	Meet Bhavin to do some revision for GCSEs				Same night			
Fri.	Get homework done and then go out with my friends, even if for an hour for a chat and kick about in the park				Same night or next morning			
Sat.	Help someone else, such as elderly person who needs some shopping doing				Same night or next morning			
Sun.	Meet friends to play a sport or go into town							

Action Plan: Long term targets

Glossary

A

Abolish – get rid of

Abuse – treating someone wrongly, harmfully or inappropriately

Activities of daily living – these include activities like eating and drinking, personal hygiene, sleeping, recreation, walking

Activity coordinator – many residential settings employ an activity coordinator to encourage individuals to participate in activities which stimulate thinking and encourage physical movement

Acute – usually short-term and curable

Aggression – behaviour that is unpleasant, frightening or intimidating

Alternative healers – individuals who use non-medical ways of supporting people with medical and social issues

Anaphylaxis – extreme allergic reaction occurring when the body is extremely sensitive to a substance

Antenatal services – midwives and specially trained doctors who care for pregnant women

Appropriate – suitable or fitting for a particular purpose

Arthritis – a condition affecting joints which is more common in older age

Assertion – behaviour that helps you communicate clearly and firmly

Assertive – confident and able to state his/her own views

Assessment – the ongoing process of gathering, analysing and reflecting on evidence to make an informed decision

Atonement – amends made for an injury or wrong

Attendee – someone who attends a session but does not live there

B

Barriers – reasons why some people cannot access health and social care provision

Basic food hygiene – a course which instructs people in the correct storage and preparation of food

Beliefs – strongly held opinions stored in the subconscious mind

Body language – our posture, position of our arms when speaking, use of gestures, eye contact, facial expression

Braille – system of raised points which is used as a form of written language for individuals who are without sight

Bronchitis – a chest infection

C

Carbon monoxide – a poisonous gas

Cardio – to do with the heart

Central stores – large stores where much of the equipment is kept

Chronic – usually long-term and may be progressive or incurable

Circumcision – male circumcision is the removal of some or all of the foreskin from the penis

Clarification – making something clear and understandable

Code of Practice – set of standards of conduct for workers and employers

Cohabiting – people living together in an emotionally and/or sexually intimate relationship

Communication – the exchange of information between people

Community care assistants – people who have usually completed an NVQ level 2 in social care or a BTEC First Diploma in Health and Social Care who provide personal care for individuals in their own homes

Community nurses – nurses who visit people in their homes and provide nursing support

Confidential – information that is secret. It has been entrusted to only the person to whom it has been communicated

Confidentiality – to be kept secret and to keep secure and private information about service users

Congenital – relating to a condition that is present at birth, as a result of heredity or environmental causes

Consent – to give permission, to allow what someone wishes

Context – the circumstances in which an event occurs; a setting

Core competencies – skills which are essential to performing a role accurately

CPD – Continuing Professional Development

Criminal Records Bureau check – a method of ensuring that people who work in health and social care do not have criminal records

Culture – a set of beliefs, language, styles of dress, ways of cooking, religion, ways of behaving and so on shared by a particular group of people

D

Dementia – condition which may occur in older people which includes memory loss and confusion

Depression – a mental illness. It can be a chronic condition or a short-term one

Deprivation – a lack of something

Description – providing a picture in words; saying what something is, how it works or what it does

Detained – kept in custody or temporary confinement

Di – Two

Diagnose – identify a medical condition

Dialysis unit – a hospital unit which contains specialist equipment for treating long term kidney disease

Dietitian – a health professional who works with individuals who need to adapt their diet for health reasons

Diffusion – the net movement of molecules from an area of high concentration to an area of low concentration

Dignity – a calm and serious manner/style suitable for the situation and to treat someone with respect

Dignity – feeling worthy of respect

Disability – a condition that restricts someone's ability to perform particular activities

Disclosure – to expose, to view or to reveal and to make known

Discrimination – to treat a person or group of people unfairly or differently from other persons or groups of people

Disease – a state in which the whole or parts of the body are not functioning properly, causing ill health

Diuretic – increasing the flow of urine

Diversity – the ways in which people are different from each other. Key differences include gender, age, social class, disability, sexuality

E

Economic – to do with money

Egocentric – centred on the self; thinking chiefly about oneself

Eliminate – to get rid of something that is not wanted

Empathy – identifying with and understanding another person's feelings and situation and putting yourself in someone else's shoes by sharing and understanding someone else's emotions

Emphysema – a chronic lung condition leading to severe shortage of breath, a dependency on oxygen, and death

Employee – a person who is employed by someone else

Employment prospects – the chances of getting and keeping a job that pays well and has good opportunities for promotion

Empower – enable someone to make decisions for themselves and take control of their lives

Emulsify – to disperse the particles of one liquid evenly in another

Epilepsy – a medical condition which affects the activity of brainwave patterns

Equality – everyone having the same chance as everyone else to obtain or achieve something and the idea of equal treatment and respect

Equality of opportunity – having equal chances and opportunities no matter what your race, ethnicity, gender, age or sexuality

Estimate – a judgement of something's value or amount

Eternity – an endless amount of time

Ethics – moral principles and philosophy

Ethnicity – the way that people belong to a particular ethnic group, where people share the same culture and way of life

Evangelistic – very enthusiastic and forceful delivery of religious message

F

Fast – going without food and sometimes drink to purify the soul and draw nearer to God

Fibromyalgia – a condition which causes widespread pain and severe fatigue

Financial burden – costs which make life difficult for people

Formal – the use of conventional language

Fulfilment – a feeling of satisfaction at having achieved something good

Functions – performs, operates

G

Gaseous exchange – when the body takes in oxygen and gets rid of (expels) carbon dioxide

Gender – the social role of being male or female

Goals – what you want to achieve in the long term; the final target

Guidance – advising and guiding

Guru – a personal spiritual teacher

H

Hale – free from infirmity or illness

Hand–eye co-ordination – the coordinated control of eye movement with hand movement. It allows the brain to process what the eye sees, so that the hand can reach for and touch or grasp an object. Many actions could not be done without it.

Hazard – an object or situation that could potentially hurt someone

Head of Room – day nurseries may be divided into separate rooms to provide support for children in the different age groups. The overall supervisor for each room is known as the Head of Room

Health care assistant – someone who works with nurses in a hospital or nursing home and delivers basic nursing support such as assisting with food, bathing and care of the skin and hair

Health visitor – a registered nurse who has additional qualifications; supporting families with young children and also older people

Hierarchy – a list of things or people arranged in order

Holistic – looking at all the different needs of the client

Holistic approach – an approach to delivery of support which takes account of all the needs of an individual

Holistic support – supporting all of the needs of an individual

Honesty – being trustworthy and truthful

Hormones – chemical messengers present throughout the body

Housing officer – a social care professional who usually works for a local authority, ensuring that individuals in need have appropriate housing

HSE – Health and Safety Executives regulate health and safety in the workplace

Humanists – believe in the importance of respect for all and celebration of life; they do not follow a religion

I

Illness – a state of poor health, sometimes referred to as ill-health

Impairment – a disability

Inappropriate – unsuitable

Independence – freedom from the control and influence of others and from the need for their support; the ability to make your own decisions

Induction loop – an electronic system which links with a person's hearing aid and enables them to hear what is being said, for example in a medical centre

Infection – illness caused by bacteria, virus or fungi, or by carriers such as animals or insects, and transmitted from person to person

Informal (support) – support which is provided by relatives and friends

Informal (language) – the use of more casual language

Inset – short for 'in-service training' when teaching staff are given training in teaching techniques or learn about new methods of teaching

Interaction – communicating with different people

Interaction – when someone or something has an effect on another

Intercostal – between the ribs

Interpersonal skills – skills we use when interacting and communicating with others

J

Jargon – technical words used by a professional person as a short way of saying things that are hard for others to understand

Judgemental – making decisions or forming opinions on the basis of something such as appearance, without proper evidence, and being too critical

L

Labelling – identifying or describing someone with a label rather than as an individual. This term is linked to stereotyping

Life stage – a distinct period of growth and development in the life span

Lifestyle – a way of life or style of living that reflects the attitudes and values of a person or group

Listening skills – listening carefully, concentrating on what is said

Literacy skills – the ability to be able to present the written word clearly and correctly and to be able to read the written word accurately

M

Macro – large or large scale

Malnutrition – not having sufficient food or nourishment for your energy needs

Manual dexterity – an ability to perform tasks skilfully with the hands so that it looks easy

Maternity – support for women before, during and after the birth of a baby

Means-tested benefits – benefits paid by the State to individuals, on the basis that their income is below a certain level

Meningitis – a serious infectious illness which can leave a person with a disability

Menopause – the natural and permanent stopping of menstruation (periods), occurring usually between the ages of 45 and 55

Micro – very small

Mobility – the ability to move around

Mono – One

Moral principle – the principles of right and wrong that are accepted by an individual or a social group

Multicultural – multi means many. Multicultural means many different cultures and groups in one area

Muslim – a member of the Islamic faith which believes in one God, (Allah)

N

Neonatal – newborn

NHS Mental Health Trust – a secondary care organisation which meets the health care needs of people with emotional disorders

Nicotine – powerful, fast-acting and addictive drug

NSPCC – National Society for the Prevention of Cruelty to Children – a voluntary organisation

Nursing assistant – someone who works with registered nurses as a support

NVQ – a qualification achieved while working in a setting - National Vocational Qualification

O

Obstetrician – a doctor who is trained to care for mothers-to-be

Occupational therapist – a health care professional who works with individuals to increase mobility and independence

Ophthalmic – care and treatment of eyes; usually provided in an out-patient clinic, but serious issues are treated in hospital

Outpatient clinic – patients may visit a clinic for a follow-up appointment after being in hospital

P

Paediatric – nursing and medical care of children

Peer group – a group of people who share at least one identifying characteristic, for example, age group, gender, job role or living environment

Permeable – allowing gases or liquids to pass through

Person centred – treating each person individually according to their needs

Phobia – a debilitating and irrational fear of something (e.g. an activity such as going outside, or living creatures such as spiders)

Physical disability – for example conditions such as arthritis which affects the joints and may worsen in older age

Placement report – at the end of your period of work experience, the setting will complete a report on your overall performance

Pollution – damage to living organisms caused by human activities disturbing the environment

Poly – Many or much

Prejudice – having a bias against a person or group of people for reasons such as their age, social class, gender, race, religion, sexuality, ability, health, disability, dress or appearance

Primary – first point of contact in health care

Private – support which is funded either through payment of fees or through an insurance company

Pro-active support – support which encourages people to make choices and retain independence

Professional bodies – organisations that set standards for, and look after the interests of, their members, who all do one type of job. One example in the health sector is the Royal College of Nursing

Progressive – happening or developing gradually

Prosperous – having success, flourishing, well-off

Proximity – being near or close to someone or something

Psychological – relating to, or arising from, the mind or emotions

Puberty – a normal phase of development caused by hormonal change, that occurs when a child's body changes into an adult body and readies for the possibility of reproduction, usually starting around 10–13 years

Public health – the field of medicine concerned with safeguarding and improving the health of the community as a whole

R

Ramadan – a holy time when Muslims do not eat or drink between sunrise and sunset in order to draw nearer to God

Rastafarian – a member of a religion which originated in Jamaica; its members avoid alcohol, and have 21 April as a special holiday to remember their founder

Rate – a measure of something compared with something else, such as litres per second or beats per minute

Reflection – looking back on actions and events to consider reasons and learn from them

Reflective log-book – whilst you are on work experience you will complete a reflective log-book of your progress

Reflex – an unlearned and quick response to a stimulus which is usually needed for survival and/or protection

Reincarnation – rebirth of the soul in another body

related to a life circumstance

Religion – a set of beliefs based on the idea of a sacred being

Repatriation – return to one's country

Resilient – able to return quickly to a previous condition and recover quickly from difficult conditions

Respect – a feeling or attitude of regard for somebody or something and to show regard for someone and treat them properly

Respite care – short-term support in a residential setting for individuals who are supported by family

Responsibility – legally or morally obliged to be responsible to take care of something or someone and/or to carry out a duty

Right – something that a person is entitled to and that a person can claim is due to them

Risk – the harm a hazard can do. The chance of suffering harm, loss, injury or danger

Risk assessment – examining something that could cause harm and then deciding whether enough precautions have been taken to prevent injury

Routine – the regular organisation and occurrence of events, for example mealtimes in a setting

Rural locations – places in the countryside where houses may be in small groups or quite isolated

S

Sanitation – measures taken to protect public health, such as supplying clean water or efficient sewage disposal systems

Secondary – second or more specialist care, often delivered in a hospital

Secular – something that has no connection to any religion or place of worship

Sedentary – tending to sit down a lot, taking little exercise

Self-concept – a combination of how you see yourself and how you think others see you

Self-esteem – how a person feels about themselves and their abilities

Sex Discrimination Act 1975 – prohibits discrimination because of an individual's gender in many areas, e.g. employment, education and provision of services

Sexuality – a sense of a person's sexual and emotional attraction to others, e.g. heterosexual, homosexual and bisexual

Sharps bin – a special yellow bin for depositing sharp objects such as needles

Sign – a posted up notice giving a direction or command

Slang – the use of informal words and expressions that are not considered standard in the speaker's dialect or language and words which are considered less polite or not correct in formal situations

Social care assistant – someone who works in a residential setting or day centre and provides support for individuals who are not ill, but find movement or daily living difficult

Social class – a group of people who share a common place in society

Social work assistant – someone who works with a social worker, providing support for individuals and families

Socio-economic – relates to social and economic or financial factors

Sound – free from defect, decay, damage, disease, injury; in good condition

Spatial awareness – understanding where things are in relation to other things

Special care baby unit – a hospital unit which cares for newborn babies with health issues

Stamina – the heart's ability to work under strain

Statutory – set up and regulated by the government (according to statute or law)

Stereotype – a fixed idea or assumption about an individual or group of people

Stereotyping – assuming something based on a fixed set of ideas

Storm and stress – the English translation of 'Sturm und Drang', a German literary movement that emphasised the volatile emotional life of the individual

Strength – the body's physical power

Stroke – when part of the body is disabled due to a blood clot or a burst blood vessel in the brain

Supervisor – a qualified member of staff who will support you during your work experience and contribute to your report

Suppleness – the body's ability to bend without damage

Surgical stitches – stitches inserted by a surgeon to close a wound created by surgery

Symbol – something such as an object, picture, written word, sound, or particular mark that represents something else

T

Targets – short- and longer-term challenges to help you meet your goal

Terminal illness – an illness where the individual does not recover

Tertiary – third or very specialist care, delivered by special hospital units, hospices etc

Therapeutic – the treatment of disease or other disorder, something that may benefit health

Tissues – a distinct type of material made up of specialised cells which have specific roles in the body

Transition – change from one place or set of circumstances to another or from one work role to another or one department to another

U

Underclass – a group of people who feel pushed to the edge of society through poverty and disadvantage

V

'Valuing people now' – a government policy which states the ways in which individuals with a learning disability should be included in society and treated equally

Verbal skills – the way we speak, for example, tone, pitch and the speed of our words

Voluntary – support which is provided by organisations funded through public donation

W

Warden – an official person in charge of a home or building who makes sure that the residents are well and happy and that everything is maintained properly

Weaning – introducing solid foods to a baby from the age of about 6 months

Welfare State – the provision of health and social care services by the State

Index